Boycotts —
Picketing —

LABOR
AND THE
LAW

LABOR

AND THE

LAW

BY CHARLES O. GREGORY

PROFESSOR OF LAW, UNIVERSITY OF CHICAGO

NEW YORK

W·W·NORTON & COMPANY·INC·

First Edition

Book Design by John Woodlock

FOR
THE EDUCATION OF R. P. McK.

CONTENTS

PREFACE   PAGE 11

CHAPTER I   PAGE 13

EARLY ORGANIZATION AND CRIMINAL CONSPIRACY

THE COMMON LAW DEVELOPMENT IN ENGLAND
THE FIRST AMERICAN CASES

CHAPTER II   PAGE 31

FREE ENTERPRISE IN ENGLAND—THE DOUBLE STANDARD

THE HOUSE OF LORDS TRILOGY—THE COMPANY CASE
THE FIRST LABOR UNION CASE
THE SECOND LABOR UNION CASE
THE LAW OF THE TRILOGY

CHAPTER III   PAGE 52

FREE ENTERPRISE IN AMERICA—CONFLICTING STATE POLICIES

THE MASSACHUSETTS DOCTRINE—A CONSERVATIVE APPROACH
HOLMES' ATTIC SALT IN THE MASSACHUSETTS CHOWDER
THE LIBERAL DEVELOPMENT IN NEW YORK STATE

CHAPTER IV   PAGE 83

THE JUDICIAL RESTRICTION OF UNIONS—THE LABOR INJUNCTION

SOME ASPECTS OF THE LAW OF TORTS IN RELATION TO LABOR UNIONS

CHAPTER V   PAGE 105

STRIKES AND BOYCOTTS—CONCERTED REFUSALS
TO WORK

THE LABOR INJUNCTION AND ITS ABUSE
STRIKES, LAWFUL AND UNLAWFUL
STRIKES AGAINST TECHNOLOGICAL CHANGE
JURISDICTIONAL STRIKES
STRIKES FOR THE CLOSED SHOP
BOYCOTTS, PRIMARY AND SECONDARY
LABOR UNION COUNCILS

CHAPTER VI   PAGE 132

SECONDARY CONSUMPTION BOYCOTTS AND PICK-
ETING—ORGANIZED REFUSALS TO PATRONIZE

MORE ABOUT SECONDARY BOYCOTTS
SOME OF THE PROBLEMS OF PICKETING
A CONCLUSION OR TWO

CHAPTER VII   PAGE 158

THE REMOVAL OF JUDICIAL CONTROLS OVER
UNION EXPANSION BY ANTI-INJUNCTION ACTS

THE SUPREME COURT AND THE CLAYTON ACT: 1914–1921
THE ANTIUNION PROMISE OR THE "YELLOW DOG CONTRACT"
CONGRESS AND THE NORRIS-LAGUARDIA ACT: 1932

CHAPTER VIII   PAGE 200

FEDERAL CONTROL OVER EXPANDING UNION
POWER—THE SHERMAN ACT I

ARE UNIONS WITHIN THE SHERMAN ACT?
WHAT THE *Coronado* CASES MEANT

CHAPTER IX   PAGE 223

THE NEW DEAL AND THE NLRA

THE NRLA—THE ACT ITSELF
THE NRLA—HOW IT WORKS

CHAPTER X   PAGE 253

THE UNIONS AND THE SUPREME COURT—THE SHERMAN ACT II

THE *Apex* CASE
THE *Hutcheson* CASE
SOME CONSEQUENCES OF THE *Hutcheson* DOCTRINE

CHAPTER XI   PAGE 289

THE NLRB BEFORE THE COURTS

THE ABROGATION OF IRREGULAR COLLECTIVE AGREEMENTS
THE DISCRETION OF THE BOARD IN AFFORDING REMEDIES
REINSTATEMENT AND INSTATEMENT IN JOBS AS REMEDIES
THE POWER OF THE BOARD AFTER COLLECTIVE BARGAINING IS
    ACHIEVED
THE EXCLUSIVE BARGAINING RIGHTS OF THE MAJORITY VERSUS
    BARGAINING BY INDIVIDUALS
CHANGE OF UNION ALLEGIANCE
THE EMPLOYER REFUSES TO DEAL WITH A UNION ALLEGED *not*
    TO REPRESENT A MAJORITY
THE UNION REFUSES TO RESPECT A CERTIFICATION BY THE BOARD
DISPUTES BETWEEN UNIONS
THE ORGANIZATION OF SUPERVISORY WORKERS
CIVIL RIGHTS UNDER THE ACT—THE EMPLOYERS' FREEDOM OF
    SPEECH AND THE EMPLOYEES' RIGHT OF ASSOCIATION—CLOSED
    SHOPS AND OPEN UNIONS

CHAPTER XII   PAGE 334

THE CONSTITUTIONAL AREA OF ECONOMIC CON-FLICT—PICKETING AS FREE SPEECH

CHANGING VIEWS ABOUT PICKETING—THE *Senn* CASE
Thornhill v. Alabama
THE *Thornhill* DOCTRINE BECOMES COMPLICATED
A NATIONAL LABOR POLICY IN THE CONSTITUTION
THE RACE ISSUE

CHAPTER XIII   PAGE 378

THE FUNCTIONING AND ENFORCEABILITY OF COLLECTIVE AGREEMENTS—ARBITRATION

CONTENTS

ISSUES ARISING UNDER COLLECTIVE AGREEMENTS—GRIEVANCES
AND THE INTERESTS OF NONMEMBERS

ARBITRATION—ITS SCOPE AND POSSIBLE LEGISLATIVE BACK-
GROUND

CHAPTER XIV   PAGE 413

WHERE DO WE GO FROM HERE?

APPENDIX   PAGE 447

TABLE OF AUTHORITIES CITED   PAGE 453

INDEX   PAGE 461

PREFACE

THE DECADE preceding the war saw the inception of truly modern labor relations law in the United States. It also gave us time to perceive that much of this law was experimental and needed to have some of the rough edges taken off. Realization of some of these shortcomings was made easier by the fact that interunion disputes, not anticipated when these laws were passed, rapidly brought them to the fore. With the declaration of war an entirely new set of controls over labor relations came into being. Some of the effects of these emergency controls have remained as lasting imprints on our labor relations setup and will no doubt loom large in the labor laws of tomorrow.

But one important immediate effect of the war was to interrupt the normal development of the peacetime law of labor relations governing the organization of workers into unions, and collective bargaining. For almost four years these laws were subordinated in importance to a system of controls established primarily to further the war effort—and nothing else. Nevertheless, everyone concerned with labor relations during the war—and their number was legion—came out of it with an extraordinarily enriched experience and with many ideas for the postwar industrial relations scene.

Now the war is over and the bars are down again. Too much water has gone over the dam for us to go back to the prewar days and pick up where we left off. In many ways the labor laws of the last decade have become unsuited for the next. The break that the war has made in the normal development has afforded an occasion for us to recapitulate our achievements in the labor laws of the past years and to ponder our mistakes with a view to profiting from them both in the future. For we realize that the ensuing years will bring new laws in this field.

It is chiefly to acquaint the responsible citizen with the mani-

11

fold problems involved in the development of labor relations laws that this book has been written. Here is a fund of basic information concerning one of the most vital and interesting aspects of modern life. This information about a not uncomplicated legal and economic field has been presented in as simple and straightforward a manner as possible for the nonprofessional and professional reader alike. It is intended to afford them an opportunity of acquiring a moderately critical understanding of this field so that they may undertake a real part in helping as citizens to make the labor laws of the future.

In a book of this size, treating so vast a field as labor law, it has seemed most essential to confine the discussion to basic matters. Naturally, it has been impossible to cover the entire subject. It has been necessary to exclude many of the details concerning important parts of the law. This has been particularly true in dealing with the work of the National Labor Relations Board. Furthermore, no attempt has been made to describe that great special field of labor relations law which has grown up in the last twenty years under the Railway Labor Act. And since this discussion has been confined entirely to the law as it touches on labor relations and collective bargaining, it has been necessary to exclude any consideration of direct regulatory legislation like the Social Security and the Fair Labor Standards acts.

The pages that follow disclose an important part of the culture of economic man as it appears through the records of the law. What those records of tomorrow may reveal will depend in no small part on the understanding we gather from these records of the past.

CHARLES O. GREGORY

CHAPTER I

EARLY ORGANIZATION AND CRIMINAL CONSPIRACY

Does this measure tend to make good workmen? No: it puts the botch incapable of doing justice to his work, on a level with the best tradesman. The master must give the same wages to each. Such a practice would take away all the excitement to excel in workmanship or industry. Consider the effect it would have upon the whole community. If the masters say they will not sell under certain prices, as the journeymen declare they will not work at certain wages, they, if persisted in, would put the whole body of the people into their power. Shoes and boots are articles of the first necessity. . . . If these evils were unprovided for by the law now existing, it would be necessary that laws should be made to restrain them.—Moses Levy, Recorder, charging the jury in *The Trial of the Journeymen Boot & Shoemakers of Philadelphia,* 1806.

THE ANCIENT struggle between capital and labor now travels under a new name—the conflict between management and organized unions. Laws governing this clash of interests are not the invention of modern times. Centuries ago in England, long before the industrial revolution, the relationship of master and servant was comprehensively defined by statute. The old craft guilds maintained strict controls over the duties of journeymen and apprentices, conceding them hardly any rights at all. Indeed, at times there were criminal statutes which placed ceilings on wages and occasionally on prices in general. And after a manpower shortage caused by the Black Death in the 1300's, it was a serious offense to entice away another's workman by offering him higher wages. These are early instances of the reflection in law of changes and developments on the labor front.

13

Not until after the industrial revolution did conditions arise that resulted in combinations of workingmen for the purpose of securing from their employers better conditions of work. By that time the centralization of production into the factory system had begun to herd wage earners into the towns and to reduce them to little more than one of the commodities essential to manufacture. These changes of condition incited them in desperation to collective demonstrations against their exploiters. Here was the beginning of modern unionism in England at a time when our country was still a group of colonies largely devoted to agriculture. And in those times began the body of law designed to control these revolutionary attempts at self-help and to keep the working class in its ordained place.

Economists of those times accepted the prevailing philosophy of the owners of enterprise. In their writings they made it clear that the best of all possible worlds was one in which these owners were left free to pay for wages and materials as little as they had to through direct dealings with the individuals concerned. These notions found ready supporters in the judges, who reflected them in their decisions that combinations of labor to secure higher wages were common crimes. And Parliament itself insured proper respect for this judicial development in suppressive statutes aimed at unionism.

But even while courts in this country were entrenching these judicial doctrines of England in our own states, labor organizations in England had begun their fight before Parliament to free unionism from the stigma of criminality. This fight was virtually won in 1875, although the substance of the victory was not assured until the Trades Disputes Act of 1906 was adopted. In the meantime American courts had embraced the English notion that unions were criminal and had already virtually discarded it by the middle of the nineteenth century. But this did not mean that unions in this country were given the same economic freedom that English unions had ultimately secured by political action. Far from it. For during the middle of the nineteenth century they were hemmed in by state statutes according them a narrow field of activity. Their leaders were constantly subjected to civil actions for damages. And during the latter part of that century our courts developed against unionism a control far more effective than any criminal device—the labor injunction.

The period from around 1890 to 1932 was characterized by the inception and growth of modern labor unions as well as by the last-ditch struggle through litigation in our courts to suppress union activities and to keep them from expanding. At the same time the country was undergoing what might be called a twentieth century industrial revolution—the inception and growth of the assembly line in mass production. During this period the craft unions were too busy to realize the implications of this important social development. Their chief preoccupation at this time was the extension of their organizations. Their efforts in this direction were largely aimed at getting rid of the labor injunction and in discouraging the use of the Sherman Antitrust Act against them in the federal arena. As industry grew into larger and larger units of a national character, most of the activities of unions began to take on a nationwide significance. Although early union attempts to abolish the labor injunction failed miserably, their efforts finally achieved the effective Norris-LaGuardia Anti-injunction Act in 1932.

This statute furnishes a fitting threshold to the New Deal period. The next few years saw legislation undreamed of a decade or two earlier. The National Labor Relations Act in 1935 guaranteed independent organization to employees in all large industries. The Fair Labor Standards Act of 1938 established a forty-hour week and minimum wages. Both of these measures were upheld by the Supreme Court in the teeth of long-established constitutional doctrine to the contrary. Social security legislation was adopted by Congress to insure workers against the ravages of unemployment and to assure them of a financially independent old age. And right in the midst of all this the CIO sprang into being with a program for

the unionization of millions of workers theretofore not practicably organizable under the laws of earlier decades.

Then came World War II with its emergency legislation
and administrative facilities for promoting labor relations and
collective bargaining. The whole world then witnessed the
most remarkable feats of production ever staged—all made
possible by the extraordinary co-operation of management and
labor during these years and by their determination to see the
job through to the end together. A program of government-
conducted collective bargaining was carried on by the War
Labor Board in such a way that the wheels of industry kept at
a tremendously high level of production with relatively little
inflation ensuing. But then came the peace among nations and
quick upon its heels a renewal of the struggle between our
industrial Titans — organized management and organized labor. What has transpired since then is a matter of common
knowledge.

Reflection over the span of years indicates pointedly how
the developments in labor law, so slow in their early stages,
have accelerated their pace. Mass production and the assembly
line were making their imprint on the total industrial scene.
These new techniques, conceived by the brilliant ingenuity of
our industrialists, inevitably brought to the fore the organizational aptitude of our most able statesmen in the field of labor
—and the great industrial unions sprang into being. This development, in turn, led to some of the violent clashes between
union philosophies—the conflict between craft and industrial
unions exemplified in some of our bitter interunion disputes.
And all of these phenomena cried out for the orderly guidance
of the law.

These changes, which are still going on so fast, present a
challenge to American political genius. Fortunately the American people are endowed with a native political ability to find
in the long run the answers to most of their troubles. And they
are able to achieve settlements of most of their internal disputes
by peaceful solutions. Never have they been faced with a greater
need to apply this knack than they are in these days. They have

in their midst organized agencies for the production of vast wealth—management and labor. But they have come to a time when the traditional laws of the market place no longer provide the final answer as to how this abundance should be divided. Now they must concentrate their political genius on the most effective schemes for solving this pressing internal problem—how to perfect the rules whereby through peaceful means the pie may be fairly divided to the real satisfaction of all at the table.

THE COMMON LAW DEVELOPMENT IN ENGLAND

Before we begin, it is necessary to understand the difference between statutes and the common law. The bulk of our law and of England's law has in the past been what is known as common law. This is the law which consists of the accumulated decisions of courts, developed by the judiciary without the aid of legislatures. The laws specifically enacted by legislatures are called statutes. They usually denote departures from, or particular developments of, certain phases of our customary or common law. Statutes usually represent changes in our law resulting from political pressures which are articulated from the people through their duly elected representatives in the legislatures. Our courts, who are the trustees of our common law, profess not to make or change the law but only to interpret and apply it as they find it to be. This they do, or profess to do, whether the law they interpret and apply be statute or common law.

In the process of applying the common law, they have undertaken during the centuries to set it forth in general and sometimes rather vague principles which, in themselves, have come to be called law. Naturally, when a bench of judges are confronted with an issue for which there is no exact precedent and which is not covered by a statute, they are compelled by tradition either to dismiss the case altogether or to deal with it on its merits in accordance with the principles of the common law. If they do the latter, the law grows and the principles themselves are modified and enriched. Thus our courts, who claim that they do not make law but only interpret it, are nevertheless able to keep abreast of the times and to dispose on its merits of almost any litigated dispute which may be presented to them.

An analysis of labor problems and of labor law may be made in terms of the institution of property. Certainly, the ownership and control of property has traditionally implied economic and political power over others. The political, constitutional, and legal departments of our social community have been devoted chiefly to insuring the integrity of property and to maintaining the complete freedom of its use. In so far as government or any substantial part of the community has attempted to modify this institution of property, it has always failed unless it could demonstrate clearly some supervening social need of recognized great importance or could overcome determined opposition through great political superiority. This leaves out of account, naturally, the recourse to violent organized revolution—a technique for the eradication of established social institutions, well known in history but fortunately still unknown for that purpose in our own country.

The traditional emphasis laid on the importance of property and its incidents in England and the United States has always in the past seemed to overshadow assertions of purely personal rights dissociated from property. This is not intended to imply that these two countries have not always cherished high ideals of personal liberty. Far from it. Personal freedom of contract has traditionally been maintained with remarkable vigor. But the practical application of this political ideal has sometimes seemed to compromise it. Thus, when English wage earners of the eighteenth century attempted through combination to effect improvements in their immediate employment conditions by direct economic action, the courts regarded them as criminals and threw their leaders in jail. Such economic action was the concerted refusal to work unless certain concessions were made—in other words, the strike. And this device consisted merely of the concerted exercise of their individual freedom of contract by all the participants in the strike acting together.

English courts were not originally acting under statutory authority when they adopted this stern position. And since they felt impelled by tradition to rest their official disapproval of strikes on some formal legal grounds, they decided to dress it up for public consumption in what they called the doctrine of criminal conspiracy. A few scholars have professed to be greatly puzzled on logical grounds concerning the inception and nature of this doctrine. They point out that there was nothing unlawful in combination itself, nothing unlawful in an individual's refusal to work, and nothing unlawful in a workingman's desire to obtain better standards of employment. How then, they asked, could the courts have put these elements together to constitute a crime, when each of the component parts was perfectly lawful according to the common law as they understood it?

The answer to this question seems fairly simple. English judges believed that the use of the economic power made possible by combination and the concerted action of working people was bad for the economy of England. Since individual refusals of wage earners to work under conditions not acceptable to them had no discernible effect on the national economy, the vice was combination and concerted action. Hence the judges found it possible to maintain the principle of freedom of contract—at least for individuals—and at the same time to declare unlawful the united efforts of workers to change the conditions under which they worked.

This result seems to have rested on the premise that the objectives of organized workers were unlawful because they interfered with the "natural" operations of basic principles of economics—the sanctions of the market. English judges took it for granted that the labor of an individual is worth only what it commands in the market. Any concerted attempts of workers to increase its value by demanding higher wages they regarded as arbitrary invasions of the employers' rights. They thought employers were compelled to resist such attempts even though the resulting strikes disrupted industry and trade. For if an employer bought peace with his organized workers by granting their demands, his competitive position in relation to other employers was jeopardized. And if all English employers were eventually compelled by strikes to concede better wages and working conditions, the consequent general rise in production costs would impair England's trade in world markets. How could English merchants hope to compete with Continental goods produced in countries officially fostering the doctrine of the utility of poverty—that workers are most productive and will work best under the constant incentive of hunger and the direst need?

These were the times when Malthus was expounding his theory that if the working people in an industrial country were allowed more than the barest means of subsistence, they would merely increase and thus provide more mouths to feed at the same marginal standard of living. And about then economists were developing the wage fund theory. This was the belief that in any national community there was available in any one year a fixed fund for wages, which ought to be distributed equitably among the working population. The first of these theories made any attempt to improve the conditions of labor seem hopeless. The second made any organized attempt by some workers to wrest from the wage fund more than their proper share seem wicked and malicious. These were the notions that led Carlyle to refer contemptuously to economics as "the dismal science."

It seems most reasonable to suppose that English judges during the eighteenth century cherished all these beliefs. How, then, could they have failed to regard the disruptive undertakings of labor combinations as anything but pernicious? And knowing, as they did, that combination and concerted action alone made possible the effectiveness of organized labor's demands, no wonder they picked upon that factor as the element of illegality involved and labeled the whole business criminal conspiracy. The idea of conspiracy as a category of illegality in other contexts was not new.

Parliament had by statute previously declared certain undertakings of business enterprisers to be unlawful conspiracies, such as combinations to buy up and hold for artificially high prices staple commodities like grain and hops. These statutes acknowledged the vice inherent in a combination of economic power sufficiently strong to do what few, if any, individual merchants could have done. And even if Parliament had not yet acted against combinations of workers, the courts found the analogies presented in these statutes aimed at merchants' combinations too apt not to use against them.

English judges of these times must seldom have been troubled by the reflection that they might be using the doctrine of criminal conspiracy to deny working people the enjoyment of their personal civil rights to combine and jointly to exercise their liberties of contract. After all, rights of any kind are relative matters. The judges were also aware that the owners and operators of industry had what might be called their personal civil rights in the ownership and administration of property. As long as the development and operation of industry was left in private hands, then it was incumbent upon government to see that industrial enterprisers remained free to prosecute their business unhampered by concerted oppression from their laborers. Industrial operators and investors of capital were providing the means of support to the nation's working class.

The fact that this new factory system of production had originally divorced wage earners from their traditional sources of livelihood, making them dependent on the system itself, hardly mattered any more. Industry must be fostered and encouraged, for it was rapidly becoming the very life blood of the nation, without which England could hardly hold her place in the world. Hence, if there was any choice to make between protecting the civil rights of the owners and operators of industry, on the one hand, and those of wage earners on the other, the courts could easily be counted on to uphold the former as against the latter. In doing so they would be supporting the interests of the dominant political class in England

and, to their way of thinking, no doubt, would be taking the obvious and only sensible course open to them. For in maintaining the law in this fashion, they were fulfilling their obligations to the group that placed them on the bench and were betraying no political obligation of any sort to the working class who did not yet enjoy the privilege of voting.

THE FIRST AMERICAN CASES

Although Parliament did eventually enact several statutes forbidding labor combinations to exercise direct economic pressure against employers, English courts had achieved this same position independently of Parliament as a matter of common law. This conclusion was important in the United States during the early nineteenth century, since it largely governed the disposition of what has been called America's first labor case. That case appears to have set the tone for the early judicial treatment of organized labor in this country.

This was the famous *Philadelphia Cordwainers'* case decided in 1806. Cordwainer is an ancient term meaning a shoemaker working particularly in cordovan leather. The journeymen cordwainers, or employees, were united in a club. They met together and presented their employers, the master cordwainers, with a schedule of sums which they claimed should be paid to them for their production of fancy tops, back straps, long boots, cossacks, and bootees—the proposed increases ranging from 25 to 75 cents the pair. The journeymen demanded adoption of this schedule—or else. The reaction of the master cordwainers was immediate. This demand was most embarrassing to them. They were trying to lower the prices of their shoes in order to compete with rival shoemakers in other cities for the expanding markets in the recently settled territories in the South and West. Their reaction took the form of an appeal to the public prosecutor.

The upshot was that the grand jury found a true bill charging the journeymen cordwainers with "contriving, and intending unjustly and oppressively, to increase and augment the prices and rates usually paid and allowed to them and other artificers" for their labor, and with preventing, "by threats, menaces, and other unlawful means," other journeymen from working at the occupation of cordwainer for wages below a fixed schedule of rates. Furthermore, they were accused of "unjustly and corruptly" conspiring not to work for a master who employed any cordwainer breaking any of their society's rules and bylaws and of preventing any other workmen and journeymen from working for such master. This indictment, of course, was a list of the charges as they were viewed by the prosecutor; but it really meant only that the workers organized, set wage rates agreeable to themselves, concertedly refused to work for less, and brought social and economic pressure on both their fellow workers and masters who ignored their schedule of rates.

At the trial of this case counsel for the defendants engaged in some wonderful flights of oratory in an endeavor to discredit the common-law doctrine of criminal conspiracy, which the prosecution insisted had been adopted intact in this country along with the rest of the English common law. He attempted to show "that the spirit of the revolution and the principle of the common law, are opposite in this case," and "that the common law, if applied in this case, would operate an attack upon the rights of man." In effect, he asked, why did we fight the revolutionary war for liberty, only to find that we are not free to combine and concertedly to refrain from work if we see fit—and that because of English law against which we had successfully conducted a revolution a few years ago?

This argument raised a square enough issue before the judge, Recorder Levy. He reflected the sentiments of property owners and businessmen of Philadelphia, the only people who could vote in the days before popular franchise was adopted. Thus he found that the views prevailing among the substantial citizens of Philadelphia were admirably reflected in the common-law doctrine of criminal conspiracy. To support his belief, he recited the principles of supply and demand economics, showing how prices and wages are regulated in the natural course of things. What the defendants were doing, he declared, was "artificial regulation . . . governed by no standard, controuled by no impartial person, but dependent on the will of the few who are interested . . . an unnatural, artificial means of raising the price of work beyond its standard, and taking an undue advantage of the public."

He said that the rule of law is not bottomed upon such principles. If it were, the commerce of the city would be ruined. He went on, "Is there any man who can calculate (if this is tolerated) at what price he may safely contract to deliver articles, for which he may receive orders, if he is to be regulated by the journeymen in an arbitrary jump from one price to another?" Concerning the workers who did not wish to join the combination or tie themselves to its fixed wage schedule, he observed that "a term of reproach is fixed upon them." The members would not work with them, and refused to board or lodge with them. The result was that everyone was compelled to join the society.

The recorder then observed that most of the answers are found in the volumes of the common law, the rules of which are the result of the wisdom of ages. As he put it, the common law says what one man may do without offense, many combined may not do with impunity.

Then he went on: "A combination of workmen to raise their wages may be considered in a two-fold point of view: one is to benefit themselves . . . the other is to injure those who do not join their society. The rule of law condemns both. If the rule be clear, we are bound to conform to it even though we do not comprehend the principle upon which it is founded. . . . It is enough, that it is the will of the majority. It is law because it is their will—if it is law, there may be good reasons for it though we cannot find them out. But the rule in this case is pregnant with sound sense and all the authorities are clear upon the subject."

The key to the practical importance of this case was revealed in the recorder's opinion. Shoe manufacturing in Philadelphia was changing from a "bespoke," or personal order, to a wholesale contract basis. With the advancing settlement of the South and West and the development of transportation facilities to these far points, shoe manufacturers on the eastern seaboard were undertaking to supply large orders of ready-made shoes to merchants in those regions. Since competition among them was already keen, and since it centered around the price contract for large future deliveries of shoes, any intervening rise of production costs in any particular locality participating in this venture might endanger the prosperity of the whole community. At any rate this is what Recorder Levy and his business friends believed.

The labor combinations were trying to force this increase of production costs in the shape of higher wage rates. Hence they were threatening with injury the welfare of the entire community. It seemed irrelevant that they were trying to defend themselves against the effects of advancing commercialism which destroyed all incentive of individual workmen to excel, in the interests of more and more quantity production at an ever decreasing price per unit. They were throwing a monkey wrench into the system and were hurting everyone, including themselves. Hence, as the recorder observed, "If these evils were unprovided for by the law now existing, it would be necessary that laws should be made to restrain them."

Within the next thirty years there followed a series of similar cases throughout the East, reflecting these sentiments. In some of them courts conceded the right to strike for higher wages but condemned strikes to compel the discharge of workmen who would not join the unions as arbitrary means "which went to deprive their fellow citizens of rights as precious as any they contended for." Shortly after that Chief Justice Gibson spoke forth in the Pennsylvania case, *Commonwealth v. Carlisle*, decided in 1821, which is chiefly significant because of what he said about combination among businessmen. Several shoe manufacturers were prosecuted for using the united front technique to depress wages. Their defense, which the court thought good, was that they were trying to resist the concerted attempts of their employees artificially to raise wages above their true market worth and to decrease high rates already secured by strikes. The court declared that a combination of employers to lower wages, aside from such a defense, would amount to criminal conspiracy as would "a confederacy among the bakers to extort an exorbitant price for bread, which everyone will acknowledge to be indictable."

This was apparent, for "The labouring classes purchase their bread with their labour, or, what is the same thing, they give their labour for the money with which they purchase bread, and it is evident the more labour is depreciated, the more of it will be required to purchase any given quantity of bread." But all combination was not unlawful, the court remarked. "The combination of capital for purposes of commerce, or to carry on any other branch of industry, although it may in its consequences indirectly operate on third persons, is unaffected by this consideration, because it is a common means in the ordinary course of human affairs, which stimulates to competition and enables men to engage in undertakings too weighty for an individual." In this modest statement the court forecast the trend which culminated in our mighty corporate enterprises, the size and economic strength of which have given rise to most of our modern labor problems.

In 1836 the New York Supreme Court, deciding *People v. Fisher,* read into an exceedingly vague statute a legal bar against labor activity comparable to that of common-law conspiracy. The legislature had enacted that "If two or more persons shall conspire . . . to commit any act injurious to the public health, to public morals, or to trade or commerce; or for the perversion or obstruction of justice or the due administration of the laws—they shall be deemed guilty of a misdemeanor." A group of journeymen shoemakers, organized in a club, were indicted under this statute for striking to procure the discharge of a workman who accepted wages lower than the minimum approved by them. If they were guilty at all under this law, it was for a conspiracy to commit an act injurious to trade or commerce.

A provision of such generality was not much of a guide. But the court readily accepted the responsibility of using it to convict the defendants. It saw the issue as one of a conspiracy to raise wages. Artificially high wages meant correspondingly higher prices for boots, which prevented local manufacturers from selling as cheaply as their competitors elsewhere. Furthermore, the community was deprived of the services of the man whose discharge was effected by the union. Such results were, in the court's opinion, clearly injurious to trade and commerce, and their causes should be punished under the statute.

These and numerous other criminal convictions of workers for taking advantage of what they regarded as their ordinary civil privilege to exercise their right to work or not work, under such terms as they saw fit, bred ill-feeling throughout the East. Mobs of laborers held mock trials of judges and hung them in effigy to show their resentment at being treated as common criminals for having done what they believed they had a perfect right to do. Juries were refusing to convict in some of these prosecutions, in spite of clearly proved cases of criminal conspiracy under the prevailing law. Even the press attacked judicial statements that the unions were of foreign origin or were mainly upheld by foreigners. These were implications that were patently false. News of these events traveled fast. The owners of the newly established textile and shoe factories in Massachusetts were as much concerned over the judicial treatment of organized labor as were the unions themselves.

In the case of *Commonwealth v. Hunt* one of their lower courts had convicted seven members of The Boston Journeymen Bootmakers' Society for organizing a strike against an employer who had hired and retained one Jeremiah Horne, a journeyman, who was not a member of the society. The indictment had charged them with having unlawfully, perniciously, deceitfully, unjustly and corruptly conspired not to work for any master who employed any workman not a member of their union, after he was notified to discharge such workman; with having compelled by these means at least one master named Isaac B. Wait to discharge Horne; and with the "wicked and unlawful intent to impoverish" and to keep him from pursuing his trade. The trial judge had instructed the jury that the indictment set forth a course of conduct amounting to criminal conspiracy. This meant that if such acts were proven at the trial, a verdict of guilty should follow.

The convicted shoe workers appealed to the highest court of the state on the ground that the indictment had not charged a crime. Its decision came down in 1842, Chief Justice Shaw writing the opinion for the court. He was no lover of unions and probably believed them to be thoroughly vicious. In other connections he showed himself unsympathetic to wage earners by preventing them from recovering damages against their employers for personal injuries due to the defective conditions of premises and appliances or because of the carelessness of fellow employees. This had the effect of lessening the overhead risks of infant industry at the expense of workers who could ill afford to bear them.

Nevertheless, he realized from reading the newspapers that Massachusetts workers would react violently if courts persisted in calling them criminals for trying to advance their interests by their refusal to work. He knew that the fortunes of many a future old Boston family were tied up in the newly built mills and that a wave of strikes, on the heels of the recent depression, could easily finish them off. Such a disaster, in turn, might have political repercussions fatal to the proposed tariff believed necessary for the protection of incipient industry. Something simply had to be done to discourage the indiscriminate use of the doctrine of criminal conspiracy against the workers!

Shaw rose to the occasion in an opinion which was a masterpiece of tact and technicality. He disregarded the adverbs in the indictment as mere recital—wishful thinking by the prosecuting attorney. All the indictment really charged, he said, was the intention of the society to induce all those engaged in the same occupation to become members of it. This was a not unlawful objective designed for the purpose of securing power. Such power, he said, might be used for useful and honorable purposes as well as for dangerous and pernicious ones. If the latter were the real ends in view, and were susceptible of proof, they should have been specially charged. For all the court could tell from the indictment, the purposes of the society might be laudable, such as discouragement of the use of ardent spirits. "Such an association might be used to afford each other assistance in times of poverty, sickness and distress; or to raise their intellectual, moral and social condition; or to make improvement in their art; or for other proper purposes." If this were so, the indictment could not support a conviction. And the court refused to assume that the workers' objectives were bad.

Everyone, including the court, knew what the union's purposes really were, even if they had not been set forth in the indictment. Hence this decision issued by perhaps the most able state judge of his time gave the doctrine of criminal conspiracy a considerable setback. Shaw had not abolished the doctrine of criminal conspiracy as some wishful thinkers think he did. But by so obviously side-stepping the real issue in the case as a matter of expedience, he discouraged the use of this doctrine for many years. And, as Dean Landis of Harvard Law School, a prominent writer in this field, has remarked about Shaw's opinion . . . "he foreshadows clearly the doctrine of a later day that the legality of a strike is to be made to depend upon the end sought to be attained."

Common-law criminal conspiracy has never again played a prominent part in the control of labor unions by American courts, although it was used occasionally after the Civil War to break up strikes. Parliament by statute formally discarded this doctrine for all time in 1875, after English labor unions had achieved substantial political power. But in America it just faded away, perhaps chiefly because the courts developed a much more effective means of control in the injunction. It had served as a formal vehicle—a legal abracadabra, if you please—in the name of which English and American judges had made labor unionists conform to the principles of classical economics.

Like most legal principles, this doctrine was an arbitrary statement of a result, and depended for its existence on the economic views of the judges using it. Indeed, it is clear in retrospect that these economic views were really the law, while the doctrine of criminal conspiracy was merely the form in which it was presented for public consumption. The fact that it was relished neither in England nor this country may partially explain why it was supplanted by other doctrines. But acknowledgment of this fact does not tell why these new doctrines reflected the same economic views adapted to conditions in a somewhat changed world. That, however, is a matter which must be told. For without it there will be lacking the very basis on which rests an understanding of modern common law concerning the activities of organized labor.

CHAPTER II

FREE ENTERPRISE IN ENGLAND—THE DOUBLE STANDARD

> One of the eternal conflicts out of which life is made up is that between the effort of every man to get the most he can for his services, and that of society, disguised under the name of capital, to get his services for the least possible return. Combination on the one side is patent and powerful. Combination on the other is the necessary and desirable counterpart, if the battle is to be carried on in a fair and equal way.—Holmes, J., dissenting in *Vegelahn v. Guntner,* 1896.

DURING the last third of the nineteenth century the courts in both England and this country evolved general principles to govern suits brought against those whose economic activities caused harm to others. The most conspicuous approach to a statement of general rules was made in what has come to be known as the Trilogy of the House of Lords. This Trilogy comprised three cases involving the activities of combinations, one of business and two of labor. These cases deserve careful consideration here, not only because they influenced the law of this country but also because they reveal much judicial double talk behind some of the law.

THE HOUSE OF LORDS TRILOGY—THE COMPANY CASE

In *Mogul Steamship Company v. McGregor, Gow and Company,* decided in 1892, a new transport line sued a combination of shipping lines which had secured control over the carriage of goods between England and the Far East. This combine

31

served all ports whereas the newcomer called at but a few. At the same time most shippers of consequence had interests in all ports, with access to both the combine's and the new company's facilities. The combination had put the screws on this new company in two ways. First, it offered kickbacks to all shippers who sent goods exclusively in its ships. In addition to this bait, it had a club. It refused to accept goods from anyone out there who patronized the new company. Under this economic pressure the shippers in the Far East were forced to the use of the combination's vessels. As a result the new company went bankrupt. It sued the combine for damages and sought an injunction against future conduct of the same sort. Its case rested on the tort theories of intentional commission of harm without justification and of civil conspiracy.

For the benefit of readers who may be unfamiliar with legal terms, a tort is merely a civil wrong. One who has sustained damage as a consequence of a tort may ordinarily secure compensation therefor against the aggressor. A maxim in the law of torts says that intentionally inflicted harm is actionable, although it goes on to state that this is not necessarily so if the infliction of harm is justifiable under the circumstances presented. The complaining company in this case showed that the damage in question had been deliberately inflicted on it by the combination and argued that it was therefore actionable.

Conceding that the combination had intentionally ruined the new company, the court nevertheless thought the other companies not liable for the damage because there was justification for its infliction. Here was a conflict between two equally protected rights—that of plaintiff to protection in the legitimate exercise of trade and that of defendants to carry on business as they see fit, as long as they observe the law. The combination of defendants here, it said, "have done nothing more against the plaintiffs than pursue to the bitter end a war of competition waged in the interest of their own trade." And when the plaintiff company claimed that the ill-will of the defendant companies rebutted just cause and excuse, the court

replied: "So to hold would be to convert into an illegal motive the instinct of self-advancement and self-protection."

The court dismissed that part of the plaintiff's action based on the theory of civil conspiracy because there was no proof of "the intentional doing of some act to the detriment of the plaintiff's business without just cause or excuse." Combination alone cannot imply illegality, it said. Suppose one capitalist had bought up all of the companies in the combination? Or suppose that they all belonged to one joint stock company? Such situations, the court said, would imply unity and not combination. And it would be an odd principle of law that would penalize the defendants in this case, just because of their combination with each other, but which would tolerate the same effects by an identical aggregation of economic power when it was all owned and controlled by a single person or a single joint stock company. Presumably the court did not choose to regard either of these latter "units" as the combinations of capital, managerial skill, and administrative capacity which they would have been, in spite of unitary ownership.

"The truth is," the court remarked, "that the combination of capital for purposes of trade and competition is a very different thing from such a combination of several persons against one, with a view to harm him, as falls under the head of an indictable conspiracy. There is no just cause or excuse in the latter class of cases. There is such a just cause or excuse in the former." Only legislation—some sort of antimonopoly act—could make unlawful the conduct of the combination in this case. Until such a statute were passed, the court could show its disapproval of the combination's potentiality for harm only by refusing to lend its aid to the combination or to any of its members in suits arising among them over matters of internal interest.

This decision of the House of Lords was remarkably important because it established so clearly the immunity with which a combination might impose very serious harm on another through the exertion of economic pressure, as long as it

was done for self-advancement and in the pursuit of gain. Here
the defendants, pooling their economic strength in a combination, had exercised ruthless compulsion on the plaintiff company, deliberately causing it great harm. But they had done
this only by concertedly refusing to deal with shippers who, in
turn, dealt in any way with the plaintiff. Such refusal to deal,
except upon terms agreeable to the members of the combination, did not involve conduct in itself unlawful, such as beating
with a club, or fraudulent misrepresentation or libel or the
types of conduct employed by gangsters in "shaking down" a
victim. Refusal to deal with another was not, in itself, a civil
wrong, whether indulged in by an individual or by a group.
It was, rather, a civil right, the exercise of which the courts
confessed complete inability to control.

By this technique the combined defendants had compelled
the shippers to become the unwilling instruments in bringing
harmful pressure on the plaintiff. This was, in effect, a secondary
boycott—a term frequently encountered in labor law. It implies the refusal by one party to deal with another unless such
other will, in turn, refuse to deal with a third—the real object of
the first party's animus. In telling the shippers that the combination would have all of their trade, or none, it let them know
that it would not deal with them at all unless they, in turn, refused to deal with the plaintiff. It was this last effect which the
combination sought—the bringing of harmful economic pressure on the plaintiff company by the shippers. For if this new
enterprise could get no customers among the shippers, it would
fold up. The end result was advantageous to members of the
combination, since they retained a complete monopoly over the
Far East to England transportation business, free from outside
competition. This was a curious consequence of a legal principle based on the notion that the otherwise wrongful deliberate imposition of harm on another is privileged as competition itself.

THE FIRST LABOR UNION CASE

Labor unions in England thought the *Mogul* case was wonderful. Even though it concerned the activities of a business group, it stood for the principle that any combination, intent on promoting the interests of its members, was free to do so by using even ruthless economic coercion against others as long as it did not engage in conduct contrary to any established category of tort or crime. Yet in the second of the great Trilogy cases, *Allen v. Flood,* the application of this broad principle to the activities of labor groups was vigorously opposed.

It seems that in 1894 a ship-repair company employed 40 boilermakers who belonged to a union of that name. These men objected when the company employed two shipwrights, who belonged to a different union, and threatened to strike unless the company discharged them. Allen, the business representative of the boilermakers' union, came down from London and put the matter up to the company. Since it did not want a strike on its hands, the company fired the two shipwrights, Flood and Taylor. This it had a legal privilege to do, as they were only employees at will and not hired under contract. The fired shipwrights thereupon sued Allen for the damage they suffered when they lost their jobs as a consequence of Allen's having compelled the company to exercise its privilege of discharge.

At the trial of this case, the judge left it to the jury whether Allen could be charged with malice, whatever that might mean. The jury went ahead and found that Allen had "maliciously induced" the employer to discharge the shipwrights and not to rehire them. Judgment against Allen for 40 pounds was affirmed by the Court of Appeal. He then appealed to the House of Lords, where his case was argued four days in December, 1895 and, in the additional presence of several lower judges whose advice was being sought, for six days in March, 1897. Plainly the last guess was going to be no snap judgment, however certain the courts below had been that the activities of the union were unlawful.

In June, 1897, these invited lesser judges dragged out their opinions for the edification of the law lords through 56 dreary pages of small print, six of them recommending affirmance and two urging reversal for the defendant. At the conclusion of these opinions there appears in the report the following understatement: "The House took time for consideration." And finally, in December, 1897, the law lords screwed up their courage and, in 114 pages of opinions, set forth their vote of six to three for reversal. Of 21 judges voting on this case, 13 believed that Allen had committed a wrong. But the nine law lords had the last say, and a majority of them apparently felt that sound policy required approval of what he had done for the union in this case.

A glance at two of the final set of opinions should give some idea of how law comes into being and of how slender are the threads with which legal theories are spun. Lord Chancellor Halsbury, the equivalent of chief justice, headed up the dissent in this case. He made it plain that all men have the right to get work and pursue their calling without molestation from others, basing this on "that freedom from restraint, that liberty of action . . . found running through the principles of our law." He said that this was like the wild duck case in which English judges long ago held that a man behaved unlawfully when he deliberately scared away wild fowl from his neighbor's decoys by firing a gun into the air over his own land. One would have to be at least a lord chancellor to see the connection between these two cases. And he declared that the jury's finding of malice clearly negatived any just cause and excuse Allen might offer as a defense against a charge of intentionally caused harm.

The theory of Halsbury's dissent is not apparent from his opinion. He could hardly have been willing to permit a common jury's finding of malice to foreclose consideration by the law lords of whether or not the labor union's objectives in this

case furnished just cause and excuse for the harm which occurred. If this factor was a matter for legitimate consideration
in the case at all, it was a most fundamental issue for the court.
And Halsbury must have known that the trial judge had no
business submitting it to the jury. What had happened was perfectly clear from the evidence. It was apparent that Allen had
not sought the discharge of the shipwrights either out of a
devilish desire to cause them harm or just to have some fun—
the presumable components of malice. He did it pursuant to
the policy of the union which was to secure to union members
as much of the available work, in terms of jobs, as possible. And
even if the union's policy to be served had been the broader
one of subjecting all employees to union membership, permitting new workers to remain on the job as long as they
joined the union, in order to insure the observance of union
standards throughout the plant, Halsbury still could not conscientiously have agreed with a verdict of malice. For the union
would be serving some economic end of its own conception
under any interpretation of the evidence.

Lord Herschell wrote the leading majority opinion. In it,
he inveighed against the idea that while inducing breach of
the employment relation might not be unlawful, maliciously
doing so would be unlawful. He also emphasized the folly of
leaving the issue of malice to a jury under the circumstances of
this case. He deplored the introduction of motive as the issue
upon which legality depended. Even if the defendant's motive
was the pursuit of his own interest, and malice were made to
depend on the means employed in accordance with the test of
what an honest and fair-minded man would do, he still did not
like it. "The truth is," he said, "this suggested test makes men's
responsibility for their actions depend on the fluctuating opinions of the tribunal before whom the case may chance to come
as to what a right-minded man ought or ought not to do in
pursuing his own interests." He just could not see why motive
should ever render unlawful a course of conduct, such as a refusal
to work for or deal with another, which, aside from motive, does

not fall within a recognized category of illegality like beating with a club or libel and slander. And he believed his position to be perfectly consistent with what the House of Lords had maintained in the ship combination decision—the *Mogul* case.

He remarked that union men "act in the interest of their class. . . . If they do not resort to unlawful acts they are entitled to further their interests in the manner which seems to them best, and most likely to be effectual." If the men believed it unfair for others to be given work that they regarded as rightly theirs, then regardless of how the law lords personally felt, they were within their rights in taking any steps not unlawful to keep such work for themselves. A man's right not to work or to determine when or where or with whom he will work "is in law a right of precisely the same nature, and entitled to just the same protection as a man's right to trade or work. They are but examples of that wider right of which I have already spoken. That wider right embraces also the right of free speech." A man may say what he pleases, as long as he does not slander or deceive or commit any of the conventional wrongs articulated through speech. Unless he thus abuses his right, "why is he to be called upon to excuse or justify himself because his words may interfere with someone else in his calling?"

Although he did not believe that Allen, the boilermakers' business agent, had to show justification for what he did, and thought that competition was neither "regarded with special favour by the law" nor "should be so regarded," Herschell nevertheless declared that if competition could be established as a special category of defense, then the present case fell within it. The object of the defendant and the workmen he represented was to assist themselves in their competition with the shipwrights. According to him a man may take steps to compete most advantageously in the use of his labor and to shut out what he regards as undesirable competition just as much as if he were conducting the business of ocean transport, like the combination in the *Mogul* case.

In concluding his 28 page opinion, Lord Herschell observed with some asperity that he was "not behind my noble and learned friend [Halsbury] in the desire to preserve individual liberty" but that he thought it "never in greater danger than when a tribunal is urged to restrict liberty of action because the manner in which it has been exercised in a particular instance may be distasteful." He then submitted "with all deference to my noble and learned friend on the woolsack that any other conclusion would run counter to principles of the common law which have been long well established," in the *Mogul* case. He apologized for the time he had taken, but justified his efforts by remarking that the position supported by his noble and learned friend Halsbury was "one absolutely novel, and which can only be supported by affirming propositions farreaching in their consequences and in my opinion dangerous and unsound."

THE SECOND LABOR UNION CASE

So the boilermakers won the last round in the House of Lords —and this second installment of the Trilogy was most pleasing to the unions. Now they seemed to be on a par with businessmen in the use of economic pressures to promote what they conceived to be their best interests. Henceforth they could wield their collective privilege to work or not to work at their pleasure and under whatever conditions they chose, as far as the penalties of the law were concerned. But their triumph was to be short-lived. For even as the learned law lords were cudgelling their wits to do right by England in this case, the final disillusioning chapter of the famous Trilogy was being fought out in the lower courts of Ireland.

There, a rural wholesale slaughterer named Leathem was asked by the meat workers' union to hire his help only from among its members. He would not do this, but offered to pay the dues and other obligations required for the installation of his regular employees into the union. The labor folk insisted upon adherence to their union's objective of placing its existing members first on the list for jobs, in preference to all nonmembers or late comers. It was also stipulated that if Leathem's workers joined up, they must nevertheless relinquish their jobs and, as new members, await their turns for further employment. When Leathem refused to comply, the union leaders threatened to bring pressure on him by taking away his best urban customer, Munce, who ran a large retail market. This they proposed to do by calling out Munce's union employees if he would not at their request discontinue purchasing his meat from Leathem. Leathem remained adamant, so they asked Munce to cease dealing with him. Since Munce did not want a strike on his hands and since he was not under contract with Leathem, he bought his meat elsewhere. Leathem then brought this action against Quinn and other members of the union to recover damages for the loss of his trade with Munce.

This case of *Quinn v. Leathem* presented an instance of what has become a typical secondary labor boycott. It was put into effect by a refusal of the unionists to work for Munce if he, in turn, did business with Leathem, whose employment policies were contrary to their interests as they conceived such interests to be. They could not bring pressure against Leathem directly by refusing to work for him because he did not employ union men to begin with. From the *Mogul* case and *Allen v. Flood* they understood that a group of employees acting in concert might lawfully refuse to work for their employer without giving any reason or for any reason they wished to give. Hence they believed that they might get at Leathem by exerting direct pressure against Munce, on whom they had some hold, so that he in turn would be forced to become the instrument for putting pressure on Leathem. They simply placed one condition on the continuance of their members' employment with Munce—his discontinuance of business dealings with Leathem—and let his self-interest take its course.

The trial and lower appellate courts in Ireland, one judge out of nine dissenting, came up with damages in favor of

Leathem. The reason they did this is not easy to determine. At the trial the jury was asked to consider (1) did the defendants wrongfully and maliciously induce the plaintiff's customers to refuse to deal with him, and (2) did the union defendants maliciously conspire to induce the plaintiff's customers not to deal with him? On the meaning of the words "wrongfully and maliciously," the trial judge instructed the jury to consider whether the defendants had gone beyond "securing or advancing their own interests or those of their trade by *reasonable means,* including lawful combination," or whether their acts were intended to injure the plaintiff in his trade, through combination, "as distinguished from acts *legitimately done* to secure or advance their own interests." He told them that a union may do acts to better itself as long as they are not "maliciously—that is to say, intentionally—done to injure a third party." Such wrongful acts occur, he said, when there has been "a conspiracy, a common intention and a combination on the part of the defendants to injure the plaintiff in his business."

This language of the trial judge was hardly the sort of stuff a jury is equipped to handle. The court might just as well have told the jury that if it did not like what the defendant unionists were up to, then to "give them the works." He did not give the jury any idea what he meant by "legitimately done" or "reasonable means." So naturally the jury supplied its own definitions from its own background of social experience. And it is hard to see how any group of jurymen in this case, trying to discharge their duty in accordance with the judge's instructions, could have failed to find the defendants guilty of an illegal conspiracy to injure Leathem.

On appeal by the union defendants, the House of Lords affirmed the judgment against them. Lord Brampton wrote the longest and most thorough opinion. He clearly thought that the real issue concerned a conspiracy to injure Leathem in his trade. But before he finally dealt with the conspiracy issue, he had already concluded that what the defendants had done was unlawful, anyway, aside from conspiracy. He and his fellow law lords believed that this case was different from the *Mogul* case because the defendants here could not justify their conduct "as legitimate trade competition." And those law lords who believed that there had been a showing of competition in *Allen v. Flood* thought that that case did not apply here because Allen, the boilermaker union's business agent, had acted individually in warning the employer of a probable strike, and he could not in his individual capacity constitute a conspiracy.

Now, if Lord Brampton was correct in concluding that the defendants could not justify their commission of harm on Leathem, and if at the same time he coupled this conclusion with the maxim of law that the intentional commission of unjustifiable harm is illegal, then the unionists were caught both in the maxim and in the doctrine of civil conspiracy. For all civil conspiracy amounts to is a tort occurring when defendants combine to achieve a lawful end by illegal means, an unlawful end by legal means, or an unlawful end by illegal means. So Lord Brampton had the unionists coming and going.

Just how did Brampton happen to conclude that the defendants in the *Leathem* case were not prompted in what they did by the instinct of self-advancement and self-protection, to borrow a phrase from the *Mogul* case? According to him, apparently, these union folk were engaged in aimless mischief and were hurting Leathem just for the hell of it. Their acts were not done, he said, "to obtain or maintain fair hours of labour or fair wages, or to promote a good understanding between employers and employed and workman and workman, or for the settlement of any dispute, for none had existence." But anyone able to read could tell from the report of the case that the union had a very definite interest at stake—not unlike that of the boilermakers' union in *Allen v. Flood*. Its endeavor to unionize Leathem's slaughter house indicates quite clearly that it was competing directly with unorganized labor for particular jobs—that it wanted to control Leathem's employment potential in order to keep its unemployed members at work. This alone seems clearly to supply the element of self-advancement mentioned in the *Mogul* case.

Furthermore, unless this union was different from all other large unions, it had another important economic interest about which nobody was very articulate in the early 1900's. The report of the case indicates that the union included in its membership the employees not only of retail butcher shops but also of slaughter yards—the equivalent in those days of packing houses. In this respect it resembled the AF of L Amalgamated Meat Cutters and Butcher Workmen of North America as it exists today. Now, in so far as the union had slaughter yards already organized with advantageous standards of employment, it had an interest in stabilizing and maintaining employment conditions in *all* slaughter yards. For in this way alone could it prevent the undermining of its already established standards in organized units by the undercutting competition between union slaughtered meat and nonunion slaughtered meat—the competitive factor being the wage differential which made nonunion meat cheaper.

This seems clearly to supply the element of self-protection mentioned in the *Mogul* case. As long as Leathem's slaughter yard and others like it were free to undersell their unionized competitors, because of lower wage rates, the welfare of the unionized employers would be hurt and they, in turn, would try to drive the union standards of their employees down to the nonunion level. This would certainly hurt the union. So by organizing the nonunion firms, it would strive to eliminate the competition of the nonunion meat with the union slaughtered meat in order to maintain the prosperity of the unionized firms and thus stabilize the security of the union men employed in them.

It is true that this attenuated but nevertheless real example of competition between union members and unorganized workers in the industry was not clearly thought out and expressly articulated at the time of *Quinn v. Leathem*. But even if it had been, it might not have played a very important part in the case, because the union placed so much emphasis on putting old union members in Leathem's jobs and almost no emphasis on the mere unionization of Leathem and his old employees. Consequently, it looked as if the only substantial competitive factor in the case was the struggle between the union and Leathem's old employees for the opportunities to work in his slaughter yard. Nevertheless, there seemed to be considerable evidence of real union interest to prevent Brampton from concluding so forcefully that the defendants were not serving any useful purpose by their conduct but were merely inflicting aimless and unjustifiable harm on the plaintiff.

Nonetheless, as indicated above, Brampton believed the defendants in this case to have been guilty of something called civil conspiracy. His extended remarks on this matter would have been most distressing to the recently deceased Lord Herschell, had he been able to read them. "It has often been debated," Brampton said, "whether, assuming the existence of a conspiracy to do a wrongful and harmful act towards another and to carry it out by a number of overt acts, no one of which taken singly and alone would, if done by one individual acting alone and apart from any conspiracy, constitute a cause of action, such acts would become unlawful or actionable if done by the conspirators acting jointly or severally in pursuance of their conspiracy, and if by those acts substantial damage was caused to the person against whom the conspiracy was directed: my own opnion is that they would. . . .

"Much consideration of the matter has led me to be convinced that a number of actions and things not in themselves actionable or unlawful if done separately without conspiracy may, with conspiracy, become dangerous and alarming, just as a grain of gunpowder is harmless but a pound may be highly destructive, or the administration of one grain of a particular drug may be most beneficial as a medicine but administered frequently and in larger quantities with a view to harm may be fatal as a poison." And he concluded that a conspiracy is "a powerful and dangerous engine, which in this case has, I think, been employed by the defendants for the perpetration of organized and ruinous oppression."

With these words before us, we should return to a statement made in the *Mogul* case by the same Lord Chancellor Halsbury who presided over the unanimous judgment of the law lords in the *Leathem* case. There he had said: "What injury, if any, has been done? What legal right has been interfered with? Because if no legal right has been interfered with, and no legal injury inflicted, it is vain to say that the thing might have been done by an individual, but cannot be done by a combination of persons." It is true that Halsbury then said he did not deny there were "many things which might be perfectly lawfully done by an individual, which, when done by a number of persons, become unlawful," referring to an instance of organized co-ordinated hissing of an actor. But trading, he said, is different from hissing and insulting. Merchants must seek the co-operation of others without whom they cannot carry on business. Yet he could not see a labor union—a lawful enterprise under British statutes—in this light, although it could function and exercise its normal purposes only in the same way a company did.

Halsbury, who could see no wrong in the *Mogul* case where the combination of defendants ruthlessly crushed the plaintiff without offering it any alternative, stoutly declared that if Leathem could not recover against the labor union defendants "it could hardly be said that our jurisprudence was that of a civilized community." And this, when Leathem's alternative of avoiding damage by complying with the union's terms was always open. Of course, the union was determined to supplant Leathem's employees with their members of longer standing who had been out of work for some time. This no doubt was regarded as thoroughly wicked, although it is of the very essence of competition as understood by sober and conservative business folk. At any rate, Chief Justice Palles of the Irish Queen's Bench Division thought his colleagues were behaving most inconsistently in the *Leathem* case. He concluded that however much he disliked what the defendant unionists had done, he could not conscientiously read the law as declared in the *Mogul* case and *Allen v. Flood* to furnish anything other than complete support for the legality of their conduct.

THE LAW OF THE TRILOGY

Now these three cases are what is called law. Just what that law is seems to defy statement in principles which judges and scholars can agree upon and consistently apply. At first it looks as if people are free to combine and in concert to inflict serious harm on others, as long as they do not indulge in conduct falling into categories of specific torts or crimes and as long as they can justify the commission of harm by showing that it was not done wantonly but was in pursuit of advantage and gain. In other words, combination is not illegal since combination alone is not a tort or a crime. Similarly a refusal to do business with another is not illegal since it is not a tort or a crime. Finally the refusal by members of a combination to do business with others is not illegal as long as it is done to serve some selfish purpose cherished by them. This is apparently the lesson of the *Mogul* case.

In *Allen v. Flood* we learn that this is still true, although Lord Herschell, who apparently did not participate in the *Mogul* decision, clearly expressed his doubt that the conduct of the defendants in that case depended on their showing any sort of justification. He thought it obvious that motive was immaterial as long as the defendants had not engaged in activity which was unlawful under any established category of tort or crime. In his opinion appears what might be called a very broad civil rights doctrine—the unquestionable right of anyone to indulge in activity not traditionally illegal and not contrary to any statute, regardless of its harmful effect on others and regardless of the actor's motives. He did not address himself to any sort of conspiracy doctrine, except to observe in passing that it is anomalous in more than one respect.

Up to this point the law seemed clear enough. The only matter still open related to the requirement for a showing of justification or excuse. Herschell took the position that such a requirement did not exist as long as the conduct leading to harm was not comprised under some established category of tort or crime or was not unlawful under a statute. But the decision of *Quinn v. Leathem* knocked all this galley west. In so far as it depended on the civil conspiracy doctrine, it undid a great deal to which the House had committed itself in the *Mogul* case. Indeed, this was virtually the reintroduction in civil dress of the old notion of criminal conspiracy, which had presumably been laid to rest for all time by Parliament in 1875.

The position that the House of Lords adopted in the *Leathem* case was simply this. If a common jury does not approve of the conduct of a group of people acting to promote their own ends, then such conduct is illegal when it causes harm to another, even though this conduct does not fall into any established category of illegality. And it still retained this position although the evidence showed clearly that the group's conduct was carried on for the purpose of advantage and gain —clearly enough, at any rate, so that under the doctrine of the *Mogul* case if the defendants had been businessmen, a judgment against them would not be sustained. In other words, the *Leathem* case was an unwholesome and rather disgraceful exhibition by the law lords of what might accurately be called both class prejudice and skulduggery. It is to Parliament's credit that the effects of this decision were wiped out by legislation in 1906.

It is difficult in commenting on these three famous cases not to insist that the prevailing law governing the conduct of all groups trying to get ahead should be embodied in the adage "What's sauce for the goose is sauce for the gander." In other words, what is good law for the activities of businessmen is also good law for the activities of labor leaders. Of course, this position seems unassailable as far as it goes. The fault implicit in this philosophy is the assumption that what happened in the *Mogul* case was desirable or even tolerable. But here arises the crux of the whole matter.

Granting that what the defendants did in the *Mogul* case was ruthless and deliberate, resulting in no benefit to anyone but themselves and only in detriment to society as a whole, who is going to make this judgment officially? Are the judges in a position to do so as a matter of common, or unwritten, law? The answer seems clearly to be in the negative. That is essentially an issue for the legislature to handle, as Lord Bowen indicated in the *Mogul* case, implying that even Parliament would find it impossible to choose adequate standards of conduct. Like most other matters of grave social policy, that is a matter with which the peoples' representatives, politically elected and responsible to their constituents, should handle. If these representatives are inept, according to popular opinion, they can be kicked out and replaced at the next popular election.

Now, in this respect, what difference is there between the conduct of traditional business enterprise and that of the new type of co-operative business enterprise called labor unionism? The answer is: absolutely none. This is no attempt to defend labor unions in what they do. Many believe with good cause that labor unions have been up to a good deal of mischief in the past and that several of their leaders are rascals who are out for all they can get. Rather, it is an attempt to persuade people to think honestly and clearly about one of the most troublesome issues confronting us all in modern times. One way of approaching the problem is to show how thoroughly mixed up on this matter were the deliberations of one of the world's most important and influential judicial bodies. Assuredly there is nothing very complicated about the common law involved in this discussion. And the duty of judges to apply it is equally simple and forthright. If the result of its application seems shocking, society has the power under our type of government to change the law. And this conclusion applies with equal force to the law as it is brought to bear on the activities of companies and of unions alike.

Let us reflect on these three cases briefly before we dismiss them for good. The combination in the *Mogul* case put the screws on the shippers of tea so that they could not avail themselves of the plaintiff's ships. Thus it suppressed competition, and in the name of competition maintained a monopolistic control of a substantial cost item in the price of tea. The plaintiff was ruthlessly eliminated, as the combination intended it should be. It could have gone elsewhere for trade. And if the public does not like the price of tea, it can drink hot water. The House of Lords said that if society does not like this, let it think up something better and enact it in legislation.

The boilermakers' business agent in *Allen v. Flood* told the employer that the union members would not work for him at all unless they could do all of his work, which they were competent to do. The employer acquiesced by discharging the two men he had employed, who were not members of the union. This was hard on them, but they could no doubt find work elsewhere. If they could not find such work, then the result would be two shipwrights unemployed instead of two boilermakers. Such a result could increase the employer's labor bill, as he might have made a better wage bargain with the shipwrights than he had made with the union. Society, therefore, might suffer to some extent through the increased price of ships. But the House of Lords, this time in a six to three vote, again said that if society does not like this, it can change it by legislation.

The union leaders in *Quinn v. Leathem* put the screws on Munce, the urban retail butcher, so that he in turn would compel Leathem, the slaughter-house man, to deal with the union on its terms if he still wanted Munce's custom. They were much more considerate than the combination of defendants in the *Mogul* case were to the plaintiff in that case. They did not try to run Leathem out of business. Indeed they wanted him to remain in business with union employees of long standing doing his work for him. Of course, they were not very considerate about Leathem's present employees whom they wanted to displace with their own unemployed members. But as far as they were concerned, it was a choice between one or another of the two sets of workmen remaining unemployed. Naturally they made the choice in favor of their own lads. Leathem's loyalty to his old employees was commendable and touching. But it is hard to see why he should expect both to have his cake and eat it in a world run on the principles set forth in the *Mogul* case. Yet here the House of Lords unanimously said that it was its business, and not society's as a political matter, to intervene on behalf of Leathem—a position which it is unthinkable Lord Herschell would have taken had he still been in the House.

It seems apparent from the perspective of years that the House of Lords deeply regretted its position in *Allen v. Flood* shortly after it was taken. Certainly it indicated in the *Leathem* case the flimsiest distinction possible between the two cases— that Allen could not in his sole capacity have constituted a conspiracy, conveniently ignoring the fact that he was speaking for a whole local union of boilermakers, and implying that his conduct was actually quite as antisocial as that of the defendants in the *Leathem* case. In any event, the latter case was an excellent chance to repair the damage done in the former, and the House did not let it slip.

In this famous Trilogy we have a suggestion of what was later to be termed in this country the *illegal purpose* doctrine— a judicial device by which courts were in a position to hold unlawful any conduct of labor unionists which was outwardly lawful but through which a union was attempting to achieve some end not judicially approved. As long as the courts were willing to reserve this power to declare any particular objective unlawful—apparently in accordance with some subjective judicial standard of how business should properly be conducted— then in the name of law they were able to crack down on any union activity not to their liking. All laymen reading this book must perceive quite as easily as lawyers do that this was an extraordinary way to administer the law—making it up as you go along and to suit your own notions of propriety.

There is nothing wrong with an illegal purpose doctrine as long as the proper body states what the illegal purpose is. That body is the legislature, speaking for the people who elected it. In England, the legislature's voice is final and controlling except in so far as the courts may find loopholes by interpretation. In the United States, the legislatures, both state and national, must stay within the provisions of our constitutions as the courts read them. But within these limits, the legislatures alone have any right to say what are the illegal purposes of trade groups, be they employer or labor groups. What the legislatures should conclude are illegal purposes is a large order. Society alone, expressing its social and economic aims politically, can supply the answer. But one thing seems already clear from our consideration of the famous House of Lords Trilogy—we cannot safely leave these delicate issues of policy to our courts alone when they are so prone to develop one law for industry, and another law for labor.

CHAPTER III

FREE ENTERPRISE IN AMERICA—
CONFLICTING STATE POLICIES

Scarce any man has the means of knowing a twentieth part of the laws he is bound by. Both sorts of law are kept most happily and carefully from the knowledge of the people: statute law by its shape and bulk; common law by its very essence. It is the judges (as we have seen) that make the common law. Do you know how they make it? Just as a man makes laws for his dog. When your dog does anything you want to break him of, you wait till he does it, and then beat him for it. This is the way you make laws for your dog: and this is the way the judges make law for you and me. They won't tell a man beforehand what it is he *should not do*—they won't so much as allow of his being told: they lie by till he has done something which they say he should not *have done*, and then they hang him for it. What way, then, has any man of coming at this dog-law? Only by watching their proceedings: by observing in what *cases* they have hanged a man, in what *cases* they have sent him to jail, in what *cases* they have seized his goods, and so forth. —Jeremy Bentham, *Works*, Volume 5, page 235, 1843.

No DEVELOPMENT comparable to the House of Lords Trilogy ever took place before the United States Supreme Court. These labor matters used to be local issues in this country. Our parallel to the famous English cases may be found in the reports of state supreme court decisions. In our leading industrial states there were two main lines of development. These may conveniently be termed the conservative philosophy—reflected chiefly in decisions of the Massachusetts court—and the liberal philosophy, set forth most typically in the decisions of the New York court and suggested in two of Justice Holmes' famous dissents in the Massachusetts cases.

Each of these state courts applied the common law. The fact

that they differed radically from each other should not be surprising since each court, in its own jurisdiction, was entitled to regard whatever it thought best as *the* common law. Indeed, that was its job. Hence, we shall see the Massachusetts court doing almost exactly what the House of Lords did in the Trilogy cases, employing the illegal purpose doctrine instead of resorting expressly to a notion of civil conspiracy. And we shall see the New York court finally adhering to Herschell's position in *Allen v. Flood*—the civil rights theory. Holmes on the other hand carved out a middle course that harm intentionally inflicted is actionable unless justified, taking a view of justification broad enough to include the normal objectives of labor unions.

THE MASSACHUSETTS DOCTRINE—A CONSERVATIVE APPROACH

Perhaps the most convenient point of departure is an American counterpart of the famous *Mogul* case discussed in the previous chapter. *Bowen v. Matheson*, decided in 1867 by the Massachusetts Supreme Court, was not a labor case, although it bore a curious resemblance to one in that it involved the supplying of sailors to ships sailing out of Boston harbor. John Bowen was engaged in housing and boarding seamen between voyages and in signing them up on out-going vessels. He complained that a combination of Boston shipping masters —his competitors—had agreed among themselves to secure control of all of this business locally, to the exclusion of all nonmembers of their combination. In short, they excluded him. To implement this purpose, he declared, each member had conspired with the others to refrain from dealing with any sea captain who hired any men from nonmembers. Since the combination controlled the great bulk of available seamen—so many, that no sea captain could man his ship without going to the combination—all shipowners and sea captains began to drop the services of nonmembers and to patronize only the members of the association. Thus the plaintiff John Bowen was faced with ruin. He asked the court to stop the association from conspiring to ruin him and to grant him damages against its members.

Judge Chapman, speaking for the Massachusetts court, ignored the allegation of conspiracy, observing that to win, the plaintiff must have set forth factually the commission of illegal acts. What the plaintiff did charge was that (1) defendants took men out of ships hiring his men, (2) they refused to ship men with his men, (3) they prevented men from shipping through him, (4) they notified the public that "they had laid him on the shelf," (5) they publicly notified his customers and friends that he could not ship men for them, and (6) they "did break up the plaintiff in his business and calling by their conspiracy, acts and doings, as aforesaid, and compel him to abandon his said business." These charges the court thought unimpressive because they did not describe any specifically illegal conduct falling within settled categories of tort or crime.

By reference to the association's charter, the court perceived that conformance to a wage schedule for seamen was the chief item of its policy. Concerning its various stipulations, as well as the matters charged by the plaintiff, the court failed to recognize anything unlawful. "If their effect is to destroy the business of shipping-masters who are not members of the association," Judge Chapman said, "it is such a result as in the competition of business often follows from a course of proceeding that the law permits. New inventions and new methods of transacting business often destroy the business of those who adhere to old methods."

Here was economic pressure on the shipowners, by cornering the market for able seamen, to compel their co-operation in eliminating Bowen. This was a secondary boycott pressure, implemented by the refusal of all association members to deal with any shipowner who dealt with the plaintiff. As in the *Mogul* case, a monopoly existed in this collective assertion of privileges not to deal with others with the object of destroying the beneficent competition of rivals offering the same commodity at a lower price. A more charitable view of the association's program might reveal an attempt to maintain a high level of seamen's wages and other working conditions, with an incidentally higher commission for shipping brokers, against the attempts of enterprisers like the plaintiff to keep both such items more nearly at the marginal level indicated by an uncontrolled market demand. This curious similarity to the normal objectives of labor unions is apparent only because the commodity in which the parties dealt was the services of men. Had that commodity been lumber, for instance, the suggestion of similarity would have been absent, although the analogy which has just been suggested would still remain in a purely economic sense.

In this case the Massachusetts court made its general position fairly clear. Since nothing the association had done fell within any established category of tort or crime, the harm it inflicted on the plaintiff in the pursuit of gain was not actionable but was justified as competition. The members of the association, individually or in concert, were free to deal with whom they wished, or even not to deal with anyone at all, if such a course promoted their interests. This seemed a fair statement of the common law, consistent with the later *Mogul* pronouncement by the House of Lords.

Hence the decision of the Massachusetts court three years later in *Carew v. Rutherford* is surprising. There a general contractor brought suit to recover $500 from a union on the ground that this sum had been illegally exacted from him. It seems that he was erecting a cathedral on contract and that he sent certain ornamental stone cuttings to be done in New York. The stonecutters' union had resolved in its bylaws that such work should not be sent out because it deprived them not only of an opportunity to earn more money but also of a chance to teach their apprentices their complete trade. Pursuant to this resolution, the union had notified the general contractor that he must not send out such work. Since he proceeded to do so, the union officials imposed a fine on him roughly equivalent to their opinion of the damages they had suffered, declaring that they would not continue work until it was paid. In order to keep his stonecutters on the job, the contractor paid the $500 fine to the union. Then he brought suit for restitution after the cathedral was completed.

The Massachusetts court, declaring the union's act to be extortion, allowed recovery of this sum on the theory of duress. This must have come as a bit of a shock to the Journeymen Freestone Cutters' Association of Boston and vicinity who in the preamble to their constitution had provided:

"Whereas in the course of human events civilization is spreading its salutary effect over the globe; and whereas societies and honorable combinations are marching hand in hand with enlightened bodies, and for their mutual support and protection certain classes of men in their respective callings do assemble and commune together, to adopt rules and regulations to govern their professions, and to develop and embrace the advantages that are derived from a thorough knowledge of business throughout this land; and whereas stonecutters heretofore, in this great and growing country, were looking on with calm indifference at the prosperity derived from such association, but have finally been awakened from their lethargy, and now behold with delight the solid advantages they may derive from a similar institution; they therefore have formed themselves unanimously into one body, to guard and cherish that trade which gives to them an honorable livelihood, and do adopt for their government the following constitution and by-laws, and to show to the world that they are alive to their moral as well as their pecuniary interest."

Although Judge Chapman for the court quoted from a criminal statute dealing with extortion, he chose to rest the civil liability of the union on the common law. From old English law, he mentioned several quaint precedents of tort liability against defendants for threatening to maim and vex one's customers and workmen so that they ceased buying and working;

against a defendant who "menaces my tenants at will of life and member, *per quod* [because of which] they depart from their tenures"; and against a defendant who frightened away wild fowl by discharging guns near a decoy pond. In order to suggest the idea of civil conspiracy, he cited the case of one who hired several to hiss and groan at an actor to persuade the manager to cease employing him. And he mentioned a line of cases wherein money was recovered from those who had exacted its payment by withholding property to which they had no right, by oppression and fraud, by abuse of legal process, by threats of a groundless prosecution and by show of force with a group of armed men. As if these precedents bound the defendants in this case from stating a condition to the continuance of their services as free workingmen, the court called their conduct "an illegal, if not a criminal, conspiracy; . . . a species of annoyance and extortion which the common law has never tolerated."

The judge went on to remark that the principle involved did not interfere with business, but protected it. "Every man has a right to determine what branch of business he will pursue," he declared, "and to make his own contracts with whom he pleases and on the best terms he can. . . . He may refuse to deal with any man or class of men. And it is no crime for any number of persons, *without an unlawful object in view,* to associate themselves together and agree that they will not work for or deal with certain men or classes of men, or work under a certain price, or without certain conditions."

In this passage the judge may seem to have talked himself out of his decision against the defendants, although if faced with this charge, he would no doubt have pointed to the phrase in italics. And this would reveal something very strange, indeed, about the state of the law. For the court's general principle is supposed to indicate what is or is not lawful. If workmen are told they may in combination lawfully refuse to deal with any man and refuse to work without certain conditions, it seems odd that when their conduct is carefully confined to such ambit, the court should still be able to find something unlawful about it.

The court here seemed to believe that the union's conduct was quite different from a strike for higher wages, which by this time it was apparently willing to condone as lawful, even if the result were an increase in wages far in excess of the $500 here involved. At first glance, this distinction may seem clear. The defendant's conduct resembled the shakedowns of the prewar racketeer days. They were using an extralegal technique to compel the payment of money which was not owed to them and which they could not have secured by suit in the courts. Furthermore a strike usually concerns future wage rates and implies an unwillingness to continue work unless the employer will pay a more advantageous scale. And such a concerted exercise of pressure obviously bears a close relationship to the exchange of something of value controlled by the strikers and which the employer is anxious to secure if a price can be determined.

But strikes are not always called to achieve only future benefits. They have been known to secure retroactive settlements as well, occasionally amounting to very substantial sums for each worker concerned. Moreover, the exaction of a money payment under circumstances similar to those in the case under discussion has in recent times been termed a reasonable exercise of economic pressure to achieve a desired economic end. In 1937 the House of Lords declared that a trade association of merchants may black-list an individual merchant who sells certain commodities at prices below an approved schedule and, by threatening to withhold their patronage from any manufacturer who sells to the proscribed merchant, may lawfully compel that merchant to pay a stipulated fine before his name is removed from the black list. The English Court of Criminal Appeal had in a similar situation affirmed the conviction of this same association's secretary for blackmail.

But the law lords took the position that, in the absence of a statute forbidding price fixing, the use of collective coercion of this sort was proper to enforce compliance with the association's schedule of prices. They then observed that the technique employed was the only way in which such coercion might be practiced. For the rebellious merchant, who was not a member of the association, had already violated the schedule. Since there was no way to insure that he and others like him would not do so again without compelling him to make amends for the past and thus really feel the penalty, the imposition of the fine was in their opinion a permissible alternative to the continuation of the black listing.

In some respects the trade association practice condoned by the House of Lords was far more questionable social conduct than that condemned by the Massachusetts court in this labor case. First, it was allowed as a device to enforce price fixing and to suppress competition in the sale of goods—a particularly reprehensible restraint of trade. And second, it depended for its success on the secondary boycott technique. The practice in the Massachusetts case, on the other hand, does not appear to have involved either of these factors. Certainly it was true there, as in the English case, that the union could hardly have insured recognition of its policy without imposing a punishment for a past offense, enforced by a concerted refusal to work.

The union's motive, then, seemed quite as reasonable as that of the English trade association in the sense that it was not just to make easy money but was to protect trade standards. And in each case the practice depended on a concerted refusal to continue trade relations—by the union to work and by the association to deal—a recourse recognized by each court concerned as lawful in itself. Hence it seems fairly clear that the Massachusetts court in this case initiated its illegal purpose doctrine under which it could declare unlawful any outwardly lawful acts of labor unions, undertaken to achieve purposes of which the court does not approve. The net result of this earlier Massachusetts litigation is no different from that in the Trilogy of English cases, although it does not expressly depend on any idea of conspiracy.

HOLMES' ATTIC SALT IN THE MASSACHUSETTS CHOWDER

In the decade commencing with 1896 the Massachusetts court
went on to establish in an important series of cases its principles
of modern labor relations law from which it did not recede
until recently. The first of these, *Vegelahn v. Guntner,* is chiefly
important because of the challenging dissent filed by Judge
Holmes. It seems that a union called a strike to secure better
wages and working hours and had established a picket line to
back up the strike, to persuade loyal workers to join them
and to discourage new employees from accepting jobs. By this
time all American courts had come around to the view—possibly as a matter of political expedience—that strikes for direct
objectives like higher wages and shorter work days were lawful.
The Massachusetts court accepted this change by regarding
these objectives as lawful, thus excluding such strikes from the
operation of its illegal purpose doctrine. The issue before the
court in this case was the propriety of an order forbidding
peaceful picketing—a patrol posted outside the employer's
premises merely to accost and speak to persons leaving and
proposing to enter the plant. A majority of the court thought
the order was proper. Judges Holmes and Field disagreed.
Field thought it unwise to prevent a striker from trying to persuade applicants for jobs not to apply, by simply relating the
truth, believing it "a dangerous principle to leave his liability
to be determined by a jury upon the question of his malice or
want of malice."

But Holmes raised some broad issues in stating what he
called the less popular view. He denied the court's assumption
that the patrol necessarily implied a threat of bodily harm to
anyone. Conceding the infliction of temporal damage and the
proposition that it is actionable unless justified, he observed
that the law recognizes justification in numberless instances.
On this issue of justification, he observed that judicial reasoning was frequently inadequate. "The true grounds of decision
are considerations of policy and of social advantage," and logic

built on universally accepted general propositions of law solves few problems. Propositions concerning public policy, on the other hand, are not generally accepted. Although a special training is required to form an intelligent opinion about them, judges nevertheless act upon them, he observed, rather as inarticulate instincts than as definite ideas. A new tradesman drives established rivals to ruin, but the courts do not call this unlawful.

"The reason, of course, is that the doctrine generally has been accepted that free competition is worth more to society than it costs, and that on this ground the infliction of the damage is privileged," as long as "the damage is done not for its own sake, but as an instrumentality in reaching the end of victory in the battle of trade." Of course, the methods of inflicting this damage must be carefully scrutinized. He went on to say that force or threats of force are not permissible. But it is otherwise with persuasion of free customers—the refusal or withdrawal of various pecuniary advantages within the defendant's lawful control, and the withdrawal of or threat to withdraw, such advantages from third persons who have a right to deal or not to deal with the plaintiff, as a means of inducing them not to deal with him either as customers or servants. As to threats, compulsion, annoyance and intimidation, words only too apt to suggest unlawfulness in themselves, "it depends on what you threaten" or how you compel, annoy or intimidate. In this respect, economic pressure and violence should be sharply distinguished.

Holmes deprecated the commonly heard assertion "that the conflict between employers and employed is not competition," and he declared: "If the policy on which our law is founded is too narrowly expressed in the term free competition, we may substitute free struggle for life. Certainly the policy is not limited to struggles between persons of the same class competing for the same end. It applies to all conflicts of temporal interests." At the peak of his dissent Judge Holmes used language which has been and still is widely quoted. He said:

"It is plain from the slightest consideration of practical affairs, or the most superficial reading of industrial history, that free competition means combination, and that the organization of the world, now going on so fast, means an ever increasing might and scope of combination. It seems to me futile to set our faces against this tendency. Whether beneficial on the whole, as I think it, or detrimental, it is inevitable, unless the fundamental axioms of society, and even the fundamental conditions of life, are to be changed. . . . One of the eternal conflicts out of which life is made up is that between the effort of every man to get the most he can for his services, and that of society, disguised under the name of capital, to get his services for the least possible return. Combination on the one side is patent and powerful. Combination on the other is the necessary and desirable counterpart, if the battle is to be carried on in a fair and equal way."

When it is considered that Holmes wrote this in 1896, its tolerance and its penetrating wisdom are those of a true legal prophet. The full significance of his position appears in the Massachusetts court's next outstanding labor case decided in 1900—*Plant v. Woods*. Previously, he had recalled the day when many people thought that strikes were wicked, as organized refusals to work. In supposing that intelligent economists and legislators have given up that notion today, he implied his belief that other judges had long since concluded that strikes for *any* purpose, aside from incidental violence and breach of contract, were lawful. He expressed the hope that they would shortly share his views on picketing. This next case, therefore, must have given him a terrible jolt.

It seems that a large local union of painters and decorators had split up—probably over the same difference of opinion that had broken up the national organization of which it had been a part. The two resulting locals each retained the same name and local number and practically the same bylaws and constitution, the only obvious distinguishing features about them being the headquarter cities of the two resulting national unions with which these locals were affiliated. The old national union had its headquarters in Baltimore, and the defendants adhered to the organization still housed there. The plaintiffs, however, were in the offshoot union headquartered in Lafayette, Indiana. Prior to this law suit the Baltimore unionists had been conducting a campaign to wipe out the Lafayette union and to bring its members back into the fold. To achieve this end, they had refused to work for any employer or contractor who also hired men belonging to the rival union. Because the Baltimore adherents included most of the best workers, the employers could not afford to ignore their demand, deciding under economic compulsion to hire only them and not to deal with their rivals. In the latters' suit for an injunction to forbid the continuance of this undertaking, the Massachusetts court took the view that the Baltimore outfit was threatening to strike for the closed shop—that is, to secure an agreement from the employers that they would hire only workers belonging to the Baltimore union, membership in which would be a condition of employment. The court thought this practice should be enjoined. It intimated that the threatened strike was unlawful under the illegal purpose doctrine because its objective—the closed shop—was in its opinion undesirable.

The court emphasized a statement made by the Baltimore unionists that if the employers did not cease hiring men from the rival union, they "might expect trouble in their business." Now strikes always cause trouble of some sort and are intended to do so. But trouble is an ambiguous term and in connection with a strike—unless evidence appears to the contrary —should be assumed to mean no more than the general economic inconvenience normally attendant upon loss of a steady and unrestricted supply of labor. The court nevertheless thought it meant more than merely ceasing work, which it called the "preliminary skirmish." This threat of trouble, it declared, meant organized social pressure to discourage the continued employment of others, physical injury to the employers' property, attempts to injure and ruin the employers' business, and violence toward applicants for employment.

This passage calls for two caustic remarks. First, the court's belief that a strike necessarily implies damage of the sort suggested is plainly incorrect. Its assumption that the strikers would as a matter of course behave illegally and commit acts of violence, and its approval of an injunction based on this assumption before any such violence occurred, indicate a serious abuse of judicial authority. These apprehensions of unlawfulness, concededly not yet committed but anticipated in order to justify the injunction, betrayed a display of power which all classes of men might well dread. Second, the court openly disclosed its purpose to protect the employers and their business. But the employers had not complained or asked the court's protection, the suit having been filed only by the members of the Lafayette union. The threatened strike, it is true, was to be against the employers if they continued to hire members of that union. But if they were willing to forego hiring the Lafayette unionists in order to retain peaceful relations with the Baltimore boys, why should the court have concerned itself with nonexistent harm to their interests?

The court said its chief concern was to preserve the equal rights of all workmen to dispose of their services with full freedom. The Baltimore lads, of course, had no quarrel with this aim. They claimed it to be the basic premise of their position. But the court declared that the motive behind the threatened exercise of their liberty of contract was all important. It all depended upon whether they employed this coercion to further their interests or merely to injure others. If it was to further their interests, then it depended upon whether they used pressure generally recognized in the business world to be legitimate, as competition, or clearly thought to be unpermissible, as extortion. While the court admitted that the Baltimore unionists were attempting to promote their interests, it nevertheless thought that the case involved the outright commission of harm for harm's sake against the employers and the Lafayette union. It thought the situation to be more like extortion than competition, and that it resembled *Carew v. Rutherford,* the "extortion" case, rather than *Bowen v. Matheson,* involving the "corner" on seamen, and the *Mogul* case. As the court observed: "The necessity that the plaintiffs [the Lafayette unionists] should join this association is not so great, nor is its relation to the rights of the defendants [the Baltimore unionists], as compared with the right of the plaintiffs to be free from molestation, such as to bring the acts of the defendants under the shelter of the principles of trade competition."

Although the court did not expressly base its decision on the "illegal purpose" of the defendants, it impliedly did so by stressing the importance of motive in judging the legality of otherwise lawful conduct. Hence this rival unions case of *Plant v. Woods* is generally taken to mean that a strike for the closed shop is unlawful. And it is clear from the opinion that the court also dealt with the case under the maxim that the intentional infliction of harm on another is actionable unless justified, choosing to regard as justification only trade competition, which it found to be absent between the parties involved.

Certainly Judge Holmes so interpreted its position, for in his dissent he was pleased that the court had made its decision depend on the presence or absence of justification. Then he inferred from this position that the difference between him and the rest of the court was simply one of degree. He perceived in the court's opinion a tacit acknowledgment of the right to strike for wage and hour adjustments as long as the strikers refrained from violence and from inducing breaches of contract.

"To come directly to the point," he said, "the issue is narrowed to the question whether, assuming that some purposes would be a justification, the purpose in this case of the threatened boycotts and strikes was such as to justify the threats. That purpose was not directly concerned with wages. It was one degree more remote. The immediate object and motive was to strengthen the defendants' society as a preliminary and means to enable it to make a better fight on questions of wages or other matters of clashing interests. I differ from my brethren in thinking that the threats were as lawful for this preliminary purpose as for the final one to which strengthening the union was a means. I think that unity of organization is necessary to make the contest of labor effectual, and that societies of laborers lawfully may employ in their preparation the means which they might use in the final contest."

He went on to add: "I cherish no illusions as to the meaning and effect of strikes. While I think the strike a lawful instrument in the universal struggle of life, I think it pure phantasy to suppose that there is a body of capital of which labor as a whole secures a larger share by that means." He declared that production is consumed "by the multitude," and that "organization and strikes" may get a "larger share" for the organized, but only at the expense of the less organized, thereby implying no belief in the old wage fund theory. His view was that wage increases won by union efforts raised the prices of commodities. Then the union men with their higher wages came to market with greater purchasing power than did the unorganized workers who remained on a relatively lower scale of wages. "They do not create something out of nothing," he declared of the unions. "But," he concluded, "I think it lawful for a body of workmen to try by combination to get more than they now are getting, . . . and to that end to strengthen their union by the boycott and the strike."

Now just because Judge Holmes declared that the difference between a strike for higher wages and a strike for the closed shop is one of degree, and not of kind, does not make that proposition true. There is a good deal of difference in kind between pressure by a group of employees to secure higher wages, and coercion exercised by the bulk of the employees in a plant to compel their employer and fellow workers to acknowledge the employment of only union members. This latter purpose is an attempt to establish overwhelming bargaining power by preventing the employer's access to an open and uncontrolled labor market and by denying nonunion labor free access to employment in his plant. Perhaps Holmes meant that there was no difference in kind between the coercive techniques used in strikes for wages and strikes for the closed shop. This, of course, is true. In each case the striking employees concertedly refuse to work. One of the chief objects of the strike for the closed shop, however, is to disable the employer from resisting future collective bargaining undertakings such as a simple strike for wages. And the court condemned it as a grab for power.

Holmes must have experienced a sardonic pleasure when he learned that the majority of his court made the legality of strikes depend on the presence or absence of justification. He knew that the only justification the court recognized was so-called trade competition. Logically he might have taken its concession that strikes for wages were lawful to imply in such strikes the presence of competition. But he probably realized that, according to the court's conception of trade competition, none could fairly be found in wage strikes, and hence the court could logically find no justification for them. Yet it declared such strikes were permissible!

It should not, of course, require the legal insight of a Holmes to perceive that the Massachusetts court was really making the lawfulness of strikes depend on its conception of legality of purpose and not upon any intelligible conception of competition at all. Even this court had finally felt obliged to concede the legality of strikes for direct benefits, like wages. This may have been because it would be politically impracticable to continue deciding otherwise. After all, it was hard to impute any illegality of purpose to a desire for higher wages or a shorter work day. However, it saw no need to extend this privilege of striking for direct benefits to any but voluntarily associated workmen. And it was determined to discourage strikes intended to spread monopolistic and pervasive unionism.

Five years later this same court again aired its views on trade competition as justification for the commission of harm, in a suit involving a closed shop contract. Such a contract requires all employees of the company in question to be members of the union as a condition of continued employment. Pursuant to the terms of this contract, an official of a local shoe workers' union required an employer to discharge the plaintiff, an employee of some years' standing who had refused to join the union after the contract was executed. In his suit for damages caused by his discharge, the union official offered as a defense this term of the contract making union membership a condition of employment. Acknowledging this defense as proper if the contract were lawful, the court made its validity the issue in the case. It concluded that the contract for the closed shop was unlawful, thus depriving the union of its defense. Thus in this case of *Berry v. Donovan* the discharged employee received substantial money damages.

The union had argued in justification of the plaintiff's discharge that its achievement and use of the closed shop contract was "a kind of competition." But the judges did not regard this as competition. This was like the previous rival unions case of *Plant v. Woods,* since the union was not trying to get the plaintiff's job for one of its existing members but wanted him to remain at work as a member of the union. "Indeed," they said, "the object of organizations of this kind is not to make competition of employees with one another more easy or successful. It is rather, by association, to prevent such competition, to bring all to equality, and to make them act together in a common interest." And they then remarked that the defense "rests entirely upon another kind of socalled competition, namely, competition between employers and the employed, in the attempt of each class to obtain as large a share as possible of the income from their combined efforts in the industrial field."

This, the judges thought, was not in a strict sense competition at all but was a struggle among interests of different kinds, not operating on the same plane of endeavor. It was not like the conflict between two tradesmen for the same customers or between two groups of workmen for the same jobs. The union achieved no *direct* benefit from this closed shop policy, said the court, but secured only increased bargaining power. Such an object "is too remote to be considered a benefit in business" so as to justify the intentional infliction of harm in securing it. If it were otherwise, the unions could force all workmen to join and would have "complete and absolute control of all the industries of the country." And then it added: "Employers would be forced to yield to all their demands, or give up business. The attainment of such an object in the struggle with employers would not be competition, but monopoly." Indeed, the more this court attempted to distinguish labor cases from the good old business competition cases like the "corner" on seamen in *Bowen v. Matheson* and the *Mogul* decision, the more alike they seemed in all their implications.

But the Massachusetts court's position is not complete without reference to one more case. *Pickett v. Walsh,* decided in 1906, is a case frequently contrasted to *Plant v. Woods,* the rival decorators' case. This suit was also between two sets of workers. The bricklayers' and stonemasons' unions wished to secure the work of pointing bricks and stones as well as of laying them. This extra work had always been done by pointers, who were not members of either of the unions and who had been persistently denied a charter by the AF of L. The unions told the general contractors by whom their members were employed that they would not work for them at all unless they could do the pointing, as well. In other words, they would do all of their work, or none. While the employers preferred to retain the pointers at this work, because they were more skillful and charged less, they had to have the bricklayers and stonemasons on their jobs. Hence the contractors were obliged to let the union men do all of the work and to let the pointers go. The pointers thereupon sued the masons and bricklayers to enjoin them from this commission of harm through their threatened concerted refusals to work. The Massachusetts court decided this case in favor of the masons and bricklayers.

This is the way the judges looked at it. They observed that "there is no question of the general right of a labor union to strike." But they mentioned several purposes for which it might not lawfully strike, citing *Plant v. Woods*—the rival decorators' case—to the effect that "a labor union could not force other workmen to join it by refusing to work if workmen were employed who were not members of that union." The *Pickett* case, however, "is one of competition between the defendant unions and the individual plaintiffs for the work of pointing." The situation is peculiar because the fight here is necessarily a triangular one, involving two sets of workmen and their employers. In this respect it is like the *Mogul* case, the court said, overlooking the same resemblance to *Plant v. Woods*. "The right which the defendant unions claim to exercise in carrying their point in the course of this competition is a trade advantage, namely, that they have labor which the contractors want, or, if you please, cannot get elsewhere; and they insist upon using this trade advantage to get additional work, namely, the work of pointing the bricks and stone which they lay." The opinion indicates that all that the labor unions have done is to say: You must employ us for all the work or none of it, and they have not forbidden the employment of a particular category of artisans doing their own kind of work, as the union did in the decorators' case.

Thus the masons and bricklayers left the employers free to make their choice between the pointers and their unions, with the understanding that if they chose the pointers they would have to get somebody else to lay their bricks and stones, well knowing that they could get nobody else. The pointers could not lay brick and stone, but the masons and bricklayers could point. And pointing is not so far removed from masonry and bricklaying that the court could fairly deny the defendants' right to compete for this work. The unions would not allow the pointers to join their organizations because of their inability to lay bricks and stones. This was disastrous to the pointers. They had either to move away or learn new trades. "But this is not the first case," said the judges, "where the exercise of the right of competition ends in such a result. The case at bar is an instance where the evils which are or may be incident to competition bear very harshly on those interested, but in spite of such evils competition is necessary to the welfare of the community."

In the court's opinion, the distinction between these two cases lay in the fact that while the defendant decorators' union in *Plant v. Woods* was striking to achieve power, the masons' and bricklayers' unions in *Pickett v. Walsh* were striking to get more work for their members. Another way to put this is to say that while in the former case the infliction of harm could not be justified as competition, in the latter case it could be. Now this is really amusing. One of the reasons for the decision in *Plant v. Woods,* the decorators' case, is that a union has no right by striking for the closed shop to deny a workman the opportunity of gainful occupation. Yet in that case the union wanted the plaintiffs to remain at their jobs, merely stipulating that they join the defendants' union as a condition of doing so. But in *Pickett v. Walsh,* the pointers' case, the unions would not permit the pointers to join their organizations at all nor to retain their employment and trade. They deliberately forced the general contractors to discard them and saw to it that they were ruined economically. Not only did the Massachusetts court place a considerable premium on utter ruthlessness in determining its conception of the proper significance of the concept "competition," but it also seems to have abandoned the principle of protection accorded in *Plant v. Woods,* the decorators' case, to guarantee all workers free access to employment opportunities of their own choosing. Furthermore, while forbidding the strike for the closed shop in *Plant v. Woods,* the court in *Pickett v. Walsh* condoned what is now recognized as the most wasteful of all union coercive techniques—the true jurisdictional strike—hardly justifiable on any theory of law or economics.

From the foregoing it must appear that the Massachusetts bench had a fairly rigid conception of competition. It plainly believed that competition could exist only between people or groups of people striving against each other on the same plane of endeavor for the same thing. Apparently its thinking on this subject ran somewhat like this. The usual object of competition is a market of some sort for the goods or services of the competitors. The purpose of the strife is to secure trade outlets through preferred access to customers. Presumably completely free competition occurs when prices are shaved so that potential customers choose the successful competitor's wares to serve their own self-interest. This makes efficiency and skill in production and distribution the most important factors in free competition.

But when a group of enterprisers competing for a certain market band together and pool their economic power to control the market, an entirely different situation results, although theoretically this is still supposed to be competition. In the first place, the members of the group are no longer competitors among themselves. To that extent, at least, their compact has eliminated competition. Their object may also be to prevent any outside competition, usually through intermediate economic pressures on persons other than such potential competitors, so that they may have the market in question entirely to themselves and be in a position to control supply and fix prices. Pursuit of these objectives by this group is competition between the group and the enterprisers outside of the group. The result, if successful, is always a suppression of competition. This is a paradox apparent to the courts but is dismissed by them with the hope that persistent new enterprise will eventually win out and break down the noncompetitive control of the combination.

According to this conception of competition, the Massachusetts court did not believe that workmen competed with their

employers but were rather engaged in a joint productive effort with them to turn out goods which neither of them could
produce alone. In its opinion, employers and their employees
were not striving against each other on the same plane of endeavor and for the same thing. It did not think matters improved by saying that they were competing with each other for
a different division of the profits from their joint enterprise.
Believing all this, the Massachusetts bench could not justify
a simple strike for higher wages as competition, especially as it
could not overlook the early judicial decisions holding strikes
for wages unlawful because they were the very antithesis of
competition. Actually, it did not try to do so. In spite of its
feeling for classical theories of competition, the Massachusetts
judges knew that strikes for wages and other direct benefits—
in brief, all collective bargaining strikes—had to be made lawful
as a matter of political expedience. And as long as it stuck to
the view that the deliberate infliction of harm on another is
unlawful, unless justified, and at the same time defined justification only in terms of competition, no other explanation seems
possible.

In *Pickett v. Walsh*—the pointers' case—the judges recognized
the familiar pattern of conduct frequently undertaken by business enterprises. Here was an instance of economic strife between two sets of workmen competing between themselves for
the same opportunity to earn money—the work of pointing stones
and bricks. Success by one group meant exclusion of the other
from this advantage. Hence, if the court was to remain true to
its own notions, it had to excuse this commission of harm
during the course of competition. But in *Plant v. Woods*—the
rival decorators' case—a different situation was apparent. Instead of trying to exclude the Lafayette unionists from jobs in
that case, the defendants wished to share the available work
with them, simply requiring that they first join the Baltimore
union. There was no competition for the exclusive opportunity
to earn money. Since this situation did not have the appearance
of conventional competition, the court concluded that it could

not be justified as such. Finally it refused to recognize any analogy between the strike for the closed shop and a strike for higher wages because it thought that the same reasons of political expedience for conceding the legality of a strike based on already existing economic power did not apply to a strike aimed at building up even greater bargaining power.

Within its own broad principles of law, similar to those developed in the English cases, the Massachusetts court seems to have been confused. Analytically both the strike in *Plant v. Woods*—the decorators' case—and the strike in *Pickett v. Walsh* —the pointers' case—can be shown to have been competition. Neither the parties nor the judges in these two cases were then sufficiently accustomed to thinking about organized labor enterprise in terms of present-day economic analysis to recognize that this was true. If they had been, they would have realized that the defendants in *Plant v. Woods* were anxious to extend their organization in order to perfect the economic advantage of all organized labor against unorganized, or differently organized, labor in the decorating industry. They were concerned in carrying on their battle of trade, if you please, against the mass of unorganized or, in their opinion, poorly organized, workers who were satisfied with employment standards below those which they thought acceptable.

Through their organization they had established better conditions of employment than those which the rival union and unorganized labor had been able to secure. If they left employers free to hire nonmembers of their union at wages below their standard rates, their security would be undermined in the long run. Such an effect is today more easily observed in an industry consisting of several units producing the same commodity, some of which are unionized and some not. The employers in unorganized units enjoy a competitive advantage over organized units, based on the wage differential which normally exists. If the union is to retain its higher standards of employment, it must go out and organize those other units. If it does not do so, the consuming public will eventually tend to purchase only the cheaper nonunion-made goods; and the organized employers will either have to abandon the union employment standards or go out of business.

This, of course, hurts the union. Naturally the union, in striving to overcome this effect, does not attempt to put the nonunion plants out of business but undertakes to eliminate the nonunion competition by absorbing it into the union ranks. Such an undertaking seems reasonably described as competition between organized and unorganized labor. Nor does strife between two unions already established in the same industry, as in *Plant v. Woods*—the decorators' case—seem much different from this, when one of them has secured high employment standards and the other has not. For in a competitive sense the more successful union is entitled to believe that it is prevented from maintaining its high standards and from achieving even higher ones just as much by the weak bargaining of the other union, over whose affairs it has no control, as it is by the individual bargaining of completely unorganized labor, over which it likewise has no control.

In the long run, the Massachusetts court, and other courts following its lead, got no further than did the House of Lords in developing a consistent body of law to govern the activities of both business and organized labor enterprise. It first enunciated a broad principle based on the maxim that harm intentionally inflicted even without recourse to specifically illegal means is actionable unless justified, stating clearly that trade competition is an acceptable justification. This was not as broad as the justification asserted by the House of Lords in the *Mogul* case—pursuit of self-interest and gain—but it meant the same thing. Then, by construing the concept of trade competition in an exceedingly narrow fashion, it held organized labor accountable for all harm it caused others through the exercise of purely economic pressures in the pursuit of self-interest and gain. And it denied the effect of this category of justification except in one case of a ruthless fight to the death, too closely resembling business competition to be treated otherwise. The House of Lords had also perverted its original broad principle of trade competition as a justification in this same fashion. But while the law lords kept an ace under the woolsack in the shape of the doctrine of civil conspiracy—to be used when everything else failed—the Massachusetts court, and others following it, invented the illegal purpose doctrine to use as a last resort. Both courts, however, failed to state any articulate standards of lawful conduct or legal objectives against which to judge the activities and motives of organized labor. This in effect promulgated a government of men and not of law.

THE LIBERAL DEVELOPMENT IN NEW YORK STATE

A startling contrast to these views occurred in the liberal philosophy developed at about the same time by the highest court in the neighboring state of New York. How the judiciary of two adjacent, highly industrialized states could have been such poles apart in their interpretations of what were supposed to be the same common-law principles must remain a mystery. At any rate, after the New York court had begun to follow the lead of the Massachusetts judges, it suddenly switched to the opposite extreme position taken by Lord Herschell in *Allen v. Flood,* the most liberal of the three House of Lords Trilogy cases.

In 1897 the New York court had decided in *Curran v. Galen* that a union was liable in damages to a nonunion employee whose discharge it secured under a closed shop contract. This contract, the court said, was invalid, declaring that while the "social principle" of organized self-help was all right, unions could not go so far "as either to intend, or to accomplish, injury to others." And it concluded its short opinion with the remark: "While it may be true, as argued, that the contract was entered into, on the part of the [employer], with the object of avoiding disputes and conflicts with the workingmen's organization, that feature and such an intention cannot aid the defense, nor legalize a plan of compelling workingmen, not in affiliation with the organization, to join it, at the peril of being deprived of their employment and of the means of making a livelihood."

Five years later this same court completely reversed its position, after a slight shift in its personnel. Thus, in *National Protective Association v. Cumming* a majority of the court, through Chief Justice Parker, established beyond any doubt the right of a union to sponsor a strike for the closed shop. Briefly he outlined the privilege of any employee to leave his job at will without stating his reasons and his freedom to disclose that he was quitting because he did not wish to work alongside of certain other workmen. If the employer wished to discharge these other workmen as the price of retaining the employee about to quit, he was at liberty to do so. "The same rule," he said, "applies to a body of men who, having organized for purposes deemed beneficial to themselves, refuse to work. Their reasons may seem inadequate to others, but if it seems to be in their interest as members of an organization to refuse longer to work, it is their legal right to stop. *The reason may no more be demanded, as a right, of the organization than of an individual, but if they elect to state the reason their right to stop work is not cut off because the reason seems inadequate or selfish to the employer or to organized society.* And if the conduct of the members of an organization is legal in itself, it does not become illegal because the organization directs one of its members to state the reason for its conduct."

Although the chief justice declared flatly "that the defendants had the right to strike for any reason they deemed a just one, and further, had the right to notify their employer of their purpose to strike," he nevertheless went on to suggest some reasons which might justify their decision not to work with certain fellow employees. "I know it is said in another opinion in this case," he declared, "that 'workmen cannot dictate to employers how they shall carry on their business, nor whom they shall or shall not employ'; but I dissent absolutely from that proposition, and assert that, so long as workmen must assume all the risk of injury that may come to them through the carelessness of co-employees, they have the moral and legal right to say that they will not work with certain men, and the employer must accept their dictation or go without their services." He pointed out that some of the workmen's compensation acts had been held unconstitutional and asked how else the men could protect themselves from the carelessness of fellow servants unless they could refuse to work with men who did not measure up to set standards of care. He then repeated that he was saying this not to justify completely the collective refusal to work with certain men but merely to point out that some obviously reasonable purposes did exist for such action.

The chief justice then derided the proposition that motive rendered the collective exercise of economic coercion lawful or unlawful. "Within all the authorities upholding the principle of competition, if the motive be to destroy another's business in order to secure business for yourself, the motive is good; but, according to a few recent authorities, if you do not need the business, or do not wish it, then the motive is bad. . . ." This reference to narrow Massachusetts conceptions of trade competition as a justification and to scattered state court decisions promulgating as law purely judicial notions of so-called "fair" and "unfair" competition, depending on the lenience or harshness of the aggressor, he meant as a contemptuous reminder that only legislatures, and not judges, had any business to inquire into motives behind otherwise lawful conduct or to declare such conduct unlawful because they thought its purpose unworthy. But even conceding the validity of this trend as sound law, he said that it made no difference in the decision of the case at hand.

This *Cumming* case was a struggle between two rival organizations of workingmen, somewhat like that described in *Plant v. Woods*—the Massachusetts case involving the struggle between the rival decorators' unions—although in some respects different. It appeared in the report that the defendants, by refusing to work for any employers hiring members of the rival union, wanted to drive the members of that union out of the industrial field of steam fitting and plumbing and to fill their places with their own unemployed fellow members. But it was also suggested that they thought that the members of the rival organization were not sufficiently up to the formers' standards of skill to make them eligible for membership in their own union—the fair implication being that they would otherwise be welcomed as members. Apparently the defendants were most concerned over the fact that their higher wages and other conditions of employment were being undermined by plaintiff's members, who were willing to work for less and were frequently chosen by employers for that reason. Hence, in so far as the defendants were attempting to take work away from the plaintiff's members, they were behaving lawfully. And in so far as they were trying merely to unionize such rivals as could qualify in their union, for the ultimate protection of their established standards, the chief justice thought that the defendants were still acting lawfully, even under the recent judicial trend toward standards of fair competition, the validity of which he conceded only for sake of the argument.

Toward the end of his opinion in the *Cumming* case the chief justice referred to the last of the trial court's findings, which read in part as follows: "I find that the threats made by the defendants and the acts of the said walking delegates in causing the discharge of the members of the plaintiff association by means of threats of a general strike of other workmen, constituted an illegal combination and conspiracy." He dismissed this as not a finding of fact, but a conclusion of law erroneously drawn from the facts. Since the findings nowhere even suggested that the defendants threatened an illegal or unlawful act, they could not possibly support a judgment "that absolutely enjoins the defendant associations and their members from striking."

This so-called finding of the trial court is of considerable interest, since it reveals in such an undisguised fashion the latent vitality of the old conspiracy formula, which even the dissenting justices of the highest New York court had the political good sense not to support openly. Justice Vann, for the dissent, saw the defendants' activity as illegal threats to destroy the employers' freedom to do business as they saw fit. His inability to reconcile defendants' acts with any conception of competition is revealed by the following statements: "Public policy requires that the wages of labor should be regulated by the law of competition and of supply and demand, the same as the sale of food or clothing. . . . Competition in the labor market is lawful, but a combination to shut workmen out of the market altogether is unlawful."

This decision in the *Cumming* case committed the New York court to a liberal view quite different from the narrow position adopted by the Massachusetts court. Another decision, five years later, revealed its complete acceptance of the legality of the closed shop. There it appeared that the defendant manufacturer had voluntarily entered into a closed shop agreement with a union. The employer had guaranteed compliance with its terms by giving a note to the union, on the understanding that this note would be paid if he violated the agreement. Subsequently he did break the contract. When the union sued him on the note, he based his defense on the contention that the agreement violated was void as against public policy because of the closed shop provision.

The highest New York court in *Jacobs v. Cohen* gave the union judgment on the note, upholding the validity of the agreement. Judge Gray, for the majority of the court, spoke of the "underlying law of human society" which "moves men to unite for the better achievement of a common aim" as a "social principle" justifying organized action. The "surrender of individual liberty" involved is, he said, "but an extension of the right of freedom of action," and unless it is specifically illegal or used merely to injure others with no ultimate purpose of selfish advantage, it is perfectly proper. Justice Vann, for the dissent, thought the closed shop agreement contrary to public policy, condemning it as a device through which the union had secured a monopoly of employment in the needle industry in New York. This abrogation of their own rights by both the employers and workers co-operating with the union, he said, "was a form of slavery, even if voluntarily submitted to, for whoever controls the means by which a man lives controls the man himself." But his voice was virtually the last note of resistance against the liberal trend in New York, at least until a kind of reaction set in around the end of the 1930's.

This account of judicial developments in Massachusetts and New York reveals the radically different conceptions of labor policy which prevailed in this country around the turn of the century. One school of judges took the position that the economic activities of unions were lawful or unlawful in accordance with the illegal purpose doctrine, which in effect meant in accordance with inarticulate judicial notions of rightfulness or wrongfulness of motive. The nearest this school approached to a helpful general principle was the acknowledgment that unions, like conventional business groups, might justify their harmful economic activities under the cloak of competition, but it took an exceedingly narrow view of competition—that of a pattern seldom reproduced outside of business circles. It failed to make allowance thereunder for most of the purely economic coercion initiated by unions intent on self-protection and gain. Instead of guiding itself by the principle that sauce for the goose is sauce for the gander, leaving the legislatures to decide as a political matter what conduct and objectives are permissible and what are not, this school of judges boldly undertook to decide these issues on their own responsibility.

The more liberal courts, on the other hand, took either one or both of two quite different positions. Some judges belonging to this school of thought believed that unions causing harm to others, while in pursuit of gain, were behaving lawfully unless they engaged in conduct specifically tortious or criminal in itself, such as assault and trespass. As long as unions refrained from specific transgressions of this sort, these judges declared them to be within the law as they found it to be, leaving the creation of new controls to the proper branch of government, the legislatures. Generally, they refused to scrutinize the purposes behind union activity, holding that if the outward conduct was lawful in itself, the purposes to be served by such conduct were none of their business as judges unless, of course, such purposes themselves were illegal under established categories of tort and crime.

This position, we may, for lack of a better term, call the *civil rights* doctrine. Some of the liberal judges, however, preferred to follow the maxim that the intentional infliction of harm on others is actionable, unless justified, taking a broad view of justification and including within it a conception of competition which covered all uses of concerted economic coercion for self-advancement and self-protection. This might conveniently be called the economic interest approach. But whatever we may choose to call these various judicial developments in nineteenth and early twentieth century America, they constituted, together with the contemporary English views, the foundation on which our modern law of labor relations has been built. They serve as a fitting threshold to the remaining chapters of this book.

CHAPTER IV

THE JUDICIAL RESTRICTIONS OF UNIONS—THE LABOR INJUNCTION

We especially object to government by injunction as a new and highly dangerous form of oppression by which Federal Judges, in contempt of the laws of the States and rights of citizens, become at once legislators, judges and executioners.—*Proceedings of the Democratic National Convention,* 1896.

THE GENERAL principles discussed in the preceding two chapters stemmed originally from litigation involving business combinations. But in the course of their adaptation to labor union cases they became somewhat confused. It is, of course, very easy to criticize the courts for applying these original principles in one way against business combinations and in another way against labor unions. But it is justifiable criticism as long as they remain on the books as accepted law. For then they should have been consistently applied. Even if they were so applied, however, the principles themselves would by no means remain beyond reproach. While courts applying these common-law principles consistently have done what they were bound to do as judges, it is not at all clear that such principles reflect a sound commercial policy in sanctioning the exercise of all kinds of economic coercion through uncontrolled combination, whether among businessmen or labor unions.

Some of these techniques have been ruthless and vicious. And it seems impossible to justify them under any conception of competition. Certainly the kinds of activities carried on by the business combinations described in the preceding two chapters are of no real service to the consuming public; and those of the unions cannot fairly be judged in any different light. Many no doubt regard such activities as the sort of competition which is the life of trade. But many more probably believe that competition of this character results in a stifling of trade and the throttling of that type of economic interplay between competing units which tends to benefit consumers in lowering prices by increased efficiency in production and marketing methods. For these activities constitute a course of conduct intended to promote the security of enterprisers through the control of production and marketing and the elimination of so-called "wasteful competition"—that is, of competition as it has been traditionally recognized in economics textbooks.

Perhaps the courts cannot fairly have been expected to hit upon a common economic theory of competition and to enforce it uniformly. Anyone who has been around must realize that there are always a variety of economic theories competing with each other in the general market place of ideas. Since many of us are addicted to one or another of such theories as the only valid one, we may find it shocking when the conclusion is suggested that the official choice of one system of economic values to prevail over all others is a political matter. No economist worth his salt would like to make this admission, any more than a priest of one church would concede that the choice of the true faith is a matter of the general consensus. Yet in so far as our legal system is concerned, the choice of our prevailing economic philosophy is inescapably a political matter. The obvious choice between economic philosophies now seems to be between substantially free enterprise, on the one hand, and a more or less controlled or planned economy on the other. Of course, these concepts are very broad verbalizations, charged in these days with a good deal of emotional content. But they do suggest attitudes and ways of thinking about our economic life. At least we may be able to agree that people subscribing to the idea of substantial free enterprise want an absolute minimum of official governmental control, while those embracing the idea of a controlled or planned economy feel otherwise, albeit these latter folk may differ radically among themselves as to the methods and degrees of control and planning.

But it does seem futile not to admit that the making of such choices is essentially a function of our political life. If it is, then such choices are not for our courts to make. They are, rather, matters for our legislatures to handle, within the framework of our state and federal constitutions. In this way alone can the choice be safely made if we are to continue as a representative government, even if the choice which actually prevails is regarded by some groups of experts as horrible and disastrous. It is theoretically possible for people in a country like the United States to become sufficiently educated to make fairly objective choices. As a matter of practical fact, most people voting on choices of this sort have only the haziest notions of what they imply, with perhaps particular convictions that the courses of action they support will best serve their own interests. And these choices at elections, as well as those made by elected representatives in response to the voting, are influenced largely by spates of rhetoric either too confusing to be intelligible or sufficiently clear to be disturbing. Nevertheless, this is the way our choices are made. Our judges should properly have no part in the matter at all.

When these policy choices have become crystallized into statutes, our courts just have to say whether or not these new laws are valid expressions of constitutional power. If they are, their job then is to interpret and apply them. Until such political changes occur, their function remains that of applying the values of the past as they are reflected in the principles of the common law. By and large, when the legislatures have not spoken, the common law leaves no room for judicial speculation about economic theories.

The inherited, unwritten common law contains categories of illegal conduct such as assault and battery, trespass, fraud and deceit, libel and slander and inducing breach of contract, as well as deeply imbedded notions about property and personal rights and their protection. Granted that it is not always easy to detect from evidence submitted in courts the absence or presence of specific illegal conduct like that just mentioned, yet it is perfectly simple to observe its complete absence in most cases of purely economic coercion. And when it is clearly absent in actions brought at common law to secure redress for harm caused by economic coercion, courts are supposed to dismiss such actions, regardless of what they may think about the implications of the coercive undertaking in question—certainly if it appears that it was initiated to promote some interest of the defendants.

Now it is true that the common law is occasionally rather vague and general, with plenty of room for judicial interpretation. Thus, a particular jurisdiction may have as part of its unwritten law the proposition that intentionally inflicted harm on another is actionable, unless justified. And a court applying this principle to a case in which economic coercion alone is shown, having found that no specific illegal act such as assault, trespass, fraud or libel has occurred, must then inquire into the crucial issue of justification. This is where it runs into difficulty about competition and economic theory in general. By and large, the only safe test the court can apply in detecting justification is whether or not the particular pressure in question was exercised to further some interest or objective of the person or group behind it.

A detail in this inquiry may well be whether or not this interest must be of *direct* pecuniary concern to the members of this group if the justification is to stand. If so, then the court's task of determining what is "direct" is a much greater problem than most people unfamiliar with our law could possibly imagine. Certainly it must be plain that the scrutiny of alleged justification in applying this principle of law gives play to the economic predilections of judges and invites them to enter upon excursions into the field of policy which is properly reserved for legislators only. Indeed, it is this danger which has no doubt led some courts to deny the principle of law under discussion and to insist that conduct harmful to others is illegal only if it falls within some clear-cut category of tort or crime such as assault and battery, et cetera, or constitutes a breach of a statute—the so-called civil rights theory.

Assuming, then, that a court should not make fundamental choices of policy in litigation involving economic coercion but should leave such matters to the legislatures, the proper judicial attitude may seem to be some kind of free enterprise philosophy. It can resemble complete laissez faire, as when the court recognizes no need for justification, or it can seem relatively limited, as when the court does require the showing of some kind of justification like self-advancement or self-protection in an economic sense—just as long, in either event, as it leaves out of consideration all theories of economics and sticks to settled categories of illegality and established rules of law as the standards to be enforced. But some people will then suggest that the courts pursuing either course have willynilly adopted the *economic philosophy* of laissez faire or free enterprise— that is, have adopted an economic value position. And the answer is that, while such a result may well be true, what the courts are really doing is to leave to the legislatures the choice of curbs, if any, to be imposed on all kinds of economic enterprise, business or labor. For whether we like it or not, the prevailing Anglo-American common-law philosophy has always been one of free enterprise.

The ideal of the common law was to build up a series of sanctions against specific types of behavior too egregiously bad to tolerate, such as assault and battery, et cetera, leaving plenty of room within which people remained free to operate at will. According to the spirit of the common law, no penalty was to be created against the use of purely economic coercion, so long as it was exercised by means which in themselves were perfectly lawful, such as buying, selling, and refusals to deal in any way with others. Perhaps the greatest confusion occurred in the common law when the courts created judicial curbs against the purely economic activities of labor combinations. Yet it must be said on behalf of the early courts that in creating these curbs, they were trying to fulfill their ideals of free enterprise by protecting business and industry—which they regarded as the life stream of society—from the most determined interferences with achievement of these ideals. Their mistake was a failure to recognize in the interests and activities of labor unions simply another type of economic enterprise—from the angle of trying to get ahead and to pursue gain, not much different from the types of enterprise they were trying to foster. It would seem, therefore, that the only way in which the courts could really be impartial, and at the same time achieve their common-law ideals, would have been to treat all purely economic activity as lawful until the legislatures declared otherwise or except in cases in which such activity did not conform to some established common-law principle requiring proof of justification.

SOME ASPECTS OF THE LAW OF TORTS IN RELATION TO LABOR UNIONS

Now it is time to examine in detail the nature of the controls which our courts have traditionally exercised over the economic activities of labor unions. From a formal point of view, these controls may be defined as convictions for the commission of crimes, adverse money judgments for the commission of torts, and injunctions restraining the continuance of injuries to property interests. Now everyone knows that in the heat of industrial conflict labor unionists frequently commit wrongful acts. If they beat up strikebreakers and representatives of management, assault them, or threaten to do so, they should be punished. And if they violate property rights by breaking windows, sabotaging a plant, damaging cars and goods and by otherwise invading tangible interests of others, they should be punished. Such conduct is obviously illegal. Society cannot compromise upon how it should be treated. But in most of our states there are more subtle categories of common-law tort liability, easily adaptable to labor cases, the desirability of which is not so clear.

Thus, some of our courts declare that conduct offensive or harmful to others, even if it is in itself absolutely lawful, becomes unlawful when done with malice. An illustration of this is the spite fence case. Two neighbors have a falling out and, just for spite, one builds a fence between their yards, anywhere from ten to thirty feet high. This sort of thing, with variations, has happened many times. Of course, the man building the fence has a perfect "right" to do it, or so several of our state courts have decided. His neighbor would have had no redress if the erection had been a building of some sort, shutting off light, air and the view in the same way. But other state courts have declared that the erection of a useless structure, just to spite one's neighbor, is tortious, the malicious motive making it unlawful. And they have made the offender remove it.

Another illustration is the man in the valley who does not like his neighbors above him on the hill. All of these people concerned are dependent on the percolating water beneath them, which they pump up for domestic use. Each has the property right, as an incident to the ownership of surface land, to pump up all of the water he wishes. The man in the valley pumps it continuously, and what he does not need, he lets run off on the surface. Since by force of gravity the percolating water constantly flows down to his pump, his neighbors on the hill soon have insufficient water for their needs. A court, holding that spite or malice makes otherwise lawful conduct unlawful, will prevent this sort of thing, although it recognizes the right of the man in the valley to take all of the percolating water if he puts it to some useful purpose. But the Wisconsin Supreme Court would not stop him when he merely wasted it to quench his spite, declaring that whatever his motive might be, it was the exercise of a property right. Indeed, it went to the questionable extent of deciding that even the legislature could not constitutionally prevent this conduct.

This sort of case may occur in the business world under

somewhat different circumstances. Thus, a rich man forecloses a mortgage on a business building in a very small town, taking the premises over himself. He fits up a place in it as a modern barber shop and then invites the town barber to leave his old stand and rent this new place. The barber refuses to do so, which is his right. Thereupon the rich man hires a couple of barbers from out of town to run his shop and enables them practically to give away haircuts and shaves until the first barber is ruined financially and has to shut down. Then the rich man leases his shop to one of the barbers he brought in and has a profitable investment. The Minnesota Supreme Court said that this was unlawful if the barber could prove that the rich man had done what he was alleged to have done. And when a small retail oil peddler refused to handle its oil on his house-to-house route, a great national oil company, which did not engage in retail sales, set up its own delivery service to undersell the peddler until he went into bankruptcy. When the company's immediate end was accomplished, it promptly sold its horses and wagons to another man who contracted to purvey its product. The Iowa Supreme Court said that this was unlawful.

Most people, no doubt, would agree that these two decisions were correct and achieved what they would call justice. They would probably justify their belief by concluding that the rich man and the oil company were rascals. But these cases are not as simple as that. They involve the lawful use of property—economic power, if you will—to advance temporal interests in a social system based on property and its free use. For surely even a rich man is free to give away haircuts and shaves. Presumably a great oil company is entitled to retail oil at as low a price as it wishes! While the defendant's motives may have been purely malicious in the spite fence and percolating water cases, in each of these last two the dominant motive was plainly commercial. The rich man wanted to lease his shop and the oil company wanted to maintain and protect retail market outlets for its product. Just as soon as the courts permit juries to speculate on the motives of these enterprisers in order to determine whether or not they were malicious, they are going to get into trouble. Indeed, there is something ironic about drawing indignant juries for this purpose from the very cross section of society which, by accepting the free haircuts and by purchasing the cheaper oil, made it possible for these instances of economic coercion to succeed.

In spite of the obvious difficulties, several of our courts believe that they can set up standards in accordance with which conduct of this sort can be judged lawful or unlawful. With the approval of some legal scholars, they are tending toward a new category of tort liability called unfair competition, under which they are trying to prevent conduct of the type just described. Some of them make recovery depend on proof of malice, although this malice frequently turns out to be simply the deliberate intention to do what was done. Other courts, recognizing this, incline toward legal controls of competitive methods which employ what they regard as the contemptible use of superior economic power. But they are taking a good deal on themselves when they try to establish reasonably clear standards of what might be considered fairness in the competitive world.

A referee of a boxing match applies a set of arbitrary rules to the fighters; but he would never think of making up such rules as he goes along or even of introducing into his decisions long-felt personal notions of what he believes is fair in the ring. Referees of sporting contests accept and conform to a set of legislated rules. They would be out of work very quickly if they did otherwise. Courts are expected traditionally to behave in much the same fashion. The rules they enforce have been long established and are well recognized. If they are to be changed, it seems best that the legislatures should make the changes. For any modifications of them strike at very fundamental social policy and should be considered and debated by our traditional policy-making branch of government. In this way such changes will become the resultant of all social opinion and will not tend merely to reflect the notions of a few judges, which vary from man to man.

Certainly courts judging the behavior of labor unionists in accordance with some standard of malice or unfair competition, which they have more or less made up for the occasion, are bound to get into trouble and produce confusion. What happened to the law lords in the meat cutters' case of *Quinn v. Leathem* may then happen to any judge. They may perceive wickedness, unfairness and malice in labor union activity no more ruthless than the conduct of the business association in the *Mogul* case, which the House of Lords thought perfectly permissible. And if courts once become well embarked on the attempt to prevent all purely economic activity which they do not believe to be fair, then all our economic life has become subject to judicial censorship and we will have slipped imperceptibly into an uncharted oligarchy.

Before examining any other categories of tort liability, we should consider one other aspect of harmful conduct which is clearly lawful aside from the motive behind it. Everyone will agree that it is lawful to spend one's own money or to withhold it, to deal freely with others or to refuse to do so. But suppose a man gives money to another to secure the murder of a third person. Here we have no trouble recognizing both crime and tort on the part of the man paying the money, for he did something more than merely pay out money. And if he had merely refused to continue a course of legitimate business advantageous to another unless such other person murdered a third, we should have an equally clear case.

Hence, we can probably afford to make the general statement that pure economic coercion, ordinarily lawful in itself when designed to secure an objective even quite harmful but not illegal in itself, becomes unlawful when exerted to secure an end which is illegal in itself. Such a principle is well established and is perfectly easy to apply as long as the court applying it is scrupulous in seeing that the objective to be secured by the economic coercion is illegal in itself when judged in strict accordance with other well-established common-law or statutory categories of tort or crime. The only possible difficulty—and it is a very real one—is that courts using this general rule may too easily slip into the habit of concluding that the objective to be secured is not to their liking and is, hence, illegal. This is the sort of thing which occurred when Anglo-American courts once used the doctrine of criminal conspiracy. It has unfortunately recurred in labor litigation as one phase of applying another very questionable category of tort liability called civil conspiracy. And it is almost exactly what happened in the development of the illegal purpose doctrine. A rule of this sort is a very dangerous toy for the courts to play with, because it enables them to conceal under the dignified cloak of legal verbiage conclusions on matters of economics and policy which only the legislatures should make.

Another tort category, adapted out of its original context to certain labor situations, is inducing breach of contract. This tort originated shortly after the middle of the nineteenth century in a case involving a once famous opera singer, Johanna Wagner. Lumley had her under contract to sing only for him in London. Gye induced her to break her contract with Lumley and sing only under his management. Now Lumley, of course, could have secured a judgment against Miss Wagner for breach of contract. But for reasons best known to him—perhaps Miss Wagner's impecuniosity—Lumley preferred to recover damages from Gye, who had started all the trouble. In a decision creating this new tort, the English courts gave him a judgment for damages against Gye. Apparently the judges believed that Gye had damaged a thing of value to Lumley, in the nature of a property right, just as obviously as if he had taken a hatchet and chopped up Lumley's coach.

Of course, the court's position might have been analogized to the rule described in a previous paragraph, except that Gye had not offered Miss Wagner money to commit a tort or crime but only to break her contract with Lumley. In any event, the tort became established for inducing the breach of any con-

tract for personal service. It has been developed in most jurisdictions to cover inducements of the breach of almost any
kind of commercial contract. Courts administering this tort
category at first required the proof of malice before recognizing
its existence in a particular case. But this has been changed,
since all that malice has finally come to mean is proof that the
inducement of the breach was deliberate and intended to further the defendant's ends. Since the inception of this tort,
however, courts have recognized justification for inducing
breaches of contract in proper instances, as when a doctor ad-
vises a patient because of the state of his health to break a
contract he has made binding him to work under precarious
conditions in the jungles of Africa.

These various categories of tort liability were not originally
used by the courts against labor unions. But when they discovered the usefulness of injunctions to control labor union
activities, the courts found that these vague and ambiguous
tort notions furnished admirable theoretical foundations on
which to rest their injunctions. In the decade preceding the
1890's American courts had followed the contemporary English
pattern of controlling the unpopular activities of labor unions
by awarding to the persons harmed money judgments in tort
actions against the unions' leaders. By this time the criminal
penalty had all but disappeared with the dwindling away of
the doctrine of criminal conspiracy, only occasional convictions
recurring at intervals under state statutes expressly prohibiting
certain defined activities of unions. Of course, neither of these
proceedings could be exercised against unions, as such, but
could be used practicably only against their leaders and members as individuals, since unions as a rule were not incorporated
and could not be sued as legal persons. But judgments for
damages and the occasional convictions under statutes were
not very effective sanctions against labor union activities harmful to others, even if they did succeed in stigmatizing so much
of what organized labor did as unlawful. Most of the time union
leaders and their constituents did not have the money to pay

judgments against them. And if they did pay, they were not in the least discouraged. Furthermore, adverse money judgments and criminal convictions usually followed the occurrence of strikes, picketing, and boycotts, and were small solace to employers for the harm which had already befallen them.

Employers and the courts needed a more adequate tool— some sort of preventive device which could be used to nip such mischief in the bud before it occurred. Criminal prosecutions and tort actions for damages were cumbersome and involved too much of the law's delay, what with lengthy procedure and jury trial. Furthermore they deprived courts of complete control over unions, because they could never be certain that juries would convict or bring in adequate verdicts against the defendants. Here was a situation crying out for a judicial technique which could insure swift and effective justice, and over which the courts might exercise a complete and exclusive control, free from the cumbersome devices of the common law and from the vagaries of common juries. The answer to this need happened along in a most fortuitous fashion.

THE LABOR INJUNCTION AND ITS ABUSE

Sometime around 1880 an equity court appointed a receiver to run a railroad which was in financial difficulties. It was the receiver's duty to manage the property in a prudent and profitable manner in order to protect the interests of investors. The railroad's employees threatened this objective by a strike for higher wages. But they did not realize that by this conduct they were interfering with the duties of an officer of a court—and of an equity court, at that.

Now the point of this story will be more clear after an interpolation explaining what an equity court is. An equity court—now usually the same judge who also sits as a court of law, except that he does not follow the same rules when exercising equity powers—is set up to do far different things from those ordinarily done by a law court. In short, it exists to "do equity," a concept which in itself requires some explanation. Equity is an historical development from the days of the early king's courts in England whereby the king's secretary, his chancellor, was ordered by the king to satisfy the royal conscience by doing justice in all cases, usually involving property, with which the king's regular courts of law were not empowered to deal under the limited common law and statutes of those days.

Eventually this duty was accorded to established equity courts which built up a body of precedent law all of their own. They were primarily concerned with litigation where money damages would not be suitable, where "the remedy at law would be inadequate," as they put it. Their judgments usually consisted of orders either to do or undo some act or to refrain from entering upon or continuing a threatened or already undertaken course of action. They did not have to use juries in reaching their judgments. They could fulfill their function of preventive justice by issuing a temporary restraining order or injunction, pending the actual trial, in order to be sure that the harm threatened could effectively be avoided if the trial ultimately revealed that the person threatening the harmful course of conduct really was in the wrong. And if the order of an equity court was not obeyed scrupulously, this disobedience was an offense which could be punished summarily as a contempt of court by the court itself, acting without a jury—such punishment being immediate imprisonment for as long as the occasion warranted.

Now to return to our story about the receiver of the railroad. He complained to the equity judge, for whom he was acting, that the strike endangered the property entrusted to him. He also asked for an injunction against the strikers, as well as for a temporary restraining order pending the necessary litigation. The court promptly issued this order against the strikers. When they ignored it, their leaders, with as many more of them as were necessary to break up the strike, were immediately jailed for contempt. Then the strike was over. The whole transaction, from strike to jail, could be counted in hours rather than in the weeks and months required in actions at law.

Here was a device for the control of labor disputes that really worked. Our courts rapidly took it over, making it a well-established American institution by the 1890's. All they required to be shown to make the injunction appropriate was an actual or threatened tortious invasion of property which, if it were not stopped or forbidden, would result in irreparable damage to the property, under circumstances indicating no adequate remedy at law. The only stumbling block—not a very serious one to the American judges—was the uncertainty of whether or not strikes and boycotts were harmful to actual property. Of course it was easy to see that strikers who broke windows and damaged buildings, machinery and rolling stock, or threatened to do so, were harming or threatening to harm property. But it was not so obvious that the purely economic pressures of unions, which caused great monetary losses to employers and sometimes to nonunion labor, were harmful to property. If they were, it was certainly in a different sense. For the harm to intangible interests of employers and nonunion labor, such as loss of production, of customers and business, and of profitable relationships, did not touch anything theretofore conventionally thought of as property.

The English courts consistently refused to issue injunctions against labor unions, even when they regarded the conduct assailed as unlawful, as long as such conduct was purely economic coercion causing harm to intangible interests of this sort. They regarded the injunction as something to prevent harm to irreplaceable tangible property interests. Thus, if the defendant proposed to cut a certain grove of old trees, claiming a right to do so, at the instance of another who insisted that the trees were his, an English court would order the defendant not to proceed with his plan, pending litigation. If, during the trial, the defendant was found to have been mistaken in his claim, the court would make the injunction permanent.

But the American courts chose to go further and to assume that intangible business interests also are property, to be protected by injunction. It seems apparent, however, that they really did not care whether or not such interests were property at all but were only concerned with declaring them to be things of value which they believed should be safe-guarded in the only practicable way to do so—by the injunction. And if this use of the injunction did not conform strictly to the traditions of equity, which recognized the use of this remedy only to preserve property from irreparable harm, then so much the worse for those traditions. Furthermore, they seemed never to have had any doubts that the remedy at law in damages for the harm done would be inadequate as long as the wrongdoer was a labor union, preferring rather to assume that wage earners would be unable to pay adverse judgments. And they completely ignored the policy behind the traditions of equity, which left people free from personal interference at the hands of the court, except in very special cases of unreasonably precipitated threatened harm to tangible property. And they disregarded the traditional assumption that the personal liberty of even a potential wrongdoer is more important to society than the fact that he might not be able to pay a judgment granted against him for the harm caused by his wrong.

Many American liberals have tried to undermine the use of the injunction against labor unions by arguing that this device is appropriate only to protect tangible property interests and that doing business and maintaining profitable relationships are not property at all. They agree with Holmes, who said in another connection: "By calling a business 'property' you make it seem like land, . . . An established business no doubt may have pecuniary value and commonly is protected by law against various unjustified injuries. But you cannot give it definiteness of contour by calling it a thing. It is a course of conduct and like other conduct is subject to substantial modification according to time and circumstances both in itself and in regard to what shall justify doing it a harm." But this argument of the liberals seems futile. And it by no means strikes anywhere near the root of the real trouble in the use of the injunction against labor unions.

In spite of the ancient tradition of equity courts to the contrary, there is a great deal to be said in favor of the injunction as a device to protect anything or any person against certain types of irreparable harm. Indeed, it is sometimes a pity that our courts do not feel more free to use the injunction where it would prevent great mischief. Of course, it is an exceedingly dangerous device and should be used sparingly, since our American social philosophy is predominantly in favor of allowing freedom of action and enterprise. Rather than to prevent people from doing or saying certain things, it is our tradition to let them act or talk, holding them accountable subsequently for damages to the injured parties if they go too far as measured by our laws. But if judges are convinced that money or punishment would not compensate the complaining victim for the harm he is likely to sustain or right the wrong against him, it would seem sensible for them to do what they can to prevent its occurrence.

The case against the use of the injunction to restrain labor union activities, however, can easily be made on the basis of its past abuse. Justice Frankfurter wrote an overwhelming indictment in his book published while he was still a professor at Harvard Law School. What he has covered in a whole book can only be touched upon here, but the substance of it can be briefly suggested. As soon as the labor injunction became established in the late 1880's almost anyone with an interest in obstructing the activities of labor unions could promptly secure temporary restraining orders for the asking. Continuance of a strike or boycott, after a restraining order or injunction was issued against it, brought down on the heads of the offenders the vengeance of the court through the exercise of its contempt power, unrelieved by the tender mercies of a jury. Hence, strikes, picket lines and boycotts were easily broken up almost before they were begun.

An employer with a strike or other union pressure on his hands went to a judge, regardless of whether or not he was actually sitting on the bench at the time, submitted to him affidavits made out by his own agents to the effect that the strikers or other union folk were about to commit or were committing, and would continue to commit, alleged unlawful acts at his plant, all of which would cause irreparable damage to his property, and prayed for a restraining order pending suit for a permanent injunction. Judges usually issued such orders on request, frequently in the absence of anyone representing the persons to be enjoined. Sometimes these orders were directed at named individuals, but frequently they were not. And in any event they all purported to restrain everyone "whomsoever," in a vague but grand manner. Obviously not much care was devoted in these transactions to legal theory or even to what was actually transpiring around the plant. And by the time the matter was set for the trial which was to determine whether or not the employer was justified in securing protection of this sort, the strike was broken up, either through the obedience of the union leaders or because they were in jail for disobedience.

As a rule, judges behaved in the same casual fashion after the trial between the two parties, when they had to decide whether or not they should grant formal injunctions and, if they decided to do so, how far they should go in preventing what kind of conduct by whom. At these trials, of course, both sides were represented and the judges took testimony, affording opportunity for cross examination. These proceedings took place before judges without juries. Frequently the evidence indicated actual or imminent violence and other unlawful conduct on the part of union members. But whether it did or did not, too many judges got into the habit of making findings of actual or threatened violence and other specifically unlawful conduct where nothing of the sort had occurred or was imminent. In these injunction suits it was customary to serve a summons only upon the leaders of the unions involved, although the injunctions were issued virtually against the world in general. Consequently, anyone violating the broad and comprehensive terms of such injunctions was punished for contempt, whether or not he had been served as a party in the suit, had had the injunction called to his attention by service of its provisions on him, or had ever heard of the injunction at all. For instance, a barber, usually patronized by railroad men, was held in contempt for violation of the broad injunction issued in the 1922 railroad workers' strike because he had hung in his window a sign to the effect that no scabs or strikebreakers were wanted as customers.

Injunctions were drawn in such technical and ambiguous legal terms that one leading state supreme court scathingly compared them to the intricately worded corporate mortgage. And there was seldom any attempt to couch these injunctive prohibitions in simple language which workmen could understand, either in English or in any of the foreign languages prevailing among large sections of our labor population. Too often the judges signing these injunctions did not draft them personally but followed the prevailing custom—perfectly proper in litigation involving less contentious issues—of permitting counsel for the complaining employers to prepare them instead. Unfortunately such injunctions left little, if any, scope for even peaceful economic coercive activity on the part of unions. And the harm occasioned to unions by this summary suppression was not undone even when appellate courts, as they seldom but occasionally did, set aside or modified injunctions because they were against the weight of the evidence adduced or contrary to established law. By that time months had passed, the possible effect of the strike or boycott was long since neutralized, and the union's investment of time, effort and money to organize the pressure was lost.

Even leading conservatives of the early 1900's inveighed against the manner in which courts issued injunctions against organized labor. They were genuinely terrified by the power judges assumed and exercised in these proceedings with such a free hand. Somewhat reasonably, they compared this sweep-ing exercise of power with the function of legislatures. It was perceived that judges issuing broad and general injunctions against all people whomsoever, regardless of whether or not they had been served with a summons to appear and defend, were virtually promulgating little statutes which declared in advance the illegality of anything done in the premises which the judges did not wish to be done. And they condemned the fashion in which these judges used their contempt power to punish all persons failing to comply with their injunctions, re-gardless of whether or not such persons had ever been served with a summons originally or had ever had the injunctions brought to their attention. Indeed, they thought this practice furthered the analogy of such injunctions to little statutes, since nonobservance of statute law is always a violation, even if the offender has never heard of the law. But even one who violated a statute was better off than some of the workers hauled up for contempt proceedings, since he had a right to a trial by jury, while the workers held for contempt were tried and punished personally by the judge whose orders they had, sometimes unwittingly, disobeyed.

But perhaps the most alarming feature of the labor injunc-tion, less obvious than the shortcomings just discussed, was the ease with which its use increasingly tempted judges to dis-pense with any well-founded independent theory of illegality. After all, the injunction was originally supposed to be a kind of remedy. And judicial remedies were supposed to operate as a control of some sort of illegal conduct, actual or threat-ened. But many courts using the injunction against the ac-tivities of labor unions fell into the bad habit of overlooking the need for proof of specific and independently unlawful con-duct, either already committed or only threatened, on which to base their injunctive orders. They came to look at much of organized labor's economic coercive activity as enjoinable in itself, without bothering to find or to state in their opinions that it was also unlawful. This was an unfortunate tendency which fed on itself. It seemed to lead many courts to grant sweeping injunctions on the basis of personal or class dislike of organized labor's economic program instead of in accordance with settled standards of law. A process of this sort lent itself admirably to the use of the illegal purpose doctrine.

Instead of pondering over the law governing certain kinds of conduct in an endeavor to determine its legality or illegality, many courts simply looked at the purpose of the conduct or at the economic context in which it occurred, disregarding completely the legal significance of the conduct in itself. And since no generally recognized body of law existed, aside from that governing various specific types of conduct, by which to judge the legality of purposes and contexts, many courts asked to issue injunctions unfortunately slipped into the custom of using as standards their own notions of what they believed to be good or bad as a matter of policy. In this way too many judges began to think of labor union activity as something enjoinable in itself. And since union leaders could not anticipate the vagaries of the judicial mind, they could not define for themselves or their followers the area of permissible economic conduct within which they were legally free to act. This unwholesome state of affairs, where labor unionists never knew just where they stood under the shadow of a brooding and undefined judicial power, involved an almost certain threat of suppression to most of organized labor's bargaining and organizational program, without benefit of any legislative declaration of policy or, indeed, of any rules of the game that might be called law.

A few of the highest state courts consistently held fairly liberal views concerning the lawful ambit of union conduct. Even these courts, however, believed that the injunction was an appropriate device with which to prevent improper labor union activities. But they were relatively generous in the scope of economic action they allowed and were also careful in the way they used their power to issue injunctions whenever they exercised it. The federal courts, like most of the state courts, took a very narrow view of what unions might lawfully do. With the exception of a few individual judges, they became almost the worst offenders in the abuse of the labor injunction. Perhaps because of this, the national political forum became the scene of the most determined fight against the continuance of this abuse. The American Federation of Labor focused on Congress such political pressure as it could muster in an endeavor to secure legislative restrictions against the further misuse by federal judges of their equity powers. In 1914, Congress passed an anti-injunction act of sorts, which was shortly copied by several state legislatures. This federal act and its state prototypes eventually proved abortive. And until the fight against its abuse fell into the more skillful hands of a few outstanding liberals under the natural leadership of Professor Frankfurter, culminating in the really effective Norris-LaGuardia Anti-injunction Act of 1932, the labor injunction remained the most critical issue in the law affecting unions.

CHAPTER V

STRIKES AND BOYCOTTS—CONCERTED REFUSALS TO WORK

I do not perceive any distinction upon which a legal difference of treatment should be based between a lockout, a strike, and a boycott. They often look very unlike, but this litigation illustrates their basic identity. All are voluntary abstentions from acts which normal persons usually perform for mutual benefit; in all the reason for such abstention is a determination to conquer and attain desire by proving that the endurance of the attack will outlast the resistance of the defense.—Hough, J., in *Gill Engraving Company v. Doerr,* 1914.

AFTER ALL of this inquiry into judicial theories and practices, it is high time to make a detailed examination and analysis of the traditional organizational and collective bargaining techniques such as strikes, boycotts, and picketing. Unions naturally try to get all they can for their constituents. Labor leaders, in their relationships toward union members, in many ways resemble business management in its relationship toward stockholders and investors. They like to achieve their ends amicably and with a minimum of trouble, preferring to remain within the law if they can at the same time get what they want. But they are occasionally tempted to take short cuts and indulge in ways of getting things done which are not always proper. While they normally have insufficient wealth to achieve their objectives through the use of money, they sometimes employ the more readily available direct methods of force and threats of violence. They do not expect society to condone such conduct. Also over some generations they have taken the trouble to develop more cumbersome but ultimately just as effective techniques of coercion through the exercise of economic pressures. The most important of these devices are built on concerted refusals to work. They range from the simple strike to fairly complicated boycott situations, sufficiently varied in their nature to require considerable detailed analysis.

STRIKES—LAWFUL AND UNLAWFUL

Combination and concerted action are the very backbone of the whole union movement. While devices like picketing and refusals to patronize are important phases of concerted action, virtually the entire structure of a union's self-help program rests on one simple practice—the refusal to work. The strike is the most simple manifestation of this practice. Indeed, it is, in a manner of speaking, its only manifestation. But the strike occurs in a variety of circumstances, some of which are exceedingly complicated.

The best-known strike is that for higher wages and for other immediate conditions of labor such as a shorter work day or any other term ordinarily embraced in a collective labor agreement. A strike of this sort is initiated by a group of employees against their immediate employer as the result of a failure on their part to achieve their objectives by negotiation. It is an attempt to compel the employer to comply with the collective demands of his employees, at the risk of suffering damage through the shutdown of his plant if he refuses to do so. In short, it is a conflict or tussle, if you please, in which the group of employees on strike pit their economic lasting power against that of the employer. These employees have something their employer wants—their labor—and they proceed on the assumption that he has something within his control they want —the ability to grant such terms and conditions of employment as they are demanding in return for their labor. These striking employees have no intention of severing employment relations with their employer, except temporarily for the duration of the strike, although the employer is free to replace them, if he can. Indeed, this recourse of the employer to the available pool of unorganized labor is theoretically one of the strongest economic assets he has in combatting a strike. And one of the strikers' chief concerns is to see that he does not gain free access to this supply of labor.

Although simple strikes are all essentially the same, whatever their objectives may be, in that they are merely concerted refusals of employees to continue work until their employer complies with some demand they have made, many courts have traditionally classified strikes in terms of their purposes. And depending upon whether or not any such court has regarded the purpose of any particular strike to be lawful or unlawful, it has accordingly declared the strike itself to be legal or illegal. Theoretically this approach is indefensible, since presumably workmen are perfectly free to associate and may concertedly refuse to work, except on such terms and under such conditions as they choose. But law, like everything else, has its intensely practical side. And it was perhaps inevitable that courts should forbid the use of the strike in pursuit of objectives thought to be wholly undesirable and hence illegal. It was not inevitable, however, that they should have carried this illegal purpose doctrine to the extremes which they did. And a proper line of demarcation between lawful and unlawful strikes pointedly illustrates these abuses of judicial power.

There are two fairly obvious analytical methods of testing the legality of a simple strike. Behind each is the realization that the strike is a powerful and compelling economic force which involves the deliberate commission of damage on another. If a strike is called to secure an objective that is, in itself, unlawful under some common-law or statutory category of tort or crime, then it seems fairly apparent that a court should declare the strike illegal. In so far as this depends on the objective being unlawful under a statute, it must appear that the statute in question was constitutional.

An illustration of this test is a strike called to secure management's co-operation in practicing a fraud against the govern-

ment, such as suppressing information to the proper authorities
about the draft irregularities or incomes of certain employees.
Since a union and its members consciously attempting by the
strike to procure such an objective would virtually be participating in its achievement if they were successful—quite as much
as one who paid money to a gunman to murder his enemy
would be participating in the murder—it seems an obviously
valid exercise of judicial power to declare the whole business
unlawful. Indeed, Justice Brandeis once made it quite plain
that a strike is unlawful if it is called to achieve a purpose
declared unlawful by legislation, when he declared that a
state court's conviction of a union official who called a strike
under these circumstances was valid under the 14th amendment of the Constitution.

The second test is not so easy to apply. It has a perfectly
sound traditional basis in a maxim of the common law which
tells us that the deliberate commission of harm on another is
unlawful unless it is justified. Justification is sometimes narrowly defined as a kind of competition, but it would be more
accurate to describe it as the pursuit of self-interest and gain.
Assuming, therefore, that a strike does not in itself involve
any conduct illegal under any category of tort or crime and
is not intended to achieve any unlawful objective, it should
be declared lawful and justifiable in spite of any infliction of
harm on the employer, if it is intended to promote the welfare
of the strikers, as they see it. And if it is not so intended, then
it may be declared unlawful.

The stock illustration of this test is the so-called sympathetic
strike. Suppose a carpenters' union strikes a general contractor
to secure higher wages, and the local streetcar workers' union,
satisfied with their own conditions of employment, strike in
sympathy with the carpenters. Many people believe such a
sympathetic strike is not quite as aimless as it may appear,
since they look upon all labor as a class, the various functional
groups of which are in a position to scratch each others' backs
at opportune times. They say that through this strike the

streetcar workers may conceivably be promoting their own interests by obliging the carpenters' union to aid them in some
future clash which they may have with their employer. These
people attempt to justify this sympathetic strike by showing
that it gives the streetcar company a reason for exerting pressure on the general contractor to make him give in to the carpenters, so that the streetcar operators will then return to
work—no doubt the richer for their conviction that they have
won the friendship and future backing of the carpenters' union,
when, as and if they ever call upon them for like assistance.

Our courts seem perfectly reasonable when they declare such
a sympathetic strike unlawful because they cannot perceive
that the streetcar operators had at stake any appreciable, or
even observable, economic interest, the pursuit of which could
amount to a justification for their action. It would be difficult,
indeed, to detect anything remotely resembling economic advantage or self-interest in such a strike. Hence, the courts seem
to be correct in concluding that a sympathetic strike is an unlawful infliction of damage, aimless and unjustifiable because
of the absence of any direct economic advantage to the group
of workers participating in it.

But this judicial position nevertheless has its dangers, since
it is not always easy to detect the absence of advantage or self-
interest on the part of the strikers. After all, it must constantly
be kept in mind that many regard the freedom to refrain from
work as a sort of civil right, not to be questioned on the basis
of its purpose or objective. Courts cannot afford lightly to
cast this conceptual position aside but should, rather, retain
it as the basic principle from which they may grudgingly make
concessions, out of deference to the existing practical needs of
the community as against the asserted economic needs and
self-interest of the strikers in question.

It might occur to some, as a possible defense of sympathetic
strikes, that our judges should place less emphasis on self-
interest and more on altruism in providing a justification for
intentionally caused harm. But they seem rightly to have made

no allowance for sentimentality in this respect. In administering this maxim, the courts have assumed that people will mind their own business and have granted them a fairly generous scope for doing just that, realizing that the general run of people will place their own interests first and will go to considerable lengths to advance these interests. All they can properly do to foster this spirit of free enterprise is to stipulate that people must not pursue their instinct of self-advancement by conduct in itself illegal and must not seek advantageous objectives unlawful in themselves. As long as people obey these strictures, however, they are and should be allowed plenty of leeway. And though, in the absence of specific legislation, our courts should not be too free in saying what are or are not lawful objectives, they certainly should be free in determining the nature of justification to take a fairly objective and realistic view of what constitutes self-protection, self-interest, and selfish gain.

Actually, the courts have gone rather far in undertaking to pass on the legality of objectives for the purpose of deciding whether or not strikes are lawful. For instance, they have declared generally that the removal of foremen whom the workers do not like is an illegal objective, rendering a strike for that purpose unlawful. Yet foremen are frequently unreasonable in their demands. They sometimes play favorites and hold grudges, and in other ways affect adversely the working conditions of the employees under them. Decisions to this effect have been justified as preventing the unwarranted invasion of management prerogative. But this reasoning seems questionable, because any strike for any purpose is a serious challenge to management prerogative, whatever that concept may be.

After all, the world is not run to define and maintain the interests of employers any more than it is to establish and enforce the interests of organized labor. By and large, such matters are either to be decided solely by management through fiat or by individual employment contracts in the absence of unionism, by the interplay of collective bargaining when the employees are organized, or by the operation of political forces through legislation. There is no divine classification of employer prerogatives free from the effects of collective bargaining. As long as a union can show that it is pressing some interest of importance to its constituents not illegal in itself, then, even if its demand reflects poor judgment or bad taste on the part of the employees, no court should undertake to declare unlawful a strike called to secure that objective in the absence of legislation enabling it to do so. Some judges apparently find it very difficult to recognize self-interest on the part of unions in particular strikes. But if they are to perform their duties, they must conquer their own economic predilections in attempting to understand and to judge the matters of interest and importance to working people.

STRIKES AGAINST TECHNOLOGICAL CHANGE

More distressing examples of direct coercion to promote the immediate economic welfare of union members, as they see it, are strikes against technological changes and the old-fashioned jurisdictional strike. The former situation occurs when an employer introduces some mechanical development into his plant for the purpose of saving labor and lowering production costs. Illustrations of this are almost numberless. Suppose a coal mine operator buys machinery which enables him to produce with half as many employees the same amount of coal formerly mined by hand. Suppose a shoe manufacturer installs machines with which one relatively untrained operator can stitch in a given time the number of shoes formerly requiring the work of 80 skilled operators. The old employees can see in these changes only the disappearance of their livelihood through immediate discharge due to technological displacement or through the transformation of their art and a cheapening of the value formerly placed on their manual skill, leading to less opportunities for work and to greatly lowered rates.

Their first instinct is naturally to strike against the introduction of changes that affect them so drastically. Such strikes,
of course, are futile, because the changes occur anyway, and
are almost always of ultimate social value. Yet these displaced
workers take small comfort from the assurance that as members of society they will benefit in the long run by getting
cheaper shoes and cheaper coal, as well as a slightly reduced
price on everything dependent for its production on coal. And
the dependent children of livery stable workers and teamsters
could hardly have been expected to foresee the millions of
future jobs coming for them in the wake of the new horseless
buggy which was putting their fathers out of work.

Courts required to pass on the legality of strikes against
technological change have been puzzled about what to do.
Indeed, they are still grappling with the problem in different
mechanical contexts, such as the displacement of live musicians
by the radio, recording devices and the theater organ. But their
judicial duty seems to be clear enough. Exasperating as such
strikes are, it is hard to see, under our law as it now stands,
how the courts can declare them unlawful by assuming that
the objective is illegal, simply because it is futile and incidentally harmful to society.

The real problem created by technological change is not
a judicial problem at all. It is, rather, one of the most acute
of our contemporary legislative problems of social security—a
matter which cannot be handled adequately without all of
society helping to finance, presumably through some sort of
taxation, a displacement wage, a retraining period and a re-
placement program. For if the consuming public benefits by
technological development, as it undoubtedly does, then it
should share the burden of paying for such benefits and not
leave the social cost almost entirely on the shoulders of displaced wage earners and their families. Indeed, a perfectly
valid argument justifying our courts in refusing to interfere
with technological strikes of any kind is the effect such strikes
might have in accelerating the type of legislation mentioned

above. After our legislatures have in this way obviated the disastrous immediate effects of technological progress, then, and only then, will even they be in a position to make technological strikes unlawful.

JURISDICTIONAL STRIKES

Courts find themselves in an almost equally difficult position when they are asked to declare jurisdictional strikes unlawful. Strikes of this sort occur frequently when the same employer hires members of two different craft unions to work for him at the same time. For instance, a general building contractor puts carpenters to hanging metal doors and the metal workers, who are engaged elsewhere on the operation, strike because they are not given this work to do. They claim that the work should be theirs because they have always installed materials made of metal, although they concede that doors have not previously been made of metal. And the carpenters claim that the work is properly theirs because they have always hung doors, even if they had always been made of wood. If the general contractor gives the job to the metal workers, the carpenters will strike. If he does not, the metal workers will remain on strike. In either event the whole operation may come to a halt.

This is a difficult situation for courts to solve. Indeed, there is no way they can properly solve it at all, since such a strike is called to secure a perfectly proper economic advantage. Yet this is one of the most wasteful and distressing of all union undertakings. The employer does not really care which union hangs his doors as long as the whole operation is completed. But here again, suppression of such strikes, either by the courts under the illegal purpose doctrine or by the legislatures, does not provide a satisfactory solution. A situation of this type obviously requires legislation creating some sort of body to make jurisdictional awards. Presumably it could be handled by compulsory arbitration. At one time the AF of L established a board of jurisdictional awards within its own organization to settle these cases among its member craft unions. It did not work very well, however, since the stronger union usually got the award on the basis of its greater political influence in the organization—a result which led the weaker union to see what it could gain by striking, since it figured that it had nothing to lose.

But as far as courts are concerned, they seem compelled to declare such strikes lawful in accordance with their own principles of common law. Indeed it would be hard to find a clearer case of what might be called conventional competition as justification for the occurrence of the substantial damage accompanying such strikes. The only possible flaw in this argument is that neither of the two unions mentioned is in a position to do all of the work usually performed by the other union. In *Pickett v. Walsh,* the Massachusetts pointers' case, the bricklayers and stonemasons were able to do all of the work in question, whereas the pointers could perform only one part of it. Under such circumstances the general contractor had a clear way out of his difficulties, while in most jurisdictional strikes he has no recourse at all.

Here again, if courts consistently refuse to interfere with these strikes, our legislatures may be compelled to develop some device like arbitration or a public board of jurisdictional awards, compelling the interested parties to seek recourse to such methods of settlement by declaring these strikes unlawful. In the meantime, developments in industrial as against craft unionism may provide a practical solution of this difficulty. For if all of the building crafts ever become consolidated into one industrial union, either through a rival CIO building trades union or a modification of the present AF of L craft setup, these matters of craft jurisdiction in the building industry would automatically disappear.

STRIKES FOR THE CLOSED SHOP

Courts have perhaps most frequently questioned the legality of strikes that have had as their objective the closed shop. Whether or not such strikes may properly be declared unlawful depends, of course, upon the legality of the closed shop itself. Now the closed shop is one in which membership in a particular union is a condition of employment. Closely allied to it is the so-called union shop in which membership in a particular union becomes a condition of continued employment beyond a certain number of days after hiring or after a collective agreement to that effect becomes operative. The legality of the closed shop and of the union shop has recently become a matter of political concern in several states.

Although it is doubtful that many voters appreciate the issues involved, nevertheless if a majority of them see fit to conclude that the closed or union shop be made unlawful in their state, that is their business. And it is hard to see on what grounds such legislation could possibly be overturned as unconstitutional. But in the absence of statutes outlawing the closed shop, it is equally difficult to understand how state courts can maintain the position that the closed or union shop is unlawful. Yet there is no question that many courts have done so in the absence of legislation, simply by declaring the closed shop an illegal objective because it is monopolistic and attaches a condition to free employment. It is probably safe to guess that just prior to the war, more of our highest state courts adhered to this position than otherwise.

If the closed or union shop is not made unlawful by statute in a particular state, then the courts of that state should not condemn a strike to secure its concession from an employer as an attempt to achieve an illegal objective. Nevertheless, several courts of last resort have done so. This seems indefensible as a matter of common law, for the closed shop is simply the control by a union of all employment opportunities at a particular place of business. As such, it is no different in principle from any of the situations where business combinations have exercised control over certain types of markets through the use of superior economic power—usually the concerted refusal to deal with others who refuse in turn to deal solely with the combination in question. These instances of economic coercion by business combinations have usually been declared lawful by our courts in the absence of statutes making them expressly unlawful. The theory of courts so deciding has been that a concerted refusal to deal with others is a common-law privilege, as long as it is not practiced to secure an end in itself illegal. But this concerted refusal to work is all that a union does in its attempt by strike to secure a closed shop in a particular plant.

It is true that it strives for complete control of all jobs in the plant, not only excluding nonunion labor from such jobs but also preventing the employer from hiring or retaining in his employment anyone but members of the union. Employees or applicants for employment who are eligible for membership in the union, but are unwilling to join, suffer no more harm than those who are compelled by business combinations either to abide by the rules of the association or to stay out of the field entirely. Indeed, unreasonable as some unions have been about entrance requirements, it is doubtful if they have ever exercised the ruthless exclusionary pressures which many business combinations, in the name of competition, have been permitted by our courts to practice against outside entrepreneurs.

The unions at least permit applicants for employment to secure jobs by joining their ranks. And the employer who is no longer free to hire nonunion employees, or to retain them as such after a certain number of days, suffers no more harm than does any of the consumers of goods whose access to markets for such goods is controlled by an effective business combination. He is in a position to get all the labor he wants through the union—as long as he meets the union's terms. If the union is not able to supply his needs, he is of course free to hire where he pleases, usually on the understanding that independently hired nonunion employees become members of the union if retained beyond a certain time. Naturally all of this deprives the employer of the advantages he might secure from being able to hire help in an unorganized labor market at whatever wage bargains he might be able to drive. But there is no particular reason why an employer should expect under our common law to have a fairly available supply of labor at advantageous terms any more than he should expect thereunder to have uncontrolled access to raw materials.

The strongest arguments against the closed or union shop have always been that it interferes both with the freedom of nonunion labor to secure employment and with the freedom of employers to secure labor. These effects, of course, are conceded. But any argument that courts should therefore declare that the closed shop and strikes to secure it are unlawful, because it leads to the enslavement of workers and to the control of industry by the unions, is sheer sentimentality. If such an argument had ever been used by the courts to break up the effective market controls created by businessmen, it would have been treated as a denial of freedom of enterprise and an invasion of the natural rights of industrial entrepreneurs. Anyone doubting this statement has only to reflect on the attitude of most businessmen toward the Sherman Act. Perhaps the trouble is that so many of us do not really believe in free enterprise at all, although we may think we do, because we are unwilling to see the courts permit the same freedom of action to organized labor as they freely accord to organized business enterprise. But we should remember that as long as the industrial world is set up to allow freedom of organization and enterprise to businessmen and investors, these same freedoms should be accorded to all. When this tolerance causes harm to consumers, the only possible remedy is by legislation.

Certainly, if our courts continue to pursue the double standard in economic life, we must inevitably expect organizations like the CIO's political action committee who will make it their business to influence the election and appointment of

legislators and judges willing to place all enterprise, including
labor unionism, on a common and consistent basis. And it is
no answer at all to say that since big business has built the
country and made it what it is today, it is therefore essentially
good and should be left in a class by itself. Organized laboring
people, whether rightly or wrongly, believe that they can
make the country a lot better both for themselves and for
others by pursuing the same techniques which big business first
made popular. Even if some of us are inclined to doubt this, it
is hard to see how we can retain our present form of government and deny the unions the chance to prove that they are
right. Certainly the courts should not do it. For this is a
legislative matter suitable for disposition only in the political
arena.

The closed shop, and strikes to secure it, have objectives of
value to unions more tangible than mere control of jobs. At
one time, before workmen's compensation acts became generally accepted, associated workers in particular plants found
it to their advantage to exclude workers who could not, or
would not, measure up to their standards of safe and prudent
conduct during everyday operations. Their physical safety was
jeopardized by workers who did not observe certain precau-
tions. And employers anxious to get their work done at any
price had no incentive to hire or retain only prudent men,
because they were not responsible in damages to their employees who were hurt either because of careless conditions on
the premises or by the negligence of their fellow laborers.

The only sure way they had to protect themselves against
such hazards was to see that imprudent workers stayed out
of their plants. By establishing standards of work, and by insuring observance of these standards through so-called entrance requirements, members of these associations could protect themselves against incompetent workers and against their
employers' tendencies to hire such labor. Furthermore, they
could in this way insure maintenance at a high level of the
standards of performance of their particular arts which con-

stituted their livelihoods. These safety factors involved in the closed shop are no longer relevant, in view of modern legislation, including workmen's compensation acts.

In any event, these factors are negligible when compared to the broader economic significance of the closed shop to organized labor. Unions have always valued the closed shop as an effective bargaining climate. The success of a strike for higher wages, to take an example, would be jeopardized if substantially all of the workers in the plant did not act as a unit. Unified action of his employees can really make an employer feel the economic pinch that might compel him to concede the union's demands. If he can retain a substantial number of his employees at work during such a strike, he has a great advantage and might successfully thwart the union's collective bargaining ambitions. Naturally, this is exactly what the employer should do under the circumstances if he wishes to defeat the strike. But this possibility provides the union with a strong economic incentive to secure the unified action of all employees for collective bargaining purposes.

The Massachusetts Supreme Court did not regard the achievement of bargaining strength as a sufficiently direct interest to justify a strike for a closed shop. Indeed, it regarded the possession of such economic power as unlawful in itself, and condemned strikes directed at this objective, although it had sanctioned not only a similar economic control but an analogous technique in achieving it when the combination in question was composed of businessmen in the case involving the corner on seamen. But even if we concede for argument that a strike to achieve bargaining power is not, in itself, aimed at an economic advantage like higher wages, it still seems clear that the closed shop has always been of vital importance to unions in protecting and maintaining its already achieved gains.

Suppose a union in a particular plant has secured advantages through collective bargaining. If the employer remains free to hire nonunion workers, his normal labor turnover may eventually enable him to supplant a great many of his union employees with men willing to work under any conditions he sees fit to impose. This may so dilute the union's strength that at the expiration of the current contract the employer may successfully refuse to renew it at all. Such a result may imply a serious lowering of employment standards, to the great harm of all of the workers in the plant. In order to avoid the undermining of economic stability in this respect—a matter quite as important as securing higher wages in the first instance— the union is compelled to seek the protection afforded only in the closed shop. The situation just described indicates how an employer in an open shop may pit nonunion and union employees against each other, thus creating a kind of competition between them, which the union may effectively combat only through establishing the closed shop.

BOYCOTTS—PRIMARY AND SECONDARY

So far, the discussion has concerned only strikes called to improve the terms and conditions of employment existing between the strikers and their employers. There are also instances of collective refusals to work by employees who are apparently satisfied with their own terms of employment— even including the closed shop—but who have economic interests at stake other than those involved in their own employment relationships. Such strikes constitute the first step in what are known as secondary labor boycotts.

A boycott is usually an organized refusal to deal with someone in order to make him change some practice which he follows. Quite frequently it is a systematic refusal to buy particular products, but it may also be an organized refusal to work. For instance, any simple strike for higher wages is a direct primary labor boycott, in which the strikers refuse to deal with their employer until he modifies some aspect of their terms of employment. A secondary labor boycott occurs when a group of employees refuse to remain at work for an employer, not because of any complaint over their labor standards under him but because he persists in dealing with a third person against whom they have some grievance. Their pressure is exerted against him in the hope of forcing him to cease dealing with the third person in question, as in *Quinn v. Leathem*, the slaughter-house case. As such, it is an attempt to secure the economic assistance of their employer to compel this third person to capitulate to the union over some issue between them, at the risk of losing the unionized employer's business if he does not capitulate.

An illustration should show clearly what all of this means. Carpenters employed in woodwork shops and those in the building trades are organized in the same country-wide union. In a given metropolitan area, say around New York City, the building trades are so well organized that general contractors employ only union carpenters. Woodwork shops around this area are, however, poorly organized. It is thought necessary by the carpenters' union that all of such shops be unionized. Certain unionized general contractors customarily purchase wood trim, such as doors and window frames, from a nonunion mill. The union officials notify these contractors that henceforth their members will not handle nonunion-made products from this mill and will discontinue work altogether if the contractors persist in buying such mill's product. Faced with this ultimatum, the contractors are likely to purchase their wood trim from union shops, preferring to pay more for their materials than to have their carpenters strike. The woodwork mill can preserve its established market only by unionizing its shop, a step it has previously refused to take. If it persists in resisting the union, it will suffer great loss and probably complete ruin. And this, of course, is exactly what the union intends should happen if the mill should refuse to capitulate.

A situation of this sort raises at least two questions. First, what can the employer against whom the union threatens to strike, or actually does strike, do to prevent this economic pressure? Second, what can the employer, who is the ultimate

target of the union's coercion, do to stop this practice? Most
of our courts have always held that the secondary boycott in
any form is unlawful when practiced by labor unions, apparently on the complaint of either of the two employers.
Simply by calling it unlawful, in itself—as if it were in a separate category of tort liability—they have concluded that it's
wrong because it's wrong, although they have universally upheld the legality of the secondary boycott when it is practiced
by business combinations. A few of our courts, however, have
concluded otherwise in the labor cases, taking some pains to
show that the majority ruling on this point does not stand up
under analysis. Some of these courts place their conclusion on
the right of working people to refrain from work for any reasons they see fit, or for no reason at all. Others have evolved
a theory of legality based upon justification, and it is this analysis which seems irrefutable. ·

In response to the first question above—what recourse has
the employer against whom the strike is threatened or actually
called—the practical answer is that an employer in this position
almost never seeks the aid of the courts, usually complying
with the union's demand in order to avoid trouble. But if—
to use the illustration of the general contractor, the carpenters'
union and the unorganized woodwork shop—the general contractor tried to prevent the strike, the union could show that
his continued patronage of the nonunion producer was hurting its interests. And the analysis tending to prove the union's
contention in this respect would be virtually the same as that
used to answer any complaint filed against the union by the
operator of the woodwork mill. In this illustrative case, the
carpenters' union could show that the nonunion mill, by
operating on lower than union standards of employment, presented a continuous competitive hazard to unionized woodwork mills and, thus, to the union carpenters employed in
them. For the nonunion mill enjoys a competitive advantage
based on the wage differential between union and nonunion
employees, which would enable it over a period of time either

to drive all union-made wood trim off the market, or to break down the union standards in already organized mills.

This conclusion, of course, rests on the assumption that consumers of wood trim will naturally buy the cheaper material if they are left free to do so. Hence it is a matter of union interest to eliminate this undermining competition in order to protect its already established gains in unionized units of the woodwork industry. Since the union is not in a position to bring direct pressure on the nonunion woodwork mill by strike, its members in the building industry do the next best thing by refusing to work on such mill's nonunion-made product.

Thus, according to this analysis, the general contractors who use nonunion-made wood trim, as well as the property owners for whom they are working, themselves profit by and support subunion labor standards when they purchase and use the cheaper material. Although the union is in no sense competing with such contractors and owners, it argues that it cannot be compelled to assist them to support and to profit by the nonunion enterprise, thus hurting its own members in their competition with nonunion labor in the unorganized mill. And the union might add that it can stabilize its established standards in the unionized woodwork mills only by insuring them against competition from nonunion mills.

While this explanation shows a real economic interest on the part of the unionized shop carpenters sufficient to justify any action they might have taken to protect themselves against the undermining effects of the nonunion enterprise, what justification does it show for the coercive activity of the building trade carpenters, whose standards of employment in their industry are satisfactory? The building trade carpenters do have a personal interest in the labor standards prevailing in woodwork mills because many of them seek employment in such mills after they become too old to continue active construction work. Aside from this, however, the only actual interest they can show is membership in the same craft union with the shop carpenters and a joint concern with them over the maintenance of employment standards for all members of their union. This identity of interest is, perhaps, more easily observed as the building up of a powerful bargaining device covering similar functional operations. A common interest achieved between building and shop carpenters, through membership in the same union, certainly distinguishes the building carpenters' threatened or actual strike from one called, for instance, by a streetcar operators' union out of sympathy for the economic plight of the shop carpenters, who are trying to establish union standards in all of the woodwork mills. Since the streetcar operators have no conceivable economic interest in the welfare of woodwork mill employees, any pressures they exert to help them could not possibly be justified as pursuit of self-interest and gain. But the coercion practiced by the building carpenters in the case under discussion does affect their interests as well as those of the shop carpenters, because they are all in the same union and in the same industry built around the same craft function.

From the foregoing account it will be apparent that the secondary labor boycott is essentially an organizational device and that it can be used only by a union comprised of workers performing at least two different phases of a common industrial function, for at least two different types of employers. This is true of the carpenters' case, and many instances of a similar sort come to mind.

Thus, typesetters, pressmen and lithographers may be organized under one union roof. But while most book manufacturers employ typesetters and pressmen, lithography is fairly specialized and is usually farmed out by such manufacturers. The union may have an advantageous contract with a book manufacturer covering the labor standards of typesetters and pressmen. But this manufacturer may have certain lithographing done at a nonunion plant. If the union believes that the operation of this other plant, on subunion standards, endangers the welfare of its member lithographers in unionized plants, it may notify the book manufacturer that its member type-

setters and pressmen will not handle the nonunion-made lithograph in his books. The manufacturer is likely to heed this
warning and give his lithograph work to a union shop in order to avoid trouble.

But whatever the factual context may be in which a secondary labor boycott occurs, it is always true, from the angle of the
workers actively implementing this pressure, that it amounts
only to a simple strike or threat to strike. In spite of the fact
that it affects, and is intended to affect, others besides the employer against whom this pressure is aimed in the first instance,
the secondary boycott, for the purpose of analytically determining its legality, should be treated exactly like a strike or concerted refusal to work. Thus, if the employees who implement
the secondary boycott by their refusal to work can show an economic interest of their own at stake, then our courts should
hold such boycotts justifiable and lawful as, indeed, some of
our courts have already done.

One of the most interesting of secondary economic pressures in other types of cases occurred when the Allis-Chalmers
foundry, in an attempt to defeat a strike by its molders, shopped
out various of its molding jobs to different foundries throughout the Middle West. At all of these other plants the molders,
members of the same international union to which the strikers
belonged, refused to work on any of the struck foundry's patterns. It is true that these other molders would not have benefited directly and immediately by the success of the strike at
the original plant. But they did have an interest in the labor
standards established at that plant because it competed with
their own employers. They were interested in having standards
of work raised as high as possible in all competing plants so
that such plants could not undercut their own employers, thus
affecting them indirectly, on the basis of any competitive advantage arising from wage differentials.

In a suit brought against the national union by the struck
plant, a federal court denied an injunction on the ground that
members of the molders' union in these various plants were

justified in refusing to work on the original plant's patterns. The court took the view that this refusal to work could not be condemned as sympathetic pressure, because the local union calling the original strike was just as free to solicit and receive aid from other locals of the same union, in its economic tussle with the employer, as the employer was to seek the aid of other plants in getting out its orders. While the court's reasoning seemed apt, the argument based upon actual interest would appear to have been preferable.

While this situation involved secondary pressure, it was not an instance of a typical secondary boycott. The national union, through the co-operation of some of its locals, was merely trying to prevent outside plants from aiding Allis-Chalmers. This was essentially a defensive course of action, inspired by the struck plant's original recourse to outside assistance. As such, it seemed quite different from the aggressive attempt to impose additional positive economic pressure on Allis-Chalmers from outside, which a typical secondary labor boycott would have implied. Most assuredly it was not an instance of a sympathetic strike because of the interest which all of the locals had in the success of the strike at the Allis-Chalmers plant. After all, the national molders' union, composed of these various locals, had a real interest in the standardization of employment conditions in all of these competing plants at as high a level as possible. This interest may seem to have been indirect. But it was sufficiently apparent to justify the members of these other locals of the same national union in refusing actively to assist the struck plant against their striking fellow members by working on its orders at these other plants.

A somewhat similar situation might occur when a large nonunion printing establishment which, in the opinion of the pressmens' union, has jeopardized the position and security of the union throughout the printing industry, seeks the aid of unionized competitors in getting out weekly and monthly periodicals during rush seasons. If the union ordered its members in these other shops not to work on any of the nonunion company's jobs, their refusal to do so would no doubt cause a good deal of damage. But this pressure would seem quite justifiable under the circumstances in view of the union's interest in stabilizing employment standards throughout the industry and by unionizing the publishing house in question. Certainly it could justify its conduct as a refusal to help that company which presents to it the most serious economic threat to its standards in other plants in the industry.

LABOR UNION COUNCILS

Other common settings for a type of secondary economic pressure through refusals to work, albeit not accurately included in the category of the secondary labor boycott but in some ways resembling it, are the local labor union council and the local allied trades union council. The building trades council affords a graphic example of the latter. It is composed of all of the craft unions ordinarily engaged in the building industry, including carpenters, bricklayers and stonemasons, electricians, plumbers, hod carriers, painters and decorators, metal workers, and the like.

Suppose that one of these unions is either attempting to secure some advantage from a particular general contractor, like higher wages, or is trying to compel him to recognize the union in the first place and to employ only members of that union for the performance of the particular work in question. Such a union, for instance, the electricians' union, may call a strike of its members at a particular building site. The contractor might easily be able to break this strike by recourse to non-union electricians hired in the open market. But in accordance with the rules of the building trades council, no members of any of the associated unions may work on a building for a contractor against whom one of the associated unions has called a strike at that place. In the face of a complete shutdown of all work on the building, assuming that the other building trades unions are fairly well represented there, the general contractor has no practicable alternative to granting the electricians' demands.

This organized pressure is obviously not a conventional secondary boycott. It more closely resembles the so-called sympathetic strike. The effective pressure brought by the associated unions, other than that representing the electricians, serves no possible direct interest of these other unions, since they are not demanding anything for themselves. A court asked to prevent continuance of this complete refusal to work might naturally conclude, therefore, that the associated unions, other than the electricians, cannot justify the deliberate commission of harm which they impose on the general contractor since they have no economic interest of their own to promote.

But this position is not obviously correct. It is far more doubtful than denying the right of the streetcar operators' union to strike in sympathy with the electricians. In the latter case there is no possible community of economic interest involved, while in the case under discussion it is arguable that all of the building trades unions, being concerned with the same industry, have an interest in all employment conditions in that industry. We may still feel certain that the other associated unions support the electricians' strike out of sympathy, in the hope that when any of them is in a similar position, the electricians will support it in the same way. Yet we must confess that if all of the building trades crafts were organized into a single industrial union, instead of in several craft unions, a conflict over electricians' rates would then be *the* union's fight, which all members of *the* union might lawfully support because of the more direct interest involved as far as their union's welfare is concerned. This argument has a considerable bearing on the case in hand. For a building trades union council, while it retains the separate craft identity of the several unions for some purposes, merges them virtually into an industrial union for other purposes. This council, including only unions engaged in the same industry, *is* an industrial union for most of the practical purposes of conducting an economic enterprise.

Certainly, under the circumstances, it would be difficult for a court to rationalize granting an injunction against the strikes of the other associated unions in this case, where they retain their separate craft identities, while denying one where all of the craftsmen involved were organized directly into one common industrial union.

Quite a different result might ensue in this situation, however, if the electricians' strike was to prevent the general contractor from installing electrical fixtures manufactured in a nonunion plant. As far as the strike by the electricians alone is concerned, assuming that their craft union comprised workers not only in the building industry but also in shops manufacturing electrical equipment, it would probably be regarded by the courts as similar to the building carpenters' strike in aid of the mill carpenters, discussed above. Such a strike would be the implementation of a true secondary labor boycott. And the interest to the building trades electricians, as members of the same union to which the shop electricians belong, would probably constitute adequate justification for their exercise of economic pressure.

But if the other unions, associated with the electricans in the building trades council, also walked out to aid these electricians in their attempt to force the general contractor to desist from nonunion-made electrical equipment, they would find it difficult, indeed, to show an interest justifying their action. They might contend that it was to their interest to build up the strength of one of their associated unions and that the electricians' union, as a whole, would be stronger if the nonunion manufacturer were organized. But this alleged interest, not concerning employment conditions in the building industry in any way, would be so attenuated as to be almost nonexistent. It could hardly be accepted as justification for the commission of harm by the other associated unions through their concerted refusal to work. Here the industrial union analogy would not apply. For if the building trade crafts were all comprised in one industrial union, then all interest between the building and shop electricians would be severed, anyway. In short, their interest would be too remote.

The local labor union council is fundamentally different from the allied trades union council situation. Instead of centering the association around a common functional or industrial interest, it sets up as the bond of unity the fact that all members of the associated unions belong to the laboring class and, as such, presumably have common economic interests against the rest of the world. Such an association includes all local unions from entirely unrelated trades and industries. It is in a position to practice powerful economic pressures in the aid of member unions, if permitted to do so by the courts.

Suppose a restaurant workers' union at a particular hotel strikes for higher wages or to organize the employer in question. To assist it, other local unions in the association refuse to serve the hotel as long as this strike exists. Presumably some sort of case could be made out for the justification of pressures exerted by other hotel service unions, by analogy to the allied trades union council activities. But if other members of the association, like the butchers', the bakers' and the candlestick makers' unions, all refused to serve the hotel or to work on products or materials destined for the hotel, they would have considerable difficulty in persuading a court that their exercise of economic pressures was justified. Their only possible interests would be the enlisting of reciprocal aid in the future and the building up of a class strength, both of which are much too attenuated by common-law principles to qualify as justification for their deliberate commission of harm against the hotel.

This expression of a class community of interest among all unions—more obviously an incident of craft as against industrial union organization in light of actual developments in this country—is frequently made apparent in so-called secondary consumption boycotts and in certain types of picketing. But what we have here been concerned with is how the practices employed in the use of the strike and the labor boycott might or might not be legally justifiable in terms of the economic interests of those refusing to work in various industrial contexts. It should serve to introduce readers to the economic analysis of justification and interest, which plays such an important role in the more complicated practices, and in the provisions of the law designed both to confine and to expand their scope.

CHAPTER VI

SECONDARY CONSUMPTION BOYCOTTS AND PICKETING—ORGANIZED REFUSALS TO PATRONIZE

> We would thereby give to one labor union an advantage over another by prohibiting the use of peaceful and honest persuasion in matters of economic and social rivalry. This might strike a death blow to legitimate labor activities. It is not within the province of the courts to restrain conduct which is within the allowable area of economic conflict.—Pound, J., in *Stillwell Theatre, Inc. v. Kaplan,* 1932.

LABOR organizations and business combinations have at least one thing in common—their most effective economic pressures to secure selfish advantages consist of concerted refusals to deal with others. The best-known union version of this technique is the concerted refusal to work, variously illustrated in the previous chapter. Business combinations practice a comparable type of pressure when they refuse to sell some commodity over which they have gained control. But another effective pressure which both groups use is the systematic refusal to patronize. This practice more strictly conforms to popular notions of the boycott. It was developed originally by business combinations, and some of these groups still use it effectively. In the past, and to some extent now, the courts have permitted them under the common law to apply pressures of this sort.

For instance, an association of master plumbers in the eastern United States set up a plan to secure for its members all of the lucrative plumbing business in their several cities. All of the members agreed among themselves not to buy plumbing supplies from any manufacturer who sold his products in these cities to any plumber not a member of the association. The up-shot of this plan, which the courts called lawful competition, was to force nonmember plumbers in these cities out of busi-ness, compelling them to become journeymen plumbers. For the manufacturers of plumbing supplies did not dare to risk the loss of patronage of the association's members by violating its rules. And an association of retail lumber dealers in Minne-sota, resenting the loss of profits involved in direct sales of lumber from manufacturers or wholesalers to consumers, agreed among themselves not to handle the lumber of any manu-facturer or wholesaler who engaged in this practice unless he paid the association a fine amounting roughly to the lost profit. The Minnesota court declared this practice permissible at common law. A similar device for making retailers observe price schedules still prevails in England, with the blessing of the House of Lords.

MORE ABOUT SECONDARY BOYCOTTS

Courts have called all of these practices permissible competi-tion under the common law. Yet they are all quite clearly secondary consumption boycotts, the threatened refusal to buy being aimed in each case directly at a manufacturer or whole-saler in order to make him in turn bring pressure on the real object of the association's dislike. In each of these instances, the members of the particular association had an economic ax to grind—or *thought* they had, as their organized expedients to protect their trade violated current notions of prevailing eco-nomic theory. Hence the harm caused by these economic pres-sures was said to be justified, since the coercion was directed at self-interest and gain, even though it amounted at the same time to a drastic interference with the free enterprise and com-petitive undertakings of others. All that could be proved against these associations was the concerted exercise of perfectly law-ful refusals to deal with others, except on certain conditions.

The combination into associations, of course, alone made this economic coercion effective. But the courts consistently maintained that this element of combination was not in itself unlawful. Indeed, in these business association cases the whole affair—combination, as well as its use to exert economic coercion—was considered by judges to be virtually a sort of natural civil right. They took this view as long as the objective was some element of gain and nobody had violated a specific category of established common or statute law, such as assault, breach of the peace, trespass, libel or fraud and deceit. Any contrary view, the courts said, would have to come from the legislatures.

In the two decades prior to the New Deal organized labor attempted to use this same type of secondary coercion, based on organized refusals to patronize, with indifferent success before the courts. In many instances courts have declared such undertakings unlawful merely because they were secondary boycotts. This was a ridiculous reason in view of the fact that they had previously conceded the legality of secondary boycotts practiced by business associations without having called them such. Under recognized principles of the common law, however, they could have distinguished many labor consumption boycotts from those of business associations, because of the attenuated interest of the participants.

At any rate, the New York Court of Appeals had no difficulty in doing so in *Auburn Draying Company v. Wardell,* a case decided around 1920. There a teamsters' union wanted a trucking company to bargain with it. But the company refused to do so. Left to its own resources, the union would have been unable to exercise effective coercion on the company. But it belonged to a local council of various labor unions which, while functionally unrelated in any way to the trucking business, were nevertheless in a position to lend the teamsters powerful assistance in the form of economic coercion. Upon the company's refusal to deal with the teamsters, all of the unions represented in the council, including electricians, butchers, iron molders and what not, agreed that none of their members would patronize any local merchant who, in turn, patronized the trucking company. This possibility of losing the trade of all organized wage earners in the locality led the retail merchants to stop using the service of the trucking company. And this, in turn, faced that company with economic annihilation as the only apparent alternative to compliance with the union's demands.

There was, of course, nothing inherent in this choice which rendered the council's action unlawful. But, according to the New York court, the vice of this plan was the lack of any direct interest on the part of any of the unions involved, with the exception of the teamsters. The council's organized pressure imposed serious damage on the trucking company. And even though it resulted from purely economic coercion involving merely the right to deal or not to deal, as the members of the council saw fit, the court thought that the parties imposing it should show that they had an economic interest of their own at stake in order to justify it. Since employment conditions at the trucking company could not conceivably affect the economic status of the electricians, butchers, or iron molders in any observable way, their organized participation in this harmful pressure on the company could not be justified. Hence it was declared unlawful as the unjustifiable infliction of temporal harm.

What the court declared unlawful in this case was the systematic action of the council in organizing the participation of its member unions, presumably by inducing all of such unions in turn to require their constituents to spend their family incomes as the council directed. Naturally the court could not undertake to prevent a particular electrician or molder from refusing to spend his income in any store for any reason. That would be too extreme an invasion of personal liberty. A court would no more go this far than it would attempt to end an unlawful strike by ordering each of the strikers back to work—an unconstitutional imposition of involuntary servitude which it would avoid by forbidding only the continuance of organized direction of the strike on the part of the union and its leaders, leaving the individual strikers free to resume work or not, in accordance with their personal choices.

The court proceeded similarly in this *Auburn* consumption boycott case. After it ordered the council to abandon its organized scheme of boycotting against any local tradesmen who persisted in patronizing the trucking company, many of the union folk in the locality might still choose personally to pursue the same policy. They were at liberty under the law to do this. But without the investigational facilities of the council, they would find it difficult to learn what merchants were dealing with the trucking company, and most of them would no doubt soon forget all about it.

The secondary pressure in this *Auburn* trucking boycott case was quite evident. In two other consumption boycott cases, this secondary effect was not so obvious. Take, for instance, the case of *Seattle Malting and Brewing Company v. Hansen,* decided in 1905 by a federal district court in California. There a brewery workers' union demanded the closed shop from a brewing company. When the company refused to comply, the union enlisted the aid of the community in exerting economic pressure to achieve its objective. It had handbills printed and circulated throughout the locality in question, notifying people that the company's brand of beer was "unfair" and should not be consumed. The effect of this campaign was to discourage saloon keepers from handling the company's beer, both because it ceased to be a good seller and because they feared that people who were sympathetic to the union would not patronize their places at all if they continued to handle it.

The court enjoined this practice because it hurt and destroyed the company's business. This was an invalid reason for declaring the practice unlawful, since all of organized labor's perfectly legitimate economic pressures are harmful and destructive, just as those practiced by business combinations are.

Nevertheless, this same decision might have been explained on the ground that the union's undertaking depended on the aid of outsiders who had absolutely no economic interest at stake in the working conditions prevailing at the brewery. In this respect it resembled the situation in the *Auburn* trucking case. The members of the community who made possible the boycott against the brewery had no more interest in employment conditions at the brewery than the members of the various unions in the Auburn labor union council had had in the standards of work at the trucking company. In each case there was "a conscription of neutrals," so to speak. The consumers, whose refusal to deal with others caused the harm in question, could not justify this imposition of damage by showing that it was designed to promote any economic interest of their own; and the union groups organizing these boycotts by neutrals could stand in no better position.

However, these two cases were not identical. In the *Auburn* trucking case, the union council which conducted the boycott against the merchants had no economic interest in the outcome of the pressure, except in so far as the members of the truckers' union itself were concerned. The brewery workers' union, which alone had initiated the boycott against the brewing company's beer, on the other hand, had a very real interest in the outcome of the pressure exerted. Thus, any organized refusal by the brewery workers alone to drink the beer in question or to patronize any saloon that sold it could not logically have been declared unlawful under prevailing principles of the common law. It was only their union's organization of the general public against the brewery which could logically have been enjoined under these principles.

One other phase of these two cases is highlighted by a third situation. In the *Auburn* truckers' case the refusal to patronize was not aimed at any particular consumers' commodity, while in the California brewers' case the boycott was aimed directly at the company's beer. In the truckers' case the direct pressure was aimed only *at merchants* who patronized the trucking company, while in the brewers' case, it was aimed at the brewing company's *beer*—a commodity of commerce. A case before the Supreme Court in 1911, *Gompers v. Bucks Stove and Range Company,* illustrates the operation of a consumers' boycott against a particular commodity—Bucks stoves—a boycott conducted by a nation-wide confederation of unions which, except for the stove workers' union, had no economic interest in employment conditions at the Bucks plant. This case combined the features appearing separately in the *Auburn* truckers' and the California brewers' cases.

The American Federation of Labor is a loose association of national and international unions, chiefly craft unions, most of which have no functional relationship to each other. This cover-all organization published in a paper circulated among these federated unions a blacklist of so-called unfair products. These were products manufactured by employers who refused in one way or another to deal with the appropriate craft unions or to make desired concessions to them in collective bargaining. In this "We don't patronize" list the AF of L included Bucks stoves because that company had refused to deal with the stove workers' union, one of the unions in the AF of L. This resulted in a sharp decrease in sales of the company's stoves to wage earners all over the country. The company naturally wanted union folk throughout the country to be free to make up their own minds about what kinds of stoves they wanted. It also desired to relieve retailers from the odium cast on them for carrying the company's line of stoves, thus making it possible for them to continue selling them. Upon the complaint of the Bucks Stove and Range Company a federal court enjoined this practice, ordering the AF of L to drop this company from its unfair list and to cease to promote what it held to be an unlawful boycott.

Samuel Gompers and other high AF of L officials refused to obey this injunction. They claimed that it violated their right of free speech. When they continued their efforts to boycott Bucks stoves, they were held in contempt of court, again at the instance of the company. They appealed to the Supreme Court, contending that what they had done amounted only to communication, or speech in written form, and that they could not constitutionally be muzzled in this way. Hence, they declared, the injunction was invalid to begin with and, since it did not thus merit obedience, no contempt was involved when they ignored it.

While setting aside the commitment on purely technical grounds, the Court clearly indicated its belief concerning the merits of Gompers' contentions that the AF of L's nation-wide boycott was unlawful. It said that the organization of the boycott itself was the unlawful element, with speech amounting only to a "verbal act" or "signal" to set in operation the boycott. Hence, it concluded at this point, the mere presence of speech in effecting this boycott did not immunize the AF of L's otherwise illegal conduct under any constitutional doctrine for the protection of free speech. Apparently the Court perceived little difference between using speech and communication for the purpose of conducting an illegal boycott and for the purpose of perpetrating libel or fraud and deceit. One who libels another may not plead in defense that he has committed this tort through the medium of speech. It is hard to see how else it could be committed. Under this view, the constitutional guaranty of free speech is reserved for the expression of opinions or statements not in themselves unlawful and not used to implement practices which are unlawful under any recognized common-law or statutory categories of tort or crime.

But why did the Supreme Court regard the AF of L's nation-wide boycott of Bucks stoves as illegal? Strictly speaking, it was not a secondary boycott, although many retailers of stoves had become reluctant to sell Bucks stoves because organized wage earners refused to buy them. The proper explanation seems to be that the AF of L had organized against the Bucks company a consumption boycott supported by a class of consumers who, with the exception of the stove workers themselves, had no

recognizable economic interest at stake in employment conditions prevailing at the company's plant. In short, this was
an instance of organized "sympathetic" pressure, little different
from a sympathetic strike. As such, it resembled the situation
which later occurred in the *Auburn* truckers' case, although
that case also involved secondary pressure. But inasmuch as
secondary pressure alone has repeatedly been shown both in
business combination and labor union cases not to be unlawful in accordance with prevailing common-law principles, this
element of sympathetic pressure remains as the determining
factor of illegality in these two cases.

All three of these situations—the *Auburn* truckers' case, the
California brewers' case and the AF of L's blacklist against
Bucks stoves—present illustrations of conduct which courts
might justifiably declare unlawful under long-established principles of the common law. Although each differs from the
others, all of them reveal the imposition of damage on others
through organized agencies having no economic interest to be
served. In the truckers' and stove cases, to be sure, the labor
union council and the AF of L were interested in seeing the
truckers' and the stove workers' unions triumph, in so far as
such victories would strengthen unionism as a whole. But this
interest through alliance was not the kind of economic interest
recognized at common law under the justification of competition and the pursuit of gain. True, the brewery workers had
a direct interest to be served. But this interest justified only the
harm caused by their own abstention from the company's
beer. It did not justify their organization of the public against
the company.

This common element of recourse to organized sympathetic
pressure in these three cases distinguishes them from practically
all of the consumption boycotts of business combinations in
which the direct economic interest of the participants was
usually obvious. Hence, it remains apparent that in so far as
labor unions have sought the aid of dissociated supporters—
such as other unions or the general public—to further their con-

sumption boycott pressures, they have violated established principles of the common law. Plain as this may be in these consumption boycott cases, people tend to lose sight of it when it comes to picketing.

SOME OF THE PROBLEMS OF PICKETING

Now picketing is a well-known union technique. Normally a patrol of union folk walks back and forth in front of a place of business which is under strike or under organizational pressure, or associated in some way with an employer whose employment conditions are the ultimate concern of the picketers. Peaceful picketing has become one of organized labor's most effective techniques for implementing consumption boycotts through the participation of the general public. Until fairly recently, most courts have discouraged the use of this device, except in very restricted situations. Originally our courts thought picketing to be unlawful under all circumstances. Unions once employed this device only in connection with strikes, both to notify applicants for employment about the existence of the strike, in the hope that they would not accept employment while the strike continued, and to induce the cooperation of employees who had remained at their jobs during the strike.

Naturally this conduct was harmful to the employer. The strikers found it effective as a means of cutting off the employer from access to the labor market, so he would be sure to suffer economic embarrassment leading to his capitulation and they would thus not have their jobs filled by other men. However, workers on strike did not always exhibit restraint while picketing, frequent brawls and fist fights giving it a bad name. Indeed, most of our courts a generation ago denied that there could be any such thing as peaceful picketing. They frequently declared that all picketing, no matter how restrained, carried with it an underlying implication of force and threatened violence which influenced people approaching a picket line to react more through motives of safety and personal welfare than out of sympathy toward the strikers' cause.

Eventually, most courts modified their views about picketing by strikers, conceding that it was lawful as long as it remained peaceful—that is, nonviolent, nonlibelous and nonfraudulent. And this definition had reference not only to the number and behavior of pickets but also to the nature of their communications to others. But lawful picketing was generally confined to actual strikers who were attempting by their strike to force their employer to comply with a demand for some lawful objective. Only a few of our courts have ever recognized the legality of what may be called "stranger picketing"—that is, picketing by organized outsiders—usually initiated for the purpose of unionizing the employer. This is not surprising in view of the reluctance of most courts to concede that peaceful picketing even by strikers was lawful.

That limited concession made a certain amount of practical sense to courts as soon as they had recognized the legality of strikes themselves. They probably decided to allow a certain amount of orderly picketing, incident to lawful strikes, for much the same practical and political reasons which led them to call certain strikes lawful in the first instance. Since strikers usually had a fairly direct economic interest at stake, sufficient to justify the harm caused by their strike, then presumably they had the same interest to be served by their picket line. Picketing by others than strikers, on the other hand, did not appear to promote an interest of the picketers sufficiently direct to afford a justification for the harm they caused. Hence, most courts would not allow picketing by nonstrikers, no matter how peaceful it was, possibly for much the same obscure reasons which led them to deny the legality of strikes for the closed shop.

An analysis of economic interests involved in various contexts of stranger picketing should be preceded by some brief comments on the nature of peaceful picketing in general— that is, on the idea that all such picketing may be a form of constitutionally guaranteed freedom of speech. This notion has become generally accepted since 1940, although it is by no means completely justified, as a later chapter will show. It is a point of view that has always had a considerable appeal to most so-called liberals. Picketing has always seemed to them a method of communicating information and, as such, a type of speech, whether it involves direct verbal contacts with others, the carrying of placards or signs containing information, or merely the conveyance of ideas implicit in a picket's silently walking back and forth or just standing in front of a plant or store, without any placard or sign, whatsoever, indicating what he believes.

It is not appropriate at this time to plunge into the issue of whether or not peaceful picketing really is *merely* speech or communication or, from any sensible point of view, can be so considered in all contexts. Certainly it is a method of communication, just as the AF of L's "We don't patronize" list appeared to be. That instance of speech or communication appeared to be an integral part of an unlawful consumption boycott, according to the Supreme Court. It may be that picketing under certain circumstances will analytically appear to be something similar when used to implement an unlawful economic pressure. If so, even though it be considered a form of speech or communication, it should arguably be considered unlawful as a part of such pressure, just as much as the federation's blacklist was thought to be.

But the primary purpose of this chapter is to describe and analyze the practical and legal effects of coercive union techniques, rather than their constitutional aspects. There are hundreds of actual court decisions affording opportunities to illustrate the application of general legal principles to picketing. The most interesting and instructive of these illustrations involve what was referred to above as stranger picketing—that is, picketing of a plant by a union group not on strike against the picketed enterprise and not formerly employed by it. For instance, a nationally affiliated union, which has already estab-

lished itself in several units of a particular industry, moves in
on a nonunion plant in this industry and sets up a picket line.
This picketing is intended to impress the employer's present
and would-be employees, as well as any of his customers that
happen by, with the union's existence and its economic aims,
in the hope that they will exert pressure on the employer by
refusing to work for or deal with him, thus leading him to organize with the union to regain their co-operation. The courts
calling this unlawful have done so on the assumption that the
picketers had no interest in employment conditions prevailing in a plant where none of them had been employed, declaring that they could therefore not show any valid justification for the harm they were imposing on the employer. They
contrasted this situation with picketing by strikers, pointing out
the obvious direct interest which such picketers had in the
employment conditions at the plant under strike.

This seems to be an incorrect application of a perfectly
good legal principle, since the union clearly had a very real
economic interest in organizing the picketed enterprise, even if
none of its members participating was or ever had been employed there. For all units in a particular industry are presumably competing with each other and selling their goods in the
same markets. And assuming that employment standards are
higher and constitute a larger portion of overhead costs in the
unionized, as against the nonunion, units in the industry, then
it becomes apparent that all nonunion units have a competitive
advantage over the unionized units, due to the wage and other
labor standards differentials existing between them. Under such
competitive conditions, the nonunion units may in time dominate the market for the industry's products by underselling the
organized units. This, of course, would hurt the unionized
employers. Moreover, it would adversely affect the organized
workers, since it is plain that a union can thrive in a competitive industry only if the units within which it is established also
prosper.

The union in question would either have to abandon some

of its already achieved standards in order to protect the unionized employers' competitive positions, or go out and organize
the competing nonunion plants in that industry. And since the
former alternative is clearly against the union's interests as it
sees them, the latter is necessary from its point of view so that
it can impose on such plants employment standards conform-
ing to those already established in the unionized units of the
industry. Stranger picketing and the secondary consumption
boycott are about the only organizational techniques practically
available to the union. The latter of these two is effective only
when it receives already organized outside support, like that
furnished in response to the AF of L's "We don't patronize"
list. Therefore a union in this position usually resorts to
stranger picketing as the most expedient organizational device.
It is the one which *is* interested in employment conditions at
the nonunion units in the industry and it is the one which does
the picketing designed to bring about the organization necessary to standardize those employment conditions.

This, at any rate, is the line of reasoning adopted by the
few courts that have declared stranger picketing lawful. As
the judge speaking for New York's highest court put it in a
case decided in the late 1920's: "Economic organization today
is not based on the single shop," implying that the aims of organized labor cannot be achieved without universal organization throughout an industry. And it is exceedingly difficult to
perceive in what respect the picketers in the type of case just
discussed lack the economic interest necessary for justification
of the harm they themselves cause, any more than do picketers
who happen merely to be on strike against their employer. One
might suppose, of course, that the strikers have a real tangible
dispute with their employer concerning, say, their wages, which
he refuses to increase in accordance with their collective demand, while the stranger picketers cannot be indulging in a
real dispute of any kind when they picket an employer whose
workers appear to be satisfied with what he is actually paying
them.

Why then, one might ask, should the courts allow a group of outsiders to descend on an employer, at peace with his employees, and create a dispute where none existed before? The answer seems clearly to be that these outsiders are affected by the state of affairs in the picketed nonunion shop, just exactly as much as they might have been affected by their own employers' refusals to raise their wages before they had succeeded in unionizing them. As the unions see it, nonunion employers in a partially organized industry are battening on nonunion labor conditions and constitute a standing offense to union folk in that industry. They do not regard the dispute involved in stranger organizational picketing as in any way imaginary. To them it is just as real as the dispute over wages between striking workers and their employers. And they can prove the grounds for their belief arithmetically in terms of dollars and cents. Indeed, they can also contend that whereas strikers are aggressively out for what they can get, the stranger picketers are out merely to protect and maintain what they have already achieved and are, therefore, behaving defensively.

No court is likely to concede that an employer refusing to grant an increase to his organized employees is less deserving of its consideration than one whose employees have not yet organized and are not on strike, although his wage and other labor standards are below those prevailing in the organized units of the industry. Yet declaring a picket line to support a wage strike lawful and in the same breath holding stranger picketing by the union concerned unlawful is practically another way of admitting that proposition to be true. The fact is that both of these employers deserve all of the consideration from the courts to which they are entitled under the law. Neither of them is any better or worse than the other from any objective standard of judging their conduct. An employer is as morally justified in denying the collective demands of his own employees as he is in refusing concessions to an outside union, under these circumstances. And there is absolutely no good reason for giving an employer more consideration by preventing stranger picketing against him under these circumstances than there is for allowing his own immediate employees to picket him peacefully. According to the only intelligible legal test, justification in either case is simply a matter of proving that the economic interests of strikers or the picketers are being served. And this can be shown quite as easily in the one case as in the other.

Another variant of picketing indicates more clearly how unions enlist the economic assistance of outsiders—members of the consuming public, who have absolutely no interest in the conditions of employment in the industry involved—under circumstances where it may appear at first glance that the picketers themselves lack any real interest in the affairs of the picketed enterprise. Suppose that a manufacturer of ready-to-eat meat products runs a nonunion shop in an industry in which a substantial number of units are organized with a union. It appears that his wage scale is as much as 40 or 50 cents per hour lower than the established union scale in some operations, while all through his shop wage rates are substantially below the approved union rates in effect elsewhere. Naturally this gives the manufacturer in question a great competitive advantage over rival unionized manufacturers. As has already been shown, this disparity in wage rates in turn has a harmful effect on the union workers, as well. For presumably the manufacturer's product is just as good as that of his competitors. And he can sell it for less, while making a greater profit, because of the wage differential. Obviously, the union has a very real economic interest in taking coercive steps to unionize this manufacturer.

The case where these facts actually occurred was *Goldfinger v. Feintuch* decided in 1937 by the highest New York court. There the union established a picket line around the plant. Since this pressure was ineffective, the union placed pickets outside of delicatessen shops purveying this manufacturer's nonunion product, in the hope of compelling them to discontinue his line. The results of this step were very gratifying to the union, because the majority of the consuming public either stopped buying the product in question or kept away from the picketed shops altogether. The manufacturer immediately began to feel the economic pinch, and he presumably approved, if he did not actually support, the action brought by a delicatessen owner to test the legality of this practice.

The delicatessen owner contended that the union had no economic interest in picketing him, because he did not have any employees (the shop being a family store run by him and his wife) and because the union showed no interest in securing employment for its members at his shop. Hence, he argued, this was not a labor dispute at all but was a case of deliberately imposed and unjustifiable harm. The court, however, thought otherwise. It pointed out that the union had a very substantial economic interest at stake in keeping the manufacturer's nonunion product off the market, where it would compete with union-made products of the same type. This interest, it said, would have justified the exertion of pressure at the plant itself. And it was sufficient also to justify its exercise at points where the nonunion product was retailed. The court did not reach this conclusion, however, without tying the shopkeeper up with the nonunion manufacturer sufficiently closely to show that he was practically participating in the latter's enterprise. And even then the court told the union that while it might picket the *nonunion product* in front of the shop, it must not appear to be picketing the proprietor himself.

Apparently the court thought that nobody should be subjected to union picketing unless he had adopted a course of action adverse to the interests of the union. Thus, it implied that it would not tolerate picketing against an influential citizen merely to enlist his aid in bringing pressure against a nonunion employer, where the picketed citizen had no economic connection of any kind with the employer. Certainly, it would seem an unmitigated affront to expose people to such pressures when they had not identified themselves in any way with the nonunion practices under fire. The New York court, however, thought that the delicatessen owner was very closely identified with the nonunion manufacturer, declaring that his ability profitably to undersell competing stores which handled union-made products, on the basis of the nonunion wage differential, indicated a "unity of interest" between the manufacturer and himself in perpetuating the former's nonunion employment conditions. It regarded the delicatessen owner as virtually a distributional arm of the manufacturer, not bound to him by any legal tie, to be sure, but even more closely welded to him, in a real sense, through their common interest in manufacturing and marketing the nonunion product, to their mutual advantage. For the manufacturer could not benefit from his low overhead costs unless his product reached consumers, and the delicatessen owner could not benefit as he did without the nonunion manufacturer to supply him.

Now this picketing was intended to create pressure on the manufacturer, through decreased retail sales, by enlisting the sympathy of ultimate consumers of the nonunion-made product. The union hoped either that consumers would not cross the picket line at all or, if they did, would refrain from buying the nonunion product in question. Both of these hopes were amply fulfilled. It was apparent that systematic picketing of this sort at all retail outlets of the manufacturer's product would sooner or later ruin him or compel him to make peace with the union on its terms. How does this situation differ from the AF of L's "We don't patronize" unfair list which was circulated to all members of all unions affiliated within the federation? Publication of that list was declared unfair because it organized the assistance and support of people who had no economic interest at stake in the labor conditions prevailing at the stove company's plant. In this delicatessen shop case, the entire success of the union's pressure plan depended upon the co-operation of ultimate consumers—people who not only had no interest at all in establishing union conditions at the manufacturer's plant but who seemed to have a very real economic interest as consumers in seeing that the plant remained nonunion, so they could buy the product in question at a relatively lower price.

Any difference between these two situations is, presumably, that while the federation's pressure through its unfair list was actively initiated and implemented by union people who did not have a direct interest in the stove workers' employment conditions—people like Sam Gompers who was president of the AF of L as well as the thousands of workers in various crafts, composing the union public—in the delicatessen shop case the pressure was actively organized only by members of the meat workers' union itself. But even this difference is minimized to some extent by the fact that the stove workers directly contributed to the support of Gompers and his fellow officials, thus creating some sort of mutual interest among them to see that the stove workers' employment conditions were improved.

It is hard to escape the conclusion that in each case the real punch behind the pressure was furnished by ultimate consumers. The fact that the roster of federated union consumers, having no direct economic interest at stake, was highly organized against the stove company in one case, while the consuming public was not organized in this fashion in the meat products case, seems somewhat offset by the fact that the federated union folk certainly had more interest in achieving success for their "cousins" in other federated unions than did the consuming public in helping the meat workers' union win their fight with the nonunion manufacturer. And it seems apparent that the California brewery workers' appeal, through circulars to the general public, was not much different, if any, from either of these two situations.

One possible explanation for the different judicial views in the federation's "We don't patronize" case and the brewery workers' case, on the one hand, and this New York delicatessen shop case on the other, is that the courts in the first two believed that any secondary pressure was in itself unlawful, while the New York court had long since abandoned that view in general, retaining it only when *organized* persons creating the primary pressure, through their refusals to consume, had no interest at stake, as in the *Auburn* truckers' case. It was somewhat puzzling to see the various judges in the New York delicatessen shop case differing among themselves as to whether or not the union's picketing amounted to a secondary boycott. Why were they concerned about this? Apparently they thought that if it were a secondary boycott, it would be like the *Auburn* truckers' case, and the picketing would hence be illegal. And it looks as if they had satisfied themselves that it was not such a secondary boycott because of the "identity" of the meat manufacturer and delicatessen owner through their "unity of interest" in exploiting nonunion labor. They were convinced that picketing against the nonunion manufacturer was all right, and they apparently went to some lengths to show that there was no difference between that situation and the one before them.

Actually the delicatessen shop case was clearly an instance of secondary pressure—a secondary boycott, if you please. The union created primary pressure against the retailer with the hope that he would cease handling the nonunion product, thus in turn bringing pressure on the nonunion manufacturer. It had an economic interest at stake in doing so, because the retailer's enterprise in distributing nonunion product was harmful to the union. Hence, even in the absence of these fictions of identity and unity of interest, the union had, in plain ordinary language, an interest for bringing pressure on the delicatessen owner. Had its members been employed there, a strike by them to compel him to stop selling the nonunion product would have been accepted as routine. Also an organized refusal by members of the particular union to patronize the retailer would have been regarded as routine.

Why, then, should there have been any difficulties over the union's picketing him, as long as picketing had been accepted as lawful along with the other coercive techniques of organized labor? Certainly, the economic interest of the union was quite as potent here as it was in most instances of stranger picketing which this court had previously thought to be lawful.

Even conceding the presence of a secondary boycott pressure in this case, it was not at all like the *Auburn* truckers' case, where the primary pressure was furnished through the organized boycott of union people who had no direct interest at stake and who were, therefore, exerting sympathetic pressure. And even accepting the fiction of the identity between the manufacturer and the retailer, the delicatessen shop case is still distinguishable from the federation's "We don't patronize" case, because there the AF of L had organized the purchasing power of unions having no direct interest at stake.

Perhaps the court was worried by the fact that peaceful picketing of any sort—and particularly in this case—"organized" the purchasing power of the public to exert a sympathetic pressure, not founded on any personal economic interest, against the retailer and, through him, against the manufacturer. Maybe the court was worried by this practical similarity between the case before it and these instances of admitted sympathetic pressure, thus perceiving for the first time this fundamental difficulty of allowing immunity to peaceful picketing under the defense of justification based on interest, when this practice depended for its success on the co-operation of a sympathetic public. If this be so, it was hardly worth worrying about, since the proper time for such speculation had been before these courts had ever committed themselves so broadly in the first place to the notion that peaceful stranger picketing is permissible whenever the picketers themselves have an economic interest at stake. At this late date such courts had to shut their eyes to the "sympathetic" incidents of stranger picketing intended to influence the consuming public, in spite of the fact that they had been developing a requirement of a rigorous "economic interest" as the price of admission to the allowable area of economic conflict. Now they must concentrate on peaceful picketing as simply a form of speech or communication, ignoring any implications of "psychological coercion" and winking at the harm that follows when the consuming public responds to picketing, whether its response is influenced by "coercion" or is simply an expression of sympathy, being in either event not founded on any perceptible economic interest in the union's affairs.

A CONCLUSION OR TWO

While the preceding analysis is involved, it must be apparent that if our courts and legislatures are going to work out a body of rules to govern the peaceful self-help activities which unions employ to promote their programs, and are going to develop these rules along the lines of economic interest, then this sort of analysis is necessary in order to understand what they are doing and what they should be doing. From the previous chapter, and the foregoing account in this one, it may be seen that unions with interests at stake are given a free hand in exerting economic pressures against enterprises conducted on a basis inimical to the interests of such unions, although they are restricted from exercising purely sympathetic pressures. But in instances where unions use peaceful picketing to make bids for the co-operation of the consuming public, depending on its sympathy for the creation of effective economic pressures, it seems that many courts lose sight of the fact that this is purely sympathetic coercion, remembering only that the union itself creating this pressure has an economic interest at stake.

A recent California decision shows more clearly how courts have in this way permitted unions, through picketing, to evade the legal sanction against sympathetic support from even organized workers having no economic interest at stake. In *McKay v. Local Union No. 1067,* a salesmen's union wanted to organize the sales employees of a large garage and automobile agency. Neither the employer nor his salesmen wanted to sign up with this union, so the union threw a picket line outside of the employer's place of business. Thereupon his unionized mechanics and other craft employees, who were perfectly satisfied with their own conditions of employment, refused to come to work because "they could not cross a picket line." No union truck driver would call at the employer's place of business, either to deliver or pick up, for the same reason. These other union workers were acting in accordance with a resolution of a local council of craft unions not to cross each other's picket lines.

Now this is a plain instance of sympathetic pressure, for the other unions had no conceivable interest in the success of the salesmen's union, even conceding the fact that some of them might possibly have had a "common industrial interest" with automobile salesmen in view of their joint concern with automobiles. Of course, this was a sympathetic refusal to work, instead of to consume. The same sort of arrangement, about not crossing the picket lines of sister unions, existed among all of the unions in the council for the purpose of organizing the patronage of their members in their capacity of consumers as well as of workers. The court, however, could not very well outlaw the personal convictions of the members of other craft unions or forbid them as individuals to refuse to cross the picket line of the immediately interested union, even though it could have enjoined active support by the other unions, as organizations, through a formal council arrangement. Actually what the California court did was to uphold the picketing as "constitutionally guaranteed freedom of speech," and it did not enjoin the sympathetic pressures imposed by the other unions.

Most of us are aware of the purely sympathetic aspects of economic pressures built up through picketing by appeals to would-be patrons of picketed enterprises. This sort of thing exists when moving picture machine operators, attempting to organize their employer or to secure some immediate advantage from him, picket the front entrance to his theater, or when a retail clerks' union, for the same reasons, pickets the entrances to a store. In all cases of this sort the picketing is done to enlist the economic assistance of customers; and even if such picketing seems futile to the casual observer, much of it is exceedingly effective, imposing considerable harm on the picketed enterprises. The assistance of the consuming public, union or non-union, is usually given without any inquiry into or knowledge of the merits of the immediate dispute involved and without any regard to such public's own personal economic interests. Any interest would-be patrons might have at stake is frequently to avoid trouble which they think might ensue from crossing the picket line. Certainly, union wage earners, in the capacity of patrons, feel this way as a matter of principle, even if success for the picketers means higher priced movies or merchandise, most of them feeling that they cannot afford to be branded as scabs for crossing a picket line. For obvious reasons, local merchants and professional men, all dependent on the patronage of the public for their economic welfare, as well as office holders out for the support of the electorate, frequently react the same way.

Naturally, this analysis is not intended as a condemnation of peaceful picketing as such. It is, rather, an attempt to make clear the issues involved in the use of economic pressures by organized groups and to show how many angles there are to the consistent administration of the only valid judicial principle of justification governing the use of harmful union pressures. Now there is nothing holy about picketing to warrant its approval whenever and however it occurs. If it is used to secure the same objectives sought by other forms of pressure and communication, then our courts ought to judge its use in accordance with the same standards employed to govern these other techniques.

Perhaps it would be more apt to say that our courts should look more at the substance than at the form of what unions and other types of pressure groups do. So far there is no reason to suppose that our courts have abandoned the practice of testing the legality of various economic pressures by inquiring into the interests of those exerting these pressures. Under this test they have professed to condone harmful economic coercion only when it is exerted in the pursuit of self-interest. In every case where courts have allowed business combinations to exert

such economic coercion in pursuit of gain, all participating in
its exercise have met this test. Of course, some participants
have been unwilling actors but they have chosen to deal with
dominant associations rather than with outsiders, in order to
retain what they regarded as the best trade. Everyone involved
was directly concerned with the economic conflict in question.

This is usually true of labor's organized pressures; but enough
has appeared in this chapter to indicate that it is not always
so. When it is not so, in clear-cut cases, our courts have not
hesitated to declare sympathetic pressures unlawful. The real
difficulty in applying this general principle arises in connection
with peaceful picketing. Even here there is no trouble when
unions use this device to notify an employer, his loyal employees and his would-be employees about the state of affairs
at a plant under strike, as well as to apprise these same people
of an economic situation harmful to organized labor's interests
in a nonunion plant. Here everybody mentioned has a vital
concern in what the unions are trying to do, whether or not
they would admit it. If the present and would-be employees in
any particular instance respond to the picketing by joining the
union and participating in the economic coercion on the employer, then they are arguably serving their own interests as
they see them and are not in any sense indulging in mere
sympathetic pressure to help bring about a change in which
they have no interest.

But courts seem to lose sight of the economic interest test
when confronted by cases in which unions use picketing to
muster and organize the sympathetic purchasing habits of
ultimate consumers, many of whom are union adherents. Apparently they rationalize their position by claiming that they
are merely permitting unions, by picketing, to publicize certain facts and to invite the consuming public to act as it sees
fit. Any pressure exerted against nonunion enterprises and
those in unity of interest with them is explained as being
directly due to the whims of enlightened public opinion. Presumably they would say the same thing when they tolerate the

sympathetic refusal of other unrelated craft unions to cross a picket line.

In this way the economic interest test is diluted and qualified in a manner which, unfortunately, promises to break down the only analytical technique enabling courts to recognize at common law a valid allowable area of economic conflict for organized labor—that is, an area stripped of all elements involving sympathy. Perhaps this would not be serious if our legislatures were still free to define this area strictly on the basis of economic interest. But quite recent constitutional developments in the Supreme Court have prevented this possibility in the picketing cases. And it threatens to do so in all instances of peaceful union undertakings to organize the sympathetic assistance of others to promote the aggressive union's own economic objectives.

J. L. LEONARD
DEPARTMENT OF ECONOMICS
UNIVERSITY OF SOUTHERN CALIFORNIA

CHAPTER VII

THE REMOVAL OF JUDICIAL CONTROLS OVER UNION EXPANSION BY ANTI-INJUNCTION ACTS

> I am not speaking of conscious impartiality; but the habits you are trained in, the people with whom you mix, lead to your having a certain class of ideas of such a nature that, when you have to deal with other ideas, you do not give as sound and accurate judgments as you would wish. This is one of the great difficulties at present with Labour. Labour says: "Where are your impartial Judges? They all move in the same circle as the employers, and they are all educated and nursed in the same ideas as the employers. How can a labour man or a trade unionist get impartial justice?" It is very difficult sometimes to be sure that you have put yourself into a thoroughly impartial position between two disputants, one of your own class and one not of your class.—Lord Justice Scrutton, *Cambridge Law Journal*, 1921.

So FAR it is apparent that our courts are primarily concerned in labor cases with defining what Chief Judge Pound of the highest New York court so aptly called "the allowable area of economic conflict." They have conceded unions the right to fight with economic weapons of one sort or another for conditions thought advantageous by them. And considering the fairly conservative economic backgrounds of most judges, they have on the whole been tolerant in permitting unions to select and pursue their own values, which are so often at odds with the opinions of people brought up on classical economics. They have insisted that these disputes must be waged only between parties with conflicting interests—a position probably dictated by the principle of law that harm intentionlly imposed through the exercise of purely economic coercion is still actionable unless justified by the coincidental pursuit of gain.

Too often, however, our courts have taken exceedingly narrow views of what amounts to justification through the pursuit of gain. Thus, they have tended to outlaw the strike for the closed shop because they could see no direct economic end to be served by it. They have usually outlawed stranger picketing because they could see no connection between employment conditions at the picketed plant and the economic interests of the picketers who were not employed there. And they have outlawed the secondary boycott, both labor and consumption, because they could not perceive the economic connection between those who activated the pressure and those on whom it was ultimately exerted.

THE SUPREME COURT AND THE CLAYTON ACT: 1914–1921

It was pointed out in Chapter IV that the adverse judicial restrictions imposed on these instances of union economic coercion were as a rule reflected in injunctions prohibiting their continuance. When during the first decade of this century the federal courts were beginning to exercise rather sweeping controls over unions under the Sherman Antitrust Act, and seemed to be using the injunction too freely against organized labor, considerable political pressure was focused on the passage of legislation to curtail the powers of courts over union self-help activities. The first systematic effort in this direction culminated in Section 20 of the Clayton Act, passed by Congress in 1914. Samuel Gompers, the president of the AF of L at that time, hailed this legislation as labor's Magna Charta. And several liberally inclined state legislatures quickly copied the anti-injunction section of the act in the belief that it would allay the abuses of judicial control over unions.

An analysis of this measure will shortly reveal how mistaken they all were. Anyone reading Section 20 of the Clayton Act would suppose that it achieves three objectives:

(1) Congress first tells the federal courts that they shall not issue restraining orders and injunctions "in any case between an employer and employees, or between employers and employees, or between employees, or between persons employed and persons seeking employment, involving, or growing out of, a dispute concerning terms or conditions of employment," unless it is necessary to do so in order to prevent injury to property rights of the complainant where no adequate remedy exists at law, and

(2) Congress then tells the federal courts that they shall not issue restraining orders and injunctions *under any circumstances* in order to prohibit persons acting in concert or otherwise

(a) "from terminating any relation of employment, or from ceasing to perform any work or labor, or from recommending, advising, or persuading others by peaceful means so to do"; or

(b) "from attending at any place where any such person or persons may lawfully be, for the purpose of peacefully obtaining or communicating information, or from peacefully persuading any person to work or to abstain from working"; or

(c) "from ceasing to patronize or to employ any party to such dispute, or from recommending, advising, or persuading others by peaceful and lawful means so to do"; or

(d) from paying or withholding from any person engaged in such dispute any strike benefits, money or things of value; or

(e) "from peaceably assembling in a lawful manner, and for lawful purposes"; or

(f) "from doing any act or thing which might lawfully be done in the absence of such dispute by any party thereto"; and

(3) Congress finally tells the federal courts that none of the acts or conduct described under (2) and its subsections shall "be considered or held to be violations of any law of the United States."

In other words, Congress declares that such acts and conduct shall not only be nonenjoinable before the federal courts but shall also be completely lawful, whether in criminal or tort proceedings under statutes or at common law.

Now all this seems clear enough. It does not require a legal education to read and understand this Section 20 of the Clayton Act. Sam Gompers was not a lawyer and he understood it plainly enough—or thought he did. But just to be sure, let us review the first part from a layman's point of view. What is "any case between an employer and employees"? It does not say "his" employees. Does it mean an employer and people who are employed, regardless of where they are employed or by whom? Incidentally, are people on strike or picketing, and thus temporarily unemployed anywhere, to be considered as employees at all in this phrase? Why did Congress include the phrase "between employers and employees" after it had mentioned the preceding phrase? What did it mean by the phrase "between employees"? And what is the significance of the phrase "between persons employed and persons seeking employment"? And what, of all things, is "a dispute concerning terms or conditions of employment"? Thus it suddenly becomes apparent that the meanings of these words are not so clear.

But Congress must have had something in mind. The second Circuit Court of Appeals thought that Sam Gompers' interpretation was correct. Two of these three judges believed that Congress, in this passage, had attempted under the first category to curtail the power of federal courts to issue injunctions in cases involving economic conflict between labor unions and business concerns, whenever the evidence showed that the particular union had some real economic interest at stake which was adversely affected by the employment practices followed by the company in question. They did not believe that this passage referred only to employers and their employees, whose employment was temporarily suspended by a strike. Rather, they thought that the word "employees" meant working people—"employables," if you will. The phrase "between employees" apparently seemed broad enough to them to include conflicts between union and nonunion "employables." The phrase "between persons employed and persons seeking employment" seemed to indicate a sufficiently broad category to include stranger picketing and other pressures by outsiders against nonunion employees at a plant. And "a dispute concerning terms or conditions of employment" they believed broad enough to reflect those actual developments in our broader common-law decisions which inclined toward the toleration of any concerted economic pressures aimed at promoting the interests of those exerting the pressure, as they saw such interests, whether or not any direct relationship of employment ever had or ever would exist between them and the employers affected.

Certainly there seems to be good reason to suppose that such was the intention of Congress, however ill-chosen the word "employees" might have been to describe the general class of wage earners and laborers. For people by 1914 were well aware of the fact that organized labor had just as much interest at stake in nonunion plants of a partially organized industry as they had in plants where unions were already established, because of the serious competitive problem between union and nonunion entrepreneurs and their respective employees, made possible by the differential between union and nonunion labor standards. To deny that the phrase "dispute concerning terms or conditions of employment" was broad enough to include organizational campaigns conducted by unions against nonunion units of partially organized industries was to shut one's eyes to the obvious facts of industrial life. Furthermore, such a denial ignored the full implications of the principle of common law allowing the imposition of harm through economic pressures in the pursuit of self-interest and gain, whether by business associations or labor unions, in strict conformance with the good old-fashioned rules of justification through competition, as they had been developed by the courts themselves.

But the Supreme Court disagreed with the lower federal court. In this case of *Duplex Printing Press Company v. Deer-*

ing, it seems that an international mechanics' union had undertaken to unionize a nonunion printing press company—the only unit, out of an industry consisting of four such companies, which was still not unionized. The union felt that organization of this fourth plant was imperative because of the adverse competitive effect otherwise brought to bear on the three unionized companies and their union employees, by the labor standard differential between the two sets of shops. Their way of exerting pressure against the company was not by strike so much as by the secondary labor boycott—members of the union refusing to repair or to work on this company's presses where they were installed or to work for anyone who used them.

This was harmful to the company. In a suit for injunction under the Sherman Act, it sought to prevent the continuance of this organized pressure. The union had relied on Section 20 of the Clayton Act as a defense, arguing that its terms covered this situation. But the Supreme Court held that Section 20 applied only in cases where the relationship of employment existed between the company and the union members involved. This seemed an exceedingly narrow interpretation of the first paragraph of Section 20, and many thought it an incorrect conception by the Court of what Congress had intended.

The second paragraph in Section 20 of the Clayton Act contains a description of the self-help economic activities which Congress declared should be available to organized labor in pursuing their objectives, free from the injunctive process and, indeed, lawful for all purposes in the federal arena. The first of these, *(a)*, would seem to any ordinary intelligent person to include not only strikes by employees against their employer, to secure some advantage from him, but also *any* concerted cessation of work by *any* employees, whether or not they are employed by the company against which the ultimate pressure is focused. This, presumably, would cover organized refusals to work by employees of enterprisers using the nonunion company's product, in order to force such enterprisers to boycott the nonunion product—in other words, the secondary labor boycott. Furthermore, it includes recommending, advising and persuading others to do the same "by peaceful means," without placing any limitation whatsoever on who may so recommend, advise and persuade or how such recommending, advising and persuading can be done, as long as "peaceful means"—that is, free from violence and force—are employed.

The next provision which was marked (b), looks as if Congress had picketing in mind—peaceful picketing and patrolling, where persons have a lawful right to be, peacefully to get or give information and in a peaceful manner to persuade others to work or not to work. Anyway, if Congress didn't mean this, it is certainly hard to figure out what it *did* mean. The next provision, (c), reads as if Sam Gompers had at last persuaded Congress to nullify the Supreme Court's views in the AF of L nation-wide consumers' boycott case, involving the federation's "We don't patronize" list published to secure the economic support of all organized labor against the Bucks Stove and Range Company. For it seems to cover anybody's concerted refusals to patronize, without limitation, and then seems to allow recommending, advising, and persuading others to do the same thing, as long as such exhortation is "by peaceful and lawful means." The next two provisions, (d) and (e) above, are not sufficiently interesting in this connection to warrant discussion. But (f) is very broad, covering any conduct by labor unionists acting in concert, which any one of them alone might have done in the absence of a labor dispute—in other words, anything anybody has a civil right under the Constitution to do all by himself!

This is what Congress seemed to say—and it is hard to believe that it intended otherwise—in (2), which is the second paragraph of Section 20 in the Clayton Act. It is true that in (a) there appeared the qualifying phrase, "by peaceful means," in (b) the words "lawfully" and "peacefully," the latter word twice, in (c) the phrase "by peaceful and lawful means," in

(e) the words "peaceably" and "lawful," the latter appearing twice, and in (f) the word "lawfully." It seems quite plain that unless Congress was just playing with words in enacting this paragraph of Section 20—a dangerous thing to attribute even to our national legislature—it intended these significant words to be construed in terms of the old and established common-law categories of tort and crime, as well as in terms of statutory categories of illegality. Surely it must have had the normal self-help activities of labor unions in mind, since such activities were a matter of common knowledge and since it realized that of these activities there were two general types—those involving rough stuff, like actual and threatened violence, fraud and libel, and those consisting of purely economic pressures, like strikes, boycotts, and peaceful picketing.

It is hard to believe that Congress meant to have the words "peaceful," "peacefully," "peaceably," "lawful," and "lawfully" construed in accordance with the rationale of the same antiunion decisions which Section 20 was presumably designed to correct. Thus, just because the conduct described in (a), as it was practiced in some strikes and secondary labor boycotts, had been held unlawful, even though it involved only purely economic coercion and no vestige of illegality under traditional or statutory categories of tort or crime, was no reason to suppose that Congress was intending to perpetuate such judicial qualifications in a statute designed to curb more judicial intemperance in labor cases. Indeed, the natural supposition would be that Congress, the Supreme Court's superior in lawmaking, was ordering the federal courts, including the Supreme Court, to abandon these factitious judicial rules of illegality and to get back to their proper business of applying the real common law, as modified by this statute and by any other statute that happened to be on the books. The same observation is appropriate for the balance of the provisions.

It is true that several of our courts had declared that there could be no such thing as peaceful picketing—a ridiculous conclusion from presumably serious professional men. Why should the courts assume that Congress intended to perpetuate such folly, unless they were so vain as to believe that only they, the judges, could sensibly declare the meaning of such words as peaceful and peaceable? In (c) Congress apparently meant to imply that publishing a national union newspaper containing a plea to union folk not to purchase particular products was a program based on "peaceful and lawful means," and it seemed to be the Supreme Court's duty to recognize this. Just because that court had previously held this practice to be unlawful was beside the point. What Congress was trying to do, apparently, was to say that the court had gone too far and that it was now establishing the law as it thought it should be. It spelled out the conduct so carefully that any intelligent layman could understand it. But apparently the Supreme Court could not.

Perhaps subparagraph (f) presents the clearest item. Here Congress said, in such unmistakable terms that only a lawyer could misunderstand its statement, that *any* persons acting in concert might do *anything,* during the course of a labor dispute, which any party to it might *lawfully* have done in its absence. In other words, the concerted self-help practices of unions were to be adjudged by federal courts in accordance with what any individual interested in the dispute might have done with impunity all by himself. Why, the sky's the limit on such freedom of action, almost. For as long as he refrained from violence and other such overtly unlawful conduct, any such interested individual was free to refrain from work, to refrain from purchasing or patronizing, to persuade others to join him in doing these things, to go where he wished as long as he did not trespass, and to enjoy all of the ordinary civil rights any American accepts quite naturally as his birthright. These are the things, then, which Congress solemnly said in subparagraph (f) that organized labor might do.

When the Supreme Court decided the *Duplex* case in 1921, however, it seemed not to consist wholly of men who could grasp this novel but simple command of the lawmakers, for a majority of the Court there held that Congress had merely intended in this second paragraph to state the law as it already existed in judicial decisions—in other words, that in exercising its solemn legislative function it was doing nothing at all. The Court read this paragraph, with emphasis on the words peaceful and lawful and their variants, to reflect those very decisions which had aroused Congress, through political pressures on it, to pass Section 20 in the first place. And the strange part of all this was that a few of our state courts sympathetic to unionism had already held the common law to be that the conduct spelled out in the second paragraph of Section 20 was perfectly lawful.

Some of their decisions acknowledged its legality under any circumstances, as a matter of civil rights, and others only when those participating in this conduct had economic interests of their own at stake. Anyhow, the Supreme Court, by its reaction to Section 20, was perpetuating those same judicial errors described in detail in the first three chapters of this book. In short, it was forsaking its proper function of interpreting and applying the established principles of common law, which traditionally governed the exercise of coercion in situations involving business associations, and was superimposing on the real common law a set of factitious rules attributable to the social and economic predilections of the judiciary.

To recapitulate for clarity, and to add one item hitherto neglected, the Supreme Court refused to concede that Congress had made lawful any of organized labor's self-help techniques described in this portion of the Clayton Act, except as to such conduct as was already considered lawful, anyway, before this act was passed. Furthermore, it held that even if this second paragraph meant what the labor unions said it meant, it offered no protection to the union involved in the case before it because none of these defendants was or ever had been employed by the complaining printing press company.

The court based this conclusion, *first,* on its interpretation of the first paragraph of the section to mean that the statute applied only in cases of disputes over terms and conditions of employment between parties in the direct relationship of master and servant, so that only the employees of a particular employer, disputing with him their own personal terms and conditions of employment, were covered by the section. And *second,* it relied on the fact that the second paragraph of the section began with the words "And no *such* restraining order or injunction shall prohibit," et cetera, thus indicating through the use of the word "such" that everything said in the second paragraph was intended solely with reference to the "restraining order and injunction" covered in the first paragraph, that is, one in a case involving, as the court read it, a dispute between an employer and his own employees who were in direct master and servant relationship with him.

Justice Brandeis dissented vigorously in this case. As he read this section, Congress was attempting to enlarge the "allowable area of economic conflict" for labor unions by making it coextensive with the pursuit and defense of union interests. For about the first time in the Anglo-American law reports, the real nature of union economic needs, as the unions saw them, was fairly analyzed and described in his opinion. He showed, as has already been related in previous chapters, how unions *do* have a vital interest in the terms and conditions of employment prevailing in the nonunion plants of industries in which they are already established. This interest is such as to compel them either to unionize these shops, regardless of the wishes of the existing employees in such shops, or to give up what they have already achieved elsewhere. He indicated how some state courts, particularly the highest court in the jurisdiction where most of the machinist union's coercive activities had been exerted, had recognized this interest and had permitted the exercise of systematic economic coercion from without to organize nonunion shops.

He insisted that this was what Congress had intended to permit in Section 20 of the Clayton Act. He suggested that if Congress were not intending to do just this, there was really no point in its having enacted this section, particularly as the presumption underlying any piece of legislation is that it is designed to change the existing state of affairs, and he pointed out this broadening of the area of economic conflict as the only possible change involved. Thus, he indicated, allowable economic conflict might occur either between an employer and his own existing employees, or between an employer and all employees economically affected by the working conditions in his shop, whether or not they were employed by him. If the former only was intended, no statute was necessary; but if the latter was to prevail, then the majority of the court was wrong in their interpretation of the first paragraph of Section 20. Naturally he gave the second paragraph of this section a liberal interpretation, for he believed that its provisions were intended for the benefit of all employees affected by the first paragraph, being all with any interest at stake, whether or not they were in the direct relationship of employment with the employer against whom their conduct was focused.

Justice Brandeis closed his opinion with a dignified reproof to a majority of the court, remarkable for its restraint under the circumstances. He said: "Because I have come to the conclusion that both the common law of a State and a statute of the United States declare the right of industrial combatants to push their struggle to the limits of the justification of self-interest, I do not wish to be understood as attaching any constitutional or moral sanction to that right. All rights are derived from the purposes of the society in which they exist; above all rights rises duty to the community. The conditions developed in industry may be such that those engaged in it cannot continue their struggle without danger to the community. But it is not for judges to determine whether such conditions exist, nor is it their function to set the limits of permissible contest and to declare the duties which the new situation demands. This is the function of the legislature which, while limiting individual and group rights of aggression and defense, may substitute processes of justice for the more primitive method of trial by combat."

It is hard to read this important chapter in the development of American labor policy without becoming disillusioned about two of our most important branches of government—Congress and the Supreme Court. Ever since this first interpretation of Section 20 of the Clayton Act, almost all educated opinion in this country has been that the Supreme Court sold organized labor down the river when it construed this section. But there is another angle to this. Several astute lawyers thought that Congress was the body which had betrayed the labor unions when it enacted Section 20. They believed that Congress deliberately made this section ambiguous, with the surface appearance of going very far indeed, but nevertheless using restrictive words like "employee" in close juxtaposition with the word "employer" and craftily inserting words like "lawful" and "peaceful," so that labor people would think, after a hasty reading, that they had achieved something substantial. These same lawyers thought that Congress had all the time actually hoped and believed that the Supreme Court would nullify by construction the liberal implications of the section.

If this suspicion were true, there would be revealed the worst kind of political chicanery. Evidence tending to support this belief was found in some of the Congressional committee reports on this section, indicating that Congress had no intention of going so far as to allow the secondary boycott. It is only fair to Congress, however, to remember that an understanding of concepts like the secondary boycott was even less clear in 1914 than it is today. Quite possibly none of the members of the committee knew what was being talked about when that group disclaimed all intention to legalize such a technique.

As Justice Pitney indicated, the spokesman for the House committee said that "the section as reported was carefully prepared with the settled purpose of excluding the secondary boycott and *confining boycotting to the parties to the dispute, allowing parties to cease to patronize and to ask others to cease to patronize a party to the dispute;* it was the opinion of the committee that it did not legalize the secondary boycott, it was not their purpose to authorize such a boycott, not a member of the committee would vote to do so." Now, if Congress had really intended to extend the provisions of Section 20 to union people not in the relationship of employment with the complaining employer—and it is very hard to see why it passed the section at all if it did not—then the italicized portion of the above quotation from Justice Pitney's opinion makes it fairly clear that Congress was legalizing exactly what the AF of L had done through its "We don't patronize" column in its federation newspaper and which the Supreme Court had previously thought to be an unlawful sympathetic consumption boycott. Hence, a rather broad interpretation of Section 20 might possibly still be consistent with Congress' denial of any intention to legalize the secondary boycott.

On the other hand, a factor to be thrown in the scales on the side of the Supreme Court is the extraordinary nature of Section 20 if it were to be accepted as most so-called liberals think it was intended. For under this broader construction, Congress went to extreme limits in allowing for union pressures. If such construction were accepted, then it must be deemed to have written into Section 20 the so-called civil rights theory of freedom of concerted economic conduct. This completely ignored that qualification of this theory based on a showing of some personal economic interest by those exerting the economic pressure, which the courts had carefully developed as justification under the common-law principle that harm intentionally imposed through purely economic coercion is actionable unless justified.

Of course, the civil rights theory had occasional support in state courts, and it had a tremendous political appeal. Furthermore it was much easier to set it forth in general statutory language than it was to draft a provision limiting the allowable area of economic conflict to those who had some actual economic interest at stake. Indeed, a reading of Justice Brandeis' dissent shows quite clearly that even he believed this al-

lowable area should be defined in terms of economic interest
rather than in terms of civil rights. He went on to declare that
such a matter was entirely in the hands of Congress, as a matter of legislative policy, and was none of the Supreme Court's
business. Nevertheless, it is possible that a majority of the Court
was influenced toward the narrow interpretation by its fear of
sanctioning the extreme latitude apparently allowed by Congress and by its refusal to believe that Congress could have
intended to go so far.

During this same year, 1921, in a case involving picketing
by outsiders, by a few actual strikers and by former employees
who had been laid off but were hopeful of resuming their employment, the Supreme Court held Section 20 of the Clayton
Act applicable. This was the case of *American Steel Foundries
v. Tri-City Central Trades Council.* The opinion outlined a
kind of peaceful picketing in which only the strikers and
laid-off employees might indulge. This the labor folk promptly
dubbed "pink tea picketing." No others were allowed to participate in this strictly limited and peaceful picketing. The
reason for this was, said the Court, that they did not fall within
the terms of Section 20, even if they did belong to a union
whose standards in other organized shops were competitively
affected by the nonunion conditions of employment in the
picketed plant.

Shortly thereafter in *Truax v. Corrigan* the Supreme Court
reviewed a decision of the Arizona Supreme Court interpreting that state's anti-injunction act which was modeled after
Section 20 of the Clayton Act. The Arizona court had refused under this statute to enjoin picketing by strikers and
others with placards containing defamatory and untrue statements about the employer in question, denying the picketed
employer the relief he requested against its continuance. The
Supreme Court took the case on appeal and held, under the
due process clause of the Constitution, that the state act was
unconstitutional as construed and applied by the Arizona
court. Now it may seem odd that the Supreme Court could

uphold the validity of a set of words in a federal statute and, at the same time, deny the constitutional validity of practically the same words in a state act. But this was not really what the Court did. In effect, it declared the state supreme court's *decision* unconstitutional in so far as it interpreted this act to prohibit injunctions against tortious and unlawful picketing. This left the Arizona anti-injunction act valid as long as it was properly construed and applied in the future.

The Supreme Court never passed on a state court decision in which a state anti-injunction act copied after Section 20 had been interpreted to mean that labor unionists might exercise coercive pressures against an employer with whom they had not been in the relationship of master and servant. Nevertheless, there is not much doubt that the Supreme Court's brusque reversal of the Arizona court in one limited respect generally influenced state courts to adopt completely the Supreme Court's narrow interpretation of their statutes patterned on Section 20 of the Clayton Act. It is true that a few state courts had, without the aid of any statute, already taken a position contrary to that of the Supreme Court concerning the area of allowable economic conflict by not requiring labor unionists to show a direct master and servant relationship between themselves and complaining employers before they were permitted to use economic pressure. These courts, of course, generally confined the area of permissible conduct to persons having some economic interest at stake. If they occasionally seemed to go farther and acknowledge the civil rights theory of complete freedom of conduct, even in the absence of an economic interest on the part of persons exerting pressures, such statements occurred in cases where an economic interest existed anyway.

The foregoing account shows the complete ineffectiveness of the first large-scale attempt to curb by legislation the abuse of judicial power against organized labor. By around 1910 organized labor's chief interest had primarily to do with extending organization. It seems fairly obvious that Congress in

Section 20 of the Clayton Act was trying to repair the defects in a judicial system which would not tolerate extended organization. All through the first three decades of the 1900's there were other manifestations of a judicial antipathy to freedom of union organization. It was not so much that our courts denied workingmen the right to organize into unions and to indulge in collective bargaining with their employers. On the contrary, if workers could form effective unions, our courts were by the early 1900's willing enough to let them bargain collectively. It was a timorous activity of this sort which the Supreme Court finally concluded Congress had provided for in the Clayton Act. All except a few state courts—and in those days the federal courts gave organized labor a very cold shoulder, indeed—used practically every feasible means to discourage extended union organization. Either they were unaware of the real economic interest unions had in organizing competitive nonunion plants, or they realized it and hoped that by thwarting the extension of unionism, the competition from nonunion plants would kill off what organization of labor had already taken place. One must remember that most of the judiciary of that day were men of the old school and that in their economics books, a labor union of any sort was virtual anathema.

THE ANTIUNION PROMISE OR THE "YELLOW DOG CONTRACT"

Perhaps the most effective judicial technique used to thwart extended organization was the so-called doctrine of *Lumley v. Gye.* This was the opera singer case which involved the tort based on inducing a breach of contract between others. Its use came about in this fashion. Many employers who were determined to stifle the spread of unionism in their own plants naturally took advantage of their relatively superior economic position in dealing with their individual workers. Anyone who believes that this attitude was wicked and unconscionable is entitled to his own opinion. But he must not feel upset if others consider him somewhat naïve. From management's point of view, what these employers did seemed most sensible, because unions were challenging their powers and interests as owners and operators of their own property. In pursuit of this end it became the custom in the 1890's and first decades of the 1900's to exact from each present employee a promise, conditioned on his remaining employed, that he would get out of any union he belonged to and would keep out as long as he retained his job. From each applicant for employment they exacted a similar promise as a condition of giving him employment.

This became known as the antiunion contract, which proponents of unionism endearingly labeled the "yellow dog contract." Both in Congress and in state legislatures labor unions then mustered sufficient political power to have this practice by employers made criminal under statute, only to have the Supreme Court declare such statutes unconstitutional under the 5th and 14th amendments in the federal Constitution. The reasoning was that this legislation invaded individual freedom of contract to sell labor and to offer employment upon such conditions as the workman and employer concerned were able to agree. In response to the argument that employers had an unfair economic advantage over individual wage earners because of their superior economic power, including the present control over the means of livelihood in an industrial system, and took advantage of such wage earners' absolute necessity to make a living on any terms available, the Supreme Court had a ready, if somewhat pontifical, answer.

Said the judges: "No doubt, wherever the right of private property exists, there must and will be inequalities of fortune; and thus it naturally happens that parties negotiating about a contract are not equally unhampered by circumstances. This applies to all contracts, and not merely to that between employer and employé. Indeed a little reflection will show that wherever the right of private property and the right of free contract co-exist, each party when contracting is inevitably more or less influenced by the question whether he has much

property, or little, or none; for the contract is made to the
very end that each may gain something that he needs or desires more urgently than that which he proposes to give in exchange. And, since it is self-evident that, unless all things are
held in common, some persons must have more property than
others, it is from the nature of things impossible to uphold
freedom of contract and the right of private property without
at the same time recognizing as legitimate those inequalities
of fortune that are the necessary result of the exercise of those
rights."

The court's logic is inescapable, granting its premises. But
this passage nevertheless was troublesome doctrine. Organized
labor has always been most keenly aware of just what the court
said in this passage. That is why it has been so anxious to
build up effective bargaining organizations to cope with the
advantage which property and its control give to employers.
This it could do only through organization. It was not anxious
to extirpate the institution of private property. Rather, it
wanted freedom of wage earners to form the organizations
necessary to achieve economic equality. This freedom it believed to be a personal attribute of every worker, not to be
interfered with by employers.

But if employers and the courts took the view that property
in an industrial system implied the control by its owners over
the personal affairs of nonpropertied people, and placed them
as private citizens in a position to dictate to wage earners what
organizations they could or could not belong to if they wanted
access to the means of livelihood, then workers could hardly
be blamed if they concluded that perhaps there was something
vitally wrong with the institution of property as it had developed. What had happened in our society was, simply, that
the control of the means of livelihood of vast masses of people
had fallen into the hands of a relatively few. This, in the court's
view, was the natural result (perhaps inevitable would be a
more accurate word) of the industrial system, wherein small
people had become divorced from their tools and personal

home enterprise and completely dependent on the machines and factories of concentrated mass enterprise.

What many individual citizens seem unable to understand about this, however, is that others resent this concentration of power in private hands—a power over the lives of wage earners that they believe should be only in the government, if it is to exist at all. A few of the more resentful believe that the answer lies in kicking over the whole system of private property. But far and away the majority of them believe that the system is big enough to contain another kind of free enterprise—labor unionism—which will retain the social premise of private property and will leave power in private hands, yet on a more equitable basis of bargaining equality. But these more temperate wage earners believe—and there is absolutely no doubt that they are correct—that these matters are essentially political.

They find it hard to understand, assuming they can muster enough political power to procure statutes protecting from the economic aggression of employers their freedom to promote their own enterprise, why the Supreme Court should declare such results of the solemn legislative process to be invalid as contrary to due process. They eventually arrive at the conclusion that, while they were quite right in supposing this whole matter to be essentially political in its nature, including the function which the Supreme Court plays, the pinch occurred because the Supreme Court was not on their side politically. This troublesome flaw could be remedied, granting sufficient political power in the hands of organized labor, by seeing that the "right" personnel was appointed to the Court. This strategy is flawless, since it reflects a rational procedure designed to correct what the unions regard as an undesirable social balance. It is, nevertheless, very easy to understand why many thoughtful people of a conservative bent should become worried about what organized labor would do with this dominant political power, if achieved, and about what it is now doing with the strong political and bargaining power which it already has.

In any event, during the first three decades of the 1900's, employers were constitutionally guaranteed their freedom to impose any conditions on employment, as long as they remained within the law as the Supreme Court saw it. At the same time employees remained free under the same principles to accept employment on any terms it was offered. Consequently, antiunion agreements flourished and extended union organization was made more difficult. The unions, of course, did not hesitate to continue proselytizing in the face of such agreements.

Take the United Mine Workers of America, for instance. During the early part of this century they were in a most precarious position. They had successfully organized several of the big fields and had introduced fairly satisfactory working standards. But these employment conditions involved substantial overhead expense to the unionized employers. These operators sold coal in the same national markets supplied by nonunion operators, and the competition was tough. Nonunion operators enjoyed a very substantial competitive advantage over the unionized mines on the basis of the wage differential between union and nonunion rates. So desperate did this situation become that the unionized operators served notice on the UMWA that unless it went out and unionized all competing mines, they would either have to break with the union or shut down. This dilemma led to systematic organizational campaigns by the UMWA against the nonunion mines, needless to say with the unionized operators' blessings.

One of the union's organizers moved in on the Hitchman mine in West Virginia. The operator of this mine had previously been organized. But his experiences with the union had been so exasperating to him that after he had defeated a strike, he opened up again with the determination that he would never again have a union in his place. To insure this, he exacted from all of his employees, as a condition of giving them employment, agreements that so long as they remained in his employ, they would not join the union—the well-known "yellow dog contract." But the organizer, circulating deviously among the men and persuading them that they would suffer wage cuts if they did not join up, secretly enrolled enough of them as members so that he could finally call them out all at once on a strike and close down the mine.

Of course, the organizer knew about the antiunion agreements. His strategy had been dictated by the practical need of keeping the men at work until he had had enough of them signed up to call an effective strike. For if he called them out one by one, as they joined up, the operator might have taken successful defensive measures. When he did call the strike, and the mine was closed, the operator brought suit in the federal courts against the appropriate union officials to enjoin them from continuing these organizational activities. His theory was that the union's organizer had deliberately induced the workers to break their agreements with him and to remain at work after they had joined the union.

In *Hitchman Coal Company v. Mitchell* a majority of the Supreme Court accepted this theory, Justice Brandeis again speaking for the dissenters. Although the court did not mention by name the doctrine of *Lumley v. Gye,* the opera singer case already referred to, that was nevertheless the doctrine it applied in this decision. Here was a far cry, indeed, from the situation where an English court cracked down on a music-hall manager for persuading an opera singer to break her legally binding contract with a rival manager! It is true that American courts had long since adopted this doctrine to prevent inducing the breach of all kinds of legally binding contracts, whether or not they were merely for personal service. But in this coal mine case it was doubtful whether any real contract existed at all.

The coal miners were employed at will, and the employer was free to discharge them at any time, for any reason or for no reason at all, just as they were free to leave his employment on the same terms. It was a little hard to see how the antiunion promises of the miners were any more contracts than

were their employment relationships to which those promises
were incidental. The New York Court of Appeals, in a similar
case some years later, thought that they were not. And in refusing to recognize, in the antiunion promise of an employee
at will, a contract, for inducing the breach of which a tort action would lie, it clearly stated that it regarded the Supreme
Court's decision in the *Hitchman* coal mine case unsound and
not in accordance with the common law.

At any rate, the Supreme Court made new law to fit the
occasion before it. This was not such a dreadful thing for a
court to do, even though its professed function is to interpret
and apply existing law and to leave lawmaking to the legislature. What seemed strange was that the court should go to
such an extreme in protecting a mere promise, not enjoying
the dignity of a contract, when that promise was wrested from
the miners by economic compulsion and was of such dubious
social validity that both Congress and some state legislatures had
declared that exaction of it from workers, by withholding employment opportunities until it was given, should be regarded as
a crime. After all, it was a well-settled part of the common law
concerning inducement of breach of contract that no contract
against public policy should be entitled to the protection of this
common-law sanction. And all this, too, in a country in which
neither state nor federal courts had hitherto allowed an action
of this sort inducing the breach of anything but a mutually
binding, dyed in the wool contract, except in a few labor cases
of the same type.

This decision led to the increased use of the labor injunction.
The antiunion promise became so popular among employers
that one judge sarcastically referred to it as "the placement for
equity's longest range injunction gun." The political bitterness
occasioned by the use of this doctrine in labor cases appeared
when President Hoover appointed Judge Parker of the federal
Circuit Court of Appeals to the Supreme Court, and the Senate
refused to confirm him because he had followed the *Hitchman*
decision in a case before his court. This was one of the saddest

pieces of injustice in senatorial annals, because Judge Parker, unlike the members of the New York Court of Appeals, *had* to honor the precedents of his superior court. Of course, it could be said that he didn't have to accept the *Hitchman* decision without question and could have shown his personal dislike of this precedent, even if he followed it. At any rate, although this incident seemed most unfair to Judge Parker, it served to tell the Supreme Court just what the Senate thought of its *Hitchman* decision, and for practical purposes discredited that case for all time as a precedent meriting nothing but contempt. Yet while this use of the doctrine of inducing breach of contract is probably defunct, there are other phases of its use.

Perhaps the most apt illustration of how this doctrine might be used judicially to prevent union self-help activities appeared in the Connecticut case of *R An W Hat Shop, Inc. v. Sculley,* involving the hatters' union. The felt hat industry is composed of two separate processes, frequently carried on in different plants. One process is the manufacture of blanks or roughs. From these the finished product is made in the second process. Although different manufacturers and employers carry on these two separate processes, the workers employed in both phases of manufacture are represented by the same hatters' union. It seems that a unionized manufacturer of blanks was under contract with a nonunion finisher to supply him with all of his output. For some reason, the blanks became difficult to procure, and the few unionized finishing plants were about to shut down for lack of them. In these circumstances leaders of the union suggested to this unionized blank manufacturer that he break his contract with the nonunion finisher and supply his product to the unionized finishing plants, thereby permitting the union employees of those plants to remain at work. They told him that if he did not do this, his union employees would strike. When, in order to avoid a strike, he complied with the union's request, the nonunion finisher concerned in this situation brought suit against the union.

The Connecticut Supreme Court, somewhat understandably,

declared that the union had unlawfully induced a breach of the contract. And yet this decision has shocking implications concerning the freedom of unions to further their economic welfare by concerted refusals to work. It opens up all sorts of speculations on the use of the injunction to prevent organizational pressures.

Obviously a labor union is entitled to no more privileges in promoting the economic welfare of its members than are businessmen who are out to achieve such ends. If a businessman secures advantage by inducing a breach of contract between his rival and one who was under agreement to furnish a scarce item of material to the latter, there is no question that he has behaved unlawfully, at least in jurisdictions where this tort has not been confined to binding contracts involving personal services. Hence, there was probably good reason why the Connecticut court should have penalized the union in this case. But the court would have to be most careful in setting up the actual facts as they occurred. Actually, the union appeared to have been concerned over the destination of the blanks, desiring them in union finishing shops for exactly the same reasons that the unionized employers wanted them.

Suppose, however, that there had been no shortage of blanks and that the union was simply anxious to organize the nonunion finisher and chose to do so by cutting him off from a supply of union-made blanks until he capitulated. Under these circumstances they would tell the unionized blank manufacturer that they would not work on any more blanks which were subsequently to be processed by nonunion labor. In order to avoid a strike, the unionized blank manufacturer would have to break his contract with the nonunion finisher—and the practical result would be much the same as it was in the actual case. Here, however, the court could hardly have regarded the union's move as unlawfully inducing the breach of a contract.

This would be a type of secondary labor boycott used as an organizational technique to compel the nonunion finisher to unionize his shop. The object of the union here would be to bring economic pressure on the finisher, through the blank manufacturer's refusal to deal with him unless he, in turn, dealt with the union. This is *not*, as it was in the decided case, an attempt to secure control of certain raw materials, at the expense of the nonunion finisher, so that unionized finishers and their union employees may continue to work. Reflection will indicate a very great difference between these two situations.

In the traditional case of inducing breach of contract which would involve liability for the tort of that name, it must always appear that the prospective wrongdoer is trying to secure for his advantage control of the item, be it personal service or supplies, which the person to whom the inducement is made is under contract to deliver to another. In ordinary union organizational campaigns the object sought is not control of a commercial commodity. It is extended unionization. Approached from another angle, it must appear in the tort of inducing breach of contract that the prospective wrongdoer specifically and intentionally has in mind the breach of the contract in question. On the other hand, in ordinary organizational drives the presence or absence of a contract between the person on whom direct pressure is exerted and the ultimate object of the union's undertaking, is purely incidental.

If this were not so, our law governing the self-help organizational and bargaining activities of unions would undergo a drastic modification. For instance, take a state like New York, where the courts have for almost half a century permitted unions to use the secondary labor boycott in extending their organization. Since its courts, in a case like this, would not interfere with the unionized blank makers' refusal to work on materials destined for completion in a nonunion shop—and vice versa—all the two manufacturers in question would have to do in order to thwart the union would be to enter into a contract with each other. Thus, by the indiscriminate judicial use of the doctrine of inducing breach of contract, the union and its blank workers would have their hands tied and would be denied recourse to a normal self-help organizational technique, just because the economic pressure involved would disrupt the performance of an existing contract.

It seems clear that if this union technique may lawfully be used to exert secondary economic pressure in the absence of such a contract, then the presence of the contract should make absolutely no difference in the lawful use of the same pressure—in the same way and for the same purpose. Any other result would place the union blank makers in a position of forced labor—collectively speaking at least—and would compel them to continue work under economic conditions which they are entitled to regard as disastrous to their economic program as a union comprising the workers in both phases of hat manufacture. Thus it would virtually put them in the position of having to continue work so that the nonunion finishing plant and its nonunion employees might remain at work, compelling them to support an enterprise which they believe to be undermining of and disastrous to their interests.

CONGRESS AND THE NORRIS-LAGUARDIA ACT: 1932

The judicial excesses in the use of injunctions were in no instances more keenly resented by organized labor than when their issuance rested, as they so frequently did, on the alleged commission by them of the tort of inducing breach of contract—chiefly of antiunion promises or "yellow dog contracts." Until the late 1920's, however, our unions did not fully appreciate the importance of co-ordinated political pressure to achieve their ends. They have become a factor of vital importance in American politics only since that time. For instance, the fiasco of the anti-injunction provisions in Section 20 of the Clayton Act showed how unimportant organized labor was politically before this period. That incident, as well as the spread of antiunion employment contracts and the closely allied judicial popularity of the doctrine of inducing breach of contract, spurred the proponents of organized labor's civil rights to draft and to have enacted a federal anti-injunction measure which might be truly effective in leaving labor unions free to carry on, unhindered by the courts, all purely economic self-help coercive activities necessary to their economic program.

Although the unions had experienced serious judicial set-backs in the early 1920's and before, they and their friends had learned much from these reverses. They realized that Section 20 of the Clayton Act had been too extreme in attempting to create an area of allowable economic conflict coextensive with individual civil rights and irrespective of fairly direct economic interests. They perceived that even if the Supreme Court had construed Section 20 to mean what those more sympathetic to unionism had thought it meant, its scope would have been too broad for general public convenience. And they concluded that a new law would have a better chance for survival before the courts if it were drawn to permit freedom of concerted economic action only by those having an interest at stake and not by those exerting purely sympathetic pressures. As for outlawing anti-union or "yellow dog contracts," it was clear that their chances were better if they abandoned the former tactic of making such promises criminal and tried merely to make them unenforceable as against public policy.

In any event, sponsors of organized labor's civil rights of free economic coercive activity backed an anti-injunction bill which was introduced by Senator Norris and Congressman LaGuardia. This bill, reputedly drafted by Professor Frankfurter, now a justice of the Supreme Court, became law in 1932. It was immediately copied by a dozen or more state legislatures, having been actually anticipated in 1931 by the Wisconsin legislators, who had had access to the bill then pending before Congress. The Norris-LaGuardia Anti-injunction Act is an exceedingly important piece of labor legislation. Its chief significance lies in the fact that it simply cancels out a small host of what might accurately be called judicial perversions.

What it accomplishes is a laissez-faire setup for organized labor's economic self-help activities, on both collective bargaining and organizational angles, by requiring the courts, in their in-

junction-issuing capacity, to keep their hands off such activities under prescribed circumstances. The point of this act
is not what it does for organized labor but is what it permits
organized labor to do for itself without judicial interference.
Perhaps its most important contribution is to guarantee to labor unions freedom from injunctive interference when they
undertake the same type of economic free enterprise which the
courts at common law had always accorded to business associations, leaving them relatively free to promote their interests
as they see them, in much the same general fashion that associated business enterprisers traditionally did. Naturally, Congress was aware that the particular self-help methods employed
by unions were not exactly the same as those used by business
associations. But it recognized the fact that these methods
were much the same as a matter of general principle, consisting
in either case mainly of concerted refusals to deal with others.

Enacted in 1932, this statute first of all prohibits the exercise
of the injunctive power by federal courts in labor cases when
the use of such power is contrary to its stated public policy.
The reservation of the power to issue injunctions against
labor at all remains only in carefully prescribed instances.
The section on public policy acknowledges the state of business organization under prevailing economic conditions and
the inability of individual workers to deal effectively with
employers thereunder. There is then declared the necessity of
permitting autonomous employee organization, choice of bargaining representatives and free use of their organizations in
collective bargaining—all independent of employer domination.
And the act also makes antiunion promises, or "yellow dog
contracts," contrary to this public policy and unenforceable,
thus rendering inducements of their breach by unions no
longer unlawful or enjoinable.

The heart of the act is embodied in sections 4 and 13. The
latter section by its broad definition of a labor dispute and by
other pertinent definitional provisions gives the act a very
broad scope. Section 4 deprives the federal courts of their pow-

ers to interfere by injunction with detailed types of union self-
help "in any case involving or growing out of any labor dispute." The self-help techniques thus protected are:

(1) concerted refusals to work,
(2) joining or remaining in a union,
(3) supporting a union or strikers financially when the sup-
     porter is interested in the labor dispute involved,
(4) lawfully aiding anyone interested in a labor dispute, who
     is party to a law suit,
(5) publicizing a labor dispute and its details, "whether by
     advertising, speaking, patrolling, or by any other method
     not involving fraud or violence"—a fairly comprehen-
     sive cover-all for picketing,
(6) assembling peaceably to organize or promote labor dis-
     putes,
(7) stating an intention to do any of the above things, and
(8) "advising, urging, or otherwise causing or inducing
     without fraud or violence" the things detailed above,
     regardless of any antiunion promises.

This program of activities, on the whole, is made nonenjoinable when undertaken by those persons, acting singly or
in concert, who are "participating or interested" in the labor
dispute in connection with which such conduct occurs. Anyone reading this section over hurriedly must be impressed by
its apparent mildness of content. Although it is reminiscent
of the second paragraph of Section 20 of the Clayton Act, it
seems on the surface to be much more restrained (which, of
course, it is). A notable difference is that Congress did not, as
it had done in 1914, make the conduct listed lawful for all
purposes, but rendered it only nonenjoinable. This was deliberate, since the real evil to be laid by the act was the abuse
of judicial equity power relating to injunctions.

The Wisconsin legislature, in the preceding year, had expressly made lawful for all purposes the conduct detailed in its
counterpart of this section. But Congress clearly had no intention of going so far in 1932, regardless of its apparent open-

handedness of 1914 in this respect. In addition to this, however, Wisconsin registered one quirk in its statute which affords no little amusement at this point. It specifically said that nothing in the act should be construed to make the secondary boycott lawful, although its legalization seemed implicit in the specific conduct actually allowed. The detailed provisions of Section 4, of course, say nothing at all about such boycotts. And that, perhaps, is why the language employed seems so mild when it is compared to the corresponding provisions in the Clayton Act —at least, as Section 20 of that act appears to the liberal eye. But the full implications of Section 4 do not become apparent until we understand the context in which the permitted conduct may occur—that is, until we appreciate the full extent of the term "labor dispute" in this new legislation.

Vitally important as are the provisions of the Norris-LaGuardia Act between Section 4 and Section 13, in which the term "labor dispute" is broadly defined, they are not particularly interesting in an account of this sort. These intervening sections forbid courts to enjoin concerted labor activities enumerated above on the theory that the participants "constitute or are engaged in an unlawful combination or conspiracy"—an obvious reference to the Sherman Act. Also they carefully hedge around the exercise of judicial equity power in those few situations arising out of "labor disputes" which Congress provides may still be controlled by the injunction.

Thus, for an injunction to issue it must appear that unlawful conduct is threatened or committed—that it implies substantial and irreparable damage greater to the complainant if it occurs than the damage the union would suffer if its conduct were prohibited, for which there is no adequate remedy in a suit at law—and that local peace officers are "unable or unwilling to furnish adequate protection." In any event, the hearing on the request for injunctive relief has to be after personal notice to all known persons against whom relief is sought, as well as to the local peace officials, allowance being made for temporary extraordinary preventive relief under carefully hedged circumstances for a brief five-day period, on condition that the complainant files a bond assuring payment of damages to the union if the temporary relief granted proves to have been unjustified and harms the union. No preventive relief at all is afforded any complainant who has "failed to comply with any obligation imposed by law which is involved in the labor dispute in question," or who does not reasonably try to settle the dispute by negotiation, through government mediation, or by voluntary arbitration. The court sitting in any case where relief is allowed must make a comprehensive finding of facts; appeals from relief granted are given precedence over other pending appeals; jury trial is allowed in contempt proceedings for violations of injunctive orders; and in contempt proceedings removal of the enjoining judge may be secured in that particular case if the alleged contempt involves a personal attack on him.

The very gist of the act—that which makes it really something—comes at the end in Section 13. Here Congress acknowledges, without any shadow of a doubt, all that Justice Brandeis and other like-minded judges on state and federal courts, had ever contended concerning the economic needs of organized labor. This section really did what many had thought Congress was trying to do in the first paragraph of Section 20 of the Clayton Act, in setting the stage for organized labor's self-help activities and in defining "the allowable area of economic conflict." Its scope majestically embraces whole industries, listing as legitimate participants in conflicts concerned with employment conditions therein "persons who are engaged in the same industry, trade, craft, or occupation; or have direct or indirect interests therein; or who are employees of the same employer; or who are members of the same or an affiliated organization of employers or employees." And this goes, whether the dispute in question arises (a) between one or more employers, including associations of employers, and one or more employees or labor unions, (b) between employers or associations of employers, or (c) "between one or more employees or associations of employees and one or more employees or associations of employees." It also goes when the situation involves "any conflicting or competing interests" in a "labor dispute." Now naturally persons or associations, including unions, are persons "participating or interested in a labor dispute" if they are "engaged in the same industry, trade, craft, or occupation in which such dispute occurs, or ha[ve] a direct or indirect interest therein," or are members, officials or agents of any such association or union. Finally, the definition of the term "labor dispute" must be quoted verbatim. It reads as follows:

"The term 'labor dispute' includes any controversy concerning terms or conditions of employment, or concerning the association or representation of persons in negotiating, fixing, maintaining, changing, or seeking to arrange terms or conditions of employment, regardless of whether or not the disputants stand in the proximate relation of employer and employee."

This is it, as the saying goes. In this definition of labor disputes and of cases arising out of labor disputes, Congress gave complete recognition to certain theretofore proscribed stranger activities of unions in fulfillment of their heartfelt need to organize entire industries so that, by standardizing employment conditions throughout such industries, they could eliminate the competitive hazard to already established standards in existing unionized units of such industries, presented by the undercutting effects of nonunion wage and labor standard differentials. But note, that in stating this "revolutionary" economic philosophy, Congress did not give organized labor a complete carte blanche as far as its economic activities were concerned. These activities, in such an economic context, it declared, should not be subject to the injunctive powers of federal courts. From this it may be implied that they were still subject to other legal procedures such as criminal proceedings and actions for damages, when appropriate. It may be assumed that all state legislatures copying this act, except Wisconsin, were addressing the same command to state courts. This qualification, however, did not detract much from organized labor's sweeping victory, for with the injunction out of the way, there remained no really effective control over union economic activities. And recently the Supreme Court has tinkered with the act in such a fashion that no legal controls at all remained over labor's nonenjoinable activities within the new area of economic conflict.

The important thing to appreciate here is just what Congress did in the Norris-LaGuardia Act and just why some people claim, with a good deal of justice, that it is the most revolutionary piece of labor legislation ever adopted by Congress, even including the later New Deal statutes. In effect, it erased the prevailing view of federal judges, both at common law and under Section 20 of the Clayton Act, that the commission of damage by labor unions indulging in economic self-help activity is unlawful unless the union people committing it were directly employed by the employer affected. It substituted for this narrow conception of possible union interest in employment conditions a much broader conception of interest, transcending the restrictive features of the immediate employment relationship. The displaced view had given scope only to such bargaining activities as strikes for what the judges thought legitimate ends, together with peaceful picketing and refusals to patronize only by such strikers to promote their strikes. And far from allowing any stranger organizational pressures, it did not acknowledge the legality of even organizational strikes by immediate employees against an employer, because the courts refused to concede that such strikes were labor disputes, concerned with direct objectives like wages and other terms of employment. As has been shown in previous chapters, this displaced view was completely out of gear with the common-law principles applied to the coercive economic activities of business organizations.

Really, the net effect of the Norris-LaGuardia Act was to establish the coercive techniques of labor unions on a par with those of business associations at common law. This was a great deal, in as much as it recognized the economic interest of associated laboring folk in the employment conditions prevailing in any nonunion unit of an industry, in the competing units of which members of the labor association were established. This interest, in turn, conceived and evaluated for all practical purposes in accordance with the union's own views of its importance and reality, operated as a complete justification for any harm imposed on such nonunion unit through economic coercion.

As far as the federal courts were concerned, this act was Congress' green light to nation-wide union organizational campaigns, both for the purpose of securing the closed shop in individual units where a union was already established, and for unionizing all units throughout an entire industry—the so-called "universal closed shop." It is as if Congress had said in this act:

"This you may do, using the techniques we have suggested, as long as you can show that your union economic program, conceived as *you* and not anyone else sees it, is affected by the existing employment conditions in the units of the industry with which you are concerned. We have instructed the judges to withhold the use of the injunction against your self-help coercive activities directed along these lines. From now on it is up to you union people to promote your own economic interests, as you see them, within the area of conflict we have defined."

Another way of looking at it is to suppose that Congress was creating laissez faire, or economic free enterprise, for organized labor as well as for big business. On the face of it, Congress left the federal courts free to use *legal* prohibitions against unions within the same area of economic conflict where it had forbidden them to exercise their equity powers of injunction. But as everyone knew that the injunction and its incidents were the only really effective controls over labor's self-help activities, this was letting the bars down almost completely.

There is one thing about the Norris-LaGuardia Act, however, that is extremely significant, particularly in comparison with the second paragraph of Section 20 of the Clayton Act, as read by the liberals. Under this liberal interpretation, Congress placed no apparent limit on the extent to which unions might have employed organized economic coercion. It made no attempt to confine the privilege of exerting pressure to those who had an economic interest at stake. Had this liberal interpretation prevailed, the stage would have been set for a veritable class war, with a union permitted to enlist any aid it could get, from any source, in putting the screws on any employer directly or through persons dealing with him, as long as such participants articulated their pressures by means of the conduct defined. This would have expanded the allowable area of economic conflict for organized labor far beyond what it was at common law for business combinations and even beyond what the most liberal state courts eventually came to think it should be for labor. In short, it would have been the exaltation of the civil rights philosophy, and the repudiation of the so-called economic interest philosophy, of organized labor's rights.

Congress made no such mistake in the Norris-LaGuardia Act. From where we now sit, it seems likely that those who drafted Section 20 of the Clayton Act, assuming that the liberal interpretation of it is correct, were obsessed by the conviction that labor unions should be allowed to do almost anything not violating traditional categories of tort and crime, such as assault and battery, trespass, fraud, and libel. The wonder is that Congress ever seriously considered sanctioning such a program, although in those days the choice between suppression and tolerance of union coercive activities revolved emotionally around issues of civil rights and not around the more sophisticated notion of pursuing economic interests. Hence, the political issue before Congress in 1914 probably was whether organized labor should or should not have the right to exert economic coercion as they saw fit, with no halfway measures even considered. Indeed, until Brandeis, in his *Duplex* dissent of 1921, took the pains to spell out a theory of justification along the lines of economic interest, it is doubtful if anyone within the legal profession had ever intelligibly expressed this economic theory in connection with labor unions.

It may appear odd to some that Congress did not provide for the secondary labor boycott in Section 4 of the Norris-LaGuardia Act. The short answer to this is that Congress did amply provide for just such a practice, although not under that name. Under Section 4 (*a*) of the act, "Ceasing or refusing to perform any work or to remain in any relation of employment" is not enjoinable if the person concerned, whether alone or in concert with others, is participating or interested in a labor dispute. Beyond any doubt whatsoever, this covers all secondary labor boycotts which any liberal state court has ever recognized as lawful. Naturally it does not include secondary sympathetic boycotts, because participants in a labor dispute must be able to show an economic interest at stake in order to invoke the protection of the act at all. The scope of the labor dispute in the act, while very broad indeed, is not that broad. It is interesting to note, however, that this section almost certainly affords protection to any labor group initiating a secondary boycott which effectively induces a breach of contract between the primary object of the union's pressure and the employer who is the ultimate object. This may not be apparent at first glance. But it would be exceedingly difficult for a federal court to explain away in this connection the word "any" as it is used twice in Section 4 (*a*).

To come back to the boycott situation, it is noteworthy that Section 4 of the Norris-LaGuardia Act says nothing about "ceasing to patronize" or "recommending, advising, or persuading others by peaceful and lawful means so to do"—which phraseology appeared in Section 20 of the Clayton Act. The explanation for this omission seems plain. It looks as if Congress did not intend to prevent the courts from enjoining secondary consumption boycotts, probably because such boycotts invariably depend on enlisting the organized aid of consumers who have no economic interest at stake and who, therefore, could not qualify as persons interested in the dispute or, indeed, even as participants of a dispute as defined in the act. Furthermore, it seems doubtful that the officials of a loose organization, like the AF of L, could qualify as participants of or persons interested in a dispute between, say, the stove workers' union and a nonunion stove company, when they organize such a consumption boycott through their federation newspaper. However, this is far from clear and will remain doubtful until the courts have clarified the act in this respect. On the other hand, had the liberal interpretation of Section 20 of the Clayton Act prevailed, it is likely that such secondary consumption boycotts would have become nonenjoinable at that time.

But Congress may have been a little subtle at this point. Section 4 (e) of the act makes nonenjoinable the following conduct of persons participating or interested in a labor dispute: "Giving publicity to the existence of, or the facts involved in, any labor dispute, whether by advertising, speaking, patrolling, or by any other method not involving fraud or violence." This is a pretty broad order, permitting publication of the facts involved in a dispute on a nation-wide scale, at least by those directly interested in the dispute. In view of the tendency of all union folk to stick together, a nation-wide consumption boycott might be effected inferentially in this way without fear of injunctive prohibition, merely by leaving out the exhortation not to patronize. Of course, no particular union has a paper which circulates generally among anyone but members of that union—all of whom are interested in the dispute and hence legitimate participants in an organized consumption boycott.

If the AF of L could carry an account of the dispute in its paper circulating among all members of all affiliated unions, the foundation of an overwhelming consumption boycott is apparent. The only thing lacking—and that might be considered something which would take care of itself—would be the exhortation not to patronize. This idea would not be difficult to get across. Now, under Section 13 of the act, it seems pretty clear that the officials of the AF of L, aside from its member unions, either have "indirect interests" in the disputes of its member unions, are "members of . . . an affiliated organization of . . . employees," or qualify under the clause which includes any "member, officer, or agent of any association composed in whole or in part of . . . employees engaged in such industry, trade, craft, or occupation." At any rate, under modern notions of constitutionally protected freedom of speech it would be fantastic to think that a federal court would attempt to suppress a publication by anybody of the facts involved in a labor dispute.

Congress may have had all of this in mind when it omitted from the act any mention of patronizing but, nevertheless, included Section 4 (e), quoted above. Hence it is impossible to say just yet what the federal courts will do with secondary consumption boycotts which organize the sympathetic public against a given nonunion employer and against all who continue commercial dealings with him. It is reasonable to suppose, however, that the courts will not extend the protection of the act to organized consumption boycotts, either primary or secondary, where the aid of the general union public is enlisted directly and indirectly against nonunion employers or against union employers having collective bargaining difficulties with their employees. Bad as such a device used to be in organizational campaigns, the way out from under was always open to the nonunion employer. All he had to do was to sign up with the union—an alternative which most employers face philosophically enough these days. But now it would be an ominous device to protect under the act. For since the National Labor Relations Act (NLRA) was passed in 1935, an employer is no longer free to sign up with a union of his own choosing. That is a matter on which his employees alone have the first and last word.

Although the Norris-LaGuardia Act will require further consideration, one final observation about it is appropriate here. This act was passed in 1932, before the New Deal period. Hence, it belongs to that time bracket in which unions were expected to, and did, depend on their own economic resources to put their programs across. Thus the act is the last monument to the spirit of complete free enterprise for unions. This act is the very epitome of union self-help, which it fostered and protected to the utmost within the philosophy of economic interest as opposed to that of civil rights. It did not in any way commit the government to intervention on the side of the unions. Rather, it removed a judicial obstruction to union self-help and economic free enterprise. It did not provide for any administrative commission or board. Rather, it left the law to take its course in the usual way, merely depriving the courts which administered this law from using the injunction in the debonair fashion to which they had become accustomed. Naturally, the significance of this act has been drastically modified since the passage of the NLRA, under which government has stepped in with guaranties of autonomous organization for employees, providing a board for that purpose.

Nowadays a union's self-interest, as it sees such interest, is no longer the only test of whether or not the exercise of certain organizational pressures against employers are lawful. The opinions of the workers in a nonunion plant are now more important than those of their employer on this matter. If these workers are opposed to the organizational plans of the union, *they* are the economic enemy, and the union may focus its pressures against them at the plant—an undertaking which, of course, stands to hurt their employer in a situation where he can do nothing about it. And if his employees are already in a different union, either an independent or an affiliated union rival of the aggressor, the same situation holds true, heightened in intensity, however, in a fashion not foreseen by Congress when it passed the Norris-LaGuardia Act.

These and other new issues will be discussed in subsequent

chapters. In the meantime, the career of the Norris-LaGuardia Act before the courts may be of some interest. Curiously enough, in spite of its clear wording, several federal district courts and circuit courts of appeal tried to read Section 13 of the act to include only disputes between an employer and his employees who were in the immediate relationship of employment with him. Incredible as this may seem, it actually happened, betraying an inability on the part of the judges concerned to understand the elementary economic facts of a society in which their own former concepts had been legislatively discarded. A more tenable position was that taken by the Old Guard in the Supreme Court—to the effect that the act was unconstitutional in defining the area of allowable economic conflict broadly enough to protect stranger proceedings from the injunction. At least they could read the act and comprehend what Congress was driving at. But their position was equally hopeless, since a majority of the Supreme Court could perceive nothing unconstitutional in Congress making the allowable area of economic conflict the same for labor unions as for business combinations, in conformance with the principle of common law that the infliction of harm on others through economic means is lawful, if justified by the pursuit of self-interest and gain.

Thus, in *Senn v. Tile Layers' Protective Union,* the Supreme Court in 1937 upheld a judgment denying an injunction against a tile layers' union which picketed a nonunion contractor at every job he got, because he worked on the job himself. The union thought this practice harmful to journeymen tile layers because it deprived one of them of potential employment. The contractor offered to unionize his two helpers, thus becoming a unionized employer, as long as he would be permitted to continue working on the job. When the union remained adamant, he refused to comply with its demands and it picketed him out of work, nobody wishing to deal with a tile layer if it meant having his premises picketed. This case arose under the Wisconsin "little Norris-LaGuardia Act," but

it involved the very same constitutional issues which a test of
the federal act would have raised. Hence, the constitutionality
and meaning of the federal act were taken for granted after this
decision. Indeed, the federal act itself was shortly thereafter
construed in the same broad fashion by the Supreme Court
in *New Negro Alliance v. Sanitary Grocery Company,* a case
where a society to achieve social justice for Negroes sent agents
to picket a grocery store in a Negro neighborhood in Washington, D. C., because the management would not employ Negroes
in responsible positions.

CHAPTER VIII

FEDERAL CONTROL OVER EXPANDING UNION POWER—THE SHERMAN ACT I

> Organization and strikes may get a larger share for the members of an organization, but, if they do, they get it at the expense of the less organized and less powerful portion of the laboring mass. They do not create something out of nothing. It is only by divesting our minds of questions of ownership and other machinery of distribution, and by looking solely at the question of consumption,—asking ourselves what is the annual product, who consumes it, and what changes would or could we make,—that we keep in the world of realities.—Holmes, C. J., dissenting in *Plant v. Woods*, 1900.

ESSENTIAL to an understanding of organized labor in this country is some knowledge of the control over big unionism and union expansion exercised by the federal government under the Sherman Antitrust Act. Since this was the only important restrictive control of labor unions ever undertaken by the federal government, and because some analogous measure may again become vitally necessary in view of the increasing power of nationally federated unions, a fairly complete understanding of it is important. It is a matter on which whole books and hundreds of articles have been written. At times it has seemed much too complicated for professional understanding, let alone for the comprehension of laymen. Yet in retrospect—from the 1940's—much of what has appeared puzzling in the past has cleared up. It is now possible to give an account of this in fairly simple and clear terms so that almost anyone can appreciate what has happened and may yet happen in the way of federal control over labor unions.

The Sherman Act, passed in 1890, is exceedingly simple in statement. The gist of the act appears in its first two sections, which read, in part, as follows:

"Section 1. Every contract, combination in the form of trust or otherwise, or conspiracy, in restraint of trade or commerce among the several States, or with foreign nations, is hereby declared to be illegal. Every person who shall make any such contract or engage in any such combination or conspiracy, shall be deemed guilty of a misdemeanor, . . ."

"Section 2. Every person who shall monopolize, or attempt to monopolize, or combine or conspire with any other person or persons, to monopolize any part of the trade or commerce among the several States, or with foreign nations, shall be deemed guilty of a misdemeanor, . . ."

The federal courts are then given jurisdiction to enforce this act, and the attorney general is empowered to initiate criminal prosecutions or to secure injunctive relief against violations. All persons injured by violations of others are allowed to maintain civil suits for triple damages against those who violated the terms of the act.

From what has been quoted above, this act must seem to be fairly simple. In order to appreciate what Section 1 does, all you have to know is the meaning of the phrase "in restraint of trade or commerce." Unfortunately, this phrase has the delusive exactness of a good many other well-known words and phrases of general import current in our language. It is probably easier to understand the phrase, "to monopolize any part of the trade or commerce," appearing in Section 2 of the act, yet that phrase is not crystal clear itself. Justice Holmes is said to have thought these two sections so general in their coverage that they were almost meaningless, amounting to little, if anything, more than a fiat from Congress to the federal courts to do right by the consuming public in protecting it from the depredations of big enterprise. It set forth no economic program at all and took no position, implying at most what English and American courts had thought as a matter of common law to be the meaning of the phrase "restraint of trade." This invitation to the courts to exploit their own economic philosophy in controlling big enterprises of all sorts Holmes is said to have considered so vague and irresponsible as to merit being declared unconstitutional.

Everyone knew why the act was passed in 1890. It was in response to popular demand aroused by the fear of gigantic industrial and commercial enterprises which threatened to seize control of the manufacturing and marketing of consumer goods of all kinds. The public perceived safety of an economic nature only in what it called competition—that grand weasel word productive of so much confusion and misunderstanding. Sympathetic politicians, and economists who were sorely afraid of what was happening to our economic life, were convinced that national economic health and the security of consumers could be possible only if something called freedom of competition prevailed. This they apparently envisaged as a multiplicity of small productive and commercial enterprises continually vying with each other for the patronage of the public by shaving costs and prices, in order that each might make his merchandise more sought after than that of his competitors. Their philosophy was rather shortsighted—albeit it reflected a most commendable social ideal—in that it presupposed natural boundaries to the practices of competition.

The boldest of our big business leaders, on the other hand, recognized no such boundaries. Through collective action and high finance their aim was to eliminate un-co-operative competitors or buy them up, in order that thereafter they might govern particular commodity markets through strict control over the amounts of goods produced and over the pricing of such goods as were released to the public. These techniques they thought of as competition—a sort of commercial conflict with other enterprisers vying with them for the same markets. And since they themselves asked no quarter, they could not understand why they should be expected to pull their punches —especially since the aim of the act was to preserve the process of competition, in which they believed themselves to be busily engaged.

Competition, of course, is a question-begging term. A state of unlimited competition in a free enterprise society logically leads to the centralizing of control in the hands of the strongest, usually through combinations and mergers of formerly separated units which had carried on independently of each other. Thus, competition carried to its logical extreme paradoxically results in the antithesis of competition—or no competition. This result has led some of our leading economists to affirm that there is no such thing as real competition in the idealistic sense of a multiplicity of small units vying for the patronage of the consumer by offering the lowest possible prices for their goods. The legalistic definition of competition which appears in the court reports is this—it is a categorical justification for inflicting damage on others while in the pursuit of self-interest and gain, so far as the means employed do not constitute a violation of any settled category of tort or crime. If this definition is accepted, it might be thought that the proponents of the Sherman Act had in mind the preservation of something quite different from the idealistic competition discussed above. It seems certain, however, that the popular conception was that they were really trying to prevent much that our courts regarded as competition, and hoped to preserve an economy of relatively small units of production and distribution.

The courts at common law had traditionally maintained a prohibition against what they called restraint of trade. This was a negative control, in that it consisted merely of a refusal to enforce contracts in furtherance of restraints of trade and did not imply any punishment or liability in damages. Such restraints commonly occurred after combinations among enterprisers had seized control of markets through the exercise of ruthless competitive practices. For instance, a group of manufacturers of a particular commodity might combine to control the supply and price of this commodity in accordance with a contract among themselves, which provided a penalty against any one of them not observing the arrangement. This contract, and the combination supporting it, effected what is known as a restraint of trade—for it negatived the freedom of economic independence of enterprise that is the kind of competition epigrammatically spoken of as the life of trade.

As long as the combination in question remained mutually co-operative and retained the economic power to discourage independent enterprise in the same industrial field, its members could charge what they wished for the commodity involved. This arrangement the courts thought bad—but not bad enough to deserve the criminal and tort penalties of punishment, triple damages and injunction. It was bad because consumers suffered as a consequence of these production and marketing controls. But the courts, albeit there were historical precedents for punishments of a criminal nature, showed their displeasure only in refusing to enforce the contract holding the combination together when one of its members, in order to promote his own welfare, violated it. The courts considered this negative concession to the interests of consumers, together with the constant theoretical possibility of new enterprise entering the field, to be ample protection for the public.

Events preceding the Sherman Act indicated that this was not so. The public simply did not agree with this optimism. If the courts would not help out combinations and trusts to keep recalcitrant members in line, these organizations had other ways of enforcing their own arrangements through the exercise of economic pressures. As for the influx of new enterprise designed to compete with the combination, that was usually either eliminated or taken in, most handily. In view of all this, it seems fairly clear that what the proponents of the Sherman Act had in mind was merely by statute to supplant the traditional negative sanction against restraints of trade with the positive penalties of criminal punishment, liability in damages and the injunction, and to empower the federal courts to substitute these positive measures in dealing with restraints of trade formerly regarded as only nonenforceable in the courts. To be more explicit, it seems that what Congress did in the Sherman Act was to make expressly unlawful those undertakings which the courts, as a matter of common law and without legislation, had always tolerated as insufficiently evil to punish but only bad enough to ignore.

If this analysis is correct—and there is much evidence in that direction—it explains the ambiguity of sections 1 and 2 of the Sherman Act. Congress apparently presupposed a fairly definite body of common law, covering those types of situations involving monopolies and market controls through combinations, trusts, mergers and agreements, which the courts thought were undesirable. Instead of trying to define in fairly express legislative terms just what these situations were, it merely comprised them in the phrase restraint of trade or commerce and gave the federal courts three clubs to use against restrainers of trade, where before they had had available only the frown of disapproval. This discussion does not relate in detail what was comprised under common law restraints of trade, as that is an undertaking not particularly necessary in this book. Suffice it to say that the phrase "restraint of trade" implied at common law the denial and suppression of freedom of independent and uncontrolled enterprise by contract and combination, and the control of supply and price of commodities through the same means. Hence it necessarily, or surely would seem to have, meant that violators of the act must have been engaged in the production or marketing of commodities. In any event, this observation is important, if it be true, when we come to deal with labor cases arising under the Sherman Act.

ARE UNIONS WITHIN THE SHERMAN ACT?

Now one of the most heated controversies of modern times was whether or not Congress intended the Sherman Act to cover the activities of organized labor. After all, the courts at one time had treated labor unions themselves, and their normal effects, as restraints of trade. If the purpose of the Sherman Act was to rejuvenate the principles of classical economics, then it might logically be used to prevent such restraints of trade as unionism was once thought to imply. The only trouble with this was that the courts themselves had by 1890 come to accept labor unionism in itself as an established social institution and had practically ceased to regard the purely bargaining functions of unions as restraints of trade.

During the first eighteen years of the act, the Supreme Court considered only business combinations as possible offenders under its terms. As to labor unions the lower federal courts were divided among themselves on this issue of whether or not the act was applicable. Even after the Supreme Court finally decided the matter in 1908, the argument has been carried on with more heat than light down to the present day. This issue still presents a most fascinating field of speculation; but extended argument on this question is a little like fighting the Civil War in retrospect—and about as profitable. Although many books and articles have been written on this matter alone, the Supreme Court gave the short answer settling the whole argument when it said that Congress did intend to have the act applied to organized labor. The Court then proceeded to do so, applying the act adversely to labor unions in a way that didn't seem sensible and thereafter refusing to apply it in many ways that would have made sense. An account of what the Supreme Court actually did do with organized labor under the Sherman Act will bear out this sweeping assertion.

The first case involving labor and the Sherman Act to reach the Supreme Court—the famous *Danbury Hatters'* case—was decided in 1908. A nationally affiliated union of hat workers was trying to organize all of the eighty or so large manufacturers of felt hats in this country. Most of them were already unionized. The few stragglers were sufficiently strong to resist the union and to offer it serious embarrassment, through competition with unionized units on the basis of lower labor standards, and chiefly the nonunion wage differential. The union had unsuccessfully attempted to organize one of these recalcitrants—Loewe's—by local strikes in Danbury, Connecticut. Thereafter it imposed on Loewe's hats a nation-wide secondary boycott, implemented through the refusal by AF of L folk all over the country either to buy his hats or to deal with merchants who sold them. An immediate effect of this boycott was a cessation of orders for Loewe's hats from merchants in other states. This involved Loewe in large losses. Taking advantage of the appropriate provision in the Sherman Act, he brought suit against the membership of the union for triple damages and secured a judgment of over a half million dollars!

One of the prerequisites of bringing a suit under the Sherman Act is to show that the federal courts have jurisdiction over your action. Loewe did this by showing that the effect of the union's boycott was to interfere with two kinds of interstate transactions—the influx of orders for new hats from merchants outside of Connecticut and the corresponding export of hats from Connecticut to merchants in other states. This was a clear showing that the federal courts had jurisdiction over the suit and that the application of the Sherman Act was proper, under the commerce clause of the federal Constitution, as far as the power of Congress to act at all was concerned.

Then it was up to Loewe to show that Congress had intended to use the act against organized labor and that the union in question had violated the act. To show a violation of the act, Loewe submitted evidence of the very same thing which he had already shown as the basis of federal jurisdiction in the first place—the stoppage of orders from without Connecticut and the interference with the fulfillment of orders from within. This, he claimed, was a "restraint of trade or commerce" within the meaning of Section 1 of the act. He was quite correct in claiming that it was a restraint in the sense that it was an interference—just as if the union people had derailed a carload of hats bound for Colorado and had burned them up or sent them back to Loewe's factory.

But, surely, this was not what the courts had meant at common law when they spoke of restraints of trade. In the first place, their usage of that term applied only to those who dealt in commodities as producers or marketers. The union dealt only in the services of working people, if it can be said they dealt in anything. Second, a restraint was in the nature of a control over supply and price—the sort of practice that hurt consumers. This phrase had never been used at common law to denote mere interferences with the transit of commodities.

The act nowhere used the term interfere or interference. Conceivably an interference of the sort involved in this case might have had embarrassing repercussions on consumers by keeping this one producer's contribution of the commodity in question from the market, thus lowering the supply appreciably enough to affect price. But no such theory was adopted in the *Danbury Hatters'* case. Even if it were, and assuming evidence had been adduced to support it, the fact remains that no such practice had ever been regarded as a restraint of trade at common law, except, perhaps, as an aggravation of a conventional restraint when practiced by a combination of dealers in a particular commodity. Thus, an association of retail lumber dealers, agreeing among themselves to boycott any manufacturer of lumber who sold over their heads directly to consumers, might well be regarded as having indulged in and having aggravated a restraint of trade in the conventional common-law sense of that term. But, clearly, no such thing was shown in this case.

It seems clear that in the *Danbury Hatters'* case, the Supreme Court accepted as proof of a violation of the act evidence merely tending to show, first, that Congress had jurisdiction under the commerce clause of the Constitution to do something to prevent what the union was up to, if it wished to do so, and, second, that the federal courts had jurisdiction in this particular case to carry out Congress' orders to prevent this, supposing such orders had been enacted at all. Naturally the Court had the *power* to say that in the Sherman Act Congress *had* given the federal courts orders to stop the sort of thing the union was doing in this case. After all, if former Chief Justice Hughes was right when he said that the Constitution means only what the Supreme Court says it means, then surely a mere Congressional statute can mean no more.

But in light of the history of the term "restraint of trade" at common law, it seems fairly obvious that the Supreme Court was in error in holding that Congress meant any interference with interstate commerce when it used those words of art in the Sherman Act. What this may be, then, is another instance of judicial interference with the development of national economic policy—a matter properly for the sole concern of Congress. Such a statement should not be construed as criticism of the Court for having decided that the act applied to organized labor at all, since the broad language of the statute seems to justify the Court in this respect. It is directed rather at the assumption of virtual legislative power by the Court in stretching the content of the phrase "restraint of trade" to include mere conduct which served only to give Congress and the federal courts jurisdiction to act at all under the commerce clause of the Constitution.

The next incident concerning the use of the Sherman Act against labor unions occurred when six years later, in 1914, Congress passed the Clayton Act. This new statute was intended to amend the Sherman Act and to make more clear the effect of certain specific practices under that act. As far as we are concerned, it was important in three respects. It allowed private parties to secure injunctions against continued violations of the Sherman Act, it purported in Section 20 to regulate the issuance of labor injunctions (as previously discussed), and it appeared in Section 6 to state the position of organized labor under the Sherman Act. Section 6 of the Clayton Act reads as follows:

"That the labor of a human being is not a commodity or article of commerce. Nothing contained in the antitrust laws shall be construed to forbid the existence and operation of labor, agricultural, or horticultural organizations, instituted

for the purposes of mutual help, and not having capital stock
or conducted for profit, or to forbid or restrain individual
members of such organizations from lawfully carrying out the
legitimate objects thereof; nor shall such organizations, or the
members thereof, be held or construed to be illegal combinations or conspiracies in restraint of trade, under the antitrust
laws."

This provision may appear on a casual reading to fix everything up for the unions as far as the Sherman Act was concerned. Actually it changed nothing for them and might just
as well not have been passed. The Supreme Court readily conceded, when it construed the Clayton Act in the *Duplex* case,
that the labor of a human being was not an article of commerce,
implying, however, "So what!" The first part of the second sentence of this section the Court recognized as Congressional
acknowledgment that labor unions, by the fact of their existence and operation, were not an offense under the Sherman
Act any more than were countless manufacturing concerns—
as long as they operated lawfully under that act and carried
out their legitimate objects. The remainder of the second sentence was akin to this, in that it prevented the Court from regarding unions *as such* to be illegal combinations or conspiracies under the Sherman Act.

In this fashion the Supreme Court dismissed Section 6 as
insignificant, because it changed nothing already conceded to
be true. It is exceedingly difficult to see how the Court could
have done anything else with this section. What the unions
wanted the Court to read into Section 6 was a pronouncement
that the Sherman Act would not apply to them at all. But Congress had very carefully refrained from saying just that, although it would have been so easy to say it if Congress had
desired that result. Conceivably the tail end of Section 6
could be read by a sympathetic judge to mean that since unions
should not be regarded as "illegal combinations or conspiracies," they could not play the role of convicted defendants
under the Sherman Act. But this would hardly be the strict

construction required in reading a modification of an already existing statute, especially when its ambiguity could be so easily resolved in the mode chosen by the Court.

Glimmerings of light began to appear when next the Supreme Court grappled with labor and the Sherman Act in 1922 in the so-called first *Coronado* case. It seems that the United Mine Workers of America (UMWA) were being sorely pressed by unionized operators to go out and organize competing non-union mines. In any event, District 21 of the UMWA struck a Coronado Coal Company mine, closing it up tighter than a drum, burning tipples and coal cars, dynamiting the mine, and behaving outrageously in general, to the company's great loss. The company might have brought suit for damages in the state courts, as the strikers had behaved in a highly illegal fashion. But apparently it preferred to proceed otherwise. The company brought suit for triple damages under the Sherman Act against District 21 of the UMWA and against the national union itself, assigning as the violation of the act the stoppage of those shipments of coal which would have been made to other states had the mine not been prevented by the strike from continuing operations.

Here again the Court was asked to construe an interference with the movement of goods in interstate commerce as a "restraint of trade or commerce" within the meaning of the act. But now the Court was on the spot! If it recognized the company's theory to be valid, then it was establishing once and for all the federal government's power and willingness to cancel out most of the tremendous gains organized labor had made during the preceding century. For if it held this stoppage of commerce to be a violation of the Sherman Act, then in the name of that act it would be declaring almost all important strikes and other union self-help bargaining devices unlawful. Reflection will show that this must be apparent, for by 1922 most of the significant units of industry in this country were producing for national markets and sent substantial portions of their output to other states. If a strike of *any* kind, for *any* purpose, were held to be a "restraint of trade or commerce" under the Sherman Act, simply because it shut down a unit of industry and thus kept its products from entering interstate markets, then in the name of that act the nationally affiliated unions established throughout American industry were finished as far as effective bargaining activity was concerned.

The Supreme Court just could not do a thing of this sort, so egregiously inept in both a political and a social sense. Chief Justice Taft realized this clearly. He said in his opinion, therefore, that the company had shown only an "indirect" restraint or interference with commerce—not the kind of direct restraint or interference which would constitute a violation of the act. He pointed out that the mining of coal was of purely local concern, showing that the union's interference was confined to production and did not touch on marketing or distribution, thus implying that the Court did not even have jurisdiction to pass on the merits of this case, whatever it might believe Congress had meant to prevent by the act. He distinguished this situation from the *Danbury Hatters'* case by showing that there the union involved had hit directly at commerce, as such. "The direct object of attack was interstate commerce." Thus he made it clear that whereas the act could be used to prevent interstate boycotts, it could not be used to stop strikes, even when they interfered with, or "indirectly" restrained interstate commerce.

In a way, this position was rather odd since the only difference between the strike and the boycott, as far as the unions were concerned, lay in their relative effectiveness in bringing pressure on stubborn employers. With either device the unions' objectives were to procure compliance with their demands through the exercise of economic pressure on the employers concerned. Practically, this meant closing employers down and keeping them closed down until they gave in. If a strike would be effective, so much the better. If it would not do the trick, as in the *Danbury Hatters'* situation, then the more cumbersome secondary boycott was necessary. The result would be the same in the long run—economic embarrassment of the employer concerned.

Certain incidental differences existed between these two techniques. If the strike was successful, the employer could not operate at all because he could not get the help to keep going. Naturally, if he could not operate, he could produce nothing to ship to customers or to markets, interstate or other. With the boycott, on the other hand, he could still operate and produce. For that matter, he could still send his goods anywhere he wished to send them. But since nobody wanted them, in view of the boycott, there was no point in sending them or even in continuing to operate and produce them. This was obviously a distinction without any practical difference.

Nonetheless, this distinction involved the Court in an admission that as long as the union technique employed in exerting pressure furnished jurisdictional grounds for federal intervention, which only the boycott did according to its views, then a violation of the act was proved. Perhaps it is expecting too much to suppose that anyone but lawyers can understand just what this means. It is legal double talk for saying that the Court was confusing on the one hand the Congressional power to act at all with having acted, on the other, in the particular statute in question to prevent the practice under scrutiny. By deliberately engaging here in this confusion— probably for the sake of maintaining the integrity of the precedents in the *Danbury Hatters'* and *Duplex* cases—the Court spoiled what was proving to be the first real economic insight displayed by judges in their application of the Sherman Act to labor.

Chief Justice Taft and his Court were skating on thin ice. They were undoubtedly glad to reaffirm any sanction against secondary boycotts, under the Sherman Act or otherwise. This was so because they regarded such boycotts as unlawful and thoroughly undesirable as bids for greater union power, since they were usually employed in organizational campaigns. But strikes were something else again. Of course, the Court thought organizational strikes, like those for union recognition and the closed shop, were just as bad as boycotts, and for much the same reasons. It was difficult, however, to use the Sherman Act as a device to suppress even such strikes, because their outward effects, such as would constitute an interference with interstate commerce, were identical to the effects of what might be called tolerated strikes—that is, strikes for higher wages, fewer hours and other immediate conditions of employment.

To understand this observation, one must realize that the Court had previously become accustomed to using the Sherman Act against unions on the basis of the outward effects of union activity, in so far as such effects might constitute restraints of trade or commerce in the sense of interferences therewith. Since these outward effects were identical in all successful strikes, calling such effects a violation in a strike thought "intolerable" from the point of view of its purpose would necessitate regarding even "tolerable" strikes to be violations of the act, because their outward effects on commerce and trade could not be distinguishable from those of intolerable strikes. But since this would be unthinkable from any practical or political point of view, the Court had to find a way to get at intolerable strikes under the act, at the same time leaving a green light for tolerable strikes. One might wonder why the Court didn't just take the position that the effects of intolerable strikes on commerce were direct, and therefore violations, while those of tolerable strikes were indirect, and thus not violations, and be done with it. But this recourse would have been too transparent, particularly when the Court saw another way of reaching the same result much more artistically.

Taft understood the purpose of most contemporary organizational campaigns of big national unions. This *Coronado* case itself indicated clearly what the union was driving at in its closed shop strike at this particular mine. It *had* to unionize all mines competing with already organized mines in national markets, in order to eliminate the hazard presented by the nonunion wage differential to unionized operators, and hence to union standards, in the organized mines. Unionized operators simply could not continue indefinitely to compete with nonunion operators who could produce coal for the same markets at a lower cost, because of their lower labor standards. So, in his opinion in this first *Coronado* case, Taft dropped a broad hint indicating that if, in a strike closing down a unit of industry producing for interstate markets, it could be proved that the actual subjective, that is, internal, intent of the union's leaders was to keep the product of this unit from entering such markets as nonunion-produced coal, then a violation of the Sherman Act would be shown.

He knew, as a practical matter, that such intent did exist in almost all organizational strikes and that it did not exist in purely bargaining strikes for immediate objectives like wages and hours, because in such instances the employees were usually already organized. Apparently he believed that if counsel for the employer could unearth evidence of such subjective intent in strike cases, then the employer deserved to establish a violation of the act by the union in question. This was a little odd, since the Court never worried about the subjective intent of the unions in cases where the outward effects of their activities constituted violations, as in the boycott cases. In such situations it simply inferred the intent objectively from the fact of restraint. It introduced the subjective intent test in the strike cases only to afford a line of demarcation between tolerable and intolerable strikes under the act.

This approach was most ingenious and could have been achieved only by a master craftsman in the law, such as Chief Justice Taft. It was nevertheless irritating to have the Court do this. It had already taken the general position that as far as unions were concerned, the application of the act to their activities should be determined on the basis of their outward observable effects on commerce, as in the secondary boycott cases. The Court did not worry about the unions' subjective intent in such cases. Judged by this standard, *all* effective strikes would either fall short of violation of the act or all such strikes would constitute violations of the act, depending on which way the Court chose to jump. But the alchemy of the law, through the use of subjective or actual intent as a catalyst, could magically render an erstwhile innocent outward effect of a strike into a violation of the act, under Taft's expert manipulation. This seems unwholesome in our law, both because it is so difficult to understand and because it gives the average labor union official the notion that the Court is putting something over.

In any event, at a new trial, counsel for the Coronado Coal Company procured a disgruntled union official, who had been badly used by his fellows, to testify that, as a matter of subjective intent, District 21 had in mind the unionizing of the Coronado mine in order to keep its product, in its nonunion character, out of interstate markets, and that by the strike it sought to keep such coal out of such markets until the mine became unionized. The testimony indicated that this was intended in order to eliminate the competition in national markets between union-mined and nonunion-mined coal, pursuant to the economic program of the UMWA. Of course, everyone supposed that this was so, anyway, and believed that the same intent was fostered subjectively by the national union, but counsel for the company was unable to secure testimony from a national official to prove it. Thus judgment was allowed only against District 21 in the amount of over half a million dollars, and the Supreme Court affirmed this judgment in 1925 in what is called the second *Coronado* case.

Now the exasperating feature of all this legal prestidigitation is that the Supreme Court was for the first time on the right track in applying the Sherman Act to labor unions. In the boycott cases it had made an egregious error by forgetting that the Congressional purpose behind the act was to prevent the suppression of competition. In the *Coronado* coal mining cases, however, the Court treated proof of the suppression of competition as the crux of the matter, even though its purpose in doing so was merely to provide a device under which it could discourage organizational or intolerable strikes under the act and, at the same time, avoid using the act to suppress bargaining or tolerable strikes.

WHAT THE *Coronado* CASES MEANT

At this point we must pause and consider just what the Court had done in the *Coronado* cases as far as long term union economic policy was concerned. By the 1920's, of course, all nationally affiliated unions were thoroughly committed to the necessity of the universal closed shop in every industry— that is, to the unionizing of all units in every industry in which a union was already established. The reason for this position was that no union could endure competition in any national market between its own union-made goods and nonunion-made goods produced more cheaply because of the lower nonunion labor standards, chiefly the wage differential. This economic program had become of such momentous importance to unions that it may be said to have become the very essence of American labor unionism itself. Certainly, this program went to the very heart of their organizational campaigns. They simply had to pursue it relentlessly if they were going to survive at all. Yet in one fell swoop the Supreme Court's *Coronado* decisions had condemned this economic program—or at least organized labor's only lawful means of pursuing it—as an offense under the Sherman Act.

Now, it is arguable that in the *Coronado* cases the Court had decided only that as long as a union, pursuant to its proved intent to prevent competition between union-made and non-union-made goods in the same national markets, succeeds by a strike in keeping the products of a nonunion plant from entering such markets, then a violation of the act exists. In the case at hand, this view would emphasize the importance only of having kept out of national markets that particular coal which would have been mined, but for the strike. But this contention seems invalid.

If it were true, then it is apparent that the Court would have created a device under which any effective strike for any purpose, tolerable or intolerable, might be penalized under the act. The purpose of any simple bargaining strike is to impose economic embarrassment on the struck employer. One way of doing this, aside from preventing continued production, is to keep his goods from being sold, if possible. And the last thing the Court wanted to do was to create a means whereby the act might be used to suppress mere bargaining strikes. Still, there may be something to that argument, where strikers intend to, and do, prevent already mined coal from entering commerce to compete with union-mined coal. This possibility will be discussed later in connection with its subsequent consideration by the Court. At any rate, it seems much more plausible to suppose that the Court was awakening to the fact that organized labor's economic program of systematically eliminating all competition between union-made and non-union-made goods in national markets was, in itself, an undertaking in the direction of that kind of price standardization and market control against which Congress had really intended to legislate in the Sherman Act. For there can be little doubt that this union economic program smacked of the type of wholesale price standardization at which the act was originally aimed.

It seems fairly clear that in 1890, when the Sherman Act was passed, not even our economists, let alone Congress, had any clear-cut conceptions of this union economic program under discussion, for at that time it did not exist in any articulate form. Hence, if Congress did not have this sort of thing in mind, it could hardly be said to have legislated against it. Furthermore, as has been suggested, the act ought not to be applied to anyone not dealing in commodities of commerce. Now, unions normally deal only in the commodity of personal service or labor. Whatever else the Clayton Act did *not* do, it certainly stated clearly in Section 6 that labor is not a commodity of commerce as far as the Sherman Act is concerned.

Thus, would it not be a fair inference to conclude that the Court's position in the *Coronado* case was at fault, since the union was concerned only with the standardization of *labor* costs in all competing mines, and not with the standardization of *coal* prices? This question certainly presents food for reflection. The only possible drawback to this is that the union *did* concern itself with the commodity of coal in its attempt to keep a certain character of coal—that is, nonunion-mined coal—from competing with union-mined coal in national markets. In a limited sense, then, it might be said that the union was dealing in the commodity of coal and not just in the commodity of labor, although the standardization of wages was its long run objective, which would be only incidentally, albeit inevitably, reflected in the price of coal itself.

There is not a great deal more to say about the Sherman Act and labor before the New Deal era. Although during this interval of seven or eight years there were several decisions of the Supreme Court involving labor unions under the act, only two are of sufficient importance to require comment in the development of an understanding of labor policy as reflected in our law. One of these cases—the *Bedford Cut Stone* case, decided in 1927—was a reaffirmation of the boycott cases. In an attempt by the national stonecutters' union to organize the big Indiana limestone quarries, all union stonecutters working on buildings refused to handle nonunion Indiana limestone. This economic pressure put an end to the export of nonunion limestone from Indiana to building contractors in other states.

On the basis of the *Danbury Hatters'* and *Duplex* decisions, the Supreme Court recognized a violation of the act. Like the situation in the *Duplex* case, this was a secondary labor boycott, effected through organized refusals to work on nonunion stone, whereas the *Hatters'* case was a secondary consumption boycott, effected through organized refusals to purchase Loewe's

hats. But their effect as alleged restraints of trade and commerce were identical as far as the Sherman Act was concerned.
It is true that if Indiana cut limestone might be regarded as a
unique commodity in itself, then the effects of the labor boycott were sufficiently widespread to keep that commodity almost entirely off the market. Such a result might cause ab-
normal price increases for the particular commodity by
rendering it scarce.

This effect, in turn, might invite applications of the view,
later expressed by the Court, that a wholesale suppression of
the marketing of any commodity, sufficiently great to increase
its price through relative scarcity, would be contrary to the
policies of the act. But this theory was not adopted by the
Court in the *Bedford Cut Stone* case. It chose simply to rely
on the fact that the labor boycott had put an end to orders
and sales of the stone in question. Furthermore, the evidence
could hardly have shown any such market restriction, anyway,
since there was plenty of stone available for those who wanted
it and no restrictions at all on its physical transportation. The
only reason it remained off the market was the refusal of contractors to order it as long as union stone setters, in turn, refused to handle it.

Justice Brandeis tried hard in his *Bedford* dissent to persuade
the Court to adopt a more sensible position. First, he invoked
the "rule of reason" which had been developed by the Court
in connection with business structures like U.S. Steel and U.S.
Shoe Machinery, contending that the union was effecting a
reasonable restraint in view of the circumstances. As he said,
it was simply trying to prevent a powerful combination of
twenty-four corporations from breaking up the union. He
stressed the fact that only stonecutters and setters were involved—all with a common industrial interest—emphasizing
that the union's only weapon was the legitimate one of concerted refusal to work in order to advance their interests
through extended organization. He warned that in this case the
Court had held that Congress, in the antitrust law, had created

"an instrument for imposing restraints upon labor which reminds of involuntary servitude." After commenting on the overwhelming concentration of economic power and dominance the court had tolerated in the *U.S. Steel* and *U.S. Shoe Machinery* cases, he concluded:

"It would, indeed, be strange if Congress had by the same Act willed to deny to members of a small craft of workingmen the right to cooperate in simply refraining from work, when that course was the only means of self-protection against a combination of militant and powerful employers. I cannot believe that Congress did so."

But even Justice Brandeis concurred in the only remaining decision left for discussion in this chapter. In the *Brims* case, decided in 1926, the Court unanimously approved the use of the Sherman Act to condemn a three-cornered working agreement between the carpenters' union, the organized building contractors and the organized operators of woodwork mills in the Chicago area. Under this agreement the building contractors agreed to employ only union carpenters and to install only union-made trim. The woodwork operators agreed to employ only union carpenters. And the union, of course, agreed that its members would work for both sets of employers and that its building carpenters would install only union-made wood trim. This arrangement was disastrous to nonunion mills in Wisconsin, Indiana, and southern Illinois, which had formerly sent the bulk of their products to the Chicago market.

In view of this wholesale market control, obviously achieved at the expense of the Chicago public in their role of consumers of buildings, the Court sustained a conviction of the union leaders under the act for having helped to destroy competition from the out-of-state mills, whether or not they were unionized. The usually dissenting members of the Court approved of this decision, apparently because the union was in cahoots with the two sets of business enterprisers in an attempt absolutely to control a large market for their mutual advantage and was not engaged merely in an attempt to exert organizational pressures. Hence, completely lacking from this situation were any of those elements that Justice Brandeis thought to be legitimate union activities.

This case, as well as the others, will receive further consideration in an analysis of the Court's position on labor and the Sherman Act during the New Deal era. Perhaps it might be thought logical to proceed immediately with this analysis. But the drastic modifications in the Court's fundamental social philosophy under the political influences of the New Deal era make it necessary first to examine the intervening course of events, chiefly certain phases of the National Labor Relations Act.

This chapter has indicated the extent to which the federal government was willing prior to 1933 to restrict the organizational activities of labor unions. Later there will appear a detailed account of its relaxation of this control. And it may be stated now that in conclusion there will be a critical analysis of what might be done, either under the Sherman Act or through new legislation, to control some of the activities of organized labor which have become fully as harmful to the interests of consumers, and to our national economy in general, as were the practices of the great corporate structures that originally inspired the passage of the Sherman Act.

CHAPTER IX

THE NEW DEAL AND THE NLRA

The history of the rules governing contests between employer and employed in the several English-speaking countries illustrates both the susceptibility of such rules to change and the variety of contemporary opinion as to what rules will best serve the public interest. The divergence of opinion in this difficult field of governmental action should admonish us not to declare a rule arbitrary and unreasonable merely because we are convinced that it is fraught with danger to the public weal, and thus to close the door to experiment within the law.—Brandeis, J., dissenting in *Truax v. Corrigan,* 1921.

WITH THE passage in 1932 of the Norris-LaGuardia Act there was ushered in a period of almost complete freedom for union expansion through economic self-help. Yet, curiously enough, that act came within three years of marking the end of the epoch in which unions were completely free to expand, under their own power as they themselves alone saw fit. This was due to the changes in political philosophy and atmosphere expressed in early New Deal labor legislation. Beginning in Section 7 (a) of the Blue Eagle NRA in 1933 and culminating two years later in the National Labor Relations Act, these far-reaching changes partially eclipsed the full significance of this earlier anti-injunction legislation. And a subsequent organizational and psychological phenomenon of major importance—the creation of the CIO in 1936—profoundly affected the way in which the Norris-LaGuardia Act and the NLRA were no doubt designed to work together.

Taken at its face value alone, the National Labor Relations Act was fundamentally different from the Norris-LaGuardia

Act because it pledged the government to aid employees in securing independent organization, free from employer interference. The earlier statute, on the other hand, had simply removed the judicial restrictions on the freedom of organized labor to impose unionism on employers by means of coercive economic self-help. Until the NLRA became law, the federal government regarded union organizational campaigns as economic struggles between unions and employers, with practically no holds barred, except for violations of the Sherman Act. In the NLRA, however, Congress virtually ordered employers to stop resisting the spread of unionism, telling them that the desire of their employees to organize was none of their business and to keep their hands off. This, quite obviously, was an epoch-making step in itself, especially since the NLRA placed no restrictions on the freedom of unions to exercise economic pressures on these same employees, whenever they saw fit to do so.

It may be hard to grasp the significance of a federal statute telling employers that they are no longer free to resist unionism in their plants. These employers had thought it was bad enough, under the Norris-LaGuardia Act, to have the federal courts forbidden to enjoin outside unions from moving in on open or nonunion shops. But at least they had been left free to fight it out with the unions, exchanging blow for blow in the economic tussle and frequently winning. Now they could not even defend themselves against what many of them sincerely regarded—and probably still do—as a menace to our national economy. This was a bitter pill for rugged individualists brought up in the tradition of American economic free enterprise. Although most employers had always thought unionism itself an invasion of employer free enterprise—and certainly respectable economic doctrine supported them in this conviction—they could understand a statute like the Norris-LaGuardia Act, which left it up to unions to achieve what they could by their own economic strength. They no doubt reasoned that that statute might possibly be described as insuring free enterprise to all—even to those illegitimate organizations dedicated to pursuit of economic advancement and gain for wage earners!

The flaw in this concession, according to these employers, was the hopelessness of working people trying to better themselves by flying in the face of generally accepted economic truths. They just couldn't lift themselves by their economic bootstraps. But, these employers reflected, if they insist on trying to do so, let them try, as long as we remain free to fight them back with economic weapons. Possibly the Norris-LaGuardia Act might have been a concession in the hope of forestalling something thought to be far worse—like the NLRA itself—since stranger things have happened in American politics. But when the NLRA finally became law, what they must have regarded as a sort of shotgun wedding with the unions was too much for most employers.

The obvious distinction between the Norris-LaGuardia Act and the NLRA must, then, be apparent. The crux of this distinction is the fact of government intervention on the side of employees and, through them, of the unions. This intervention, no doubt, was as much the result of increasing union political power as the expansion of union self-help facilities had been three years previously under the Norris-LaGuardia Act. Now it is easy to suggest that Mr. Roosevelt was using the NLRA to make a bid for the support of organized labor in 1936. But it is just as easy to reply that the Republicans may have been thinking about the 1932 election when they passed the Norris-LaGuardia Act. Such motives are merely realistic recognitions of organized labor's political strength. It should be kept in mind that organized labor all during this period meant the American Federation of Labor. Both of these statutes were passed before the CIO appeared over the horizon. This fact is very important to a complete understanding of what the NLRA now means in our national labor scene as compared to what it probably was intended to mean when it was drafted and enacted as law.

Prior to 1935 there were other unions besides those affiliated with the AF of L. But it is common knowledge that they were of relatively minor economic and political significance. Naturally the various unions under the AF of L roof had occasional fights, chiefly craft jurisdictional disputes of the sort described in previous chapters, but their mutual relations were cordial, indeed, when compared to those between latter day AF of L and CIO unions competing for influence in the same industrial fields. The feeble guaranties of independent unionism in the NRA days of 1933—possibly interpreted by industry as the writing on the wall—had scared many employers into forming ERP's, or employee representation plans. These constituted a type of "independent" union more or less under the domination of management. These so-called company unions had absolutely no economic or political significance of any sort and were obviously fostered by management as a bulwark against outside, really independent, unions. Hence it is fairly clear that it was the political power of the AF of L which achieved the enactment of the NLRA. And it seems apparent, in retrospect, that in passing the NLRA, Congress was doing its best to provide the AF of L with the means to promote the unlimited expansion of its member unions, free from the interference of employers. In the year of 1946 this reflection may seem very odd, indeed. Yet if the CIO had not come along, that is almost certainly what the NLRA, in effect, would have been.

The inception and rise of the CIO has drastically changed the whole picture of American labor organization as it was probably foreseen by Congress in 1935. Whether or not anybody in Washington had information to the contrary, not available to Congress, we shall never know. The fact remains that the original plan of creating the NLRA for the sole convenience of the AF of L never materialized. It is possible, of course, that Congress anticipated the rise and growth of vigorous independent unions as the result of the guaranties in the NLRA—sufficiently numerous and strong to furnish real competition for the AF of L unions through adequate but lower labor standards. But the AF of L unions would have remained free under the NLRA to proselytize and persuade employees in plants all over the country to choose them as their bargaining representatives. As long as they could do this, while employers were compelled to refrain from interference, they would have had all they needed to become firmly established. The competition arising from the CIO, however, was more than Congress and the AF of L had bargained for. It inevitably transformed the anticipated effect of the NLRA into something far different.

Before a discussion of the NLRA, its provisions and its effects, however, one last additional point is necessary. Not only were employers now forbidden to bring pressure on their employees to keep them out of unions. They were also forbidden to tell their employees that they must join and be represented by any particular union. This was of the utmost practical importance. Up to the passage of the NLRA, unions had customarily aimed their organizational pressures at employers and had counted on ultimate employer capitulation to win recognition and to secure collective agreements in their plants. Formerly an employer, who could no longer hold out against the organizational pressures of a union seeking recognition in his plant, would capitulate to the union and sign up with it. Naturally, it seldom occurred to him in those days to consult his employees' wishes on such a matter. Thus frequently large groups of employees found themselves represented by unions which they did not want.

As soon as the NLRA became law, however, an employer could no longer do this. He was compelled to keep his hands off of union organizational matters pertaining to his own employees, no matter what his personal notions in the premises might be. And a corollary of this change was that unions attempting to organize a plant would no longer bring pressure against an employer but would exert their influence only on his employees. Now if there was only one strong union in the field seeking the right to represent a group of employees for bargaining purposes, this would be no serious disadvantage. Practically, under such circumstances, the AF of L unions would have been much better off than they had been before the NLRA became law, since the real opposition to their organizational drives had always come from employers. This was now canceled out by the new statute.

But when the CIO came into the field, competing almost everywhere with the AF of L unions for bargaining rights, and when healthy independent unions began to crop up, subtlely encouraged by co-operative employers anxious to keep out either of the two big affiliated union systems, it appeared that the NLRA was something of a boomerang for the AF of L. The fact that its affiliated unions could no longer properly exert pressures directly against employers, with the hope of compelling their capitulation, became a matter of great practical importance. Henceforth these unions were supposed to confine their pressures to employees only. We shall see that they frequently did this by methods which were disastrous to the helpless employers. Thus, they initiated boycotts and other pressures, shutting down plants completely in the hope that the employees, who had selected CIO or independent unions, would shift their allegiance to the AF of L. And they also hoped, by exerting these pressures, that the employers concerned might frankly urge their men to reconsider their first choice in order to secure peace and industrial stability. Certainly, the importance of the employees' option was embarrassing to AF of L unions when employers were anxious to sign up with them simply to forestall the CIO—employers incidentally, who would no doubt have resisted the AF of L as much as they dared under the NLRA, had that organization continued to be the only strong federation of nationally affiliated unions.

THE NLRA—THE ACT ITSELF

But interesting as these speculations may be, it is now high time to examine the NLRA briefly and see just what it provides. In the first place, it sets forth a series of findings and a statement of policy by way of an inducement to the subsequent detailed provisions. Thus it notes that "the denial by employers of the right of employees to organize and the refusal by employers to accept the procedure of collective bargaining lead to strikes and other forms of industrial strife or unrest." These in turn are stated to be a burden upon and to obstruct commerce, chiefly by interfering with the flow of raw materials and manufactured goods and by likewise diminishing employment and wages substantially enough to upset market demands for those same goods not otherwise directly affected by strikes and labor unrest.

It goes on to state that "the inequality of bargaining power between employees who do not possess full freedom of association or actual liberty of contract" and employers who do enjoy these privileges burdens and affects the "flow of commerce" and helps to bring about business depressions by lowering wages and the purchasing power of workers and "by preventing the stabilization of competitive wage rates and working conditions within and between industries." Finally it is asserted that "experience has proved that protection by law of the right to employees to organize and bargain collectively" protects commerce and promotes its flow by removing "certain recognized sources of industrial strife and unrest," by encouraging collective bargaining and its incidents and by restoring equality of bargaining power between employers and employees. This "experience," aside from the empirical observations in general by members of Congress, may have been based on the results of the Railway Labor Act of 1926 and 1934—a measure which in several ways anticipated for the railroads what the NLRA did for industry at large. And it cannot be gainsaid that whatever else the Railway Labor Act may have done for or to our national economy, it certainly did put an end to the disruptive organizational strikes for a good many years.

In brief, Congress finds that the strife over organizational activities of unions causes so much harm to the national economy that the best way to secure relief to the body economic is to let employees organize as they see fit, especially since the fruits of organization—collective bargaining by strong unions —is socially and economically desirable for the common good. And Congress adds (for under the federal Constitution it *had* to justify all it enacted in this statute as a regulation of commerce among the states, usually spoken of as "interstate commerce") : If we guarantee to employees the right to organize and bargain collectively, this will do away with all the trouble that organizational activities have hitherto imposed on commerce, whatever additional effects it might have. Hence, Congress goes on to say:

"It is hereby declared to be the policy of the United States to eliminate the causes of certain substantial obstructions to the free flow of commerce and to mitigate and eliminate these obstructions when they have occurred by encouraging the practice and procedure of collective bargaining and by protecting the exercise by workers of full freedom of association, self-organization, and designation of representatives of their own choosing, for the purpose of negotiating the terms and conditions of their employment or other mutual aid or protection."

To implement this policy Congress proceeded to enact the important substantive provisions of the NLRA. In Section 7 it declared:

"Employees shall have the right to self-organization, to form, join, or assist labor organizations, to bargain collectively through representatives of their own choosing, and to engage in concerted activities, for the purpose of collective bargaining or other mutual aid or protection."

This provision tended to summarize in declaratory form what Congress had been driving at in its statement of public policy. Next, in Section 8, comes the backbone of the act, in so far as it is designed to prevent employers from interfering with the desire of employees to organize. This section declares that "It shall be an unfair labor practice for an employer"

(1) to interfere with employees "in the exercise of the rights guaranteed in section 7"; and

(2) it makes it an unfair labor practice for employers "to dominate or interfere with the formation or administration of any labor organization or contribute financial or other support to it."

This provision was intended to prevent the formation of company unions, such as the old ERP's in the post-NRA days after 1933, and to insure absolute independence of employee representation in true collective bargaining. It did have a proviso, however, to the effect that under certain conditions, an employer may permit employees to confer with him during working hours without loss of time or pay, apparently on union business.

The next subdivision, (3), of this section makes it an unfair labor practice for an employer "by discrimination in regard to hire or tenure of employment or any term or condition of employment to encourage or discourage membership in any labor organization." This was designed to prevent employers from refusing to hire, or from refusing to retain in employment if already hired, any applicant for a job or presently employed worker because of his existing membership in any union or his desire to join one, or because of his refusal to join any particular union approved by the employer. It was also aimed squarely at the antiunion or "yellow dog contract." But it did contain one exception to this—very necessary for union approval of the measure as a whole—permitting an employer, who had entered into a closed union shop agreement with a union duly representing his employees, to require membership in such union of any applicants for jobs, or of already hired employees, who had refused to join the union when the agreement was made. And when an agreement condoned the hiring of nonunion employees, but denied the employer's right to retain them in his shop after a stated time unless they joined the union—the so-called union shop contract—this exception allowed the employer the same latitude.

The next provision, (4), made it an unfair labor practice for an employer "to discharge or otherwise discriminate against an employee because he has filed charges or given testimony under this Act." This subsection insured immunity from discriminatory treatment to employees who invoked the provisions of the act against employers, or who assisted fellow employees or a union in doing the same thing. It was broad enough not only to prevent discharge of an employee for such conduct but also to prevent the imposition on him of petty revenge such as demotions, layoffs, assignments to undesirable work and denial of promotion.

Finally, the last subdivision, (5), of this vitally important Section 8 makes it an unfair labor practice for an employer "to refuse to bargain collectively with the representatives of his employees" duly chosen pursuant to other provisions in the act. This was an exceedingly important measure, which has given rise to much bitter discussion. But its purport seems plain enough and quite consistent with the other strictures of Section 8. It was never intended to compel an employer to enter into an agreement with a union and, if it had been so drafted in plain words, it is doubtful if any court in the land would have enforced it. Clearly it was intended to compel an employer merely to meet and negotiate with the representatives of his employees, chosen by them for collective bargaining purposes. Congress apparently believed that when the parties get that far, they usually come out with a contract and begin living together on a more or less rational basis.

This provision was never intended to subject employers to impossible conditions. They were left free to reject any union bargaining proposals as long as they themselves offered counterproposals in good faith. Anyone familiar with practical labor relations can appreciate how necessary Section 8 (5) is, for he

knows how easily an employer could set at naught his compliance with the rest of Section 8, merely by refusing to deal with
the union his employees selected to represent them. Such stall-
ing conduct quickly discourages employee interest in unionism, and frequently has done so, thus permitting an employer
to achieve indirectly the very objectives denied him under the
other provisions in Section 8.

Now these restrictions on employers are not self-executing.
Indeed, Congress provided very elaborate machinery for their
administration and enforcement. This consisted chiefly of a
board of three men, the National Labor Relations Board, with
all of the assistants such an agency might need, including counsel, field examiners, investigators, hearing officers, review officers, attorneys, and regional offices with similar types of assistants in them. This setup is one of the much-discussed
administrative agencies or boards so essential to the New Deal
program and so hated by all lovers of free enterprise. Actually,
such administrative boards are commonplaces of the past, not
much different in their operation from agencies like the Interstate Commerce Commission and the Federal Trade Commission.

Their function is to implement legislation of Congress in
particular situations which Congress could not have anticipated
in all their details and could not have provided for with sufficiently specific provisions if it had. The idea behind the administrative agency is the execution of the legislature's general
will in a multitude of particular instances, far too numerous
for the courts to handle directly. The legislature is supposed to
establish standards of a general nature in a statute creating and
empowering an administrative board, leaving discretion to the
board in applying these standards to actual cases arising under
the act. In theory, the legislature does not delegate any legislative power to the administrative board, the functions of that
agency being merely to carry out the legislature's will. This, of
course, is perfectly good theory. And it would be impossible for
any government to concern itself with many aspects of a mod-

ern industrial society unless it could use administrative agencies to get its work done.

The National Labor Relations Board and its staff exist to see that employers refrain from the "unfair labor practices" described in the act. Its intervention is invoked either by one or more employees in a plant, who complain that they have been the victims of unfair labor practices on the part of their employer, or by a union either seeking or already having bargaining rights in a plant and complaining of the same offenses on its own behalf or for individual or collective employees in the plant. Naturally the board and its agents have to conduct investigations and hearings to be sure that the complaints are well-founded. Any other course would be contrary to constitutional requirements of due process of law. These inquiries are usually initiated by the board's filing a complaint against the employer charged with unfair labor practices.

The board has jurisdiction only over employers engaged in what the Supreme Court calls interstate commerce. This is because Congress itself can act under the Constitution only pursuant to the powers there accorded to it. When it passed the NLRA it purported to act under the commerce clause of the Constitution in an attempt to regulate commerce and free it from the troublesome effects of organizational strikes. Hence, the strictures in the NLRA were addressed only to employers concerned with national or interstate commerce. Now just what that is depends upon what the Supreme Court says it is. Some people believe the founding fathers had made it fairly plain that commerce among the states covered practically all gainful enterprise, whether or not such enterprise occurred entirely within one state and was independent of all outside markets, either for raw materials or for distribution of finished products. The Supreme Court, however, says it means commerce *between* the states. For years it has held enterprises to be engaged in such commerce only if they actually operate across state lines in carrying on their business. Thus, manufacture or coal mining wholly within one state was not thought to be the kind of commerce Congress could constitutionally regulate.

This was the old transportational concept of commerce, and under it the NLRB would have had little enough to do. But nowadays, while it has not yet gone back to fundamental ideas of commerce among the states, the Supreme Court has considerably broadened its old transportational concept of commerce into a brand new one, the wheels of which may nevertheless still be heard clicking over the rails.

The Supreme Court now says that even if an employer is not himself engaged in transportational interstate commerce, yet if his products, or any substantial part of them, are destined for export to other states (and whether by him or his vendee is immaterial) or if his raw materials are brought in from other states (also whether by him or his vendor is immaterial), then he is sufficiently closely related to interstate commerce to make him subject to the NLRA and thus to bring him in under the board's jurisdiction. This is for the reason that a strike at his place of business, caused by his interference with his employees' organizational desires, would affect either the importation of raw materials or the export of finished goods, or both, to the extent that he would have consumed or produced them had his plant not been struck. A moment's reflection will indicate that in an interdependent industrial society, such as ours, it would be difficult to find an employer not covered by the NLRA, according to this test. Happily, the Supreme Court has protected the board from being completely flooded with work by concluding that employers come under the act only when they are substantially concerned with interstate commerce, leaving the definition of that term conveniently (or inconveniently, depending on your point of view) up in the air for future reference.

THE NLRA—HOW IT WORKS

In any event, the first thing the board does in complaint cases arising under Section 8 of the act is to determine whether or not the employer charged with violation is concerned with interstate commerce. If in the opinion of its agents it is not sufficiently concerned to sustain the board's jurisdiction before a court, then no complaint issues. But when the board believes it has jurisdiction, and its preliminary investigation indicates a violation of this section by the employer, the board presses charges against him in complaint proceedings. At a hearing before one of the board's trial examiners, with the assistance of other board agents, a record of testimony is built up for the board's edification. The employer has ample opportunity to confront witnesses testifying against him and to offer evidence of his own. At these hearings the strict rules of evidence prevailing in ordinary law courts do not control, although the Supreme Court requires the board to rest its findings and orders on substantial evidence. Nevertheless, as it does with most other administrative agencies, the Court allows the board considerable leeway in drawing inferences from hearsay, self-serving testimony and rather circumstantial evidence, the test being whether or not there is any testimony or evidence at all which might reasonably be construed to support the board's conclusion. A staff of review agents goes carefully over the trial examiners' reports and presents the edited records, with proposed findings and rulings, to the board for final action. Usually the board allows argument before itself if the employer requests such consideration, the present practice being to supply the employer in advance with a copy of the proposed findings and rulings before the board's final order is entered.

Now the board cannot enforce its own orders at all. It can only issue these orders and, if the employers against whom they are directed refuse to obey them, it has to request the appropriate federal Circuit Court of Appeals to do the actual enforcing. At that time, the employer is enabled to secure a complete judicial review of the board's entire record, including the matter of jurisdiction in the first place. In addition, he has the privilege accorded in the act, under rather technical circumstances, of seeking a review of the board's order as a person aggrieved, even before the board has sought the court's aid in enforcing the order. These opportunities are supposed to, and do, furnish the employer with additional constitutional guaranties of due process. The judicial review also tests whether or not a fair hearing was had, whether the findings and rulings rest on substantial evidence, and whether the board's exercise of discretion and its interpretation of the act in applying its provisions were sound and accurate. If the reviewing court concludes that the board's order is in good shape, it enters judgment requiring the employer to obey it. Then it holds its contempt power in readiness to compel compliance with its judgment. Otherwise it refuses to enforce the order. In either event, the employer or the board, in accordance with the outcome, may ask to take the case on up to the Supreme Court. And the Supreme Court consents to hear the case if it believes, from a preliminary investigation, that the judgment below was incorrect.

The board's powers are rather extensive in issuing orders against employers who have violated Section 8, although they are somewhat vaguely outlined in the act. Its most obvious sanction is the "cease and desist" order, requiring the employer to abandon practices in violation of Section 8 of the act. Section 10 (c), establishing the board's complete remedial powers, reads as follows: ". . . then the Board . . . shall issue and cause to be served on such person [the employer] an order requiring such person to cease and desist from such unfair labor practice, and to take such affirmative action, including reinstatement of employees with or without back pay, as will effectuate the policies of this Act." From this it is apparent that the cease and desist orders are only one part of the board's remedies. Its power to require employers to make whole any employees against whom they have discriminated is most important. Indeed, the board's remedial power is perhaps most frequently invoked in this direction, although that body always has to preface specific orders of reparation by findings of unfair labor practices which are subjected to cease and desist orders as a matter of course.

Now anyone reading the language quoted in the preceding

paragraph will perceive that it is rather vague. What is required, in the board's opinion, to "effectuate the policies of this Act" depends a lot on what the board regards such policies to be and how far it believes it ought to go in recommending their enforcement. Obviously it cannot order the employer's "tail to be pulled out by its roots," even if in the exercise of its discretion it believes such a course would be appropriate. No court would enforce any such decree of vengeance. Indeed, the Supreme Court has made it amply clear that the board's function is only remedial and not punitive, and that the only force which can be directed at the employer is by a circuit court of appeals in contempt proceedings for his refusal to obey the court's judgment enforcing the board's order. What, then, is the proper conception of remedy for the board to entertain? Originally it was thought that the board, being composed of experts in the field of labor relations, should be left free to define its remedial scope as a matter of discretion. But a majority of the Supreme Court would have none of this, holding that the courts should define the area of the board's discretionary power by refusing to enforce orders which they believed went too far.

Here we can begin to see some of the faults of the administrative process. Congress cannot think of everything in advance, so it sets forth general guides and standards, empowering an agency to fill in the gaps in accordance with these general standards. Although theoretically this is not the delegation by Congress of its legislative powers, yet it looks somewhat like it. In any event, this particular board is presumably best equipped to deal with these matters. Now most people would dislike being subject to commission rule under the auspices of a busy Congress which might hesitate a long time before it specifically authorized some of the things done by the board under the general authority expressed in the act. This is where the Supreme Court comes in—that branch of our government which has the last word on most of our affairs. It readily concedes that the measures appropriate for effectuating the policies of the NLRA are matters of board discretion, but it insists upon reviewing this exercise of discretion to see that it is reasonable. In other words, what Congress meant the board to do in the act, and what the board may do under it, depend upon what the Supreme Court may at any time believe to be reasonable. This, of course, probably works out all right in the long run, although it depends entirely on where you sit economically and socially whether or not you agree that this observation is true.

At any rate, in exercising its remedial powers, the board frequently orders the reinstatement with back pay of employees discharged as the result of discrimination. It has also read into these words the power to instate, that is, order the hiring of applicants for employment who were denied jobs because of similar discrimination on account of their union interests—victims of so-called blacklists—with pay from the time they were denied employment to the time they were offered it pursuant to the board's order. This order to hire with back pay has been sustained by a sharply divided Supreme Court, authority for this remedy being found in the act only by somewhat circumstantial implication. The board has also read into its authorized remedial powers the right to order an employer to put in writing and sign any collective agreement reached with a union as the result of mutual negotiations. This position was unanimously sustained by the Supreme Court on the theory that such refusal is a violation by the employer of his obligation to bargain collectively. As Chief Justice Stone pointed out, any self-respecting businessman would be shocked if one of his fellow industrialists refused to conclude a bargain or contract already arrived at between them by reducing it to writing and would, no doubt, regard the whole transaction as spurious. He could see no difference when the party of the other part was a labor union.

Another important and entirely different aspect of the board's work is its handling of the so-called representation cases. It will be recalled that the NLRA guarantees to employees the right "to bargain collectively through representatives of their own choosing." And Congress backed up this guaranty with an elaborate machinery to make sure that employees got the opportunity to assert their choice. In Section 9 it provided that a bargaining representative selected by a majority of the employees in an appropriate unit "shall be the exclusive representative of all the employees in such unit for the purposes of collective bargaining in respect to rates of pay, wages, hours of employment, or other conditions of employment." Thus, a union so selected by a majority of the employees to represent them in dealing with their employer has *exclusive* rights of bargaining out terms and conditions of employment for *all* of the employees in the unit, regardless of whether or not they belong to the union. It is true, as the act goes on to say, "that any individual employee or a group of employees shall have the right at any time to present grievances to their employer"; but this inscrutable proviso means little, if anything, more than enabling minority employees to gripe. For if the employer bargains with them on their grievances, he is very likely to get into trouble with the certified union which has under the act the exclusive bargaining rights for all employees in the unit.

Now just what is meant by an appropriate bargaining unit? The act gives no ready answer, leaving that one for the board to decide in specific cases and instructing it to conclude whether, "in order to insure to employees the full benefit of their right to self-organization and to collective bargaining, and otherwise to effectuate the policies of this Act, the unit appropriate for the purposes of collective bargaining shall be the employer unit, craft unit, plant unit, or subdivision thereof." It would take a whole book to describe what these words have been and could be construed to mean.

Congress first tells the board, when it fixes the appropriate bargaining unit, to have in mind the fulfillment of the employees' best interests in getting all they can through collective bargaining. This may not mean that the board should do all it can to create the most effective and formidable collective bargaining mechanism possible when it decides what the unit shall be, but it certainly reads as if it did. If that is what it means,

then Congress has committed itself to the view that the creation
of strong bargaining power in the hands of organized labor is
definitely a social good. Such a position may well be valid, but
it nevertheless carries in its wake about as much potential
industrial conflict in bargaining for advantageous terms of employment as the act sought to avoid through obviating organizational strikes and boycotts. Yet it is hard to see what else Congress could have said in creating standards to guide the board
in the performance of its duties. The board has to take charge
of these organizational details. Congress could hardly have told
it either to do what it wished or to see that weak bargaining
power resulted from its designations of appropriate units. And
when Congress told the board to effectuate the policies of the
act generally in this connection, it probably wanted the board
to guard against any possibilities of subtle unfair labor practices by employers.

Here are a few illustrations. Take an automobile plant with
a variety of job classifications—some highly skilled, like tool and
die makers, some less skilled like polishers, and the rest either
semiskilled or virtually common labor. Suppose this plant is
owned by a company having three similar plants in different lo-
calities. And we may also assume that in each of these plants
there are foremen, supervisory and managerial employees, office
workers and a research and scientific staff. In representation
proceedings the board has the task of deciding whether or not
a majority of all of the employees mentioned above shall have
the opportunity to select an exclusive collective bargaining representative for all of them. The tool and die makers may prefer
to choose their own bargaining representative—a craft union.
And if the choice is left to all of the employees, most of whom
are either semiskilled or unskilled labor, it is certain that it will
not be a craft union. The research and scientific staff will probably prefer to keep out of the unit altogether, feeling that no
union yet chartered could possibly appreciate their problems
or do them justice, while at the same time handling the affairs
of common laborers.

The managerial employees, of course, will no more want to be represented by a union than any craft or industrial union will wish to represent them along with the production workers. This is obviously because organized labor on the one hand, and management on the other, are in antagonistic positions, comprising the two groups ultimately destined to bargain with each other. The foremen and some other supervisory employees, while definitely on the side of management, are not so sure but what they would benefit from organization and collective bargaining. Yet they are reluctant to be represented by a union composed substantially of production workers, over whom they have direct daily supervision. Their mutual interests are far from common and these lower down supervisory workers would be greatly outnumbered. On the other hand it is doubtful if the production workers as a whole would want company men like foremen in their ranks. The chances of company influence filtering through would be too great. For that matter, the company would not like to take a chance on having its foremen lined up in the same union with the production workers, because of the compromise of management prerogative which this might entail. And while office workers might need and desire the benefits of organization, their problems again are different, and it might be embarrassing to have them in the same union with the production workers because of their close contact with management.

Besides all of these issues, the board has to ponder the advisability of designating all four of the employer's plants in a single bargaining unit as against separating them into four different plant units. For all it can tell, the employer might plan to break up the union representing the employees in plant no. 1 by shutting down that plant for a while and distributing its allotted production temporarily among the other three plants. This technique is not new. If there were any evidence indicating that the particular employer had ever tried anything of the sort as a means of discouraging unionism, the board would probably decide that the employer unit—all four plants in a sin-

gle bargaining unit—would be the most appropriate designation
it could make. Under this designation, the union would be the
same in all four plants and would bargain at the same time for
the employees in all of the plants at once, leaving the employer
no opportunity to play the workers of one plant off against
those of the others. The employer might thus be deprived of a
perfectly ethical collective bargaining recourse—the efficient use
of his economic resources to counteract the pressure behind demands made by a union established at one of his plants. But,
after all, the designation of the appropriate unit is not made
with his interests in mind.

These illustrations will become more helpful with an understanding of the problems involved in board-conducted elections.
As part of the board's function in handling representation issues, Congress empowered it to investigate these controversies
and to "certify to the parties, in writing, the name or names of
the representatives that have been designated or selected" by
the employees in an appropriate unit. In connection with this
the board "shall provide for an appropriate hearing upon due
notice . . . and may take a secret ballot of employees, or util-
ize any other suitable method to ascertain such representatives."
Pursuant to this authority, the board ordinarily holds elections
so that the employees in the unit designated may choose their
bargaining representative or even vote to have none at all. In
these elections the majority choice governs as it does in ordinary
political elections. This does not mean, of course, that a bargaining representative, or union, cannot be chosen unless it has
the support of a majority of the employees in the particular
unit. The board's conception of majority choice is the choice
signified by a majority of the eligible voters in the unit who
actually vote. Thus, in a unit of 1000 employees eligible to
vote, 201 may elect the exclusive bargaining representative for
all, if only 400 cast valid ballots.

At first blush some readers may think this unfair. But it is
hard to see how else the board could have handled this matter,
particularly as most political elections are run on the same basis.

The point is that unscrupulous employers, in an attempt to circumvent the NLRA, will sometimes discourage employees from voting at these elections and, judging from past experiences, may be able to frighten away more than half of the eligible voters from the polls. If the board required the support of a majority of the eligible voters in a unit to elect a bargaining representative, an employer might in this fashion prevent any union from being selected by his employees. To obviate this possibility, which would be an unfair labor practice in itself, the board has developed the conception of majority choice just outlined.

Board elections of this sort are usually held at the plants and are conducted by the board's agents. A list of eligible voters in the unit designated is previously compiled from the pay roll of a few weeks preceding the election. As the description of the unit designated by the board normally excludes supervisory workers, office help and practically everyone but production and maintenance employees (and even the latter in some craft units), it is just as easy to ascertain in advance who may be privileged to vote as it is in ordinary political elections under modern methods of registration. The board provides official ballots, on which appear the name or names of the bargaining representatives, or unions, up for election.

It is convenient to assume, for present purposes, that only one union is up for election. In such a case the ballot contains the name of that union in one column and the category "No union" in the other, thus enabling the employees to accept or reject the union which some of their fellows wanted enough to have the board hold the election. If a majority of the employees voting designate "No union," then the whole business is over and collective bargaining does not occur in that unit—at least for the time being. But if a majority of the eligible employees vote for the union, then it is certified to the employer as the exclusive representative of all of the employees in that unit for the purposes of collective bargaining. Then the employer and the dissentient employees have to abide by this choice—the former to bargain with, and the latter to be bargained for by, the chosen union, whether they like it or not. And again the similarity to ordinary political elections must be apparent.

The importance of the board's responsibility in designating the appropriate bargaining unit must now be clear. If, in the illustration that has been used, the board designates a plant-wide unit, the tool and die makers will inevitably be represented in collective bargaining by the union that the mass of the production workers wanted. On the other hand, if the board designates the tool and die room as a separate bargaining unit, they may select their own craft union to represent them. If the research and scientific staff are included in the plant-wide unit, they will inevitably be bargained for by the production workers' union, whether or not they want collective bargaining at all. And if the board establishes an employer unit, comprising all four plants, instead of designating separate plant units, the chances are very good that the production and maintenance employees in one of these plants—say, plant no. 3—who either want no union at all or some independent or affiliated union of their own separate choice, will nevertheless be represented by the union appealing to the production workers in plants nos. 1, 2, and 4, simply because they are outnumbered at the ballot box.

Some very striking situations of this general type have actually occurred, perhaps the most notable one being the West Coast stevedores' case. There the board at one time designated the whole West Coast as a single bargaining unit, thus transcending not only mere employer limitations on the appropriate unit, but also port and sectional limitations. In this way Harry Bridges' CIO union, numerically the largest on the coast but by no means the strongest in several of the ports, secured bargaining rights for the whole coast, although the competing AF of L union could easily have won several separate cities if the board had designated port units.

On the whole, the board has handled this matter of designating appropriate bargaining units with great skill and understanding. It has patiently inquired into the historical and economic factors involved, such as the background of unionism in the plant, company or industry in question and employer sentiment on unions in general, before making its decision. It has done some odd things, however, in attempting to be perfectly fair in this matter. Yet it must be remembered that Congress gave the board no guides for its handling of representation issues and it had to make up its own rules and regulations for settling these controversies as it went along.

Thus, a question arose in the board as to how it would determine whether a small craft group in a large plant should be designated as the separate bargaining unit or should be included in a plant unit. Two members of the three-man board thought it was fair to let the employees in the craft group decide that matter for themselves, thereby virtually deciding in favor of the craft unit. For if this issue had reached the controversy stage among the employees in the plant, it is apparent that the union competing for the plant unit, probably a CIO industrial union, and the union striving for bargaining rights in the craft group —no doubt an AF of L craft union—would be at such loggerheads that the craft group, if given the choice, would inevitably elect to be a separate unit with a craft union as their representative. Actually, such a method of resolving this particular issue may have been sound. However, that would be true only on the assumption that the board had already decided for other reasons that the craft unit was appropriate under the circumstances and merely concluded that if the employees in the craft group really wanted to go in with the plant unit, they should be given the opportunity to say so in an election for that purpose.

This whole matter of representation proceedings has been complicated by the rise of the CIO. When Congress enacted the NLRA, it anticipated recourse to the act chiefly by AF of L unions, although it probably foresaw some development of independent unions under it, as well. Naturally, there would have been some strife between AF of L and independent unions com-

peting for bargaining rights in particular plants, and even a
certain amount of such conflict was inevitable among AF of L
affiliates. But the knock-down-and-drag-out scraps between AF
of L and CIO unions, commonly spoken of as jurisdictional disputes (an unfortunate application of a term which, by usage,
connotes disputes between craft unions competing for jurisdiction over work exclusively desired by each) have made the
board's work exceedingly difficult. The plight of employers in
these interunion disputes is even less enviable than that of the
board, since their places of business have become the battle-
fields on which these conflicts have raged. For they must remain
disinterested onlookers while their employees make up their
minds in accordance with the board's parliamentary procedures.

According to theory, all of these situations can be adequately
handled under the board's procedures. When only one union
is seeking bargaining rights in a plant, a majority of the employees probably want it as their bargaining agency, and an
election may be unnecessary on a show of membership cards. If
it is necessary, however, an election is held in a ballot showing
"X union" and "No union." Then the employees take it or
leave it. If two unions are at the same time seeking bargaining
rights in a plant, it usually means that among the employees
each has its supporters and members who are trying to establish
their own union as the exclusive bargaining representative,
even if some employees in the unit want neither. Why, then,
cannot the board simply hold an election and have the matter
decided immediately? The answer to this question is that the
board is subjected to terrific pressures from either or both unions to defer the election pending campaigns for new members,
neither union seeking the election until it feels sure it can win.
Naturally, a state of confidence in one union is bound to imply
a state of doubt and grim determination in the other. And
while the first now pushes for an early election, the second tries
to defer it until it can shift the balance through more vigorous
campaigning among the employees. And when competing unions campaign, they really do turn on the heat!

Originally, under the board's procedures, an employer in such a situation, although his business might be suffering from the tug of war going on in his plant, was compelled to sit by with his hands folded. Later the board adopted a rule permitting him to petition for an election. Although this enabled the employer and the board to bring matters to a head, it did not relieve the board from these pressures exerted on it by the unions. The employees themselves are protected under the act only from employer influence and are left completely exposed to almost any lawful pressures which the competing unions or fellow employees may wish to exert. For when Congress attempted to create an orderly procedure to govern these matters, it did not modify in any way the privilege of unions to use self-help techniques like picketing, or even boycotting—any activities declared nonenjoinable in the Norris-LaGuardia Act—to influence employees on issues concerning representation. Thus, while the effect of the NLRA had been to eliminate the need for recourse to these union pressures to persuade an employer, they were still available for use at his place of business in ways very harmful to him, in current efforts to persuade his employees. For instance, if the stronger of two competing unions can place an economic embargo on his plant and can keep it shut down until the employees are willing to choose it as their bargaining representative, that union is at liberty to do so in strict accordance with federal law, as far as Congress and the NLRA are concerned.

But eventually elections are held in even these tough cases. The ballots are marked "X union," "Y union," and "No union," or "Neither." Sometimes a third union, perhaps an independent which has some following in the unit, also appears on the ballot. If either of the unions secures a majority of the votes cast, it is certified as the exclusive bargaining agency, and there is an end to the matter. But if a majority are cast for "Neither," then both of the unions seeking bargaining rights are definitely out.

Suppose, however, that of 1000 votes cast, X union secures 425,

Y union 350 and "Neither," 225. Under these circumstances the board conducts a "run-off" election, placing only X and Y unions on the ballot and dropping the category of "Neither." Now, unless there is a tie vote, one of the two unions is bound to be chosen. This seems fair, since a majority of the employees have already signified a desire to be represented by some union, and the only question remaining is which one. But suppose again that in the first election, X union had secured 375 votes, Y union only 300 and "Neither" 325. Then the board would conduct a run-off election between X union and no union at all, dropping Y union from the ballot. This again seems fair, since a majority of 700 of the employees have signified that while they do not want Y union, a majority of 675 of them have signified that they do want some union. Then if the employees who originally supported Y union still do not want X union, they may join forces with those originally voting for Neither and still keep X union out. Naturally, practical difficulties of all sorts arise in these run-off elections, and whatever the board decides to do in resolving these difficulties, it is invariably wrong from one side's point of view.

This skeleton outline of the National Labor Relations Act and of the board's duties under it, with the accompanying comments indicating the practical difficulties unforeseen when it was passed, should give an approximate idea of the act and how it works. If the board members interpret the act broadly and appear too ruthless in pressing charges against employers, it must be recalled that they are trying to do what Congress has ordered them to do, as they see it. Any group of three men on such a board is inevitably bound to do questionable things, particularly when they are acting under a statute like the NLRA, so broad in its general policy directives and so meager in its specific directions. They are virtually put on their own to make practical sense of general instructions ordering them to guarantee to employees autonomous organization, representatives of their own choosing, and good faith collective bargaining, to boot. They are under constant fire and pressure from employers and competing unions, from politicians and from the press. Obviously they cannot please everyone, and it is small wonder that some of the best of them, in their endeavor to achieve a balanced system of labor relations, end up by pleasing nobody.

The enforcement activities of the board are confined to orders concerning unfair labor practices and restitution such as reinstatement of discriminatorily discharged employees, with or without back pay. The board has a staff of lawyers constantly engaged in pressing these orders before the courts. If the courts think the board has gone too far in construing and applying the act, they will refuse to enforce its orders, concluding either that the board has no jurisdiction over the matter involved, or has incorrectly read and applied the act, or has taken an exaggerated view of its discretion in prosecuting the provisions of the act.

The board does not attempt to enforce its decisions in representation proceedings, as such, since these rulings concerning appropriate bargaining units, the details of elections, and certifications of exclusive bargaining representatives are not technically orders at all; and under the statute it has the power to seek enforcement only of its final orders. But if any employer refuses to bargain with a duly certified union, he has presumably violated Section 8 (5) of the act. The board's only recourse to command respect for its certification in such a case is to issue a complaint against the employer and, after the appropriate hearings and findings, to enter a cease and desist order directed at his unfair labor practice. If *this order* is not obeyed the board may then proceed in a Circuit Court of Appeals for its enforcement, but this is the first opportunity that it has to secure observance of any ruling or decision on its part growing out of purely representation proceedings.

By parity of reasoning, a union adversely affected by the board's rulings and decisions in representation cases has no opportunity to secure relief through judicial review, since under the act a "person aggrieved" (and by definition a union is a "person") may air his grievance in court only if he is appealing from a "final order" of the board. And since the board never makes final orders in representation cases, but only in those arising out of unfair labor practices, the union or anyone else adversely affected by these representation rulings can do nothing about it. While this statement is absolutely true of disappointed union parties in representation proceedings, it is not practically true of employers. For if an employer dislikes the way the board has handled a representation case affecting his plant, he can get the whole matter reviewed in court by refusing to bargain with the certified union. The board is then obliged to file charges against him under Section 8 (5) for a refusal to bargain collectively and ultimately to take him before a court when he refuses to obey its order to bargain.

Indeed, employers have in this fashion occasionally enabled adversely affected unions to get before the court the board's rulings in representation cases, where the unions themselves had no way of securing judicial review. For instance if the board, in the stock illustration, had designated the employer unit covering four plants, thus brushing aside a bona fide independent union at one of these plants, this independent would have no way by itself of securing judicial review of what the board had done, even if it had been a party to the proceedings and no matter how arbitrary and unfair the board's designation might have appeared. But if the employer felt inclined to do so, he could refuse to deal with the certified union in the particular plant in question, thus subjecting himself to a cease and desist order for his unfair labor practice in violation of Section 8 (5). By ignoring this order, he could force the board to take the matter to court. At that juncture the independent union could intervene and, with the employer, could argue that the board's designation of a single employer unit covering all four plants was arbitrary and unjustified. If the reviewing court agreed with this view, and its judgment was sustained by the Supreme Court, the board's error is corrected. Then the board is compelled to start the representation proceedings all over again.

Everyone will agree that this is a circuitous approach to justice. And all that has just been related may sound as if the board were rather highhanded—an inference which is quite unjustified in a case of this sort, for it has to decide these representation proceedings in one way or another. If the arbitrary nature of these proceedings is anyone's fault, it should be attributed to Congress either for not having provided more precise guides in the first place, or for not allowing adversely affected parties direct recourse to judicial review, as in the unfair labor practice cases. Now, judicial review of administrative rulings may easily become a fetish, but so far it is the only known safeguard against the arbitrary abuse of administrative power by those who wield it. At the same time it happens to be in accordance with our ideals of due process and with strict constitutional theory tolerating the extension of the legislative prerogative through administrative commissions in the first place. Interests of real value, both to employers and to unions, are jeopardized by the lack of judicial review in representation cases. Though such review would be an exasperating and time-consuming recourse in most instances, in the long run much bitterness might be avoided and even some justice achieved by allowing it directly.

So much for an introduction to the scope of the NLRA and the activities of the board under it. At a later stage there will be a description of some of the decisions of the federal courts dealing with how the act should apply in a variety of circumstances and how the board should function—without which account one's comprehension of the subject would be less than complete.

CHAPTER X

THE UNIONS AND THE SUPREME COURT—THE SHERMAN ACT II

But it is not necessary to cite cases; it is plain from the slightest consideration of practical affairs, or the most superficial reading of industrial history, that free competition means combination, and that the organization of the world, now going on so fast, means an ever increasing might and scope of combination. It seems to me futile to set our faces against this tendency. Whether beneficial on the whole, as I think it, or detrimental, it is inevitable, unless the fundamental axioms of society, and even the fundamental conditions of life, are to be changed.—Holmes, J., dissenting in *Vegelahn v. Guntner*, 1896.

THE PRECEDING account of federal control exercised over organized labor under the Sherman Antitrust Act up to the 1930's indicated a pronounced bias against union expansion and the growth of nation-wide bargaining strength. With the passage of the Norris-LaGuardia Act in 1932, this policy began to crumble. For in that act Congress virtually invited unions to exert a variety of economic pressures in organizational campaigns and in collective bargaining. Of course, Congress made it clearly understood—or so most lawyers thought— that this act rendered the economic pressures described simply not enjoinable, leaving them subject to all other sanctions. In Congress' opinion, the courts had not abused their powers in actions at law or in criminal proceedings against unions, either at common law or under statutes like the Sherman Act. The abuse of power had been in issuing injunctions. And Congress was preventing a continuance of such abuse by virtually eliminating the equity jurisdiction of federal judges over labor unions.

Since the injunction had long been the only effective control over union organizational and bargaining exuberance, most people regarded the Norris-LaGuardia Act as an official approval of organized labor's self-help techniques formerly subject to the injunction. Lawyers knew that the change was one of form and that all other sanctions, except the injunction, were still available. But the temper of the statute made many conservative members of our bar decidedly uneasy. This feeling was tremendously heightened by the passage of the National Labor Relations Act in 1935. Many lawyers thought this measure would be declared unconstitutional and so advised their clients, urging them to act on that assumption in dealing with their employees. Nevertheless, the political climate in which such statutes could become law was a strange one, indeed, for the continued existence of the doctrine developed by the Supreme Court against labor unions under the Sherman Act. The conservative bar, therefore, prepared for a last ditch stand to salvage what it could from the older law and to see to it that the Supreme Court cleared the air by declaring some of these new measures unconstitutional.

Up until late 1936 it looked as if these lawyers were going to have their way. The Supreme Court had declared several New Deal measures unconstitutional. In a New York minimum wage case, it maintained the traditional position that state legislatures could not invade freedom of contract, however much the economic and social conditions of sweated labor required standards of work below which no employer and his employees might lawfully agree to go. President Roosevelt had had no opportunity to make appointments to the Supreme Court during his first four years. While the popular approval of the New Deal philosophy registered by the election returns of 1936 practically insured—in the tradition of Mr. Dooley— the acceptance by the Supreme Court of the recently enacted social legislation, he decided to play it safe. Although the court packing bill eventually miscarried, it may well be that it had something to do with modifying judicial views toward such legislation. At any rate the Court declared a new minimum wage statute constitutional, overruling the classical precedent against legislation of this type. And in 1937 it upheld the validity of the National Labor Relations Act. Now the question arose: Could the same Court, entertaining this new attitude toward social legislation affecting labor, continue to honor its own institutional precedents regarding the use of the antitrust laws against unions? The answer was not long in coming.

THE *Apex* CASE

While the hosiery workers union was fairly well established, it was anxious to eliminate nonunion competition by organizing all open shops left in the industry. A union force, augmented by a small number of employees on strike, seized the Apex company's nonunion hosiery plant in Philadelphia. This sit-down strike and seizure was intended to force unionization on the employer, although it was a technique hardly in accordance with the NLRA or with the law of the land in general. Besides locking up the plant, and breaking windows and machines, the union people deliberately refused to let the employer ship 134,000 dozens of manufactured hosiery, approximately 80 per cent of which were destined to out-of-state customers.

All of this was highly illegal under Pennsylvania law, and theoretically local judges would have condemned it. But the company preferred recourse to the federal courts, possibly believing that it would thus obtain more important treatment, and it sought to have the union's conduct enjoined under the Sherman Antitrust Act. In this attempt the company was at first successful, but the Supreme Court later reversed the Circuit Court of Appeals. Thereupon the company sued the union's officers for triple damages under the Sherman Act, assigning the conduct described above as the violation of that statute. The trial court gave the company a judgment for about $750,000. This judgment the Circuit Court of Appeals reversed because interstate commerce had not been substantially restrained—the company's product being only around 3 per cent of the national output of silk stockings—and because there was no evidence indicating an intent to restrain commerce.

When this case of *Apex Hosiery Company v. Leader* reached the Supreme Court in 1940, the judgment in favor of the union folk was affirmed. Justice Stone, speaking for a majority of the Court, condemned the union's conduct as both tortious and criminal under the laws of Pennsylvania. He pointed out that the federal courts did not have general jurisdiction over the case, since all of the parties involved were citizens of Pennsylvania, observing that they had only the limited jurisdiction to dispose of it under the Sherman Act. Whether or not a violation of its terms could be shown depended upon what Congress had intended when it passed that act. He conceded at once that Congress had jurisdiction under the Constitution to pass legislation penalizing the union's sit-down strike and seizure, since this conduct had effected an interference with interstate commerce, not only in preventing the shipment of already packed stockings but also in stopping continued production by shutting down the plant. The question remained whether or not Congress had actually exercised this power in the Sherman Antitrust Act. A majority of the Court thought it had not done so.

Certainly the union's interference with commerce in this case would have justified Congressional legislation making its repetition unlawful, quite as much as the unfair labor practices of employers had justified the passage of the NLRA—and for the same reasons. Closer analogies perhaps would be statutes aimed at train robbers and hijackers tampering with interstate trains and trucks. These would in effect be policing statutes and the alleged purpose of the NLRA was not much different, since it was to maintain a free flow of commerce by outlawing the causes of disruptive organizational strikes. Justice Stone obviously thought it fantastic to suppose that Congress had ever passed the Sherman Act as a policing measure to insure the free flow of commerce or that the act could be used to prosecute or to sue for triple damages a band of robbers who had derailed an interstate train. He believed it was passed to prevent market restraints.

Hence, in spite of the evidence indicating the union's intention to keep the silk stockings from entering interstate commerce, he thought it clear that they were merely bringing pressure on the company to make it capitulate to the union and were not trying to exercise any kind of control over the silk stocking market. No doubt he meant to imply that there was no evidence of a specific intent on the part of the union people to exercise any control over the marketing of silk stockings. Even though their ultimate intent was to eliminate nonunion competition in national markets between union-made and nonunion-made silk stockings, and even if their interference with production and the shipment of already packed stockings was to further this intent, there was no such evidence in the record. The Court could hardly assume it.

Justice Stone curtly dismissed the union's argument that the Sherman Act was never intended by Congress to apply to organized labor. He went on to show that Congress had in mind "the prevention of restraints to free competition in business and commercial transactions which tended to restrict production, raise prices or otherwise control the market to the detriment of purchasers or consumers of goods and services, all of which had come to be regarded as a special form of public injury." According to him, Congress wanted to prevent restraints of trade, as they were known to the common law. It added the words "or commerce among the several States," not to denote another kind of forbidden restraint but merely as the means "to relate the prohibited restraint of trade to interstate commerce for constitutional purposes, so that Congress, through its commerce power, might suppress and penalize restraints on the competitive system which involved or affected interstate commerce." Such restraints the states could not prevent because of their interstate character.

This was all masterly analysis; but the opinion then verged into fiction. Justice Stone said he thought it was significant that the Supreme Court had never used the Sherman Act against anyone—capital or labor—unless it found "some form of restraint upon commercial competition in the marketing of goods or services." In this statement, he was plainly wrong, since there is not the slightest indication of any such restraint in any of the famous boycott cases—the *Danbury Hatters'* case, the *Duplex* case and the *Bedford Cut Stone* case. Then he went on to say that the Supreme Court had refused to apply the Sherman Act in cases of illegal local strikes, like this one, where the resulting shutdown had prevented substantial interstate shipments of products, "but in which it was not shown that the restrictions on shipments had operated to restrain commercial competition in some substantial way." This implies that if such an effect were shown, a violation of the act would be proved. No previous Supreme Court labor decisions support this implication that a local strike keeping from national markets an amount of the national total of any product large enough appreciably to upset the price and supply of that product would be a violation of the Sherman Act. Justice Stone's statement is on a par with the proposition that a court will not convict a man for the murder of someone whose money he has embezzled, unless it is shown that he took a large enough sum to cause the death by shock of anyone similarly situated. No such case as this has ever arisen, and the implication that the conviction for murder would stand, if it did arise and was proved, is completely speculative.

The opinion does return to more solid ground, however, when Justice Stone generalizes from the application of the Sherman Act to business combinations, although his observation that the only restraints prohibited by the act in such cases are those "which are so substantial as to affect market prices," becomes accurate only when he adds "or otherwise to deprive purchasers or consumers of the advantages which they derive from free competition." But he still fails to show that any such consideration was material in any of the Supreme Court's decisions against organized labor under the Sherman Act, especially in the three well-known boycott cases he discusses.

The opinion next comes back to the *Apex* situation and Justice Stone points out that it was not like the *Brims* case, previously discussed, where the union co-operated with two sets of employers to control the supply and price of wood trim in the Chicago area building industry. The object of the hosiery workers union was simply "to compel [Apex] to accede to the union demands"; and the resulting nonaccess of Apex hosiery to interstate markets "was not intended to have and had no effect on prices of hosiery in the market." Here he might well have added that even if such an effect were observable, there was no precedent of the Supreme Court in labor cases under the Sherman Act to indicate that it would have made the slightest difference.

The normal effect of labor unionism to restrain competition among union members in the sale of their services, he remarked, never has been regarded as unlawful under the Sherman Act and never can be, because of Section 6 of the Clayton Act, which states that "the labor of a human being is not a commodity or article of commerce" and that labor unions are not in themselves "illegal combinations or conspiracies in restraint of trade, under the antitrust laws." Then Justice Stone proceeds to make the most remarkable statement in his whole long opinion. After reciting that "successful union activity . . . may have some influence on price competition by eliminating that part of such competition which is based on differences in labor standards," he declared:

"Since, in order to render a labor combination effective it must eliminate the competition from non-union made goods, . . . an elimination of price competition based on differences in labor standards is the objective of any national labor organization. But this effect on competition has not been considered to be the kind of curtailment of price competition prohibited by the Sherman Act."

At this point we might ask Justice Stone: How about the second *Coronado* case? That was a local strike case, where the Supreme Court accepted evidence of the union's subjective intention to do this very thing—to eliminate in national markets the competition between union- and nonunion-minded coal, due to the wage or labor standard differential—as conclusive proof of a violation of the Sherman Act.

Justice Stone's answer to this question is a quotation from the Court's opinion in the second *Coronado* case, indicating that the "purpose of the destruction of the mines was to stop the production of non-union coal and prevent its shipment to markets of other states than Arkansas, where it would by competition tend to reduce the price of the commodity and affect injuriously the maintenance of wages for union labor in competing mines." This answer, in effect, is as if he had said: "When a union shuts down a nonunion mine by a strike so that it cannot operate and send nonunion coal into national markets to compete with union coal—and it can be proved that such was its intent—that is a violation of the Sherman Act. *But,* if a union shuts down a nonunion mine by a strike *in order to compel its unionization* so that, after unionization, its product can no longer compete with union-mined coal in its former nonunion character—even if its intent to do this can be proved —that is only a normal objective of unionism and is not a violation of the Sherman Act." His proposition that the second *Coronado* decision was still good law had the props kicked out from under it by his inconsistent statement quoted above in the separate paragraph.

If Justice Stone's distinction of the *Apex* case from the second *Coronado* case is sound, then all the Apex Company had to do to secure a judgment was to prove that the union shut down the factory and held up the already packed stockings in order to keep the company's product from competing with union-made stockings in national markets. But the elimination of such competition was exactly what the union was seeking in the *Apex* case, just as that was the objective in the *Coronado* case; and in each instance the union involved sought this end by unionization of the company. No big union is going to shut a plant down by a strike merely to keep its product permanently out of the market. That is utterly ridiculous, since the union's interest is equal to the employer's in having the plant operate. The employees have to eat and must earn wages to do so.

These two strikes were intended to achieve unionization of the enterprises involved. If the strikers at the Coronado mine kept already mined or potentially mined coal from reaching interstate markets, just as the strikers at the Apex plant kept the already packed and potentially manufactured silk stockings from reaching such markets, it was simply for the effect this might have in imposing economic embarrassment on the two employers. There is little doubt that the Supreme Court rested its decision against the union in the second *Coronado* case on proof of subjective intent that the union was trying to organize the Coronado mine so that its product would not henceforth compete with union-minded coal in its nonunion character. Yet this very purpose Justice Stone declared in his *Apex* opinion to be a perfectly lawful incident of labor unionism and, when carried into action, not an offense under the Sherman Act. It is a pity that he did not simply overrule the second *Coronado* case as outworn doctrine, instead of paying it lip service as a valid precedent and then undermining it, leaving it balanced on a distinction less palpable than that between Tweedledum and Tweedledee.

But this is not all. Justice Stone seemed very confused about the labor union boycott cases under the Sherman Act—the *Danbury Hatters'*, the *Duplex*, and the *Bedford Cut Stone* cases. He had neatly distinguished between the incidents of jurisdiction, such as interfering with interstate shipments, on the one hand, and actual violations of the Sherman Act through market restraints suppressing competition, on the other. Then he unfortunately overlooked this very distinction in his analysis of these boycott cases. This confusion became most apparent when he implied that the *Retail Lumber Dealers'* case and the *Danbury Hatters'* case were identical.

The retail lumber dealers' association throughout the eastern states had undertaken to prevent sales by lumber manufacturers directly to consumers. In order to obviate the loss of retail profits by such sales over their heads, the members of this association agreed to boycott any manufacturer who made such direct sales to consumers. The consequent forced elimination of such sales was the deliberate suppression of competition between manufacturers and retailers for the same market and, as the Supreme Court had held, a plain violation of the Sherman Act.

But the *Danbury Hatters'* case was not at all like that. The only common element in these two cases was keeping goods from crossing state lines. Thus, the retail lumber dealers' boycott prevented shipments from manufacturers either directly to consumers of lumber or to themselves, while the embargo of the hatters' union discouraged out-of-state orders for Loewe's hats. While the lumber dealers were interested in controlling the retail lumber market, the hatters' union had no interest at all in the marketing of hats but was only trying to cut Loewe off from his customers so that he would capitulate to the union's organizational overtures in order to escape the economic pinch placed on his business. And in the *Duplex* and *Bedford Cut Stone* cases the unions there concerned were likewise merely trying to bring organizational pressure to bear on the employers involved and were not trying to control the markets for printing presses and cut stone.

Justice Stone creates the impression in his *Apex* opinion that the vice in the *Retail Lumber Dealers'* case was the boycott which interfered with shipments of goods from one state to another. Then he seems to say that since this same effect is present in the three labor union boycott cases, they also involve violations of the Sherman Act, and for the same reason. Yet it is apparent that the *Retail Lumber Dealers'* case showed a real market restraint, whereas none was present in these other three cases. In other words, his conclusion that these four boycott cases involved violations of the act rests entirely on the fact that in each there was an interference with the mere passage of goods from one state to another.

This confusion is aggravated by his claim that these boycott cases are distinguishable from the *Apex* case, which involved only a local strike and sit-down seizure instead of a secondary boycott. If these three labor union boycott cases involve violations of the Sherman Act because of the interferences with interstate shipments present in them, then to exactly that extent the *Apex* case itself also reflects a violation of the act. And if we conclude that there is no violation of the act in the *Apex* case, then it is equally clear that there is none in the three boycott cases. For it makes no difference whether the interference with the passage of goods from one state to another occurs as a consequence of economic pressure created in the same state where the goods are produced, as by a strike, or in a different state—as by a secondary boycott. By the same token, it makes no difference whether the effect of the local strike is to prevent shipments of goods by denying the facilities for their production or by preventing already manufactured goods from being loaded on railroad cars and hauled away.

The fact remains that a secondary boycott is just a more complicated way of pursuing the same objective that a union seeks in organizational strikes. In so far as each device involves interferences with the shipments of goods across state lines, they are identical when viewed under the terms of the Sherman Act. And there is no more reason for using the subjective intent test of the *Coronado* cases in the strike situations than in the boycott cases. Hence there is every reason to suppose that the *Coronado* test no longer has any significance in our law. For if this test shows only that a particular union is attempting to eliminate nonunion competition, either by organizing a nonunion concern or by keeping specific already manufactured nonunion goods from entering commerce, that is a union objective which the Supreme Court now concedes not to be contrary to the Sherman Act.

In discussing these boycott cases Justice Stone made two other remarks which should be questioned. He said that in each of them "the activities affecting interstate commerce were directed at control of the market *and were so widespread as substantially to affect it.*" This was not true, and there was nothing in the reports of these cases which made this element of substantial effect an operative factor in the decision of any of them. In each of these three labor union boycott cases the Supreme Court recognized a violation solely because of the fact that the union concerned had prevented the shipment of goods across state lines, irrespective of any effects of such interferences on any markets.

Then he went on to say: "That the objective of the restraint in the boycott cases was the strengthening of the bargaining position of the union and not the elimination of business competition—which was the end in the non-labor cases—was thought to be immaterial because the Court viewed *the restraint itself,* in contrast to the interference with shipments caused by a local factory strike, to be of a kind regarded as offensive at common law because of its effect in curtailing a free market *and it was held to offend against the Sherman Act because it effected and was aimed at suppression of competition with union made goods in the interstate market.*" Just what he meant by the phrase "the restraint itself," in the middle of this quotation, is hard to say, unless he meant the sort of interference with interstate commerce which would justify the assertion of power by Congress in the first place. If so, it is a frank admission that in the three labor union boycott cases the Supreme Court had confused the incidents of jurisdiction with violation of the Sherman Act. But the italicized portion at the end of this last quotation is more serious. There he attempts to justify the decisions in the three labor union boycott cases by reasoning that contradicts his main position earlier in the *Apex* opinion. He sets forth as the violation of the act in these cases the very thing he had just declared cannot any longer be construed as a violation of the act. That thing is the elimination of competition between union- and nonunion-made goods, which he had just said was a normal and lawful objective of any nationally organized labor union.

It is, of course, easy to sit back and criticize a Supreme Court justice's opinion. But when a member of the Court writes a long and involved opinion like that in the *Apex* case, trying to reconcile the irreconcilable and to make it look as if the Court's policy had always been consistent, he makes such criticism infinitely easier. This long account of the opinion is included to acquaint readers with the sort of thing our Supreme Court does when it tries to keep its output politically and socially up to date and at the same time consistent. Actually, it seems clear that in the three labor union boycott cases under discussion the Supreme Court had confused jurisdiction with substantive violation of the act, and had incorrectly decided against the unions on the former grounds.

Justice Stone would have made it easier for himself and for the bar in general, to say nothing of employers and unions, if he had simply declared that in the past the Supreme Court had fostered incorrect views about the application of the Sherman Act to labor unions and is now starting afresh with the correct view. Almost everything he says in his opinion about Congress' real intentions in the act seems extraordinarily lucid. He gets in hot water only when he tries to reconcile his views with previous decisions of the Court. If he had simply abandoned his regard for consistency by overruling the three boycott cases—the *Danbury Hatters'*, *Duplex* and *Bedford Cut Stone* cases—as well as the second *Coronado* case, the air would have been clearer, and he would have obviated much confusion.

Chief Justice Hughes, speaking for the three dissenting members of the Court in the *Apex* case, thought that Justice Stone's discourse about jurisdiction and the attempt to make the Sherman Act a policing measure was unsound. He felt that if employers could be prevented by the NLRA from provoking organizational strikes obstructive to interstate commerce, as the Court had held they could be, then combinations of employees could be prevented by the Sherman Act from initiating such obstructive organizational strikes, as well. Quite obviously, he might be right. But the fact remains that in the NLRA, Congress spelled out carefully just what it intended to do, and why, clearly creating a deterrent to prevent employers from provoking disruptive strikes by their unfair labor practices. Now Congress created no such stricture against labor in the Sherman Act, although it could have done so in that act or in a separate statute, by analogy to the NLRA.

Chief Justice Hughes contended that Congress had already done this in the broad and general terms of the Sherman Act. Thereby the chief justice seemed to confuse the incidents of jurisdiction with actual violations of the act as it was intended to apply. Could he possibly have thought that Congress had intended in the Sherman Act to exercise its complete constitutional powers to prohibit all conceivable interferences with interstate commerce by unions? Could he have been willing to use the Sherman Act to prevent all strikes and boycotts in plants purchasing raw materials through or sending their products into interstate commerce—in short, practically all strikes and boycotts in modern industry? Although his opinion seemed to indicate such possibilities, he finally disclaimed this position by drawing the line where unions conspire "directly and intentionally to prevent the shipment of goods in interstate commerce either by their illegal seizure for that purpose, or by the direct and intentional obstruction of their transportation or by blocking the highways of interstate intercourse."

Now the unusual thing about the *Apex* case is Justice Stone's remarkable statement to the effect that the organizational pressures of labor unions, intended to eliminate the competition between nonunion-made and union-made products of the same industry, are not unlawful under the Sherman Act. He repeatedly insists that the Sherman Act was intended to prevent market restraints and was designed to preserve free competition in national markets, emphasizing the enormity of any attempt to control prices. Yet in almost the plainest instance of conduct affecting prices and eliminating competition between commodities based upon price differentials, he refuses to recognize a violation of the act, dismissing this union economic program as "the objective of any national labor organization." Justice Stone thus side-stepped the unpleasant task of labeling virtually all of national unionism, in itself, as one gigantic and wholesale offense under the Sherman Act. But it was years too late for such a drastic step, anyway, if it ever was even theoretically possible after Section 6 of the Clayton Act had been passed in 1914.

His position is perhaps best supported by the argument that under this economic program, unions are interested in leveling off not so much the *prices* of commodities produced throughout a given industry as *wages* and other *working standards.* These are really the things they want to standardize. And it would be convenient for purposes of discussion to assume that a standard union *wage* level is the crux of the whole matter. The unions wish to eliminate the differentials existing between union and nonunion wages in all industries in which they are established. In so far as the competitive price differential between the union-made and nonunion-made products of a given industry reflect the wage differential between union and nonunion rates, *to that extent* the unions are trying to eliminate competition through restraints involving the control of commodity prices. Aside from this, unions exhibit no real interest in standardizing the prices of the products in any given industry, leaving employers relatively unhindered in making the most of other competitive factors like efficiency in management, advertising and incentive plans, as long as union employees' toes are not stepped on in the process. In effect, this is what the significant statement of Justice Stone fairly implies.

He also said that employees in combination, by securing

standard wage rates in a unionized shop, could not be assailed under the Sherman Act for attempting to restrain competition among themselves in the hiring out of their labor. None of these propositions is obvious. Indeed, at one time such practices leading to the standardization of wages among the employees of a given shop or between all units in a given industry were very definitely regarded as restraints of trade at common law. The theory used to be that an employer was entitled to get his labor at the lowest price he had to pay in the labor market, just as he was entitled to get his raw materials in the same competitive fashion. And the old judges maintained this right of the employer in both situations as an incident of owning property and of free enterprise in operating it productively. As has been shown, early violations of this right were treated not only as restraints of trade but as criminal conspiracies.

The only adequate explanation for a change in this view is the passage of time with the consequent modification of political and social views concerning the rights of working men to band together for self-protection and mutual advantage. For this result the determined efforts of organized labor leaders and outside sympathizers are no doubt responsible. At any rate, these older views are now a part of ancient history in our social culture. And it can hardly be wondered that our law, including Supreme Court decisions, has reflected this change. It would be impossible, politically and in every other way, for our Supreme Court now to outlaw this principal plank in organized labor's economic program, although it was possible for it to do so twenty years ago in Taft's time, in the second *Coronado* case. And this is true, even if the idea of competition is still exalted as desirable in our economy and even if it is impossible to detect any analytical distinction between competition among businessmen, on the one hand, and among laboring people on the other. But much water has gone over the dam since 1925. By 1940, after the *Apex* decision, speculative lawyers began to wonder if there were really *any* normal labor union practices that might be regarded as violations of the Sherman Act. For they found it exceedingly difficult to take Justice Stone at his word, after reading the heart of his opinion, that the three labor union boycott cases and the second *Coronado* case were still valid precedents and good law.

THE *Hutcheson* CASE

It was not long before their misgivings were justified, although not many lawyers, if any at all, foresaw the extraordinary manner in which their premonitions would be fulfilled. It seems that in 1939 the carpenters' union had an old-fashioned jurisdictional dispute with the machinists' union over which of the two should get the work of dismantling certain machinery at the Anheuser-Busch plant in St. Louis. The company gave the work to the machinists' union. Thereupon its employees belonging to the carpenters' union went on strike and picketed the plant. In addition to this, the officials of the carpenters' union, through circulars and their union paper, requested all their friends and members to quit buying Anheuser-Busch beer.

This latter move was a secondary boycott, somewhat like that in the *Danbury Hatters'* case. And if that historical precedent was still good law, it looked as if the officials of the carpenters' union were caught, since the company sold its beer in interstate commerce and its interstate sales were drastically affected by the boycott. In any event, Hutcheson, the president of the carpenters' union, and his fellow officials actively promoting the boycott in question, were indicted and prosecuted criminally for having violated the Sherman Act. The federal district court held that no violation of the act was shown. Thereupon the prosecution appealed this judgment to the Supreme Court.

Justice Felix Frankfurter wrote the majority opinion for the Supreme Court in this case of *United States v. Hutcheson*. The judgment in favor of the union's leaders was affirmed. He observed that an indictment may be validly drawn under one statute and at the same time another statute, not referred to therein, "may draw the sting of criminality from the allegations." Thus, if an offense under the Sherman Act alone were found to have been absolved by the terms of Section 20 of the Clayton Act—the statute which was in some ways intended to amend and to modify the Sherman Act—then an indictment charging that offense could not stand up. He pointed out that a portion of Section 20 described certain conduct customarily engaged in by union people for purposes of extending organization and of collective bargaining and made it specifically non-enjoinable. He also reasoned that this paragraph "relieved such practices of all illegal taint by the catch-all provision, 'nor shall any of the acts specified in this paragraph be considered or held to be violations of any law of the United States.'" In short, if the actions of the four indicted union leaders in pursuing this secondary boycott amounted to conduct fairly described by this portion of the Clayton Act, then such conduct was not only not enjoinable but was not even illegal in any sense whatsoever. That is to say, it did not amount to a violation of any law of the United States, including the Sherman Act, under this concluding catch-all clause.

The only drawback about this theory of Justice Frankfurter's —indisputably correct as far as it went—was the Supreme Court's previous decision in the *Duplex* case, back in 1921. Then it was held that Section 20 of the Clayton Act did not apply to the sort of situation now before the Court. Hence, it seemed impossible to use the concluding catch-all clause for the purpose of deciding that Hutcheson's boycott was not a violation of the Sherman Act and was therefore not subject to any of its three adverse sanctions—particularly those of liability for triple damages and of criminality.

The Court knew very well that the *Duplex* case, not having been expressly overruled, was still an existing precedent. The effect of Section 20 under a standing decision of the Court was, first, to relax the antipathy of federal judges toward the self-

help techniques of unions only when the laboring folk concerned were the immediate employees of the employer pressing charges against them and, second, that even then the self-
help techniques to be tolerated were those already considered
lawful. As one of the supporters of this section had explained
when it was pending before Congress as a bill, this measure was
not intended to make the secondary boycott either nonenjoinable or legal. And Justice Frankfurter must have known
this.

He no doubt believed that his predecessors on the Court had
been hopelessly wrong when they narrowly construed Section
20 of the Clayton Act. Nevertheless, he knew that as long as the
Duplex case remained on the books, it settled once and for all
the meaning of Section 20. Naturally, the Supreme Court itself could at any time overrule the *Duplex* decision and declare
that its 1921 interpretation of Section 20 was incorrect. But
this course would also indicate that the Supreme Court as an
institution could with facility vary the meaning of certain
words whenever it wished to do so. Such a course might be
thought unwholesome, since it would advertise the fact that
our law is unstable and unpredictable and can change with the
shifting personnel of the Supreme Court. Obviously, the Court
as an institution would stand to lose prestige if this fact became too generally known. It is therefore usually most reluctant to overrule its own precedents, no matter how little its
new members like what former incumbents said and did some
years ago.

The fact remains, then, that under the existing interpretations of the Sherman Act, Hutcheson and the other officials of
the carpenters' union who had activated this boycott were
guilty and were not eligible to invoke the protection of Section 20 of the Clayton Act. Justice Frankfurter's way around
this impasse was through the provisions of the Norris-LaGuardia Anti-injunction Act. First he pointed out the similarity between the labor union conduct described in this second paragraph of Section 20 of the Clayton Act and that described in

Section 4 of the Norris-LaGuardia Act. He concluded that Congress in the Norris-LaGuardia Act was talking about the same sort of labor union conduct it had mentioned in the former act.

Next he pointed out that Congress, in Section 13 of the Norris-LaGuardia Act, had very clearly made the protection of that act available to labor unionists engaging in the conduct described in Section 4, whether or not they were or ever had been the immediate employees of the employer at whom such conduct was directed. Hence, he declared, one now reading the federal statute law should conclude that labor unionists engaging in nonviolent, nonfraudulent and nonlibelous economic pressures directed at an employer—as such pressures were comprehensively described in both Section 20 of the Clayton Act and Section 4 of the Norris-LaGuardia Act—are entitled to all of the protective features provided in both acts. This intermediate conclusion, of course, set the stage for the denouement. So far, at least according to Justice Frankfurter, it was Congress and not the Supreme Court that had introduced the change.

Now all of this circuitous effort was spent in trying to get at the concluding catch-all clause in Section 20 of the Clayton Act—"nor shall any of the acts specified in this paragraph be considered or held to be violations of any law of the United States." For the purposes of the *Hutcheson* case, Justice Frankfurter got at it by deciding that Congress itself had in the Norris-LaGuardia Act *redefined* the conduct set forth in the second paragraph of Section 20 of the Clayton Act, with reference to employees and nonemployees alike. In this way, he declared, Congress had given this catch-all clause a new vitality. This was virtually writing it into the Norris-LaGuardia Act, itself, as the concluding clause of Section 4 of that act. Naturally, if this clause had been so inserted by Congress, everything would have been exceedingly simple, indeed. But Congress had not done this, so Justice Frankfurter and a majority of the Court lent Congress a helping hand. With this clause read into the act, so to speak, all labor union conduct fairly described in Section 4 was not only nonenjoinable in federal courts but also became absolutely lawful for all purposes under federal law. Hence, as the boycott initiated by Hutcheson and his aids was clearly nonenjoinable under Section 4 of the act, it automatically became lawful even under the Sherman Act.

In all fairness to Justice Frankfurter and his associates, it should be stated clearly that they did not write the concluding catch-all clause of Section 20 into Section 4 of the Norris-LaGuardia Act. What they really did was to write sections 4 and 13 of the anti-injunction statute back into Section 20 of the Clayton Act! Many lawyers were profoundly shocked, regarding this as a sort of judicial legerdemain, to be explained only by the desire of the Court to free organized labor entirely from the inconvenience of the Sherman Act. Laymen may find it difficult to appreciate just what was objectionable about Justice Frankfurter's technique. Had his opinion been simply a straightforward disavowal of the *Duplex* decision, followed by a new interpretation of Section 20 of the Clayton Act to mean substantially what sections 4 and 13 of the Norris-LaGuardia Act quite clearly did mean, the American bar would probably have been disturbed but not shocked. Such a course would have suggested that the Court had dealt injustice to the labor unionists involved in both the *Duplex* and *Bedford Cut Stone* cases. How much neater if the Court could continue to honor its own precedents, implying that it was right all the time in the *Duplex* and *Bedford* cases, and then put the responsibility on Congress for having overruled these decisions in the Norris-LaGuardia Act. This would save everybody's face. The *Duplex* case would be dead for all time, yet it would have been Congress, and not the Court, which had done the killing.

Now we ought to pause here just to see what was going on. Everybody knew that the real abuse leading to both Section 20 of the Clayton Act and the Norris-LaGuardia Act was the intemperate use of the labor injunction. Shortly after Section 20 had been declared abortive in 1921, Justice Frankfurter—

then a professor in the Harvard Law School—led the fight to replace this measure with a thorough-going and honest anti-injunction act. The new bill, which became law in 1932, was sold to Congress on the representation that it was an anti-injunction act, and nothing more. It was intended to displace Section 20, as if that abortive measure were erased from the books, and was certainly not designed to overrule the *Duplex* decision in order to make that section an honest law after eleven years of shame.

When this new bill became the Norris-LaGuardia Act in 1932, it contained a section declaring that "all Acts and parts of Acts in conflict with the provisions of this Act are hereby repealed." Since Section 20 was the only law in conflict with this new statute, it is hard to see why this repealer clause didn't wipe it right off the books. If such a result was not intended by Congress, how can we possibly explain its desire to have two statutes covering the same matter—one in great detail but lacking a clause rendering nonenjoinable conduct generally lawful, and the other in highly ambiguous language, with no effective detail but including such a clause. The only conceivable explanation would be to keep alive the concluding catch-all clause in Section 20 in order to make the nonenjoinable conduct in the later statute generally lawful.

But if Congress had really wanted this result, all it had to do was to add a clause on the end of Section 4 of the 1932 statute, making the conduct there described lawful for all purposes. It knew that this had been done by a previous Congress in Section 20, and it knew that the Wisconsin legislature had done the same thing nine months previously in its state anti-injunction act. Its decision not to include such a clause in the Norris-LaGuardia Act was apparently deliberate. For the picture of Congress passing a law with the intention of overruling a Supreme Court decision merely to revitalize a clause of a former statute so that it, in turn, may be operative in the new statute is ludicrous. Look at it this way. When the new statute becomes law, instead of automatically repealing the old statute, it instantaneously overrules a previous Supreme Court decision and leaves the old statute no longer a conflicting act and, hence, not repealed—all to re-create a mere clause of the old act that Congress could easily have put into the new statute had it wished to do so. Such, unfortunately, is the stuff that law is sometimes made of; and it may be some consolation to laymen that lawyers themselves find it thoroughly mystifying. Justice Roberts, in his dissenting opinion in the *Hutcheson* case, thought it ". . . a process of construction never, as I think, heretofore indulged by this court." And he added: "I venture to say that no court has ever undertaken so radically to legislate where Congress has refused so to do."

Justice Frankfurter had other reasons for his conclusions in the *Hutcheson* case. "To be sure," he says in one part of his opinion, with reference to the Norris-LaGuardia Act, "Congress expressed this national policy and determined the bounds of a labor dispute in an act explicitly dealing with the further withdrawal of injunctions in labor controversies. But to argue, as it was urged before us, that the *Duplex* case still governs for purposes of a criminal prosecution is to say that that which on the equity side of the court is allowable conduct may in a criminal proceeding become the road to prison. It would be strange indeed that although neither the Government nor Anheuser-Busch could have sought an injunction against the acts here challenged, the elaborate efforts to permit such conduct failed to prevent criminal liability punishable with imprisonment and heavy fines. That is not the way to read the will of Congress, particularly when expressed by a statute which, as we have already indicated, is practically and historically one of a series of enactments touching one of the most sensitive national problems. Such legislation must not be read in a spirit of mutilating narrowness."

It would be rash to suggest that Justice Frankfurter was unfamiliar with the purpose of the Norris-LaGuardia Act, which he himself had helped to draft. But it is hard to understand how he could have forgotten that it was introduced and passed only as a measure to prevent the continued abuse by federal judges of their equity power in issuing labor injunctions. Apparently he did forget that the act on its face was never intended to deal with the *legality* of the union conduct which had traditionally been suppressed so summarily by these injunctions without all of the procedural guaranties afforded in actions at law and in criminal prosecutions. He spoke of "that which on the equity side of the court is allowable conduct" and of Congress' "elaborate efforts to permit such conduct." Now, in the Norris-LaGuardia Act, Congress did not set out to allow or permit any conduct, of any kind. It was not concerned with validating the activities of organized labor.

It was merely concerned with seeing that labor unionists were fairly tried by the federal courts for whatever they did do, lawful or unlawful. Of the three techniques available for calling labor unionists to account—actions for money damages, criminal prosecutions, and suits for injunctions—Congress believed that the first two were not misused by the federal courts, while the third was abused so badly by them that they could no longer be completely trusted with it. If unions indulged in certain specified conduct, even if it happened to be unlawful at common law or under a statute, the federal courts were no longer free to stop it by injunction but could deal with it only in criminal prosecutions or in actions for damages. And Congress felt so strongly about this that it included a separate section forbidding the use of the injunction even when labor unions were guilty of conspiracies, quite obviously having in mind violations of the Sherman Act. Thus while employers were deprived of their favorite weapon, the injunction, this does not mean that they were deprived of all of their recourses to the courts. Declaring illegal conduct nonenjoinable and no longer subject to the equity powers of judges does not make it lawful.

The conduct of Hutcheson and the other leaders of the carpenters in persuading the union members and its friends to quit buying Anheuser-Busch beer so that they might win in their jurisdictional struggle with the machinists was a secondary consumption boycott. This was a device considered lawful by few state courts and traditionally regarded as unlawful by the federal courts. Could a statute designed to make such conduct merely nonenjoinable make it allowable or permissible? The answer is no! For as far as these characteristics are concerned, a statute of this sort leaves such conduct exactly where it was, simply freeing it from the adverse effect of the injunction. You cannot properly say that as far as equity courts are concerned, the conduct has become allowable. All you can say is that equity courts are no longer permitted to pass on such conduct at all. Hence the additional reasons for the *Hutcheson* decision seem completely misleading.

In spite of all that has been said here, the *decision* itself in the *Hutcheson* case is consistent with the main position taken by the Court in the *Apex* case. This was not an attempt by the carpenters' union to gain control over the market for a particular brand of beer. It was, rather, an attempt to compel Anheuser-Busch to give certain work to the carpenters as against the machinists. The conduct of Hutcheson and his fellow unionists was certainly a violation of the Sherman Act according to the Supreme Court precedents in the *Danbury Hatters'*, *Duplex*, and *Bedford Cut Stone* cases. But those precedents seem so plainly in error that the Court should have overruled them. Then it would have had before it the legality of the secondary boycott in question simply under the Sherman Act *and entirely aside from Section 20 of the Clayton Act*. The resulting opinion would then have resembled the better portions of Justice Stone's opinion in the *Apex* case, improved by the absence of lip service to these old boycott precedents. This would have left the Court free under the Sherman Act to deal with union practices designed to prevent actual market restraints, and it could have reached its decision by a sound and intelligible method.

In his opinion, however, Justice Frankfurter virtually took organized labor entirely out from under the Sherman Act. This,

in effect, repealed that act as far as labor was concerned, on the
strength of the Norris-LaGuardia Act. He did leave one loophole suggesting a further possible application of the Sherman
Act to labor unions—in situations like the *Brims* case where
the Chicago carpenters, building contractors and woodwork
mills co-operated to control an entire local market. "So long
as a union acts in its self-interest," he said, *"and does not
combine with non-labor groups,* the licit and the illicit under
§ 20 are not to be distinguished by any judgment regarding
the wisdom or unwisdom, the rightness or wrongness, the
selfishness or unselfishness of the end of which the particular
union activities are the means." In this passing hint he suggested that unions conspiring with employers to control the
supply and price of commodities for their mutual benefit, thus
departing from normal union bargaining and organizational
activities, might still be regarded as offenders under the Sherman Act.

At this point it seems quite plain that he blundered, even
conceding for argument the validity of his *Hutcheson* opinion
as a whole. What the carpenters' union did in the *Brims* case
with the connivance of the contractors and the mills, it could
easily have done alone. Simply by refusing to allow its building carpenters to work on nonunion or out-of-town wood trim,
the union alone could have achieved identically the same result as that actually reached in the *Brims* situation. Such conduct would fall squarely within the description of activities
rendered nonenjoinable in Section 4 of the Norris-LaGuardia
Act.

Then under Justice Frankfurter's rationale the union would
be completely immune from attack under the Sherman Act.
If its conduct created a market control over supply and price
of commodities repugnant to the protective features of the
Sherman Act, according to Justice Stone's views in the *Apex*
case, that result would be most unfortunate. The ease with
which unions could then circumvent Frankfurter's loophole,
simply by effecting their market restraints through conduct

described in Section 4 of the Norris-LaGuardia Act, makes his anchor to leeward seem attached to the sheerest gossamer. Certainly, implicit in this possibility of evasion, is this proposition. If the Court retains as gospel the doctrine of the *Hutcheson* case, then labor organizations can safely afford to forget the Sherman Act and may impose market restraints almost at will.

SOME CONSEQUENCES OF THE *Hutcheson* DOCTRINE

Subsequent events have indicated that the views of Justice Frankfurter are likely to endure and that unions sufficiently strong to control the marketing of goods in whole areas will be able to exclude competing goods and to promote unreasonably high noncompetitive prices, thus insuring their restricted memberships steady employment at attractively high wage rates. An instance of this sort has recently occurred in *Allen Bradley Company v. Local No. 3, IBEW,* decided in 1945. This Local No. 3 of the International Brotherhood of Electrical Workers, AF of L, comprises practically all of the production and installation electricians employed in the New York area by local manufacturers of electrical equipment and by contractors and firms undertaking to install such equipment.

This local union was a close corporation, indeed. It had conquered the ravages of the depression and the terrific impact of the decline in building on the employment of its members, by imposing the closed shop on virtually all local employers of electricians. It would not permit anybody to do electrical work in this area unless he belonged to the union. And it would not accept new members unless there was more work available than the existing members could handle. By having its installation members refuse to handle any equipment manufactured by outside shops, thus discouraging its importation, the local insured a plentiful supply of production work for its members employed in New York shops. This practice eliminated from the New York area the competition previously afforded by out-of-state manufacturers, some of whom were organized by the same national union with which Local No. 3 was affiliated. The upshot of all this was that the unionized New York producers had the entire market to themselves. Thus they could, and they did, charge local consumers of their products far more than they charged outside consumers for the same articles. Local consumers were helplessly caught in this squeeze because union installation electricians refused to handle outside products, and there were few nonunion electricians available. Needless to say, the union was in a position to charge all that the traffic could bear for the services of its members.

In this *Allen Bradley* case several of the out-of-state electrical equipment manufacturers brought suit against the union and its officers under the Sherman Act to have this situation declared illegal and enjoined. Extensive hearings were held before a master appointed by the federal court. On the basis of his findings, these companies won the first round, securing an injunction against the continuance of this practice. Then the second Circuit Court of Appeals reversed this judgment and dismissed the complaint, holding that under the Supreme Court's statement of the law in the *Hutcheson* case, Local No. 3 had not violated the Sherman Act. Judge Clark, writing the majority opinion for the Circuit Court of Appeals, thought that the union was engaged in promoting its economic security through the exercise of conduct fairly described in sections 20 of the Clayton Act and 4 of the Norris-LaGuardia Act and therefore it remained immune from violation of the Sherman Act under the Supreme Court's doctrine of the *Hutcheson* case. He considered the possibility of sustaining the injunction, in part, on the basis of Justice Frankfurter's statement in the *Hutcheson* case that connivance between a union and several employers to control a commodities market would still constitute an offense under the Sherman Act. Certainly the evidence revealed a type of market control and elimination of competition that the Sherman Act was intended to discourage. But Judge Clark concluded that the findings in the case did not show any such connivance. Thus he did not see how he could sustain the injunction in any respect without derogating from the Supreme Court's position in the *Hutcheson* case.

Furthermore, he plainly doubted the significance of Frankfurter's alleged loophole, showing that it was the merest dictum, or side remark, which had been put in such a way as not necessarily to imply a violation of the act if connivance with employers were proved. And he obviously thought that taking this loophole seriously would only create trouble, because it would be so easy for the union to achieve exactly the same results without the connivance of employers. After all, the union had an interest in creating a monopolistic market control beneficial to the employers, since the security of its members depended entirely on their prosperity. If it could lawfully achieve and maintain this control with the employers' connivance (assuming it to have been present), so much the better; but if it could not, then it would achieve it without any help.

A majority of the Supreme Court, however, agreeing with Judge Swan's dissent in the Circuit Court of Appeals, held that the findings did show connivance and approved a limited injunction to prevent its effect. Justice Black, speaking for the Supreme Court, indicated clearly that the *Hutcheson* doctrine is here to stay and that a labor union is perfectly free under federal law to create and maintain any kind of market control, as long as it achieves this result without the connivance of employers and entirely through the exercise of conduct fairly described in sections 20 of the Clayton Act and 4 of the Norris-LaGuardia Act—including, of course, the secondary boycott. Now a fair reading of the findings of fact in this case makes it very doubtful, indeed, whether any connivance existed between the employers and the union. Any conclusion to that effect seems the sheerest inference which, of course, it was certainly the Court's privilege to draw.

Furthermore, as Judge Clark had pointed out, if the union continues its boycott with the same net result, carefully avoiding connivance with employers, then the district court would be powerless thereafter to enforce the injunction in contempt proceedings for the simple reason that it would not then have been disobeyed. Plainly he deprecated the ease with which a union might circumvent a judicial decree while appearing outwardly to ignore it. He must have felt sure that Local No. 3 would continue to boycott in order to maintain the prosperity to its members—forewarned, however, that it must meticulously avoid all connivance with employers. And he probably supposed that the employers would then batten on this market control so conveniently laid in their laps, although they would all be guilty under the Sherman Act if they themselves had helped to engineer it. He might have added that unions would become very coy about executing any collective agreements with employers which might be construed as connivance with them. This prospect of unions deliberately preferring to pursue the path of economic coercion as the safe and legal course, while eschewing the more pacific methods of negotiation and agreement as unsafe and unlawful, certainly emphasizes the paradox implicit in the Supreme Court's modern version of the Sherman Act.

A curious feature of this New York electricians' case is the Supreme Court's approval of an injunction against a labor union under the Sherman Act. According to Section 5 of the Norris-LaGuardia Act, such a course is forbidden against "persons participating or interested in a labor dispute" when their offense is assailed "because of the doing in concert of the acts enumerated in Section 4 of this Act," such as strikes, picketing, and boycotts. The issuance of the injunction in this case can only be explained under one or the other of two assumptions. The first is that the union was not engaged in a labor dispute when it exercised its boycott. And the second is, regardless of this, that it was enjoined from continuing to do things over and above the sort of conduct described in sections 20 of the Clayton Act and 4 of the anti-injunction act.

The phrase labor dispute is a complicated term of art, the scope of which is not limited in any way by the illegality of the means employed or the objective pursued. Roughly, a labor dispute occurs whenever a combination of working people or their representatives resort to self-help coercive economic pressures in order to achieve some objective which they conceive to be of advantage to themselves. On this point the district court thought that there was no labor dispute involved in this case. Judge Clark thought that Local No. 3 was engaged in a labor dispute. And the Supreme Court did not touch expressly on this matter at all. But it is hard to see how the Supreme Court could avoid conceding the existence of a labor dispute without also taking the rather absurd position that after Local No. 3 had consummated the results of an admitted dispute in an agreement with the employers, the dispute suddenly evaporated. Thus, while the union is striving for economic advantage through the use of the boycott, it remains immune from injunction. But after its nonenjoinable coercion has successfully terminated in an agreement—the normal objective of all labor disputes—it suddenly becomes subject to the injunction. If this were the rule, there would certainly be a considerable premium on dilatory union tactics—that is, the maintenance of economic coercion which is about to become a contract but which never results in one. The point is that the union's chief aim, and the one it would pursue to the exclusion of all others, would be to maintain the boycott.

Exactly the same observation is appropriate concerning the enjoinability of conduct on the union's part over and above that described in Section 4 of the Norris-LaGuardia Act. If the union by acting alone in the exercise of its secondary boycott remains immune from injunction and its activity becomes enjoinable only when it is merged in agreements or understandings with employers, then naturally it will be reluctant to reflect such otherwise successful and effective economic pressure in these agreements. Justice Black does not discuss this matter in his opinion. But he does indicate, without explaining why, that a collective agreement embodying the promise "not to buy goods manufactured by companies which did not employ

the members of Local No. 3" would not, in itself, be unlawful
under the Sherman Act. The actual offense in this New York
electricians' case, he says, is the mutual effort of the union and
the employers to police the agreed-to boycott and to see that it
works smoothly. But since Judges Clark and A. Hand, as well
as Justice Murphy of the Supreme Court, thought that there
was no evidence establishing this offensive conduct, and since
everybody apparently concedes the union's ability to get results
without recourse to anything more than the conduct described
in Section 4 of the Norris-LaGuardia Act, the whole matter
seems somewhat up in the air. And it still appears odd to see
an injunction popping up against the purely economic activities of a union in the year 1945, after all that Congress and
the Supreme Court have said and done about that remedy in
labor cases.

This is the confusion that the Supreme Court has created
by its own excess of ingenuity in using the Norris-LaGuardia
Act to resurrect the concluding catch-all clause of the repealed
and out-moded Section 20 of the Clayton Act. As a result organized labor is now free to create and maintain the most
flagrant of market controls—concededly in violation of the
Sherman Act when construed according to the principles laid
down by Justice Stone in the *Apex* case—as long as it relies on
its own resources and does not connive with employers. And
apparently it is now a matter of indifference to the Supreme
Court that unions may effect market controls in an area with
no intention of organizing the employees in outside plants,
the normal objective of any nationally affiliated labor union.

In the case of *United States v. American Federation of Musicians,* which involved Petrillo's union comprising "virtually
all musicians in the nation who make music for hire," the
Supreme Court has said that the union might with impunity
conspire to prevent the use of canned music by radio broadcasting stations, in tavern juke boxes, and even in the home,
through coercion exercised on record-making companies by
the refusal of union members to make musical recordings.

This, of course, was not an attempt to improve the working conditions of men employed by record manufacturers and radio stations but was, rather, an undertaking by the union to drive these enterprises out of business unless they would provide unnecessary employment for its members. This secondary boycott was enforced not in a local, but in a national, market. In another case—*United States v. International Hod Carriers', etc., Council*—the Supreme Court allowed a union to prevent the importation from a sister state of cement-mixing trucks, designed to lower the cost of building through the saving of labor, unless the contractors proposing to use these trucks hired just as many laborers as they had before, thus defeating the whole point of the technological improvement in question and depriving property owners of the normal benefits flowing therefrom. This is challenging, indeed, when one reflects how important technological progress can be as a factor in real competition.

Similarly, the Court has permitted a union to discourage the general use of cheaper prefabricated and improved building materials by condoning a building carpenters' secondary boycott focused against such materials produced in other states by employees organized in a rival union. There the Court acknowledged that rival union factions are free to fight out the new interunion dispute—a struggle between conflicting economic and political union ideologies—with the channels of interstate commerce as their battleground, quite regardless of the effect on consumers' markets. These are the cases of *United States v. Building and Construction Trades Council* and *United States v. United Brotherhood of Carpenters and Joiners,* both decided in 1941.

In a suit under the Sherman Act, the Court has even permitted a union to drive an employer completely out of interstate commerce, not because he refused to deal with the union on perfectly satisfactory terms but because the union cherished a long-standing grudge against him. This was the outstanding fact in *Hunt v. Crumboch,* decided in 1945. During a strike conducted by the truck drivers' union against this employer some years ago, one of the union members was killed. An officer of the company was tried for his murder and was acquitted. Later on the union succeeded in organizing all of the trucking companies in the area and secured an agreement from the large chain store using their services, and for which this same employer had trucked interstate for fourteen years, that it would patronize only carriers organized with the union. Then, although the employer in question earnestly sought an agreement with the union, the union refused to deal with him or to permit its members to work for him because, as it said, he was a murderer. Hence, under its agreement with the union, the chain store was compelled to cease patronizing this particular employer, Hunt. Then he had to look elsewhere for whatever uncontrolled business he could find. This is arresting, because it illustrates the use of union power completely to eliminate an interstate business and, in a slight degree, to lessen competition, on the basis of personal dislike and not in pursuit of organization or improved working conditions—the normal economic objectives of labor unions.

All of these restraints on markets and enterprises, assailed under the Sherman Act as such, were tolerated by the Supreme Court because they were imposed by unions through the exercise of coercive economic conduct fairly described in sections 20 of the Clayton Act and 4 of the Norris-LaGuardia Act. This state of affairs directly stems from the doctrine of the *Hutcheson* case. It is true that even Justice Frankfurter dissented in the truckers' case just discussed, apparently because he believed that the immunity implied in his *Hutcheson* opinion should be available to unions only when they are trying to promote what he seems to regard as legitimate interests, such as organization and improved employment conditions—in short, when they are engaging in legitimate labor disputes. Possibly he has forgotten that "the licit and the illicit under § 20 are not to be distinguished by any judgment regarding the wisdom or unwisdom, the rightness or wrongness, the selfishness or unselfishness of the end of which the particular union activities are the means," as he had so deftly put it in the *Hutcheson* case. But this intriguing suggestion of a belated illegal purpose doctrine has little appeal to the majority of the Court, which insists upon taking his *Hutcheson* opinion at its face value. Indeed, from Frankfurter's concurrence in the other cases following the *Hutcheson* decision it is hard to believe that he himself places much confidence in it. Anyway, four years earlier in the case of *Milk Wagon Drivers' Union v. Lake Valley Farm Products, Inc.,* the Court had committed itself to the view that a labor dispute is still a labor dispute, regardless of the disputants' motives or the illegality of their objectives.

What has happened here, as Justice Roberts indicates in his dissent, is the creation of an impossible situation. As he says, "This court, as a result of its past decisions, is in the predicament that whatever it decides must entail disastrous results." If this were not such a serious matter, it would be amusing. The Supreme Court is mired so deeply in its own complicated circuitry of words that it cannot get out gracefully unless the infusion of new members enables a break from its present position or unless Congress saves the day with a statute, comparable in effect to the Sherman Act but directed at the market restraints of organized labor. The latter solution will be exceedingly difficult, because Congress will perforce have to maintain tolerance of certain types of union market restraints which the very existence of large, powerful, nationally affiliated unions itself implies. In any event, to quote from Justice Jackson's dissent in the *Hunt* case:

"With this decision, the labor movement has come full circle. The working man has struggled long, the fight has been filled with hatred, and conflict has been dangerous, but now workers may not be deprived of their livelihood merely because their employers oppose and they favor unions. Labor has won other rights as well, unemployment compensation, old-age benefits and, what is most important and the basis of all its gains, the recognition that the opportunity to earn his support is not alone the concern of the individual but is the problem which all organized societies must contend with and conquer if they are to survive. This Court now sustains the claim of a union to the right to deny participation in the economic world to an employer simply because the union dislikes him. This Court permits to employees the same arbitrary dominance over the economic sphere which they control that labor so long, so bitterly and so rightly asserted should belong to no man.

"Strikes aimed at compelling the employer to yield to union demands are not within the Sherman Act. Here the employer has yielded, and the union has achieved the end to which all legitimate union pressure is directed and limited. The union cannot consistently with the Sherman Act refuse to enjoy the fruits of its victory and deny peace terms to an employer who has unconditionally surrendered."

There remains only the task of suggesting what should be done about this state of affairs. Briefly, if the Supreme Court abandoned its unfortunate doctrine established in the *Hutcheson* case and adhered faithfully to the best of what Justice Stone said in the *Apex* case, it could even yet achieve substantial justice under the Sherman Act. In the alternative, however, the next move seems to be up to Congress. It would be impertinent to say that Congress should do this and that, and so and so. At a later stage there will be presented briefly a practical program of the measures which some reflective people believe should be promulgated, either under the Sherman Act itself, or under a law of that type specifically directed at organized labor. In conclusion, it seems almost unnecessary to observe that the Supreme Court has done the labor unions a real disservice in vesting them with the worst curse of modern times—too much economic power over others. Congress will be compounding that curse if it does not provide appropriate controls over that power. Unless something is done, it seems too plain for argument that the grapes of wrath will ferment until the whole keg blows up. And the wine that spills may be bitter to the taste.

CHAPTER XI

THE NLRB BEFORE THE COURTS

It is idle to feel either blind resentment against "government by commission" or sterile longing for a golden past that never was. Profound new forces call for new social inventions, or fresh adaptations of old experience. The "great society," with its permeating influence of technology, large-scale industry, and progressive urbanization, presses its problems; the history of political and social liberty admonishes us of its lessons. Nothing less is our task than fashioning instruments and processes at once adequate for social needs and the protection of individual freedom.—Felix Frankfurter, 1927, appearing in *Law and Politics,* page 234, 1939.

A HOST of problems have arisen before the National Labor Relations Board since the act was passed in 1935. Much of the board's work has required judicial scrutiny, since only the federal appellate courts can enforce its orders. This joint administrative and judicial process reveals how some of the gaps in the act are filled in by nonlegislative interpolation. At the same time it suggests a few items which require the attention of Congress in some well-considered amendments.

So that the board might have the power to make readjustments in the cases arising before it, Congress authorized it to issue cease and desist orders and "to take such affirmative action, including reinstatement of employees with or without back pay, as will effectuate the policies of this Act." But the board's powers have not proved to be as wide as they appear in this grant. According to the Supreme Court they are strictly remedial and not punitive. Within the proper scope of authority, however, the Court has construed the board's orders most sympathetically. Thus, it has gone far to recognize orders disestablishing company-dominated unions, upholding the board's findings whenever they were based on substantial evidence— "such relevant evidence as a reasonable mind might accept as adequate to support a conclusion."

•

THE ABROGATION OF IRREGULAR COLLECTIVE AGREEMENTS

Early in its career the board received a setback from the Supreme Court. Although this difficulty was later straightened out, at the time the decision in question came down it threw doubt on much that the board had assumed it could do as a matter of course. In effectuating the policies of the act, the board naturally supposed that it was free to set aside agreements that it concluded had been reached contrary to its provisions, whether or not the union in question was company-dominated and was subject to being disestablished. Nevertheless, it found that its assumption was not completely justified.

A company with 38,000 employees made a collective agreement with an AF of L union on behalf of its members only, while board proceedings, initiated by a competing CIO union, were still pending. Before the board had completed its investigation, 30,000 of these employees had joined the AF of L union. The board ordered the company to set aside this contract, apparently finding that it was arranged between the company and the AF of L union, regardless of the employees' right to choose their own bargaining representative. The board could not find that the employer had dealt with a company-dominated union, since AF of L unions are hardly in that category. But it did find that the company had ignored the formalities of the act and had made the contract without consulting its employees, thus influencing thousands of workers to sign up with the union which had so rapidly succeeded in getting a good contract. In its opinion, the employer could not lawfully choose the union to represent any or all of his employees, regardless of their wishes expressed pursuant to the provisions of the act, thus setting at naught the policy that workers should be represented by unions of their own choosing. Apparently the company had done all this in order to side-step the CIO union, preferring to deal with the AF of L if it had to bargain collectively with either.

The Supreme Court, in *Consolidated Edison Company of N. Y. v. NLRB,* refused to enforce the board's order, chiefly because the AF of L union was not a party to the proceedings. Against the board's protest that this made no difference, the Court pointed out that in prior cases where contracts had been set aside under somewhat analogous circumstances, the unions had been found to be company dominated. This was not true here. Furthermore, the contract was advantageous to the employees covered—actual members of the AF of L union—and had achieved in the plant an industrial stability which would be completely disrupted if it were now set aside. Since the whole purpose of the act was to keep commerce on an even keel, this policy could best be served by letting things stay as they were, enforcement of the board's order inviting total disruption of the stability already established. For these reasons, the Court thought, its decision was imperative.

But none of these reasons answered the board's objection that the company had seriously interfered with independent and autonomous organization in the plant. The board remained unimpressed by the fact that so many employees had joined the AF of L union voluntarily, for it knew that they were naturally affected by the AF of L union's success in so promptly having achieved recognition and a desirable contract. All the board could see in the Court's decision was acquiescence in allowing an employer, through connivance with the union it preferred, to thwart the completely free choice by its employees of an exclusive bargaining representative. It knew that if the employees had been left to choose a representative under methods prescribed in the act, they still might have selected the AF of L union. But it also knew that they might have chosen otherwise, after having considered the merits of both competing unions. It simply objected to this opportunity for a completely free choice having been foreclosed by the employer's self-serving action, when matters pertaining to representation were none of its business under the act. And it wanted to afford an opportunity for a free choice by undoing the mischief and letting everyone really concerned—the employees and the two competing unions—start all over again pursuant to the proper procedure in the act.

From this account one might suppose that the board set too high a premium on the rights of the CIO union as an enterprise in itself, aside from the interests of the employees themselves. But many of the employees in the plant had preferred the CIO union; and, given equality of opportunity with the adherents of the AF of L union in the plant, they might have convinced a majority of their fellows to support their choice. They could not, however, compete with an accomplished fact. And the board's position that they should not have to do so may well imply greater emphasis on actual employee choice and less on the rights of competing unions, as such.

In any event, the Court subsequently modified its position in this type of case, upholding a board order that set aside a contract executed under similar circumstances. Eventually, Congress intervened during the war to deprive the board of its power to set aside contracts achieved in this fashion when it appeared that they had been in existence for a stated appreciable length of time and, because of the independent and undominated character of the contracting unions, there had been established stable collective bargaining in good faith. Possibly such a measure was justified to obviate the disruption of industry during a war. Yet it clearly remains so completely in conflict with the basic policy of the act as to invite employers openly to select the unions with which they prefer to do business.

THE DISCRETION OF THE BOARD IN AFFORDING REMEDIES

Originally the board claimed complete discretionary authority to effectuate the policies of the act, not subject to judicial check as long as it granted only those remedies contemplated by Congress. But the Supreme Court held otherwise, declaring that the board's discretion should be judicially defined, if necessary.

This issue first arose in a case involving a sit-down strike with incidental physical violence in and around the plant. Because an employer had discouraged the independent organization of his employees, they called a strike, seizing the plant and proposing to hold it until he dealt fairly with them. Most of the employees remained inside the plant, while the rest of them aided and abetted from outside, chiefly by supplying provisions. The employer's attorney formally discharged all of the employees inside the plant, shouting at them through a megaphone. When the sit-down seizure finally ended and work was resumed, the employer took back some of the strikers but refused their old jobs to several others, including a few who had stayed outside the plant as part of the supply line and, therefore, had not been formally discharged. All of these strikers who had been denied re-employment filed charges with the board. After a hearing the board ordered their reinstatement, with back pay. It was found that they had been denied their old jobs because of their union activities and that the employer had in the meantime fostered a company-dominated inside union. This was the celebrated *Fansteel* case—*NLRB v. Fansteel Metallurgical Corporation.*

The Supreme Court refused to enforce this order, a majority declaring that the board had gone too far when it required an employer to take back into his shop men who had, by their "highhanded proceeding without shadow of legal right," forfeited any claim to continued employment. Plainly these members of the Court could not believe that the act "abrogates the right of the employer to refuse to retain in his employ those who illegally take and hold possession of his property." This was the first expression of opinion by the Supreme Court that the sit-down strikes and seizures of 1937 were illegal. Naturally this view was not surprising, although some prominent liberal lawyers had stoutly maintained that such conduct should be deemed the lawful retention by these strikers of their "property" in their jobs, as tangibly manifested by their physical place of employment. But the novel and revolutionary disregard by the strikers of the institution of property—and real property, at that—was probably even less distasteful to the members of the Court than the opinions of a few legal scholars that such conduct was defensible and arguably lawful. At any rate, in spite of evidence supporting the board's findings that the employer refused to take back the complainants because of their union activities, a majority of the Court thought the company nevertheless free to reject these former employees for *any* reason, as long as their conduct had given it a valid reason for doing so. Naturally, the majority judges did not put it this way, but that is what their decision amounted to.

Justice Reed pointed out for the dissent how unwholesome he believed this position to be. As he warned: "Friction easily engendered by labor strife may readily give rise to conduct, from nose-thumbing to sabotage, which will give fair occasion for discharge on grounds other than those prohibited by the Labor Act." Obviously he feared a view of the act permitting an employer to goad an ardent union employee into some indiscreet conduct, verbal or other, in order to create a convenient reason for getting rid of him. Such a view he clearly perceived in the majority's decision. He was not impressed by the argument that the employees could have sought relief from the employer's original unfair labor practices by recourse to the board instead of unlawfully taking matters into their own hands. He preferred to take a more practical view of the industrial scene as it actually exists, realizing that workingmen and their supervisors do not always behave rationally in their mutual dealings. He felt that the board was in a position to make an expert survey of these matters and should be allowed to decide when it would or would not be suitable to continue the employment relationship, whatever the parties to a dispute had been doing.

"The point is made," he observed, "that an employer should not be compelled to re-employ an employee guilty, perhaps, of sabotage." And he continued: "This depends upon circumstances. It is the function of the Board to weigh the charges and countercharges and determine the adjustment most conducive to industrial peace. Courts certainly should not interfere with the normal action of administrative bodies in such circumstances. Here both labor and management had erred grievously in their respective conduct. It cannot be said to be unreasonable to restore both to their former status."

The decision of the Court, nevertheless, established the view that the board's discretion in administering its powers of granting affirmative relief is subject to judicial limitation. Since this decision, the board has voluntarily refrained from pressing the matter, refusing to reinstate employees who are not taken back after a strike because of their egregiously bad conduct. But it seems probable, in view of the changes in personnel on the Court, that if this issue were to arise again squarely before the Supreme Court, a majority of the bench would take a more generous view of the board's discretion and might conceivably accord it complete discretionary authority in ordering affirmative relief.

REINSTATEMENT AND INSTATEMENT IN JOBS AS REMEDIES

The Supreme Court has allowed the board a fairly generous scope in construing its remedial authority under Section 10 (c) of the act. Congress had there empowered the board, in dealing with unfair labor practice cases, to issue cease and desist orders "and to take such affirmative action, including reinstatement of employees with or without back pay, as will effectuate the policies of this Act." Except for a narrowing of the board's discretion, no real difficulties ensued concerning reinstatement of employees discharged because of union activities. One of the earliest Supreme Court decisions under the act dealt with a board order requiring reinstatement of several employees who had gone out on a bargaining strike and were thereafter denied the right to return to their jobs on the ground that they had in the meantime been filled by other men. Evidence showed that the employer had taken back most of the strikers but had replaced with others only those men who had actively led the strike. It also indicated that the employer had not been guilty of any unfair labor practice prior and up to the time of the strike but was only unwilling to concede the fiscal demands of his employees.

The board concluded from the evidence that the employer's real reason for having replaced the rejected employees was his desire to get rid of them because of their union activities. It then ordered the employer to reinstate them with back pay, discharging the newly hired employees, if necessary, in order to make room for them. This order the Supreme Court declared to be proper. At the same time it asserted the employer's right to replace strikers with outsiders and to refuse them their old jobs, as long as it appeared that the strike itself was not preceded and occasioned by any unfair labor practices on his part and that he had replaced the strikers in good faith and not merely to conceal his desire to be rid of ardent unionists. This result seems faithfully to reflect the Congressional mandate as it was expressed in the act.

But it is not so easy to perceive such conformance to Congressional will in another instance of affirmative relief granted under this provision. The board construed it to include authority for the "instatement" of applicants for employment, who were denied jobs because of their union interests and affiliations, together with pay from the time they applied for work until they were offered jobs. In this particular case of *Phelps Dodge Corporation v. NLRB* it so happened that the two applicants in question had at one time worked for the company and had voluntarily left their employment at its plant. While this fact has no legal significance, it is nevertheless a matter of interest in the case.

The company's denial of employment was certainly an unfair labor practice in violation of Section 8 (3) of the act. The real question, however, was whether or not the board could order the affirmative relief of instatement and back pay. This raised a variety of issues before the Supreme Court, all subordinate to the main consideration of just what Congress had intended in this section. It was one thing to require a renewal of employment relations where they had already existed on a mutually satisfactory basis—at least until the employee in question had shown an interest in unionism. But it was quite another thing to require the employment of somebody with whom the employer had never maintained such a relationship at all. The former was a drastic modification of the employer's traditional freedom of contract.

But the latter seemed almost a revolutionary step, imposing a contractual relationship where none had ever existed and under circumstances which suggested no standards or terms of employment to govern its inception. Furthermore, Congress had seemed to indicate its trepidation in providing even reinstatement with back pay by expressly mentioning this remedy, apparently implying that it wanted no misapprehension as to how far it was empowering the board to go in the matter of taking affirmative action. For this reason, many people believe it impossible to suppose that Congress would have empowered the board to impose the relationship of employment where it had not existed before, without spelling out this power in unmistakable terms instead of leaving it to be inferred. Certainly it seemed a more revolutionary modification of freedom of contract than Congress would ordinarily leave to an administrative agency's conception of what was necessary to "effectuate the policies of this Act."

In spite of all this, an astonishingly strong case can be stated in support of the board's position. The discriminatory practice in question is plainly unlawful under Section 8 (3) of the act and is subject to a cease and desist order. It resembles in effect the antiunion or "yellow dog contract" so unpopular in this country, and it smacks of the antiunion blacklist. But a cease and desist order seems ineffectual against such a practice because its enforcement is so practically difficult to imagine. Suppose an employer is staffing a shop and rigorously rejects all applicants with union records. By the time a cease and desist order is issued against him, and has been declared enforceable by judgment of a court, his shop is presumably manned.

He can then afford to promise that he will not do it again. And even if he later repeats this offense with new applicants during the course of normal turnover, it is arguable that such instances are entirely new discriminations exercised against different people and, as such, the proper subjects for new complaints rather than violations of the outstanding cease and desist order. Otherwise, the existing order and judgment will virtually have acquired the force of a statute—a somewhat novel concomitant of administrative orders. If, however, such a cease and desist order and the enforcing judgment were to be given this effect, how would the contempt incurred in violating them be purged? The most obvious method would be by undoing the harm done—hiring the rejected employee in question and making him whole financially. Certainly this would appear to be effectuating the policy of the act by striking directly at the offensive practice and undoing it entirely.

A majority of the Supreme Court decided that Congress had given this power to the board. It was not disturbed by the fact that the rejected applicants were not employees, within the meaning of the act. It had been suggested to the Court that the clause "including reinstatement of employees with or without back pay" marked the extreme limit which Congress had set on the board's authority to order affirmative remedial action. The Court rejected this notion. In his opinion Justice Frankfurter observed in this connection:

"Reinstatement is the conventional correction for discriminatory discharges. Experience having demonstrated that discrimination in hiring is twin to discrimination in firing, it would indeed be surprising if Congress gave a remedy for the one which it denied for the other . . . To differentiate between discrimination in denying employment and in terminating it, would be a differentiation not only without substance but in defiance of that against which the prohibition of discrimination is directed. But, we are told, this is precisely the differentiation Congress had made. It has done so, the argument runs, by not directing the Board 'to take such affirmative action as will effectuate the policies of this Act,' *simpliciter,* but, instead, by empowering the Board 'to take such affirmative action, including reinstatement of employees with or without back pay, as will effectuate the policies of this Act.' To attribute such a function to the participial phrase introduced by 'including' is to shrivel a versatile principle to an illustrative application. We find no justification whatever for attributing to Congress such a casuistic withdrawal of the authority which, but for the illustration, it clearly has given the Board. The word 'including' does not lend itself to such destructive significance."

While one may instinctively distrust this conclusion, it is almost impossible to deny the force of what Justice Frankfurter said. Justice Stone, for the dissent, however, observed:

"The Congressional debates and committee reports give no hint that, in enacting the National Labor Relations Act, Congress or any member of it thought it was giving the Board a remedial power which few courts had ever assumed to exercise or had been thought to possess, and we are unable to say that the words of the statute go so far . . . Authority for so unprecedented an exercise of power is not lightly to be inferred. In view of the use of the phrase 'including reinstatement of employees,' as a definition and enlargement, as we think it is, of the authority of the Board to take affirmative action, we cannot infer from it a Congressional purpose to authorize the

Board to order compulsory employment and wage payments not embraced in its terms."

Plainly, instatement of applicants for employment who had been refused jobs because of their union affiliations is an arguably sound and valid affirmative remedy. And if Congress had been pressed to include it in Section 10 (c), it would have found it difficult to deny while allowing for reinstatement of discriminatorily discharged employees. But if this matter had been squarely raised on the floor of Congress, the enormity of such a drastic innovation might well have jeopardized passage of the whole act or, at least, of the granting of any but carefully outlined and restricted affirmative powers to the board. Certainly, it seems quite distinguishable from such affirmative action as requiring an employer to execute in written form an agreement he has reached with a union, in strict compliance with Section 8 (5) of the act making a refusal to bargain collectively an unfair labor practice. Yet approval by the Court of an order requiring such action has been thought by many to constitute a compelling precedent for reading the power of instatement into the affirmative action authorized in Section 10 (c) of the act.

THE POWER OF THE BOARD AFTER COLLECTIVE BARGAINING IS ACHIEVED

Another case of the utmost importance in its implications shows how pervasive the power of the board really is, even after the apparent policy of the act has been fulfilled. A perusal of the act might reasonably lead one to believe that its purpose was to insure organization free from employer control, as well as good faith bargaining thereafter between the employer and the duly selected bargaining agency representing the employees—and nothing more. Hence, it might come as a surprise to find the Supreme Court concluding that the board may still dispose of a complaint, claiming discrimination in his discharge, filed by an employee in a completely organized plant which is covered by a fairly bargained contract between the employer and a union.

At any rate, in a case of this sort brought before the board —NLRB v. *Newark Morning Ledger Company*—reinstatement of the discharged employee, with back pay, was ordered. The Circuit Court of Appeals at first had refused to enforce this order, taking the position that the purpose of the act—to guarantee independent organization and good faith collective bargaining—had been achieved and that the effect of the act in this particular plant was exhausted. The board, it said, should concern itself only with matters of public importance, the avoidance of disruption due to an employer's interferences with the organization of his employees and his refusal to bargain collectively. And, the court continued, it does not have the power to enforce private rights after these objectives had been achieved, suggesting that employees working under a collective agreement must look to its terms for enforcement of their rights by way of arbitration or recourse to the courts. In this particular case the contract included a provision against discriminatory discharge. And the Circuit Court of Appeals believed that the discharged employee should pursue her rights in the fashion conventionally developed in the law to deal with breaches of contract.

On a re-hearing, however, the court changed its mind, concluding that, after all, the policy of the act was broad enough to give the board authority to see that genuine collective bargaining *continued*, even after it had been auspiciously begun. Such bargaining, it pointed out, is never in a state of quiescence. Each contract is normally for a year's duration. After it is executed, the parties frequently begin speculating on improvements and continue chaffering all through the term of the current agreement. If the employer remains free to discourage such experimentation on the part of his ardent union employees, he is in effect interfering with their right to bargain collectively as set forth in Section 7 of the act, denial of which right is made an unfair labor practice in Section 8 (1)

of the act. Action by the board to prevent such a practice, as
well as to remedy harm flowing from it, the court finally
thought to be a matter of public concern and not just the enforcement of a private right. Hence, it proceeded to enforce
the board's order of reinstatement and back pay.

One of the judges then on this court—W. Clark—filed an
exceedingly arresting dissent, pointing out in a most learned
discourse what he believed to be the vice in the position taken
by the board. He cited numerous authorities indicating that
Congress had never intended to give the board more power
than to see that employees in a unit were enabled to organize
and bargain collectively with their employer. By referring to
instances where Congress had either provided an administrative
forum in which employees might seek adjustment of grievances,
as under the Railway Labor Act, or had in open hearings considered the possibility of a similar device for industry in general while the NLRA was still pending as a bill, he sought to
prove that Congress had carefully refrained from empowering
the board to do more than get employers and their employees
together, in the first instance, as a going concern. Their inability to get together, he pointed out, was the difficulty
prompting the act in the first place. And that, he thought, was
the difficulty Congress had adequately resolved by passing the
act. He did not question the wisdom of Congress' some day
empowering the board to do more, signifying that such a matter of policy was solely the concern of Congress. But he plainly
believed it unwise for the board and the courts to read additional power into the act on what he regarded as the most
circumstantial and inferential authority where, in his opinion,
Congress had deliberately withheld such authority, leaving
matters of this sort for disposition in already existing forums
in accordance with the provisions of the contract.

This is an exceedingly fundamental issue, going directly to
the heart of government by means of administrative agencies
acting under Congressional authority. It is unfortunate, therefore, that the Supreme Court approved the circuit court's final

judgment merely by refusing to hear the case, thus refraining from comment on the matters aired in the opinions just discussed. Oddly enough, most people had taken it for granted that the board had the power under the act to prevent and remedy discriminatory discharges under any circumstances. But the arresting considerations set forth in this case challenge such complacence, while the Supreme Court's blunt refusal to comment on the matter leaves us only to believe that the general impression was probably correct, after all.

THE EXCLUSIVE BARGAINING RIGHTS OF THE MAJORITY VERSUS BARGAINING BY INDIVIDUALS

Under the act, the bargaining agency or union chosen by a majority of the employees in an appropriate unit is the exclusive representative of *all* of the employees in that unit. Section 9 (*a*) of the act makes this plain. At the same time it implies in a proviso that individual employees or groups of employees may still have dealings of some sort with the employer, actually stating that they "shall have the right at any time to present grievances" to him. Unfortunately, in the first decision of the Supreme Court under the NLRA, Chief Justice Hughes created the impression, without stating clearly what he meant, that some leeway had been provided in the act permitting employers to bargain and contract with individuals. Employers inferred from his language that they remained free under the act to make individual arrangements with employees, aside from collective arrangements with the bargaining representatives of their employees as a whole. But if such a practice were tolerated, it could easily wreck the act. And eventually the Supreme Court had to straighten out this misconception.

In one case—*National Licorice Company v. NLRB*—an employer refused to deal with a committee of his employees who predominantly supported an AF of L union, and the men went out on strike in protest. When they returned to work, after their strike had failed, the employer circulated among them a form of individual contract, declaring that only those who signed would receive a proposed increase in wages. About 85 per cent of the employees signed this contract which contained a clause committing each of them thereafter not "to demand a closed shop or a signed agreement by his employer with any Union." In complaint proceedings the board ordered these individual contracts to be set aside, regarding them as a manifestation of unfair labor practices. The Supreme Court thought that the board's order should be enforced but modified it so that the employees might claim any rights which they had secured under them. It believed that such individual contracts "set at naught" the policies of the act and thus violated a public right in organization and collective bargaining.

That case seems fairly simple and clear. In the next one of this kind to reach the Court, however, it appeared that about 75 per cent of the men in a plant had voluntarily executed individual contracts with the employer, agreeing to serve for the terms of the contracts in return for stated conditions of employment. These contracts contained nothing against unionism, and the employees not executing them were in no way harassed by the employer. A CIO union petitioned the board for an election at the plant. The employer contended that the individual contracts constituted a bar to this petition because they showed a majority of the employees already committed contractually. Nevertheless, the board held an election which the union won, being thereupon certified to the employer as the exclusive bargaining agency for all of the employees in the unit concerned, most of whom were already under individual contracts. The employer then refused to bargain with the union. Thereupon the board, in complaint proceedings, found it guilty of violating the act and ordered it to bargain with the union. This order was enforced by the Circuit Court of Appeals, with the Supreme Court's approval.

In his opinion for the Court in *J. I. Case Company v. NLRB*, Justice Jackson set forth an illuminating discussion of collective agreements, comparing them to railroad rate schedules under which individual contracts are made by shippers. As he pointed out, employees working under collective agreements make individual contracts of simple employment, benefiting automatically therein by the terms set forth in the collective agreement. But, he added, the act makes no provision for the concurrent existence in a plant of the collective agreement together with individual contracts reflecting terms of employment different from those effected by the collective agreement. Practically, individual bargaining is sometimes necessary and lawful, he remarked, citing situations where collective agreements expire and are not renewed. It may not be permitted to interfere with the policies of the act, however. Hence it cannot be taken to preclude collective bargaining. And whenever an employee stands to gain more from the collective agreement than from his individual contract, he is free at all times to claim the advantage, in spite of his personal agreement to the contrary.

In answer to the argument that unusually competent employees may lose by conformance to the collective agreement alone, Justice Jackson replied that individual contracts extending greater privileges are in conflict with the "practice and philosophy of collective bargaining" which "looks with suspicion on such individual advantages." Special treatment of this sort is frequently an attempt on the part of an employer to breed a dislike for unionism and it lays employers open to the suspicion of unfair labor practices. An unusually competent worker may express his dislike of collectivism by voting against it. If he is outvoted by his fellows, he ought to conform to the majority rule, Justice Jackson suggesting that he then contribute his special talents to compensate in the collective scheme for the shortcomings of less competent employees. "We cannot except individual contracts generally from the operation of collective ones because some may be more individually advantageous." Of course, he goes on to say, an individual employee may bargain and contract with the employer for some advantage not covered in the collective agreement, although he cannot barter away therefor any advantage secured him in the collective contract.

But when the real showdown comes, Justice Jackson admits that the net legal effect of advantageous individual contracts concurrent with a collective agreement is to be left to state courts in suits on such contracts and to the board in unfair labor practice proceedings. The Court refused to enforce that part of the board's order entirely eliminating these individual contracts, modifying it to lop off only those contracts that violated the policies of the act. Hence we see that while the Court frowns heavily on individual contracts purporting to exist alongside of collective agreements, it concedes for the time being the theoretical possibility that they are lawful.

This is a most troublesome subject. It seems inevitable that under a statute vesting the chosen representative of a majority of the employees with exclusive bargaining rights for them, these rights will some day be declared all-inclusive. For the distinction between exclusive *collective* bargaining rights and any other kinds of bargaining rights seems pregnant with mischief, as long as we are to have collective bargaining as the prevailing policy. Perhaps the only solace for the unusually competent employee is an incentive system which attaches a bonus premium to extrastandard production. But unions dislike this system and may be able to exclude from plants any consideration of such a trend.

In this field, one further development challenges our consideration. An employer recognized a labor union as the exclusive bargaining representative of his employees in a certain unit, 75 per cent of them having requested him to do so. The union proposed a contract providing for an increase in wages. And a date was set for collective bargaining. Two days before that date the employees who belonged to the union approached the employer and stated that they were not interested in the union if they could secure certain wage increases without it. The employer took this under consideration and told them shortly thereafter that they could have the requested increase. All of the union employees accepted the increase and informed the employer that they "did not need the union, and we would rather stay out." Later that day the employer informed the union representatives, who were not employees of his but were full-time union officials from outside, that the union no longer represented a majority of the employees in the unit and he would not negotiate with the union unless it were established otherwise by an election. On complaint of the union the board found that the employees' defection had been induced by the employer's conduct in dealing directly with them. Thereupon it ordered the employer to cease and desist from violating the appropriate parts of the act and to bargain with the union. This was the fairly recent case of *Medo Photo Supply Company v. NLRB.*

The Supreme Court upheld this order of the board. It did so not because the offer of increased wages came from the employer (which was not true, anyway) and not because the employer bargained with the employees only when their revocation of the union's authority was extended to include their agreement to abandon collective bargaining altogether. Rather, the Court said, the employer's vice was bargaining with the employees directly at all, after their proposal to break up the union to which they still belonged and which had not yet been repudiated by them, if he would give them an increase in wages. This was going over the head of the already recognized exclusive bargaining agent of the employees with a vengeance. Chief Justice Stone said for the Court: "That it is a violation of the essential principle of collective bargaining and an infringement of the Act for the employer to disregard the bargaining representative by negotiating with individual employees, whether a majority or a minority, with respect to wages, hours and working conditions was recognized by this Court in *J. I. Case Co. v. Labor Board.*" Such bargaining "would be subversive of the mode of collective bargaining which the statute has ordained." Here indeed was a rapid development in legal theory. Only seven weeks had elapsed between these two decisions of the Supreme Court.

The Court refused to state whether the employees were foreclosed for any particular length of time from revoking their designation of a bargaining representative or whether any special formalities were required for such revocation. It said simply that until effective revocation occurred, the employer had to bargain with such representative exclusively. The employer contended that if he withheld the requested increase from the employees, such course would have been as much a prounion influence as granting it was said to have been an antiunion influence. But the Court answered this by saying that his proper course was to have avoided bargaining directly with the men at all. And their consent to such bargaining did not make any difference because a public right only was involved, which their actions could not affect. Thus, while the board's order and the Court's decision may appear to be aimed at assisting an outside union that is not wanted in by either the employer or his employees, it is actually directed at vindicating the public interest in a stable labor relations procedure and at prevention of its abuse as a lever both to secure personal advantage and to encourage antiunionism. At the same time, it is apparent that there remains little, if any, possibility of individual employment contracts and collective agreements currently existing in the same bargaining units.

Closely related to these cases is another appearing about the same time, in which the Supreme Court declared that an employer was forbidden under the Railway Labor Act to vary the terms of a collective agreement, as it affected certain employees, by individual bargaining with them. This ruling was made in *Order of Railway Telegraphers v. Railway Express Agency, Inc.* A railway express company and a telegrapher's union had agreed that each employee should receive an additional sum per unit for every freight car of a certain type dispatched. Because of unforeseen traffic conditions, these extra payments threatened to become so huge that the company and the individual telegraphers agreed between themselves to relax the provision in the contract. Later these individual employees sought to have such extra sums paid them in conformance with the contract—in the case of one telegrapher amounting to around $40,000. The Court upheld awards by the adjustment board in their favor on the theory that this individual bargaining was unlawful and not binding on the employees, although it conceded that a similar modification of the contract, bargained between the company and the union, would have been proper and effective.

Similarly, it appears that an employer may not of his own motion grant wage increases to his employees, in the absence of bargaining with the union representing them, without violating the policies of the NLRA. Such unilateral action is a denial of collective bargaining and tends to discredit the union in the eyes of the employees, as it no doubt was intended to do. And in spite of the proviso in the act—"That any individual employee or a group of employees shall have the right at any time to present grievances to their employer"—it seems a foregone conclusion that the Supreme Court would regard an employer's adjustment of any such grievances directly, and not through the accredited bargaining agency, also a violation of the act. The principle of majority rule in collective bargaining carries far, and the Supreme Court is apparently determined to see that it is rendered effective in controlling the interests of employers and employees alike under collective agreements.

CHANGE OF UNION ALLEGIANCE

Another angle of the majority rule idea appears where the employees in a bargaining unit decide during the course of an agreement between the employer and an accredited union that they want another union to represent them in dealing with their employer. Congress was absolutely silent on this matter.

The board has undertaken with rather hard-boiled determination to fill in the gaps of the act in this respect. Here

its ultimate solution appears to be perfectly fair to all concerned, even if in particular cases it may seem to lean in the
direction either of the employer's or of the contracting union's
interest. A typical situation is the popular or unanimous decision by the employees in a unit, right in the middle of the
stated term of an existing agreement, to get rid of the accredited
union and to affiliate with another union. A majority of them,
through a committee armed with a petition, approach either
the employer or a board representative, or both, requesting
substitution of their new choice as the proper bargaining
agency. Less typical, perhaps, but nevertheless a frequent occurrence, is the decision of a majority or all of the employees
in a unit either to change unions or to forsake all union
representation, after such a union has been accredited to the
employer but before collective bargaining between this bargaining representative and the employer has culminated in a
contract or has even commenced.

When the board first dealt with cases of this sort, it was
under great pressure to adopt a theory of substitute unionism.
To support this theory of substitution, its proponents argued
that the board should make possible true and desired representation for the employees in a unit, as they wanted it at the
time their desire had crystallized. Of course, the intolerable
situation resulting from representation by a bargaining agency
that the men no longer want and that they have openly repudiated is apparent. After all, the union was only their agent,
so to speak. And ordinarily if a man loses faith in his agent,
he lets him go and gets another whom he can trust. Refusal
to allow substitution of unions would place too much emphasis
on the interests of the incumbent union, as such, and would be
neglecting the interests of the employees, who were all that
really mattered.

But there were important considerations militating against
this theory of substitution, not the least of which was consideration for the employer who has presumably secured rights
in the existing contract, on which he may have based his

plans for the term stated therein. Of course, his convenience in this respect could be served by insisting on the stipulated duration of the present contract, simply altering any union recognition clause to reflect the change in bargaining agency. It would not be so simple, however, to dispose of the accredited union's rights if substitution were to occur, assuming that the union is an outside organization prevalent in the particular industry involved.

Unions like the AF of L and CIO are, after all, enterprises which must conduct their affairs on some sort of businesslike basis. Such unions put a great deal of time, effort and expense into organizing plants and bargaining out contracts. They are not simply agents working on a commission basis, to be hired or fired at the will of their principals. As a matter of fact, it may be recalled from preceding chapters that a union has just as much interest in organizing a plant, for the benefit of the whole national union, as the employees in the plant have in securing the advantages of local collective representation. They stand to lose a considerable investment and much advantage by being summarily booted out in the middle of a contract term. Conceivably some assessment of damages to a rejected union might operate as a condition to substitution, but this would inevitably raise awkward financial problems.

But there are more potent considerations leading to a denial of substitution of this sort. The work of an already busy board would be tremendously increased by having to conduct additional representation proceedings, especially under what would inevitably be heated circumstances. Then, adoption of a theory of substitution would encourage pirating by out unions trying to get in. Actually, this is the connection in which the issue of substitution first arose—a CIO union working from outside having persuaded the employees in a unit to repudiate an AF of L union, right in the middle of a subsisting contract term, on the contention that it could do more for them than the incumbent union had done. Such a possibility of wholesale industrial warfare is not pleasant to contemplate. In any event, the board decided against the theory of substitution, taking the position that once the majority of the employees in a unit had made up their minds, they would have to stand by their choice for the duration of the contract, usually one year, just as any public electorate has to put up with their choice on election day. The time for reflection comes before the choice is made, and no intermediate change of mind is recognized except in extraordinary circumstances leading the board in its discretion to permit substitution—a situation perhaps analogous to grounds for impeaching an elected political representative of the people.

For some years the board has held rigorously to this view. And it accordingly insists that the employees' majority choice must stand, once it is made, even if they change their minds before bargaining has culminated in a contract or has even begun. So far, the Supreme Court has not spoken on this issue. The circuit courts of appeal have approved the board's position, intimating that employees in a unit may not abandon their deliberate majority choice until some reasonable time —probably a year, but possibly less—has elapsed. This salutary position will no doubt impress employees with the responsibilities entailed in their original choice of a bargaining representative. And it implies a future judicial confidence in the exercise of the board's discretion over such matters. This also reflects approval of the board's view that an employee election of a bargaining representative is not merely a choice of an agent for the conduct of personal business affairs but is, rather, a participation in a large scheme of industrial democracy, which carries with it all of the responsibility such a privilege should involve.

This policy the board extends to cover contracts with automatic renewal clauses, subject to reopening provisions which permit either the employer or the union, by timely notice, to end the contract at the expiration of the current term. The board has been lenient in recognizing circumstantial notice of intention to reopen contracts. But it is firm in compelling employees in a unit to continue adherence to the original bargaining agency, when notice of a desire to change bargaining representatives is filed after an automatic renewal clause has taken effect by its terms. Its policy as a whole enables the employees in a unit freely to substitute another union at the expiration of a normal contract term. And since nothing in currently existing law can prevent the employees from courting a new union during the term of the old contract or, for that matter, can prevent an out union from selling itself to the employees during this period, a little forethought enables a smooth and effective substitution at the end of the contract term, if it is desired.

THE EMPLOYER REFUSES TO DEAL WITH A UNION ALLEGED *not* TO REPRESENT A MAJORITY

Consistent with the board's position in all of these cases is its policy in the somewhat related situation, where an employer disclaims any obligation to bargain with a representative chosen by his employees because such union no longer represents a majority among them. All during the war this was a most troublesome issue. A union would win an election and be certified to the employer as the exclusive bargaining agency. Then the employer would refuse to bargain with the union, probably because he didn't like the particular union his men chose. Naturally this attitude would tend to discourage many of the employees. They would either drop out of the union or join up with another—one perhaps more to the employer's liking —in the hope that they could get something done. In such cases, the board has consistently refused to entertain petitions from either the employer or the out union to hold new elections, even if it can be demonstrated beyond doubt that a majority of the employees are no longer behind the certified union or have shifted their allegiance to the other union. Its position in this respect rests on the assumption that the employer's original refusal to bargain with the certified union was an unfair labor practice. And the evidence in such cases usually justifies the board's inference that the original refusal of the employer to bargain was calculated to cause defection among the employees by implying that their first choice of bargaining representative was unwise.

In *Franks Brothers Company v. NLRB* the Supreme Court upheld the board's position in these cases, recognizing that an employer's refusal to bargain "disrupts the employees' morale, deters their organizational activities, and discourages their membership in unions," and stating that "for these reasons, a requirement that union membership be kept intact during delays incident to hearings would result in permitting employers to profit from their own wrongful refusal to bargain." It suggests, however, that the employees themselves are not to be saddled with a permanent bargaining representative in such cases, without regard to new situations that may develop. In this connection it cited a circuit court decision, *Great Southern Trucking Company v. NLRB,* in which it was stated that after the certified union was given a chance to show what it could do in real bargaining with the employer, a majority of the employees might then be able to substitute a new union if they still desired to do so. "But," as that court declared, "until the Company purges itself of its unlawful conduct in violating our decree [to obey the board's order to bargain], the employees' true desires 'are matters of speculation and argument.'"

THE UNION REFUSES TO RESPECT A CERTIFICATION BY THE BOARD

When an outside union fails to respect the board's certification of another union duly chosen by the employees in a unit as their bargaining representative, real trouble often follows. Here occurs a head-on collision between the policies of the NLRA and the Norris-LaGuardia Act. The case of *NLRB v. Star Publishing Company* is a neat illustration in point.

A CIO union proceeds to go out and organize a newspaper company. An election is held under board auspices and the employees in the circulation department vote to become a part of the entire unit. There follows a contract between the certified union and the company. Then the AF of L teamsters' union demands from the company the right to represent the employees in the circulation department. When the company hesitates, the teamsters declare that they will refuse to allow any more papers to be delivered. This forces the company into action. It asks its circulation department employees if *they* can get the papers delivered. When they confess their inability to do the job, the company shifts them to other parts of the plant. Then their jobs in the circulation department are given to members of the teamsters' union.

This provokes a bitter complaint from the CIO union. In response to this, the board orders the company to fire the teamsters and put the original circulation men back in their old jobs. When the company stands pat, the board asks the Circuit Court of Appeals to enforce its order. Having no option under the law, this court then requires the company to obey the board's order, although it knows perfectly well that its compliance will spell the end of its operations. This was exactly what happened. As soon as their men were discharged and the old men were reinstated, the teamsters' union slapped on its boycott again and the company shut up shop.

The obvious reason for this is the irreconcilable conflict between the NLRA and the Norris-LaGuardia Act. Under the former statute both board and court were compelled to require the employer's observance of the CIO union's right to jurisdiction over the circulation room. On the other hand, under the anti-injunction act the federal courts are forbidden to enjoin defiance of or interference with the board certification by the out union, as long as its obstructive tactics are confined to conduct described in Section 4—striking, boycotting, and picketing. Thus, any union which competes for bargaining rights in a plant and loses a board-conducted election can then turn around and picket the plant or subject it to a boycott in an effort to impress the employees with the folly of their choice. Indeed, there are instances in which the defeated union has openly declared that if the employers, to whom the winning unions are certified, so much as presume to bargain and contract with the only unions lawfully entitled to recognition, they will subject them to economic pressures causing them great financial loss.

This is obviously a ridiculous situation; yet it is recognized by the Supreme Court as the only possible result under our federal statute law as it now stands. The Circuit Court of Appeals enforcing the board's order against the newspaper company readily acknowledged the employer's plight and remarked "that such an argument should be submitted to Congress but not to us." In view of recent Supreme Court decisions, however, it appears that the out union in a case of this type has no lawful interest to be served by such conduct, since both the employers and the employees are compelled to continue observance of the board's certification until the allotted contract period has expired or, if no bargaining has yet taken place, until it occurs and culminates in a contract. Since such pressure by the out union can serve no purpose but revenge, perhaps it should not be regarded as a labor dispute in any legitimate or statutory sense of that term. For in such a way alone can the federal courts surmount the restrictions of the Norris-LaGuardia Act and compel respect by injunction for the policies of the NLRA and for the board's certifications thereunder. Their only alternatives are to revive the illegal purpose doctrine—a recourse plainly incorrect under the anti-injunction act—or to leave things as they are. Congress could easily relax the Norris-LaGuardia Act to permit injunctions against this egregiously bad union conduct, perhaps allowing the out union some scope for the exercise of economic pressure toward the end of an existing contract term in order to persuade the employees concerned to change bargaining agencies.

DISPUTES BETWEEN UNIONS

The last case discussed is an instance of the new type of so-called jurisdictional dispute. That it is not properly termed a jurisdictional dispute at all is apparent from the issue involved. In the true jurisdictional conflict, the question is, which union is going to get certain available work—the carpenters or the machinists? But here, in what should properly be called an interunion dispute, the question is, who is going to represent certain employees—an AF of L or CIO or some independent union? This phenomenon is largely a consequence of the creation and development of the CIO. It has already been suggested that since Congress did not foresee such a gigantic rival to the AF of L when it enacted the NLRA in 1935, it could not very well have framed that statute properly to take care of the kinds of interunion disputes which have occurred. Even if Congress could have foreseen the conflicts between these two huge federations of unions, it is far from certain that it could appropriately have legislated against interunion disputes in a statute like the NLRA, or would have wanted to do so if it could. After all, Congress' chief concern in the act was to facilitate independent organization and to encourage collective bargaining. And interunion disputes have little connection with either of these policies.

Possibly the prohibition by the act of certain unfair *union* labor practices might have been feasible. However, unless the enforcement of such prohibitions were rigidly confined to insuring free organization of employees, by preventing unions from putting too much pressure on them at the organizational stage, the act would tend to lose its identity as a measure to guarantee union civil rights and would take on the appearance of a union control device. If such a control statute is required, it should be separately conceived and should be enforced either by a separate agency or directly through the courts, as the Sherman Act is supposed to be administered. For its purpose would be essentially different from that of the NLRA itself.

It is true that in some of the situations which have been discussed, interunion disputes are intimately concerned with and profoundly affect both initial organization of employees and subsequent collective bargaining. These are matters of direct concern under the act. Conceivably the board might undertake to administer sanctions against such practices, although private parties, if permitted to do so, could more easily procure injunctive relief directly from the courts. But suppose the AF of L carpenters' union boycotts prefabricated building material, refusing to let its members handle this product because it is made by employees organized in a CIO union. The object of this boycott might be to supplant the CIO union or to discourage the manufacture of prefabricated building materials, or both. Perhaps these objectives are not socially desirable and possibly Congress should outlaw the use of union economic pressure to achieve them. But it is hard to see how a sanction against the first of these two objectives would be consistent with any labor policy now current in this country. At any rate, it is not the sort of undertaking that the board could, or should be asked to, assume.

Aside from the courts, it is hard to imagine just what sort of forum could handle these cases. The danger of setting up any deterrents at all against interunion disputes might outweigh any advantages to be gained. Indeed, if unionism is to be accepted as a conventional form of enterprise, how can its conventional competitive techniques be suppressed any more than those of traditional business enterprises? All of these considerations apply with equal force to the old-fashioned jurisdictional disputes occurring between craft unions enrolled in the same federation, as well as to the new type of interunion power struggles developing between industrial unions in the same system, such as that recently looming between the United Automobile Workers and the United Farm Equipment Workers, both national CIO unions. The answer to the difficulties arising from the conflict mentioned above, between the AF of L carpenters and the CIO woodworkers, may lie in the extension of CIO organization to include unions offering labor to install CIO manufactured products. In any event, it is apparent that the act is not the proper vehicle, nor the board the proper forum, for the disposition of these matters, and the board has astutely left them for Congress and the courts to handle.

THE ORGANIZATION OF SUPERVISORY WORKERS

Another phase of the act, not as yet passed on by the Supreme Court, concerns the organization into unions of supervisory workers such as foremen. A plain reading of the act seems to indicate that any group of people who are employed by others in industry or gainful occupation, with the exception of agricultural and domestic labor, are to be regarded as employees for the purpose of enjoying the protection and privileges of its terms. For all one can tell on a straight reading, the provisions of the act are available to bookkeepers, professors and school teachers, plant superintendents of a widespread corporate organization, et cetera. Of course, Congress carefully stipulated that the act should not govern when the employer is the United States, any state or a political subdivision thereof, any railroad or other enterprise subject to the Railway Labor Act, or any labor organization. As to other employers, they are not covered by the act unless they are engaged in the vast field of commerce among the states. While these exceptions may seem numerous, it is manifest that the coverage of the act is most comprehensive.

Yet the board held until recently that it would not make its representation facilities available to supervisory workers in their attempts to organize and bargain collectively. Nevertheless, the board always defended such workers in their efforts to accomplish by themselves what it had refused to do for them, issuing complaints against employers guilty of interference with supervisors who attempted to create unions among themselves for the purpose of collective action. In exceptional instances, where the history of collective bargaining warranted such action, as in the maritime trade and in the printing industry, the board had even afforded its representation facilities under the act to supervisory workers.

It is apparent that the board has always recognized its statutory power under the act to treat supervisory employees exactly the same as any other employees in industry. At times this has seemed doubtful, in view of the emphasis placed on that provision of the act which leaves it up to the board to designate "the unit appropriate for the purposes of collective bargaining." But this section clearly reveals no intimation that Congress intended to deny any group of employees all of the privileges accorded under the act, including the benefits of representation proceedings. It merely recognizes the practical difficulties involved in individual situations concerning the size, pervasiveness, and functional nature of bargaining units from the angle of convenience in collective operations, leaving the exact *coverage* of the unit up to the board's discretion in each case.

Until recently the board claimed that this discretion was broad enough to let it veto the appropriateness of any particular type of employees to combine and to bargain collectively at all, as far as their right to invoke the provisions of the act was concerned. But a careful reading of the act makes this surmise seem entirely speculative. Naturally, Congress was not acting in a vacuum when it passed the NLRA. It knew that management in the plants affected would have no great desire to organize and bargain collectively with itself. No need of such an extraordinary undertaking existed, if indeed it would be possible at all. Nevertheless it is hard to believe that Congress did not intend to afford all of the act's facilities to any class of workers included in the defined term employees, as long as such workers themselves felt the need for such facilities and requested them.

It has been argued that since the term employer includes "any person acting in the interest of an employer, directly or indirectly," all supervisory employees are in fact employers, and hence are not eligible as employees for the protection of the act. This argument is supported by the board's customary ruling that unfair labor practices exercised by supervisors, including foremen, are automatically attributed to the employer, whether or not such practices were authorized. But it seems most reasonable to conclude that the section defining employer was intended only to make employers responsible for the conduct of their supervisors, in order to obviate an easy evasion of the act through the difficulty of proving top management's authorization of foremen's conduct toward production employees. To exclude supervisory workers such as foremen from the protection of the act, on the basis of the definition of the word employer, would seem an extraordinary inference in light of the competing broad definition of the word employee, particularly in view of the apparent purpose of Congress' definition of the former term.

Congressional intent is not a thing to be lightly construed. It is highly questionable administrative technique for a board charged with effecting a statutory command to narrow its scope on the ground of discretion. That is the wrong way for the board to learn from the courts the real scope of its administrative power, since the party aggrieved then has no way in which he can secure judicial review of the board's position. The correct procedure is for the board to assert power in close cases and to have its proper functions defined by court decisions which pin the board down to a prescribed course on the basis of judicial interpretations of Congress' intent.

Actual conditions in industry show a possible need for collective representation of supervisory workers. Yet even if this were doubtful, it has never been the custom in this country to make workers pass a needs test as a condition to collective action. Of course, it may be bad policy to permit organization on the management side of the fence, particularly as equality of bargaining power between production workers and management seems already to have been achieved without whittling down management's strength any more by dividing it against itself. Foremen and supervisory workers, although low down in the scale of management, are nevertheless management's direct contact with the production workers and are the only practicable means of directly relating management's policies to the working force. Employers have a hard enough time, as it is, dealing with production workers' unions.

If foremen organize for collective bargaining and choose as their representatives the same unions that represent the production workers—a perfectly tenable procedure under the act, as it reads, and one already in effect with plant guard unions— top management would certainly be hard pressed. It could escape some implications of this impasse by appointing personal representatives to deal directly with unions over grievances. Even then it would be likely to get from its foremen colored and biased versions of what had happened in the plant, and it would have lost almost all direction over actual operations. And if the foremen created independent unions to represent themselves collectively, such unions would be under constant temptation to work along with the production workers' unions, such as co-ordinating strikes and not crossing each other's picket lines.

Indeed, such co-operation might be thrust upon them. The head of one large union of production workers has publicly declared that the first time the foremen's union pulls a strike in any of his plants, shutting down operations when his men want to work, his union will either break the foremen's union or take it over—lock, stock and barrel. On the other hand, the foremen have no real voice in shaping management policy and are at best in a sort of unenviable limbo between real management and the workers. Although they have usually fared well in an economic sense, they may still be permitted to feel that they are the forgotten men in the huge units of industry in modern mass production and to take collective action for more recognition of the abilities which placed them above the hourly paid employees.

Organization of supervisory workers is really a live issue and it is charged with dynamite. Congress has started something in the act which has no easily perceptible logical limit. A majority of the board has finally concluded that foremen may enjoy all of the facilities of the act, including representation proceedings. And it has taken this step somewhat hesitantly, hinting at possible board control over subsequent activities of foremen's unions, through the exercise of what it calls de-certification, if such unions abuse the privilege of collective action. This suggestion of control over the conduct of a certified union certainly invites speculation on just what the board thinks its powers are. A majority of the board's members had until recently narrowed the unqualified guaranty of the act concerning "designation of representatives of their own choosing" by disclaiming any intention of certifying a union already representing production workers in a plant as the agency to represent the foremen in the same plant. But it is probably only a matter of time until even this restriction on the free choice of organized supervisors to organize as they please is generally removed.

So far, it appears, no group of supervisory workers in a manufacturing plant has asked the board to go quite this far. The supervisory, clerical and technical employees in the soft coal industry, however, have put this point up to the board and have secured a favorable decision. These employees have never been included in the bargaining units comprising the production and maintenance workers, which units are represented by John L. Lewis' United Mine Workers of America. They have organized in an allegedly separate union called the United Clerical, Technical and Supervisory Employees of America. While this union is nominally separate and independent, it is chartered by District 50 of the UMWA and hence is under the tutelage of the production workers' union.

The board, with one member dissenting, has apparently as

a matter of discretion allowed this virtual affiliation of a supervisory workers' unit with the same union representing the production workers in the industry. Although its decision not to
have done so would have been understandable and would have
made a certain amount of sense, yet it would have implied an
arbitrary and somewhat questionable interpretation of the act
as it now reads. Indeed, this whole matter of supervisory workers' unions is a critical one. And until the Supreme Court has a
chance to pass on it and to define the extent to which Congress
has committed itself in allowing employees to select unions of
their own choosing, it is perhaps too early to contend that Congress should have legislated more carefully and should now
hasten to clarify the act in this respect by a suitable amendment.
In the meantime the *Packard* and *Jones & Laughlin* cases, involving this matter, are on their way up to the Supreme Court.
At the same time Congress has passed the Case bill depriving
supervisory workers of the act's representation facilities, leaving
them to the primitive organizational process of trial by combat.

CIVIL RIGHTS UNDER THE ACT—THE EMPLOYERS' FREEDOM
OF SPEECH AND THE EMPLOYEES' RIGHT OF ASSOCIATION—
CLOSED SHOPS AND OPEN UNIONS

Another phase of board policy deals with the civil rights of employers and workers in connection with organization and collective bargaining under the act. From the very inception of
the act, the board has taken the position that an employer must
not interfere with the organizational aspirations of his employees, although outside unions have remained at liberty to
speak freely to them in ways best calculated to induce their
affiliation. Of course, an employer's interest in the organizational plans of his employees is manifest. It is not surprising
that it has been impossible for many employers to keep silent
on these matters. But when they have spoken to their employees, or have put statements in their pay envelopes and no-
tices around the plants, concerning the worthlessness or wisdom

of organization as well as the propriety of one kind of union as against another, with comments on the propaganda of unions aspiring to representative rights, the board has reserved the right to treat such conduct as unfair labor practices.

Employers ordered by the board to discontinue such practices believe that they are being denied their constitutional rights of free speech. But recourse to the courts has shown merely that employers cannot use the cloak of constitutionally guaranteed freedom of speech to cover their attempts to discredit unionism or any particular union. At the same time the courts have made it plain that an employer is perfectly free to remind his employees that in organizing and selecting a union to bargain for them they are making a solemn choice, allowing him to comment in a dispassionate fashion on such things as the Wage Stabilization Act and on their past relationship together, as long as he makes it clear that the choice of a bargaining representative still lies in their hands and that he will abide by it honestly.

The board executes this policy in particular cases pursuant to its discretion, which is the only way it can practicably proceed. A blanket denial of employers' rights to speak to their employees on matters of such mutual interest would pervert real freedom of speech. Furthermore it would create an unbalanced relationship between a group of employees and their employer, on the one hand, and between these same employees and outside unions "wanting in," on the other. An absolute freedom for employers to say anything they wished to their employees, either bluntly and crudely or skillfully concealed behind protestations of impartiality, would imperil the policies of the act. As long as the board's exercise of discretion in these cases remains subject to judicial review, there is little real danger to anyone's constitutional rights of free speech or freedom of association in this quarter.

A moment's reflection indicates that implicit in the closed shop is the issue of the individual employee's right of association upon terms mutually satisfactory to himself and to those with whom he might be associated. This aspect of the civil rights of employees has an important bearing on the board's powers and administrative techniques, and it is well illustrated by the Supreme Court's decision in *Wallace Corporation v. NLRB.*

Here, two unions, an independent and a CIO union, were disputing over bargaining rights in a small plant in West Virginia. In order to facilitate settlement of this dispute, the board approved an agreement between the two unions and the employer to hold what is called a consent election, dismissing as part of this truce certain unfair labor charges pending against the employer. This device enables the board, with the consent of all parties concerned, to allow an opportunity for the choice of a bargaining representative without first having to iron out pending disputed issues such as unfair labor practice charges. It is a time-saving device, well justified in view of the board's tremendously large agenda. No harm can ordinarily attend its use, as long as all parties interested consent to it in advance.

At any rate, the election ensued and the independent union won. Thereupon it received immediate certification from the board to the employer as the exclusive bargaining representative. In the bargaining which followed, the employer granted to the independent a closed shop which meant, of course, that all employees in the plant must belong to the contracting union as a condition of continued employment. Those employees who belonged to the CIO union thereupon applied for membership in this independent, which accepted some of these applications but turned down others, apparently because of their militant CIO activities. Because they were refused admission to the union, these rejected applicants filed a complaint before the board.

In the proceedings which followed the board came close to accusing the employer of virtual connivance in advance with the independent union. Indeed, the board found as a fact that when the employer granted the closed shop to the independent, he knew that the independent planned to exclude certain of

the CIO employees from membership, thus insuring their discharge from the plant. This employer, of course, took the position that under the appropriate proviso in the act, he had no
choice but to discharge the employees who had complained to
the board because they did not belong to the union enjoying
the advantage of the closed shop provision. He disclaimed any
right to interfere with the manner in which the independent
administered its business, contending that he was legally obliged
under the contract to take the list of union members, as the
independent gave it to him, and to act accordingly.

The board, however, formally found that the employer had
been guilty of two unfair labor practices. First, he had "set up
and maintained" the independent "to frustrate the threatened
unionization of [his] plant by the CIO." Second, he had agreed
to the closed shop provision with foreknowledge that the independent would use it to exclude certain of the former CIO
members from employment in the plant, by refusing them membership in the independent. On the basis of these findings, the
board ordered the employer to reinstate the discharged employees with back pay, to abrogate the contract and to disestab-
lish the independent, denying it future recognition in any way.
The Circuit Court of Appeals, concluding that the board's
findings were supported by substantial evidence, gave judgment
enforcing this order. The Supreme Court agreed to review the
case "because of the importance to the administration of the
Act of the questions involved."

Speaking for the majority of the Supreme Court which sustained the board's order, Justice Black observed that the settlement agreement among the parties, leading to the consent election, "plainly implied that the old employees could retain their
jobs with the company simply by becoming members of which-
ever union would win the election." He went on to show that
prior to the execution of the final contract, the business manager of the independent had told the employer that the independent must use the contract to protect itself against boring
from within by CIO-minded employees, whose membership

might ultimately endanger the independent's majority control. Then he observed that the evidence submitted to the board clearly supported its findings that the employer had systematically engaged in unfair labor practices *before* the agreement concerning the consent election, as well as subsequently thereto and prior to certification itself.

In response to the employer's and the independent's objections that the board could not go behind this settlement agreement and certification, Justice Black declared that nothing in the act or in administrative procedure generally prevented it from doing so, while considerations of public interest in carrying out the policies of the act occasionally made such a recourse imperative. He dismissed as irrevelant the judicial doctrines prevailing in ordinary litigation between private parties, which compel them to maintain a position once it is taken on any aspect of a case. Such notions of estoppel, however appropriate they might be in litigation between parties dealing at arm's length over some disputed private interest, he believed inapplicable to the situation where an overworked administrative board, trying to speed up its work, invites a course of action on the basis of assumed facts in the hope that a final settlement of a troublesome dispute would more promptly ensue. This was especially true, he thought, where the board is administering a public right in the interests of public convenience. He entertained no doubts whatever concerning the propriety of the board's inquiring behind the settlement agreement and certification when it was put on notice by an unfair labor practice which occurred subsequent to these events.

Concerning the employer's denial of such subsequent unfair labor practice, in view of its commitment under the closed shop provision of the contract and of the proviso in the act which tolerates the closed shop, Justice Black was brief and to the point. No such argument is acceptable, he declared, even conceding lack of control by the employer over the union's admission requirements, if it is offered to sustain the conclusion that "the contract is valid and the company must discharge non-union

members, regardless of the union's discriminatory purpose, and
the company's knowledge of such purpose." A bargaining agent
is required under the act to represent the interests of *all* workers in a unit, not just its own or those of its members. He conceded that such a union may require membership for continued
employment if it has secured a closed shop provision in its contract with the employer. But it must allow all of the employees
in the unit to become members. Otherwise the whole policy of
the act would be defeated. And as for the case in hand, it was
as much a violation of the act for the company to secure the
discharge of the CIO minority through collaboration with the
independent as it would have been for it to discharge them directly because of their union interests. "To permit it to do so
by indirection, through the medium of a 'union' of its own
creation, would be to sanction a readily contrived mechanism
for evasion of the Act."

A substantial minority of the Court dissented in this case.
After outlining the background of bitter dispute preceding the
arrangement for the consent election, Justice Jackson, for the
minority, pointed out that the CIO union had first suggested
the consent election to the employer. Its proposal was made on
the understanding that "when we prove a majority and become
the exclusive bargaining agency for all your employees, that as
a condition of employment all eligible employees must become
members of Local Union 129, U.C.W.O.C.," CIO. Thereupon,
with the approval of the board, the company agreed to the consent election and to grant the winning union a union shop,
which all parties conceded to mean the closed shop. The independent rigidly held the employer to this commitment, and
the employer seemed bound to comply with his promise to concede the closed shop. That the employer knew of the independent's intention not to admit the CIO members into their union
was in Justice Jackson's opinion unimportant, because he felt
that the union's plans were none of the employer's business. Of
course, the board made them the employer's affair by penalizing
him for having granted the closed shop and for having there-

after complied with this provision of the contract, in view of his knowledge that the independent planned to get rid of the CIO men. But the minority thought this course to be a dangerous assault on the policies of an act which required an employer to keep his nose entirely out of union affairs.

According to them, the board might properly have qualified the arrangement for the consent election, or even the later certification of the independent, with the warning that it would retain jurisdiction over the complaints of unfair labor practices pending before the consent election was held and would prosecute them if the victorious union used the closed shop provision in its contract to get rid of fellow employees by refusing them membership. But the board did not do this. Instead, by its approval of the consent election, it lulled the employer into a sense of obligation to do the very thing he had done. Then it placed the burden on the employer to police the independent union and see that it observed the spirit of the act. This, the dissenting justices thought, was very hard on the employer, declaring that the least the Court could do was to hold the board to its word.

Justice Jackson had more to say of a most fundamental and arresting nature. He described the closed shop as a device permitting a union to exercise on fellow workers certain discriminatory influences which, while "unfair when exerted by the employer in his own interest, . . . are fair and lawful when enforced by him as an instrument of the union itself." And he continued: "A closed shop is the ultimate goal of most union endeavor, and not a few employers have found it a stabilizer of labor relations by putting out of their shops men who were antagonistic to the dominant union, thus ending strife for domination. It puts the employment office under a veto of the union, which uses its own membership standards as a basis on which to exclude men from employment." In his opinion Congress gave the board no power "to supervise union membership or to deal with union practices, however unfair they may be to members, to applicants, to minorities, to other unions, or to employers. This may or may not have been a mistake, but it was no oversight."

If the board had nevertheless exercised its discretionary power in advance by making the validity of the certification contingent on an open union under any closed shop contract, he observed, its order might have been proper in the absence of express authority from Congress. As it was, it went too far. The result of this decision, he added, might appear to be a victory for labor, since the employer was required to make back-pay awards of several thousands of dollars. But in reality it is a setback for organized labor, as it compels employers to pry into the affairs of all unions seeking the advantages of the closed shop, placing upon them the task of policing union activities at the peril of incurring the wrath of the board if they fail to do so.

The real fight between the majority and the minority of the Supreme Court in this case concerns the administrative techniques of the board less than it does its powers under the act. But the statement of the minority seems rather farfetched, although the employer certainly appears to have been badly used. It was, perhaps, his bad luck that the only criterion he was allowed, by which to guide his own conduct under the act, was a conscience nicely attuned to the plainly stated policies of Congress as set forth in the act and as construed up to that time by the Supreme Court. Naturally, businessmen like to behave in accordance with fairly clear-cut legal standards. The employer in this case seemed to have conducted himself righteously in strict accordance with the letter of the law as it appears in the books. But now he knows that the act, and the board's administration of it, are not to be legalistically construed in accordance with good lawyerlike traditions. Now he knows that the policy stated by Congress as the introduction to the substantive measures of the act is an important and integral part of the act itself.

It is hard to believe that this decision will compel employers to pry into union affairs or to police closed shop contracts. Few cases are likely to arise where an employer will have skated on such thin ice as this employer did, with apparent realization of the fact. What the board did here may seem harsh and somewhat inconsistent, but it was nonetheless inescapable. It had dismissed the pending unfair labor practice charges and agreed to the election on the assumption that a bitter dispute would be settled. Even if it foresaw the possibility of a closed shop contract for the emergent independent, it could hardly be blamed for not anticipating a closed union, as well, and for not guarding against it in advance. Such foresight is required of corporation and conveyancing lawyers when they are playing the game of business. Why should the board be so mechanically disabled from insisting upon compliance with the spirit of a law that embodies, to quote Justice Jackson in another case, "the recognition that the opportunity to earn his support is not alone the concern of the individual but is the problem which all organized societies must contend with and conquer if they are to survive?" The board's duty is to maintain the public interest in freedom from the disruptive effects of labor disputes. Had it acted differently in this case, it is manifest that the dispute at the plant in question would have been renewed with bitterness.

A majority of the Court clearly believed that the board had followed the only course consistent with the policies of the act. While this majority rested its decision on evidence showing that the employer had deliberately lent his co-operation to a union of his own fostering, in order to get rid of the undesirable employees, it nevertheless went far to suggest that no union may practice discrimination against fellow employees by denying them membership in a closed shop secured under the provisions of the act. How the Court thinks this sort of thing can be prevented when the employers in question are innocent of co-operative unfair labor practices remains uncertain and, perchance, to be seen. Where such employer practices do occur, the Court leaves the board free to press the matter. But where they do not occur, it is difficult to see *how* the board can proceed against *whom*, since the act has no sanctions against labor organizations and neither mentions nor forbids unfair labor practices by unions. Obviously, the dissenting members of the Court fear a doctrine under which employers will observe the terms of a closed shop provision at their peril. If they are right, then employers will have an excellent reason for combatting the closed shop with all their resources. Then those who succumb will be compelled to share with their unions the task of checking on the eligibility of every applicant for union membership.

Perhaps the Supreme Court may be willing to invent a doctrine compatible with some of the civil rights developments under the Constitution, to be discussed hereafter, under which it will entertain suits brought by excluded employees directly against offending unions. What the nature of such suits might be is highly speculative. In the meantime, unless Congress takes this situation under advisement with a view to creating direct sanctions forbidding unfair practices by unions against employees—to be administered by the board, by a new agency, or directly enforceable in the courts—some members of the Supreme Court not unreasonably fear that the employers concerned, however innocent, will become the objects of attack for having tolerated unconstitutional practices in their midst.

CHAPTER XII

THE CONSTITUTIONAL AREA OF ECONOMIC CONFLICT—PICKETING AS FREE SPEECH

> Because I have come to the conclusion that both the common law of a State and a statute of the United States declare the right of industrial combatants to push their struggle to the limits of the justification of self-interest, I do not wish to be understood as attaching any constitutional or moral sanction to that right. All rights are derived from the purposes of the society in which they exist; above all rights rises duty to the community. The conditions developed in industry may be such that those engaged in it cannot continue their struggle without danger to the community. But it is not for judges to determine whether such conditions exist, nor is it their function to set the limits of permissible contest and to declare the duties which the new situation demands. This is the function of the legislature which, while limiting individual and group rights of aggression and defense, may substitute processes of justice for the more primitive method of trial by combat.—Brandeis, J., dissenting in *Duplex Printing Press Company v. Deering*, 1921.

IN OUR society the legislatures should be the sole arbiters of policy in regulating the self-help activities of labor unions. Our courts should be occupied in construing and applying the law, without undertaking to make it as well. Of course, when they find that their predecessors have been mistaken in interpreting the law, they can hardly be blamed for overruling the older decisions. But even this is unsettling. In effect it is really changing the law under the guise of re-establishing the true law. Certainly this seems to be so when the courts overrule old precedents on the basis of social and political changes which have occurred during the intervening years. According to strict judicial tradition, such changes in the law should be made only

334

by the legislatures, but all judges do not agree with this limitation on their powers. These nonconformists admit that they should not *change* existing law. They deny that an old decision *is* law when in their opinion it ceases to reflect present social needs. If enough of these nonconformists sit together as a court of last resort, they have the power to discard the established precedent and to say what the true law now is, and that is their official job. Hence, it is apparent that the tradition against judge-made law really means no more than the judges want it to mean. In the meantime, our highest courts wield an enormous power over all of us, enjoying a position which enables them to leave the imprint of their own social and economic beliefs on society in the name of that much abused and misunderstood institutional standard of conduct and behavior—the law.

We are supposed to live "under a government of laws and not of men." In our federal government, Congress is the appropriate body under the Constitution to make our national policies and to crystallize them into law. In each state the legislature performs a similar function locally. Who is to say what these respective spheres of legislative influence are? The theory is that the federal Constitution makes this clear. The practice is that the Supreme Court sets these boundaries, doing so in the name of the Constitution. In the commerce clause of the Constitution the founding fathers probably attempted to give the federal government far more legislative power over the internal affairs of states than a states' rights dominated Supreme Court would ever concede. Hence the Court has prevented Congress from exercising its full powers under the Constitution, allowing it only such scope as it could enjoy on the tether of the interstate commerce theory. It is true that in recent years the Court has found this tether to be fairly elastic. But apparently it still thinks that Congress is not sufficiently mature to read the Constitution on its own.

Even more restrictive has been the Court's refusal to let Congress and state legislatures pass valid laws aimed at correcting what these policy-making bodies regarded as social evils. While it occasionally conceded that some of these attempted changes were proper exercises of power, the Court more frequently declared them invalid because it thought them to be deprivations of liberty or property "without due process of law." Yet these statutes involved no more nor less due process than many other statutes validly modifying interests of liberty and property in the Court's opinion. The accuracy of this observation is illustrated by recent decisions of the Court declaring valid several types of statutes consistently discarded as invalid by previously constituted majorities of the same Court. In other words, the constitutionality of social legislation has turned out to be a function of at least two variables—the meaning of the phrase due process at any particular time in any particular context, and the shifting personnel of the Supreme Court, with the different social and economic views of the various judges.

Until recent years, the customary pattern had been for a relatively conservative Supreme Court to deny the constitutionality of liberal social legislation enacted by Congress or state legislatures on behalf of what might roughly be called minority and underprivileged groups. Much of this legislation affected labor. Although most of it concerned such things as minimum wages, maximum hours and child labor—matters in which unions used to display little interest, because they dealt only in marginal standards affecting nonorganizable labor—occasionally some of it did touch unionism, such as laws against the antiunion or so-called "yellow dog contracts." Although there were scattered state laws making union self-help techniques criminal, and while the Sherman Act in the federal arena had a similar effect, it apparently never occurred to the Supreme Court to question the constitutional validity of these laws. From the Court's point of view, the real question was not whether legislatures could *deny* to minority and underprivileged groups their alleged but somewhat dubious rights to help themselves out of their economic plight. Rather the question was whether or not legislatures had the constitutional power to give them a boost by creating previously nonexistent rights in their favor. The constitutional presumption seems to have been against the underprivileged and those who supported them, while it was in favor of those who were against them from the start.

During the last few years, the Supreme Court seems to have become aware of what might be called an erstwhile dormant potentiality within the Constitution. It has discovered a power within itself to reverse the traditional attitude of former incumbents on the Court toward legislation affecting minorities and the underprivileged. Now it embraces all manner of social legislation in its stride, and it reserves its constitutional strictures for legislatures attempting to deny the assertion of rights by those referred to above as minorities or the underprivileged, including organized labor. Apparently the present Court is quite as sensitive to the temper of the times as the personnel of that institution always have been. At any rate, the Court has within the last few years exhibited a tendency not only to foster legislation directed at improving the conditions of labor and strengthening unions, but also to invalidate legislation aimed in the opposite direction—all in its role as guardian and interpreter of the Constitution. While the ultimate goal of the Court is a matter of speculation, its progress to date, as reflected in the picketing cases, affords an exceedingly provocative basis for a few shrewd guesses.

CHANGING VIEWS ABOUT PICKETING—THE *Senn* CASE

Not many years ago picketing of any kind was generally held to be unlawful as a tort. Indeed, in 1909 the California Supreme Court in *Pierce v. Stablemen's Union* indicated this as the basis for holding illegal what it regarded as a perfectly proper secondary boycott, merely because an appeal to consumers had been communicated through a picket line. Apparently it made no difference to courts generally that the picketing was by strikers who were attempting to secure higher wages, or by strangers to an employer who were attempting to organize his plant—so-called stranger picketing. Nor did it seem to matter that the picketing was peaceful—that is, without violence, fraud, or libel. By the 1920's most courts perceived a difference between peaceful picketing by strikers, who were conceded to have some interest to serve, and by outsiders, who "had no legitimate interest" to serve because they were bent only on organization. The former was generally regarded as lawful and the latter, unlawful—a dichotomy suggestive of the way in which various courts had lined up on strikes for the closed shop as against strikes for higher wages. Toward the end of that decade, however, several of our liberal courts had taken the position that all peaceful picketing was lawful, conceding that the same kind of interest was served by stranger picketing as by the strike for the closed shop—the elimination of competition between union and non-union labor standards. The law reports published during this period reveal a picture of complete confusion on peaceful picketing. While some of our appellate courts were stoutly declaring that there was and could be no such thing as peaceful picketing and that inherent in all picketing lay a threat of force and violence, other courts were firmly maintaining that picketing could be and frequently was peaceful and free from all suggestion of violence and that, as such, it was merely a form of communication analogous to speech.

All through this period it was taken for granted by most people that picketing could be forbidden or restrained and that its toleration in any form was a matter of judicial or legislative grace. Certainly the manner in which the Supreme Court had grudgingly conceded in 1921 that there could be such a thing as a limited peaceful picketing on the part of strikers and, possibly, by laid-off former employees, fairly implied this to be true. Of course, there had been occasional intimations that peaceful picketing should be protected under the sheltering category of "freedom of speech." Yet it is doubtful whether many impartial people took this notion seriously or regarded it as more than rhetoric.

In 1937, Justice Brandeis made everyone give this matter serious thought by an assertion he made in *Senn v. Tile Layers'*

Protective Union, a case arising under Wisconson's "little Nor-ris-LaGuardia Act." Senn was a nonunion tiling contractor who conducted from his home a two-bit enterprise with the aid of a couple of helpers. In 1935, for instance, his net earnings from this business were about $1500, half of which was attributable to work with his own hands. The tile layers' union proposed that he unionize his business. Senn was willing to co-operate with the union by signing up his helpers, but he himself could not join under its rules and still continue to work on his own jobs. Indeed, he was not even eligible for membership in the union as a journeyman worker because he had never served an apprenticeship under a master tiler. As his business was so small that he could not continue to operate it unless he himself were allowed to work on his own jobs, he refused to accept the un-ion's proposal.

The union, on the other hand, took the position that he should not contract for jobs as an entrepreneur and at the same time work on them as a tiler, because he would then be depriv-ing a union tiler of employment. Furthermore, continuance of his business as a nonunion tiler was in their opinion detrimental to their interests because it undermined the labor standards established by the union. Therefore the union picketed Senn's home and the various premises at which he had undertaken til-ing jobs. As a result, he found himself virtually out of work and he brought a suit to secure an injunction against this peaceful stranger picketing. Under the state anti-injunction act the trial court denied Senn's request, and he appealed.

The Wisconsin Supreme Court affirmed the judgment below, holding that the picketing which ensued was not enjoinable under their anti-injunction act, a provision of which rendered all nonenjoinable conduct lawful for all purposes. Senn there-upon appealed this decision to the Supreme Court on the ground that the state anti-injunction act was unconstitutional. This appeal was doubly important, since on its outcome infer-entially depended the constitutionality of the Norris-LaGuardia Act itself, upon which the Wisconsin statute had been modeled.

In a five-four decision a majority of the Supreme Court held the state act constitutional, affirming the judgment in favor of the union.

When the Wisconsin court had upheld the validity of the state anti-injunction act in this case, it had also decided that the union's conduct was lawful for all purposes under the statute. The Supreme Court in affirming this decision merely declared that a state act having that effect in a stranger picketing case of this sort was not going too far as a matter of constitutionality. Justice Brandeis said, in part:

"Clearly the means which the statute authorizes—picketing and publicity—are not prohibited by the Fourteenth Amendment. Members of a union might, without special statutory authorization by a State, make known the facts of a labor dispute, for freedom of speech is guaranteed by the Federal Constitution. The State may, in the exercise of its police power, regulate the methods and means of publicity as well as the use of public streets. If the end sought by the unions is not forbidden by the Federal Constitution, the State may authorize working men to seek to attain it by combining as pickets, just as it permits capitalists and employers to combine in other ways to attain their desired economic ends."

This statement, and particularly the second sentence, has been sadly misconstrued by most American lawyers. They read Brandeis as having said that picketing—at least, peaceful picketing—is freedom of speech entitled to the guaranties of the federal Constitution. But a re-reading of this quotation will show that he did not say that at all or even imply it. He said simply that unions may make known the facts of a labor dispute, as a matter of free speech—a constitutional right they naturally enjoy with all other Americans—without saying *how* they may do this. He had just said that there is nothing so obviously wrong or inherently illegal about "picketing and publicity" that would prohibit the state under the federal Constitution from making it a nonenjoinable and lawful technique.

This statement he apparently believed necessary in view of

the fact that a state law suddenly making libel or assault and battery lawful would almost certainly be declared unconstitutional. The most he did was to concede that peaceful picketing was not that bad and that it was sufficiently innocuous so that a state legislature, having the power to "regulate the methods and means of publicity as well as the use of public streets," was free under the federal Constitution to use this power to permit unions to communicate the facts of a labor dispute by picketing. In other words, granting that unions are entitled as a matter of right under the Constitution to enjoy freedom of speech in disseminating information, the state legislature is not going too far under the 14th amendment when it declares that one of the ways in which they may enjoy this privilege is by peaceful picketing.

What Justice Brandeis actually said, therefore, is a far cry, indeed, from the proposition that peaceful picketing is a form of constitutionally guaranteed freedom of speech. Actually, he intimated that this was a somewhat dubious proposition, but declared nevertheless that a majority of the Supreme Court would not deny a state's power to make picketing a permissible form of communication if that is the way that state wanted it as a matter of local policy. The minority of the court, however, thought that the state no more had the power to do this under the due process clause than it would have had to pass a law legalizing libel or assault and battery. At best, the actual issue in this case was close enough, since even peaceful picketing had always been under a cloud.

Thornhill v. Alabama

It was somewhat astonishing, therefore, to see the Supreme Court in 1940 come out with a decision in *Thornhill v. Alabama* that peaceful picketing is a form of speech entitled to constitutional protection and that under the 14th amendment no state legislature could pass a valid law prohibiting it, because such a statute would be a denial of freedom of speech.

Alabama had passed a statute putting picketing on a par with loitering and making it a misdemeanor. As a consequence of his activities on the picket line, one Byron Thornhill was sentenced either to three days' imprisonment or to pay a fine of $100 and costs. After his conviction under this statute had been affirmed by the state supreme court, he appealed to the Supreme Court on constitutional grounds. Thereupon the Supreme Court told Alabama, and any other state interested, that they were not allowed to make peaceful picketing unlawful, even if they wanted to do so as a matter of local policy. Thus, within the brief span of three years peaceful picketing—a concept dismissed by many courts as a contradiction in terms and regarded as tortious in some or all of its contexts—suddenly became transformed not only into something that was proper and lawful but also something that was above the law.

The Court's general method of approach, while not exactly orthodox, was certainly reasonable enough. Justice Murphy noted that in the 1st amendment to the Constitution, Congress is forbidden to pass any law "abridging the freedom of speech, or of the press." While the 14th amendment—which operates as a constitutional control over states—says nothing about freedom of speech, it forbids any state to pass or enforce any law abridging the "privileges and immunities of citizens" and goes on to say that no state shall "deprive any person of life, liberty, or property, without due process of law." He then remarked that it was proper in defining the word "liberty" in the 14th amendment, to refer to the 1st amendment to see what such liberties are. In this way freedom of speech is read into the 14th amendment as one of the liberties of which a state may not arbitrarily deprive any person. So far, then, it is plain that no state may constitutionally pass a law denying freedom of speech. The question then becomes, does a state statute prohibiting even peaceful picketing deny this protected freedom of speech? Obviously, the answer to this question depends upon whether or not peaceful picketing is, in itself, merely speech and nothing more. The Supreme Court must be understood to have decided that it *is* speech—a pure matter of communicating ideas or information—and nothing more.

Of course, ordinary speech is a vehicle for committing some unlawful acts, such as libel and fraud. Thus it is apparent that quiet and orderly picketing may be a medium for committing the same torts, as when picketers carry libelous or fraudulent placards. Naturally, the Court concedes that some instances of picketing may be prohibited, as when it is accompanied by violence or threats of violence, fraud, libel, et cetera, just as a state may prohibit any "wrongs" committed through the medium of speech. But when truly conventional speech—and this includes platform and soap-box talks, placards and handbills, newspaper and periodical matter, skywriting and radio addresses, and books like this one—is devoted to the frank discussion of anything, regardless of how annoying or even harmful it may be to some people, it cannot constitutionally be suppressed or penalized as such if it does not contain any element which would place it within one of the settled categories of illegality, such as libel or fraud.

Does this necessarily mean that our courts and legislatures are forbidden to recognize or create any new categories of illegality under which otherwise lawful speech may be penalized? Apparently not, for speaking the truth may occasionally invite severe constitutional reprisals in times of war. Both courts and legislatures have successfully undertaken to make unlawful certain instances of speech containing true statements about the private affairs of others. And under some sort of category called unfair competition, certain branches of our state and federal governments are tending to prevent business enterprisers from adversely criticizing competitors' wares.

Aside from these exceptional situations, however, the constitutional presumption is against the creation of new categories of illegality covering the medium of speech. The reason for this is plain. We believe as a people that there is no irrevocably established method of running society and that our community, our social and our economic ways and customs are matters of value, about which opinions may differ. We believe that anyone has the right to be as critical as he wishes in expressing his opinions about these things, with any interpretations he pleases to put on them. For it is our conviction that in this way alone can we grow into a fully matured society and make it possible to embrace new and better principles of social life. We think it important to have publicized any shameful conduct which may affect some or all of us adversely. And we live in the constant hope that the resultant of competing ideas on these matters may produce a better world. In fact, we have committed ourselves in our Constitution to the conviction that freedom of speech is one of the most priceless heritages we possess.

But the whole of our law is a practical compromise between complete freedom of action and expression, on the one hand, and the common convenience of all, on the other. Our arbiters of policy, called legislatures and courts, have stated for us in laws the rules by which we shall live together. Some of their rules seem foolish, and occasionally they are so repressive that we either have them changed through political action or our courts throw them out as unconstitutional. Nevertheless, we have to live by laws. In general the test of their validity is whether or not they have the support of the majority. This does not mean that valid laws may be freely enacted against minority groups, although it very definitely does mean that minority groups are obliged to recognize most of the ways of life deemed appropriate by the majority. If certain conduct amounting essentially to speech or communication is thought by the majority to be so undesirable that it had better be suppressed by legislation, then the burden of proving that such legislation is an unconstitutional interference with freedom of speech is clearly on a court undertaking to declare it invalid. This is especially true if behind the conduct in question there has been a considerable background and tradition indicating that it is tortious and wrongful, such as there is behind slander and libel as well as behind orderly and peaceful picketing.

Conceding for argument that peaceful picketing equals pure speech, this by itself need not necessarily involve the proposition that a legislature cannot regard it as a socially undesirable form of speech. Nor need it follow that our local legislatures should be denied the constitutional power either to suppress it entirely or, short of that, to regulate it. The real difficulty seems to lie in the Supreme Court's belief that peaceful picketing is merely speech—the dissemination of information and nothing else. It sees in legislation suppressing peaceful picketing a denial of the right of free speech, even if such legislation makes no attempt to prevent unions from publicizing information concerning their disputes through any of the customary channels of communication. Perhaps everyone should accept this as an authoritarian statement of the truth, because the Supreme Court has said it is so.

But it is confusing to keep up with the changing fashions of the Court. Only 29 years before, in 1911, it had told Sam Gompers that he should not use the AF of L newspaper to say that the Bucks Stove and Range Company was unfair to organized labor. In 1921, it had grudgingly conceded the legality of peaceful picketing by strikers, implying that peaceful stranger picketing was still unlawful at common law. And it was but three years before in the *Senn* case in 1937 that the Court had split wide open, five to four, on the proposition that a state legislature had the constitutional power under the 14th amendment to make peaceful stranger picketing lawful at all—four of the Justices believing that such picketing was so inherently illegal that, like libel, it could not constitutionally be made lawful even by legislation. Within three short years, however, the Court discovered that legislatures could not even make peaceful picketing of any sort *un*lawful, because it turned out that all the time it was just plain speech, the dissemination of information, and nothing else!

Not many people would agree to support legislation denying unions the freedom to publicize labor disputes altogether. Indeed, many states have perceived a sufficiently great need for publicity of this sort that they have even made peaceful picketing a nonenjoinable medium for that purpose. While no state has attempted completely to prevent unions from publicizing matters of interest to them, some have tried to stop them from doing so by picketing of all kinds in various situations, leaving them free to pursue the conventional channels of disseminating information. In response to this, the unions renewed their traditional objection that they do not have access to the controlled press or to other effective mediums of publicity. They claimed that if they were prevented from picketing—the only form of publicity within their reach—they would virtually be denied the right to communicate information at all. Now this has always been a strong practical argument in favor of allowing unions the privilege of peaceful picketing. Any court or legislature might well have heeded it before denying the right of all picketing.

But some legislatures and courts, as a matter of policy, nevertheless have taken the position that picketing in all forms —or short of that, all stranger picketing—should be forbidden, believing that the unions should be required to create some access to the other available forms of expression. In such situations the unions have had the political task of breaking this position down, an undertaking not at all hopeless in view of the progress they have made in many states during the past years. But whether or not the unions were politically successful in this venture, at least the matter remained a close issue for local action until the Supreme Court threw the 14th amendment into the scales on the side of organized labor.

It seems plain enough to many disinterested people that picketing, even peaceful picketing, is not at all just speech or the dissemination of information but is, rather, a type of coercion and is intended as such by its users. Most people who are either sympathetic to organized labor or are sufficiently open minded to realize that unions have a perfect right to strive for advantage have learned to tolerate peaceful picketing. Many others, however, even disinterested persons, remain unable to see anything but a kind of coercion which they find socially offensive. Almost all disinterested citizens, however, must wonder how people who are directly exposed to peaceful picketing react to it.

How does the loyal employee, who wants to stay at work during a strike, react to picketing, and why? If he finally decides to stay at home during the strike, rather than cross the picket line, does that mean he has been convinced of the merits behind the union's cause? And how about an applicant for employment during a strike, who decides not to cross a picket line, although he may need the work? How about prospective customers who decide not to enter a picketed store? Are they persuaded to go elsewhere by the merits of the union's cause, assuming that they even know what the cause is, let alone its merits? And how about property owners who would give work to nonunion jobbers but who prefer to deal with union contractors in order to avoid having their premises picketed? Are they inclined to this decision because they are convinced of the merits behind the union's cause? And when the members of other unions, unrelated by any common economic interest to the picketing union, refuse to enter picketed premises, are they reacting to personal intellectual conviction concerning the worth of the picketers' cause, or are they merely reacting to some tacitly understood signal that their sympathy is expected and must be given pursuant to established labor union policies?

It is hard to believe that the reactions here recounted are all expressions of intellectual conviction as to the worth of the picketing unions' several causes. In the first place, no real attempt is made on picket lines to describe what grudge the union has against the employment or commercial policies of the picketed employer. And there is usually no attempt to define what the picketers want, and why. What even peaceful picketing usually boils down to is a simple process of proscription. The picketed person is bad because he is either not doing what we, the picketers, want him to do, or because he is doing something which we don't want him to do, and such information is thrust at passers-by, whether they want it or not. Such a procedure is, indeed, a dubious venture into the world of ideas and opinions, and hardly seems to be the sort of thing contemplated by the constitutional guaranty of free speech. Rather, it suggests a sort of psychological embargo around the picketed premises, depending for its persuasiveness on the associations most people have in mind when they think about picketing. Hence it is likely that people hesitate to cross picket lines more because they wish to avoid trouble and to escape any possible scorn that might be directed toward them for being antiunion, than because they are persuaded intellectually by the worth of the picketing unions' cause. And if it were possible to conduct a carefully prepared Gallup poll on these various subjective reactions to picketing, it seems safe to conclude that this guess would be confirmed.

At any rate, granting that a state legislature or court may express local economic and social values by allowing peaceful picketing, should they not be left free under the Constitution to conclude that some or all of such picketing is of too dubious social merit to be tolerated? Is it so very clear that peaceful picketing is purely and simply speech—the dissemination of information, and nothing more—that a state legislature or court is forbidden to conclude otherwise and to regulate it for the purpose of preventing that part of it which is thought not to be simply speech but, rather, psychological coercion or the organization of disinterested sympathy? And is a state legislature so obviously behaving unconstitutionally if it persists in viewing even peaceful picketing as an unwarranted interference with the freedom of its citizens to make up their own minds, in any way they may see fit, about whom they will deal with, what they will sell, and why?

Because of the prevailing sentimentality about peaceful picketing, any discussion of this subject is compromised if it seems to be defending antipicketing legislation. But, surely, it must be apparent that the issue at stake is much larger than whether or not unions should be allowed the privilege of peaceful picketing. The real issue is whether or not the Supreme Court has any defensible right, on the basis of an arbitrary assumption that peaceful picketing *is* simply speech, to forbid a state to reach a contrary conclusion on this very dubious proposition and to protect itself against something it does not like. The Supreme Court has always had an extraordinarily great power in its hands to control the affairs of states under the 14th amendment of the Constitution. In past years many believe that it abused this power in denying states the right to enact certain types of social legislation intended to benefit labor. The Court still has this power, and real liberals perceived its wise use in the Wisconsin tile layers' case. But in the *Thornhill* case it looks as if the Court were again beginning to abuse its extraordinary power, although now in the other direction. This provokes the unhappy reflection that the Court is destined to be swayed more by political pressures and its economic and social predilections than by dispassionate considerations of the correct use of political power within the states, regardless of what values local legislatures may entertain.

Naturally, it must be conceded that the Court's most sacred mission is to protect at all costs the right of every person to speak freely and to advance his social, economic, and political views whenever he wishes to do so. The Court enjoys its extraordinary power of judicial review under the 14th amendment chiefly to see that freedom of speech and other civil liberties are maintained. But this should not give the Court a free hand to slap the label of speech on social conduct as dubious in its nature as peaceful picketing is and, thereby, to deny to the states the power to regulate it on the basis of contrary notions about its nature. Here is a situation, perhaps, where true liberals might paraphrase Voltaire by saying that they hate what the Alabama legislature did but they will defend to the death its right to do it, leaving the ultimate outcome to local enlightenment and the political process.

THE *Thornhill* DOCTRINE BECOMES COMPLICATED

To get on with our story, however, it shortly appeared that all was not so clear on the Potomac. In 1941 the Supreme Court handed down two picketing decisions on the same day, Justice Frankfurter speaking for the Court in both cases. In each one he reaffirmed the doctrine of the *Thornhill* case, but he gave it some slight twists which indicated that he had been thinking the matter over somewhat reflectively. As he succinctly put it in one of these cases: "A union of those engaged in what the record describes as *beauty work* unsuccessfully tried to unionize Swing's beauty parlor. Picketing of the shop followed." Swing secured an injunction against this peaceful stranger picketing by the "beauticians' " union and the Illinois Supreme Court upheld it as proper. Upon the union's appeal to the Supreme Court under the 14th amendment, however, this decision was set aside as unconstitutional on the basis of the *Thornhill* case. This was also an illustration of the fact that the Supreme Court may use the 14th amendment to set aside decisions of state courts as well as to invalidate the acts of state legislatures.

This decision in *American Federation of Labor v. Swing* was not surprising after the *Thornhill* case. Nevertheless, it changed the common law of many states which had long before conceded the legality of peaceful picketing by strikers but had always held that since strangers to the picketed employer had no direct interest in his employment policies, they could not therefore justify the harm caused by their picketing. Justice Frankfurter took the trouble in this case to point out something which might seem irrelevant under the absolutism of the *Thornhill* case. He observed that under the 14th amendment a state could not prevent workers from stranger picketing "by drawing the circle of economic competition between employers and workers so small as to contain only an employer and those directly employed by him," noting that the "interdependence of economic interest of all engaged in the same industry has become a commonplace." Thus, while the presence of interest on the part of peaceful picketers seemed unnecessary under the *Thornhill* doctrine, Justice Frankfurter suggested that at least it makes the application of that broad doctrine more palatable.

In the case of *Milk Wagon Drivers Union v. Meadowmoor Dairies, Inc.,* decided the same day, it appeared that a milk wagon drivers' union had combined a little bombing, hijacking, and hatchet work with the picketing of companies organized by a rival union. An Illinois court issued an injunction forbidding violent, but permitting continued peaceful, picketing, although a master in chancery who heard the case had recommended enjoining all picketing because of the union's behavior. The Illinois Supreme Court overruled the trial court and extended the injunction to forbid all picketing for the duration of the dispute in question, resting its decision on the master's findings that any picketing this union did was perforated and colored by the violence it had committed.

Upon the union's appeal, a majority of the Supreme Court voted to sustain the Illinois judgment, Justice Frankfurter stressing the importance of leaving to the local courts this matter of drawing inferences from the evidence. As he observed, the Illinois court had concluded that even peaceful picketing, undertaken as part of the same dispute in which extreme violence had occurred, would carry over with it a "momentum of fear from past violence" and might persuade others not so much by enlightenment but rather by caution. He thought that it would be an abuse of the Supreme Court's power to deny the Illinois court the right to draw this inference from the evidence and then to conclude that future so-called peaceful picketing by this union in this dispute would not really be peaceful, at all, and should be enjoined. The minority justices of the Supreme Court were furious with this decision, claiming that the *Thornhill* case had collapsed on the first attack against it. They contended that the only proper way to avoid future objectionable picketing in this dispute was "in the maintenance of order, not in denial of free speech." It was this latter remark which prompted Frankfurter to rejoin that nothing in the 14th amendment "prevents a state if it so chooses from placing confidence in a chancellor's decree and compels it to rely exclusively on a policeman's club." Quite obviously, the picture of peaceful picketing as speech, simon-pure, was becoming a bit cloudy.

The next picketing case before the Supreme Court, decided in 1942, arose in Wisconsin. This was the case of *Hotel and Restaurant Employees' Union v. Wisconsin Employment Relations Board*. In 1937, the legislature of that state had modified its "little Norris-LaGuardia" anti-injunction act, substituting a narrow definition of the term labor dispute for the broad definition it had adopted in 1931. Under the former definition, which incidentally had furnished the basis for the *Senn* tile layers' case, peaceful picketing was made lawful even when the direct relationship of employer and employee did not exist between the disputants. Under the new provision, however, the legislature afforded a legal status to picketing only in a "controversy between an employer and the majority of his employees in a collective bargaining unit," concerning bargaining or the designation of representatives. Thus the legislature withdrew completely its approval of peaceful stranger picketing as a lawful and nonenjoinable activity.

Then it made expressly unlawful any picketing of a business or of its customers and business visitors, such as truckers, in the absence of a labor dispute "between an employer and a majority of his employees." On top of all this the legislature's new employment peace act designated certain union conduct as unfair employee labor practices, subject to prohibition by a board whose order could be enforced in the state courts. Among these unfair union practices were picketing the domicile of an employee and engaging in any picketing "unless a majority in a collective bargaining unit of the employes of an employer against whom such acts are primarily directed have voted by secret ballot to call a strike." The legislature was sufficiently cautious, however, to state in a separate section that nothing in this statute shall "be so construed as to invade unlawfully the right to freedom of speech." Just what this could have meant in a statute which all but expressly rendered peaceful stranger picketing unlawful, especially since it was enacted before the *Thornhill* case was even dreamed of, remains a matter of conjecture.

Be that as it may, under this new statute the highest Wisconsin court affirmed a judgment enjoining a union from *all* picketing because of its violence during the course of a bargaining strike called in defiance of an arbitration award. Then the union appealed to the Supreme Court under the 14th amendment. Since this injunction had been granted to enforce an order of the state labor relations board under the employment peace act, the union assailed the constitutionality of that act. In some ways this situation resembled the *Meadowmoor* case because the injunction forbade *all* future picketing, peaceful or other. Nevertheless, the Supreme Court sustained the Wisconsin injunction without any dissent, certainly not because it thought the employment peace act constitutional on its face, but because the Wisconsin court had not denied any freedom of speech in its judgment enforcing that act.

Indeed, Justice Frankfurter pathetically pointed to the clause in the statute which forbade any construction of its terms to deny freedom of speech, possibly regarding that section to be in effect a repeal of any provision in the act making peaceful stranger picketing unlawful. The somewhat similar provision in the Wisconsin anti-injunction act, referred to above, has not yet come to the Supreme Court's attention under the 14th amendment. Nor is it likely to do so, since the highest Wisconsin court has interpreted it—how, is anybody's guess—not to forbid peaceful stranger picketing. And the Supreme Court traditionally accepts a state court's construction of any of its local statutes. Aside from one later close call, avoided because no issue of free speech was raised before the Supreme Court on the record, the Wisconsin antipicketing legislation has so far endured. This is indeed a tribute to the sagacity of a legislature famous in the past for its bold and farseeing experiments in social legislation.

Shortly after these Wisconsin cases came down, the Supreme Court issued simultaneously two other picketing decisions which indicated not only a drastic modification of the *Thornhill* doctrine but also an extraordinary use of the Constitution in thwarting developments of labor policies by state legislatures. In one of these cases, *Bakery and Pastry Drivers Union v. Wohl*, the union in question was an organization of bakery wagon drivers. Many of the employers of bakery wagon drivers around New York City became unwilling to retain drivers as employees because of the expense involved in paying taxes under the New York and federal social security laws. Hence many of these drivers were forced to leave the union and to comply with a proposal that they buy the trucks at a fairly nominal figure and peddle the bakery products independently, thus freeing the employers from the obligations of paying social security taxes and workmen's compensation premiums on their account, and even for automobile liability insurance on the trucks. The profits made by these new independent peddlers were substantially lower than the wages they had formerly earned as employees.

The drivers' union, fearing the loss of their previously achieved high employment standards, put on a campaign to lessen the undermining effect of this independent competition by requesting these peddlers to work only six instead of seven days a week and to hire an unemployed union member for the seventh day at from $6 to $9 for his services. Since each of the two peddlers involved in this case earned around $35 a week working all seven days—and all of that not clear profit—they refused to comply. Thereupon the union peacefully picketed in the vicinity of the bakeries where these two peddlers bought their wares, carrying placards which bore the names of the peddlers in question and truthfully told a few of the facts involved. Also it occasionally sent pickets to follow the trucks in order to plead with some of the peddlers' customers. The New York courts enjoined this picketing because they concluded that no labor dispute existed within the meaning of their "little Norris-LaGuardia" anti-injunction act, almost identically similar to the federal act. From the judgment of the highest New York court the union appealed to the Supreme Court.

The only question before that Court was whether or not there had been a denial of the right of free speech under the 14th amendment. The Supreme Court had to accept the interpretation which the New York court placed on its own statutory definition of the term labor dispute. Taking the case on that basis, it set aside the New York court's judgment on the ground that it amounted to a denial of free speech under the Constitution. Justice Jackson for the Court said he could see "no substantive evil of such magnitude as to mark a limit to the right of free speech" which the unions sought to exercise. Although, as he remarked, "A state is not required to tolerate in all places and all circumstances even peaceful picketing by an individual," the peddlers' "mobility and their insulation from the public as middlemen made it practically impossible for [the union] to make known their legitimate grievances to the public whose patronage was sustaining the peddler system except by the means here employed and contemplated," concluding that "those means are such as to have slight, if any, repercussions upon the interests of strangers to the issue."

Justice Douglas, speaking for Justices Murphy, Black, and himself, wrote a somewhat biting concurrence. "If the opinion in this case means that a State can prohibit picketing when it is effective but may not prohibit it when it is ineffective," he said, "then I think we have made a basic departure from *Thornhill v. Alabama*." His chief concern was the majority's implication that if, in its opinion, the New York court had correctly concluded that no labor dispute was really involved, then it would have been free to enjoin the picketing. He did not see how, under the *Thornhill* decision, a state could be allowed to draw this line. He went on to remark, with engaging candor, that "picketing might have a coercive effect" and that "picketing by an organized group is more than free speech, since it involves patrol of a particular locality and since the very presence of a picket line may induce action of one kind or another, quite irrespective of the nature of the ideas which are being disseminated."

This seems a remarkable concession from the liberal wing of the Court. It narrowed the whole issue down to who may make the judgment of whether peaceful picketing only persuades on the merits of the union's contentions, or merely coerces because of its very existence—the state legislatures and courts or only the Supreme Court? Justice Douglas apparently thought the majority of the court was doing something else— that while it was conceding peaceful picketing to be at least free speech, it was making the constitutionality of the New York court's judgment depend on whether or not the union was engaged in what has come to be known as a labor dispute. He feared that what the majority of the Court had done was merely to take issue with the New York court's narrow definition of a labor dispute, thus escaping its constitutional obligation to uphold peaceful picketing whether or not the union had any economic interest to pursue in its conflict with the peddlers.

Whatever significance this fact may have had concerning the constitutionality of the New York court's judgment, it seems plain that the bakery drivers' union had a clear labor dispute with these independent peddlers and, for that matter, with the former employers whose goods these peddlers were distributing. It is true that these peddlers were not themselves employers. But they fostered a practice most harmful to the interests of the union—a practice in which the former employers themselves had an important economic interest in supporting because of the money they saved in escaping the necessity for paying social security taxes on delivery employees, workmen's compensation premiums, upkeep expenses of their trucks including liability insurance, and high union wages. Thus these former employers used the independent peddlers to get their products distributed more cheaply than the union would do it. It was at this point that the union found ample economic justification for exerting picketing pressures in the vicinity of the bakeries themselves.

It seems perfectly clear, on the basis of all that was said and decided in *Goldfinger v. Feintuch* (this was the New York case in which the meat workers had picketed a delicatessen shop selling nonunion products) that the bakery drivers' union had a perfectly legitimate justification peacefully to picket *both* the independent peddlers and the former employers from whom they bought their goods. These former employers and the peddlers certainly had a unity of interest in conducting their mutual affairs as they did. They had a great competitive advantage over union bakeries and drivers on the basis of very substantial overhead cost differentials. Analytically, the two cases are not identical, but the bakery drivers' union had quite as clear an economic interest at stake as the meat workers' union had had. And there were equally compelling reasons why the New York court should have refused to enjoin the union from any peaceful picketing of the bakeries or peddlers. But that was a matter of local policy, of peculiar concern to the New York court and legislature—at least, until the Supreme Court took it out of their hands under the 14th amendment.

The other picketing case decided by the Supreme Court on the same day as the New York bakery drivers' case, showed clearly the direction in which the Court was headed. In *Carpenters and Joiners Union v. Ritter's Cafe,* a Texas restaurant operator named Ritter let a contract to a nonunion contractor for the erection of his dwelling house about a mile and a half away from the business section of town, where his restaurant was located. Since the carpenters' union resented this, regarding its interests in higher union standards to be endangered, it peacefully picketed Ritter where such pressure would do the most good—in front of his restaurant. As a consequence, Ritter's unionized restaurant employees refused to come to work, union truck drivers ceased deliveries of supplies, and union patrons stopped eating at his cafe—not because any of these folk had anything to gain from Ritter but because they would not cross a "sister" union's picket line.

Now it is hard to deny that any nonunion building operation threatens to undermine union standards in this industry. And in this case the carpenters' union had a real economic interest at stake, justifying their exertion of peaceful economic pressures against competing nonunion enterprisers. Indeed, all union interests in the building trades are represented by such high rates that many people cannot afford to build unless they can find nonunion contractors. But in spite of our prevailing ethics of free enterprise and competition, affording the carpenters' union a justification at common law for focusing economic pressure against Ritter and his nonunion contractor, the Texas courts thought that this pressure could not be exerted by picketing Ritter's restaurant. The highest state court affirmed an injunction forbidding the union to picket the restaurant. But it did not prohibit picketing at the building under construction or publicizing the situation in any way other than by picketing the restaurant. From this judgment the union appealed to the Supreme Court, claiming a denial of free speech under the 14th amendment.

In this case the Supreme Court decided that the Texas court had the constitutional power to enjoin the peaceful picketing in question. Through Justice Frankfurter a majority of the Court enunciated a most intriguing analysis of why it reached this conclusion. Fundamentally, the Court regarded the conflict as a personal fight between Ritter and the carpenters' union concerning Ritter's labor policies *as a house builder and not as a restaurant owner*. The union had no dispute with Ritter concerning his employment policies at his restaurant. Picketing of his restaurant, however, implied that it did.

As the opinion puts it, patrolling at that place led to the

"conscription of neutrals"—that is, members of the public, both union and general, who might exhibit some concern over low employment standards in restaurants but who had no interest in the employment standards of carpenters. Justice Frankfurter thought that the Texas court should be allowed, under the 14th amendment of the Constitution, to insist that picketing should be confined to the undertaking with respect to which the dispute existed and that by injunction it could "insulate from the dispute an establishment which industrially has no connection with the dispute."

He urbanely conceded that "as a means of communicating the facts of a labor dispute, peaceful picketing may be a phase of the constitutional right of free utterance." And then he made a statement much too revealing not to quote in full.

"But," he declared, "recognition of peaceful picketing as an exercise of free speech does not imply that the states must be without power to confine the sphere of communication to that directly related to the dispute. Restriction of picketing to the area of the industry within which a labor dispute arises leaves open to the disputants other traditional modes of communication. To deny to the states the power to draw this line is to write into the Constitution the notion that every instance of peaceful picketing—anywhere and under any circumstances —is necessarily a phase of the controversy which provoked the picketing. Such a view of the Due Process Clause [in the 14th amendment] would compel the states to allow the disputants in a particular industrial episode to conscript neutrals having no relation to either the dispute or the industry in which it arose." Then out of abundant caution he observed that the New York bakery drivers' case was not inconsistent with this because there, "in picketing the retail establishments, the union members would only be following the subject-matter of their dispute."

The minority of the Court in this five-four decision—Justices Black, Douglas, Murphy, and Reed—now realized that in spite of the majority's protestations to the contrary, the cat was out of the bag. The *Thornhill* doctrine, as the Court had originally promulgated it, was gone. With some reason, they could not understand why peaceful picketing should be subjected to any regulation at all, if it were really speech—the dissemination of information—and nothing more. They could not perceive why the rest of the Court should concede that Texas had the power to prevent the union from conscripting neutrals—strangers to the grievance—by the device of peaceful picketing when they freely admitted that the union had an absolute constitutional right to undertake the enlightenment of these very same neutrals by pursuing "other traditional modes of communication."

To their way of thinking—and their logic appears faultless—this position meant that the majority of the Court did not really regard peaceful picketing as constitutionally protected speech at all, but rather as some sort of coercion depending on communication for its effect. They realized that the eating public and the house dwelling public are more or less identical and that restaurant patrons were no more neutral than potential home builders. And they knew that this identity was not obscured by the fact that some of these members of the public were unionized restaurant workers, truckers, or wage earners in general. Union programs are addressed to this public, and it is this public's influence that might persuade either a nonunion contractor that he should employ only union carpenters or Ritter that he should deal only with union contractors. If peaceful picketing is *really* only communication, why should not the union be constitutionally protected in communicating the facts to the public in its role of potential diners as well as in any other role?

If the basic assumption of these four minority justices was valid—that peaceful picketing really is constitutionally guaranteed free speech—they are absolutely correct and the majority of the Court is absolutely wrong in drawing any line at all around the union's constitutional rights. But the real trouble is that it is extremely difficult to treat this basic assumption as a valid one. The fact is that it is simply a species of coercion traveling under the guise of speech for the purpose of enjoying constitutional immunity from state regulation. Any candid labor leader would, in all probability, confess this off the record.

The union's purpose in this *Ritter* case was patent. It wanted to put Ritter on an embarrassing spot by creating in front of his restaurant what the Texas courts thought to be a kind of nuisance. The union members knew full well that if enough patrons and members of other unions refused to enter his restaurant because of their reluctance to cross a picket line, he would eventually try to appease the union by calling off his nonunion contractor—that is, unless he could first stop the picketing. After all, it is hard to imagine restaurant patrons who might be prospective home builders reaching the intellectual conviction that Ritter must be a good person to avoid in all connections—including that of restaurant keeper— simply because he did not want to pay any more than he had to for his home.

It is quite apparent that a majority of the justices felt this way. It is hard to understand the Court's present position as being anything but a retreat from the *Thornhill* case, and this can mean only that the majority no longer believe peaceful picketing to be speech—the dissemination of information— and nothing more. For if they do still believe that peaceful picketing is free speech, then they have entered on the monstrous undertaking of denying this liberty constitutional protection whenever they see fit to do so. As the minority complains, the majority can't have it both ways. Peaceful picketing either *is* or it is *not* an instance of free speech under the Constitution. If it is, then the union's right peacefully to picket Ritter's cafe should have been upheld. But if it is not? Here is the critical question. For if it is not, then what business has the Court dealing with such matters at all?

The Court has frequently admitted in the past that local labor policy is a state's own concern and none of the federal government's business. While the power of Congress to act on these matters has been expanding under the influence of increasing union political strength, the federal courts have not legitimately acquired any more power over the affairs of states than they have ever had. Federal courts do secure jurisdiction over the internal affairs of a state when it enacts or enforces a law contrary to the guaranties of the 14th amendment of the Constitution. Thus, in these picketing cases, the Supreme Court acquires jurisdiction over what the states have done if antipicketing legislation or court decisions result in the suppression of freedom of speech. But if no freedom of speech issue is involved in such statutes or decisions, then the Supreme Court has no power to act at all.

Perhaps some people see nothing wrong in letting the Supreme Court tell states what a desirable internal labor policy is, with orders that they should stay within the limits of that policy. The thing that is wrong with this is that states have the right to make these decisions themselves, under their own political processes—except where they really violate some constitutional guaranty that the Supreme Court has the power to enforce. The Court abuses that power if it nevertheless dictates decisions of policy under an assumption of jurisdiction to review which it does not constitutionally enjoy. In other words, it is beginning to look as if a majority of the Court had reasoned itself out of passing on state peaceful picketing laws at all under the 14th amendment.

The most recent picketing case of importance decided by the Court, in November, 1943, indicates that it has no intention of retreating further from the ambiguous position taken in the *Ritter* case. In *Cafeteria Employees' Union v. Angelos,* a cafeteria workers' union picketed two restaurants run by the proprietors, without any employees at all. The proprietors sought and secured injunctions against this peaceful picketing. The New York Court of Appeals upheld these injunctions on the ground that no labor disputes existed between the union and the two proprietors. This was because there were no employees with respect to whom employment conditions could become an issue. On the union's appeal to the Supreme Court under the 14th amendment, the New York decision was reversed as a denial of free speech. The union had insisted that a labor dispute did exist, within the broad definition of such disputes in the New York anti-injunction act. What it was after was to force these proprietors to hire employees they did not want. Its first interest was that the very existence of cafeterias run without any employees created a competitive situation harmful to cafeterias who did hire union employees. This was for the reason that the absence of such employees lowered their overhead costs and enabled them to dispense food more cheaply than the union enterprises. Secondly, it wanted more jobs for its members.

A NATIONAL LABOR POLICY IN THE CONSTITUTION

Here was a situation almost identical with the Wisconsin tile layers' case in 1937. It is difficult to understand how the New York court failed to see that under its state anti-injunction act labor disputes were involved. Possibly the judges were influenced by the fact that the picketers carried banners which denounced the proprietors as "unfair" to organized labor and said that the cafeterias served "bad food," telling prospective customers that by patronizing them "they were aiding the cause of Fascism." After all, peaceful picketing is supposed to comprise only nonviolent picketing from which are absent the elements of libel and misrepresentation. But as Justice Frankfurter, after noting that the peaceful character of the picketing was unquestioned, said about these banners: "And to use loose language or undefined slogans that are part of the conventional give-and-take in our economic and political controversies—like 'unfair' or 'fascist'—is not to falsify facts."

This must have led the New York courts to wonder just what Justice Reed had meant when he generously conceded in the *Ritter* case: "We do not doubt the right of the state to impose not only some but many restrictions upon peaceful picketing. Reasonable numbers, quietness, truthful placards, open ingress and egress, suitable hours or other proper limitations, not destructive of the right to tell of labor difficulties, may be required." At any rate, whatever moved the New York court to construe its anti-injunction act as it did in these cafeteria cases, the Supreme Court is supposed to be bound by the state court's construction of its own laws. So likewise the New York court is just as entitled to construe its broad anti-injunction act narrowly, as the Wisconsin court is to construe its narrow anti-injunction act broadly.

Now that the Supreme Court has assumed the power to dictate the allowable area of economic conflict with respect to peaceful picketing within the several states—a power which even Congress has not yet undertaken to assert—there seems to be no good reason why it should stop at that point. For it seems a small step from this position for the Court to conclude that strikes and secondary boycotts are also fundamental personal freedoms of labor unionists, reasonably falling within the term "liberty" as it appears in the 14th amendment. As a matter of fact, reflective people would agree that such conduct fits more easily within that term, since they perceive the freedom of workers in operation in their refusal to work, when they don't want to, or to patronize any enterprise or commodity they don't like—all of which is purely passive conduct—while they might regard even peaceful picketing as unwarranted intrusion and aggression. Indeed, it may be argued that the Court will take the next logical step of writing Section 4 of the Norris-LaGuardia Act, along with Section 13, directly into the Constitution by embracing all union activities there described within the meaning of the term "liberty" in the 14th amendment. It is true, of course, that peaceful picketing was brought within that term only under the guise of speech, this step seeming plausible because of the Court's established use of the 14th amendment to afford protection to freedom of speech. Strikes and boycotts are not informational techniques, although secondary boycotts are closely allied through the use of "unfair" and "We don't patronize" lists. But that seems immaterial, partly because they are fundamental freedoms, and partly because we now know that peaceful picketing—already ensconced in the 14th amendment—is, practically by the Court's own inferential admission, no more an "informational technique" than these other pressures are.

This suggestion might seem utterly fantastic to some readers. If so, all they have to do is recall what the Court did with the Sherman, Clayton, and Norris-LaGuardia acts in the *Hutcheson* case. The transformation of conduct criminal under the Sherman Act into conduct absolutely lawful for all purposes—just through the means of an anti-injunction statute—seems much more improbable. Yet that actually happened with respect to any union undertaking which is put into effect by any of the means described either in Section 20 of the Clayton Act or Section 4 of the Norris-LaGuardia Act. Of course, the Court could not successfully afford constitutional protection to all strikes and boycotts, any more than it has been able to justify protection for all peaceful picketing. What it could do, consistently with what it has already done in the picketing cases, is to guarantee immunity to all strikes and boycotts within the area of allowable economic conflict evolved for peaceful picketing. That is, it could require proof that any particular strike or boycott served some economic interest of the union exercising the pressure, and that with respect to this interest the object of the union's pressure was competitively taking an antagonistic or harmful position.

The union would have to show the same economic relationship between its own interests and the enterprise placed under its coercive pressure that the Supreme Court has come to require in the peaceful picketing cases. In other words, any showing that the purely economic coercion of unions—at least, if it is articulated through the types of conduct appearing in Section 4 of the Norris-LaGuardia Act—amounts to a labor dispute within the meaning and scope of Section 13 of that

act would entitle such unions to the protection of the due
process clause of the 14th amendment in exercising such pressures. This is exactly what the Court *has* done with peaceful
picketing. It is hard to see how it can logically avoid doing
the same for all other economic techniques employed by
unions if it is called upon to do so. Such a development would
virtually be writing Section 4 of the Norris-LaGuardia Act
into the Constitution—where Section 13 of that act has already been enshrined for the picketing cases. As two able
authors have so aptly put it:

"The desideratum of uniformity [of state labor policy]
would have been achieved at the price of crystallizing into a
constitutional amendment a law 'which explicitly applies only
to the authority of the United States Courts "to issue any restraining order or injunction."' The wand which in the
Hutcheson case touched the Sherman Act now appears to have
touched the Constitution, to complete the metamorphosis."

It is not only the egregious invasion of states' rights under
the cloak of constitutional power to preserve civil liberties
which would make this step so appalling. Such a pre-emption
of power would be distressing enough in its assumption that
state legislatures or courts, and even Congress, are unable to
figure out these matters of labor policy or cannot be trusted
to achieve a uniform liberal labor policy, because they can't
appreciate as clearly as the Supreme Court can the importance
of adopting a unified liberal program of this sort for the whole
country. But think of the appalling task the Court would be
taking on in defining the allowable area of economic conflict!
The very thought of this undertaking, which the Court has
already assumed in the picketing cases, was most upsetting to
Justice Reed. Dissenting in the *Ritter* case, he said:

"We are not told whether the test of eligibility to picket is
to be applied by crafts or enterprises, or how we are to determine economic interdependence or the boundaries of particular industries. Such differentiations are yet to be considered." He saw in clear outline the task of the Court as one

of checking on each state court's definition of the allowable area of economic conflict in every peaceful picketing case appealed under the 14th amendment. He would take small comfort in being told that the area allowed is the same area defined in Section 13 of the Norris-LaGuardia Act, for there it is loosely described and can receive "definiteness of contour" only after numberless applications in specific cases. If the Court adds to the task it has already assumed in picketing litigation, the same issue in relation to strikes and boycotts, its work will indeed be multiplied. And the confusion within the states will become thrice confounded.

Aside from what may happen in the future, there are several embarrassing incidents of the Court's present attitude toward peaceful picketing. Now peaceful picketing, even if it is mere communication, causes a good deal of harm. In the absence of legislation, the infliction of harm can validly be no objection to peaceful union coercion, any more than it ever has been to those coercive effects of business undertakings called competition. But justification of some sort is always necessary for immunity in such instances of the privileged infliction of harm.

Suppose Congress wishes to pass a law making enjoinable the peaceful picketing by a losing union in a plant where the employer has bargained with the certified union after an election held under the NLRA. Presumably, such a statute would be unconstitutional under the 1st and 5th amendments, according to the present state of the law. Such picketing falls squarely within the allowable area defined in Section 13 of the Norris-LaGuardia Act. Yet it is in plain derogation of Congress' mandate in the NLRA, for the employer may never lawfully yield to such pressure and the employees may not do so during the life of the existing contract. Apparently they will have to sit back and accept any resulting damage, unless the Supreme Court thinks up another exception to the *Thornhill* doctrine. The same remarks apply to peaceful picketing used by labor organizations in old-fashioned jurisdictional strikes and in the modern interunion disputes—activities which Congress and state legislatures might reasonably wish to forbid. And think how futile any attempt through new legislation may prove to be in preventing unions from achieving pervasive market controls or in making them abide by the parliamentary methods devised to relieve a worried public from the inconvenience of traditional trial by combat!

Another perplexing situation, which has ensued from the *Thornhill* case, is best illustrated by a California decision. In *McKay v. Retail Automobile Salesmen's Local Union,* a large automobile agency had about 30 salesmen whom a salesmen's union wished to organize. It was immaterial that these 30 salesmen did not wish to be represented by this outside union. Upon the employer's refusal to bargain with the union, it peacefully picketed his premises. Although this peaceful picketing could not in itself possibly hurt the employer, it served to insulate him from his already unionized mechanics and from all deliveries by unionized teamsters and truck drivers, none of whom would cross the picket line of a sister union. Here was a situation that amounted to sympathetic coercion, pure and simple. The California court's refusal to enjoin the picketing—decided upon after the *Thornhill* case but before the Supreme Court's later qualification of that case—could not have been rationalized as acknowledging a legitimate labor dispute within the allowable area of economic conflict defined in Section 13 of the Norris-LaGuardia Act. It is true that the picketers had an interest at stake within this area, but the pressure harming the employer was the refusal of his mechanics and of teamsters, who had no quarrel of any sort with him, to enter his premises. Quite obviously, their refusals to deal with him were not inspired by any intellectual convictions they had acquired because of the picketing. Their refusals to enter were in pursuit of an interunion agreement not to cross each other's picket lines—as plain an instance of sympathetic support as could be imagined. Here, indeed, was a "conscription of neutrals," as Justice Frankfurter put it in the *Ritter* case.

The permissible area of economic conflict as defined in the Norris-LaGuardia Act, and the whole policy of the liberal common law on which this was based, exclude sympathetic pressure. Thereby a show of economic interest is required as a justification for the infliction of harm involved in the exertion of this type of economic coercion. The only way in which the California court could deal with this situation practicably—at least, under the present position of the Supreme Court on picketing—would be to enjoin the mechanics and the teamsters from heeding and refusing to cross the picket line on the ground that they were concertedly exercising sympathetic pressure, with no interest at stake. But "that way madness lies," because such a course would involve maintaining the peaceful picketing by the salesmen's union as constitutionally guaranteed freedom of speech and, at the same time, eliminating the only response sought from the enlightened public by this constitutionally guaranteed appeal. But this just couldn't be done with any semblance of balance. Consequently, under the current rulings of the Supreme Court on picketing, unions are now in the position where they can agree in advance upon the infliction of sympathetic pressures, each of which are in pursuit of the class war. Yet such sympathetic pressures are excluded by the statutory definitions of the term labor dispute. Moreover, our most liberal judges of the past, like Holmes and Brandeis, all agreed that they were beyond the pale.

THE RACE ISSUE

But enough of picketing. If this discussion seems to imply a bias against peaceful picketing in all situations, then it has been misunderstood. The criticism is of the Supreme Court's assumption of power under the Constitution. The danger implicit in this judicial undertaking to mold a pervasive national labor policy is too alarming to ignore. American society must agree that the right to have our labor policies shaped by the frank and open political process in our state and national legislatures, instead of by the paternal benevolence of the Supreme Court, is much too important to pass by default.

The Supreme Court has recently had occasion to use the 14th amendment of the Constitution for a different purpose, one closely allied to the protection of free speech. But apparently it preferred to side-step the constitutional issue in favor of a more technical and less explosive approach. This was a situation involving racial discrimination by unions in the administration of their internal affairs—a matter with which the California court has dealt squarely as a constitutional issue and which the Supreme Court can hardly avoid treating in that fashion much longer. It appeared that the locomotive firemen's brotherhood was bargaining with railroads to exclude Negro firemen from securing the advantages of seniority normally arising from the contracts between the railroads and the brotherhood. It was clear that under the terms of the Railway Labor Act a majority of the firemen, who happened to be white, had lawfully selected the brotherhood as their bargaining representative in spite of the fact that this union excludes Negroes from membership.

Under the present state of the law it is impossible to say that such discrimination on the part of the union is illegal. The act does require, however, that the bargaining representative selected in any unit must represent the interests of all workers in the unit. Since there was a substantial minority of Negro firemen, their interests were administered in the same collective agreements negotiated between the railroad and the union to govern the employment conditions of the membership. Now one of the most important items in railway labor agreements is that concerning seniority. Under previous agreements the Negro firemen enjoyed the advantages of seniority along with the white firemen. But the brotherhood made new agreements with the railroads advancing several white employees over the heads of Negroes who had already established preferences, in many cases supplanting them with whites having less seniority. Two reasons apparently lay behind this step.

One was that the union wished eventually to exclude Negroes entirely from the unit in question. The other was that since Negroes were not promotable to the job of engineer, it was thought appropriate to advance white firemen to seniority positions from which they could eventually be promoted to that job.

A Negro fireman named Steele brought suit in the Alabama courts requesting an injunction against the union and the railroad employing him, to prevent them from putting this new scheme into effect. When the Alabama court held that an injunction could not be issued, since all bargaining had been in strict compliance with the Railway Labor Act, the Supreme Court agreed to pass on the case as "one of importance in the administration of the Railway Labor Act." It then decided in *Steele v. Louisville and N. R. Company* that what the railroad and the union had agreed to do was an improper disregard of the Negro firemen's established seniority rights and could not lawfully be put into effect under the Railway Labor Act.

Chief Justice Stone, speaking for the Court, likened the bargaining power of the union to the lawmaking power of a state legislature, hinting obliquely that such power cannot constitutionally be used to prefer the rights of some over others on the basis of any arbitrary classification. But he made it plain that the Court had decided as it did because the union had violated the Congressional intention to have the chosen union represent without discrimination all employees in the unit for which it was bargaining representative, whether they were or were not members of the union.

While he conceded that unions might have rules of eligibility for membership, he could not conceive of Congress' placing complete bargaining power in the hands of a union selected by a majority of the employees in a unit, with the idea that such a union might then lawfully use its power to promote the advantage of union members at the expense of nonunion employees in the same unit. He made equally plain the Court's astonishment to find that any railroad would suppose it could enter into a collective agreement of this sort and expect it to be lawful. He thus implied that the railroad might have to compensate the Negro firemen who had in the meanwhile sustained losses under the new agreement. He did not broach the issue presented when a union enjoying exclusive bargaining rights secures a closed shop contract and then arbitrarily excludes certain employees in the unit from membership on the basis of race, creed, or economic belief. Yet on that very same day—December 18, 1944—the Court handed down *Wallace Corporation v. NLRB* wherein it upheld the Labor Relations Board's order designed to prevent precisely this sort of thing as an unfair labor practice on the part of an employer.

Justice Murphy apparently detected some circumlocution in the majority opinion, for while he concurred in the *Steele* decision, he came out boldly against "the cloak of racism surrounding the actions of the Brotherhood in refusing membership to Negroes and in entering into and enforcing agreements discriminating against them." He thought that any construction of the Railway Labor Act allowing this practice would render the act unconstitutional—a sufficient reason in his mind for construing the act otherwise. He deprecated a decision "solely upon the basis of legal niceties" while the Court remained "mute and placid as to the obvious and oppressive deprivation of constitutional guarantees." He concluded: "Racism is far too virulent today to permit the slightest refusal, in the light of a Constitution that abhors it, to expose and condemn it wherever it appears in the course of a statutory interpretation."

He, no doubt, highly approved of a California decision appearing two weeks later in which the state supreme court, on square constitutional grounds, enjoined the operation of a closed shop contract secured by a union which would not admit Negroes to membership. In this California case of *James v. Marinship Corporation,* a union of boilermakers and shipbuilding workers, chosen as bargaining representative in a large unit, had set up a "Jim Crow" union for Negro workers. They were refused admission to the brotherhood itself and were forced in its collective agreement with the employer, under pain of discharge if they did not comply, to join this auxiliary union and to pay dues. It is true that the California court approached this case somewhat conventionally. First, it stated the fundamental issue to be "whether a closed union coupled with a closed shop is a legitimate objective of organized labor." After this invocation of the illegal purpose doctrine, the court denied the legality of a monopoly which "affects the fundamental right to work for a living," observing that "the discriminatory practices involved in this case are, moreover, contrary to the public policy of the United States and this state," with specific reference to the 5th, 14th, and 15th amendments of the federal Constitution.

This might not seem a very sturdy avowal of constitutional guaranties against racism. But the court was not in a position to do much more than it did, since it could not exercise the same power of review over the private actions of the employer and the union which the Supreme Court can exercise over state legislative and judicial acts under the 14th amendment. In finding the illegitimacy of objective by recourse to the federal Constitution, however, the California court did all within its power to treat the practice in question as an offense under our fundamental law, making it plain that unions are too closely concerned with the control of opportunities for livelihood any longer to "claim the same freedom from legal restraint enjoyed by golf clubs or fraternal associations."

On the same day this case appeared, the California court decided another—*Bautista v. Jones*—which is much less easy to reconcile with the trend of constitutional developments in the Supreme Court. It seems that almost all of the milk dealers around Los Angeles had agreed with the milk wagon drivers' union to employ only its members in distributing its product.

These same dealers supplied two independent peddlers with milk to distribute to their own customers on their own routes. Believing that competition from such independent sources harmed the interests of its members—particularly since these peddlers did not have to observe social security laws pertaining to employees and could hence undersell union-delivered milk, thus suggesting to dealers the economic possibilities of distributing through independents—the union requested these peddlers to hire union men to do their work. The peddlers would not do this but offered to join the union, an overture which the union promptly turned down because it existed for promoting the interests of employees and not of enterprisers, or, as the court called them, of businessmen workers. Since the peddlers insisted on combining the operations of entrepreneur and worker, the union intimated to the big milk dealers that its members would refuse to work for them if they continued to supply these peddlers with milk, its frank intention being to compel such peddlers either to become milk wagon drivers like its members were, to hire drivers and remain only as entrepreneurs, or to go out of business altogether. And when the dealers obeyed the union's request, the peddlers sued for an injunction.

So far, it seems impossible to distinguish the situation from that involved in the Wisconsin tile layers' case, except that there the union exercised its pressure through the device of picketing. But in a four-three decision the California court granted an injunction, ordering the union to discontinue this pressure. Quite obviously the majority judges believed that unions were going too far when they used economic coercion against small businessmen who operated without any employees, exhibiting an almost sentimental concern for American institutions like the milkman, the barber, the plumber, the watchmaker, the groceryman, the service station operator and, of course, the farmer, all of whom, they feared, unchecked unionism might destroy. Every one of these people, they declared, are businessmen workers who run enterprises and at the same time work on them with their own hands. Surely, they contended, these people have the constitutional right to conduct free enterprise without interference from labor unions, intimating that at least the state of California could not be prevented under the federal Constitution from maintaining this right by issuing injunctions against unions which actively disputed its maintenance.

In view of the prediction that the Supreme Court may extend its already existing constitutional power to prevent states from declaring strikes and secondary boycotts unlawful, it seems arguable that the majority judges on the California court were mistaken. This milk peddler case closely resembles the cafeteria workers' and bakery drivers' situations already discussed in this chapter. If this California case were taken up to the Supreme Court on constitutional grounds, that Court would find it difficult indeed to distinguish them. It is true that these established precedents involved pure stranger picketing and that the California milk drivers' case did not. But it seems rash to suggest that stranger picketers could enjoy a stronger constitutional immunity than would actual employees who threaten to strike their employers unless they, in turn, cease dealing with someone else.

For according to the way the law now stands, there seems to be no conceivable constitutional way for the California courts to prevent the milk drivers from picketing both the independent peddlers and the milk dealers who supply them, since such picketing would be protected as free speech. It would seem ludicrous for the Court to uphold the right to engage in such picketing while at the same time it left the state of California free to enjoin a strike which the picketing is intended to support, even if it transpires that this particular strike happens simultaneously to be effecting certain secondary economic pressures. The only test we now have is whether or not the union is participating in a labor dispute, within the meaning of Section 13 of the Norris-LaGuardia Act. Can there be the shadow of a doubt that the California milk drivers' union could qualify under this test? It made a clear showing that its economic interests were adversely affected in several ways by the competition afforded through the independent milk peddler system. Without any doubt, its picketing activities would fall squarely within the area of constitutional protection now established by the Supreme Court.

Perhaps the correct note on which to conclude this chapter was sounded by one of the dissenting judges in the California milk drivers' case, when he said that "so long as the theory of free enterprise [previously] defined is applied to activities of capital it should equally be applied to those of labor." And, he went on: "I am not suggesting that competitive activities of labor organizations may not be subject to reasonable control but I am definitely opposed to the application of a double standard which would deny to organizations of one character activities which it condones in the other." His main objection was the court's undertaking to supply any controls in the absence of legislation and in conflict with existing principles of the common law governing free enterprise for all. Even he may be surprised some day to see the Supreme Court not only agreeing with him but also embossing his sentiments with the insignia of constitutional protection from any state interference.

When and if this happens, the circle will indeed have been completed. For it was not many years ago that our courts were prohibiting types of social legislation and labor union activity now thought reasonable, because they interfered with the constitutional rights of free enterprise believed necessary for the economic existence of employers and nonunion workers. As soon as organized labor's techniques of economic coercion are similarly enshrined as free enterprise on a pedestal of constitutional immunity from even Congressional or state legislative regulation, we shall live again in a climate of economic absolutism similar—but converse—to that experienced a generation ago. From this dubious fate the Supreme Court alone can save us by yielding back to our legislatures, both federal and state, the power to deal with these matters as they see fit. In this course lies the only hope that over the years the patient example of liberal thought and action will eventually be reflected through the democratic political process in an enlightened labor policy and a balanced industrial way of life.

CHAPTER XIII

THE FUNCTIONING AND ENFORCE-ABILITY OF COLLECTIVE AGREEMENTS—ARBITRATION

An agreement upon wages and working conditions between the managers of an industry and its employees, whether made in an atmosphere of peace or under the stress of strike or lockout resembles in many ways a treaty. As a safeguard of social peace it ought to be construed not narrowly and technically but broadly and so as to accomplish its evident aims and ought on both sides to be kept faithfully and without subterfuge. In no other way can confidence and industrial harmony be sustained.—Sibley, J., in *Yazoo & M. V. R. Co. v. Webb*, 1933.

And therefore it is a law of nature, *That in every controversy, the parties thereto ought mutually to agree upon an arbitrator, whom they both trust; and mutually to covenant to stand to the sentence he shall give therein.* For where every man is his own judge, there properly is no judge at all; as where every man carveth out his own right, it hath the same effect, as if there were no right at all; and where is no judge, there is no end of controversy, and therefore the right of hostility remaineth.

An arbitrator therefore or judge is he that is trusted by the parties to any controversy, to determine the same by the declaration of his own judgment therein. Out of which followeth: first, that the judge ought not to be concerned in the controversy he endeth; for in that case he is party, and ought by the same reason to be judged by another; secondly, that he maketh no covenant with either of the parties, to pronounce sentence for the one, more than for the other. Nor doth he covenant so much, as that his sentence shall be just; for that were to make the parties judges of the sentence, whereby the controversy would remain still undecided. Nevertheless for the trust reposed in him, and for the equality which the law of nature requireth him to consider in the parties, he violateth that law, if for favour, or hatred to either party, he give other sentence than he thinketh right. And thirdly, that no man ought to make himself judge in any controversy between others, unless they consent and agree thereto.—Thomas Hobbes, in *The Elements of Law*, chapter XVII, 6 and 7 (1640).

IN SPITE of the developments in labor relations and collective bargaining over the last ten years, it is safe to say that there is still no settled American law governing the status of collective labor agreements and their enforceability. This case of arrested development may not have been particularly serious before 1935, when the NLRA became law. But now that the government has committed industry to a far-reaching program of virtual compulsory collective bargaining, we must establish some feasible techniques for the interpretation, application, and enforcement of collective agreements.

One explanation of the absence of such a development may be that the enforcement of contracts has traditionally been a concern of the states. And they have unfortunately followed no trend toward a uniform theory adapted to the adequate settlement of claims arising from collective agreements. Nor are they in a position to do so effectively. On the other hand, Congress has created the conditions that have resulted in thousands of new collective agreements, and it is in a position to provide some uniform method for their application and enforcement. It is true that under our federal state system of government, Congress is traditionally supposed to keep its hands off of matters pertaining to the interpretation and enforcement of contracts. But we are faced with a practical and unprecedented situation of Congress' own making. And it may have to provide the solution by exercising the same powers with which it created the NLRA in the first place—the cause of these numerous collective agreements.

The use by Congress of its commerce power seems most appropriate in this situation. Many present-day collective agreements have very decided interstate implications, some of them covering the various units of industrial empires which spread from coast to coast. It is certainly as tenable to suppose that Congress has the constitutional power under the commerce clause to provide a uniform method for the administration of these collective agreements as it was to assume that it could originally impose on industry under the NLRA the conditions which led to universal organization and collective bargaining. If it was necessary to guarantee independent organization and collective bargaining for the purpose of protecting commerce from the disruptive effects of strikes concerning organization and recognition of unions, then it is equally necessary to protect commerce from the ravages of disputes concerning the application and enforcement of the resulting agreements.

Congress and the state legislatures have so far refrained from spelling out any procedures for the enforcement of collective agreements. They have left that job to the courts, and the judges have the most rudimentary notions about what is required. But even if the courts had clearer conceptions of an adequate procedure, there are good reasons why they could do little about it without the aid of legislatures. One reason is that labor unions have no separate legal status such as corporations enjoy. Since they are not persons in the eyes of the law, they have no standing before the courts as parties in suits to enforce contracts or as parties being sued under their terms. In many states, unions may enjoy the benefits of legal personality through incorporation, as long as they are willing to assume the responsibilities which such a step entails. A few unions have already found it convenient to incorporate. But most of them seem reluctant to abandon some of the advantages of loose and informal association and look with suspicion at the consequences of incorporation, such as disclosure of their internal affairs. This situation can be corrected only by legislation creating a status for unincorporated unions as legal persons, to sue and be sued without the formality of incorporation. In the absence of such legislation our courts may simply decide to treat unions as legal persons for certain purposes, as indeed a few have already done. But this involves a process of judicial legislation which few courts relish and which affords no promise of a uniform development fitted to the needs of the occasion.

Another reason for the rudimentary development in our

common law regarding the enforceability of collective agreements is the tendency of lawyers and judges to think about these agreements in terms of conventional contract law. In a sense they *are* contracts. But, strictly speaking, they are not contracts at all in light of what that term traditionally signifies. As one court has said, the collective agreement "resembles in many ways a treaty." This characterization is exceedingly apt. For the rigors of collective bargaining with strikes, boycotts, and picketing frequently suggest warring factions, each anxious to make peace with the other on a basis of selfish personal advantage. Indeed, the highest court in England has supported this analogy by declaring that collective agreements are not enforceable in a court but only by the immediate parties, fairly implying that unions can hope to secure compliance with their terms only by striking. This counsel of despair sacrifices most of the stabilizing advantages inherent in written collective agreements. For if these undertakings fail to keep the parties on a fairly businesslike basis of mutual give and take, much of their contribution to civilized progress is lost. Fortunately, our courts do not share the hopeless attitude of the House of Lords, although their attempts to provide redress under these agreements are still far from satisfactory.

Judicial developments in this country concerning the enforcement of collective agreements fall roughly into three categories—none of them according to an unincorporated union, as such, actual participation in litigation. Under one category, collective agreements between a union and an employer result in a *custom* or *usage* which is to be reflected in the individual "contracts" of employment made by each worker with the employer. This theory implies the nonexistence of any contract between the union and the employer—a view possibly explained by the fact that under judicial conceptions of its status, the union is not in a position to offer any obligation in return for the benefits conceded by the employer. Practically, the agreement becomes effective only when each individual employee contracts with the employer to receive for his labor the terms of employment which it recites. Generally, this means that each employee must have the terms of the agreement in mind when he is hired and must stipulate that they are to control in his case. It is really inaccurate to call the individual employment relationship a contract, since each worker is actually employed only at the will of his employer. Of course, an employee suing for back wages always brings suit on the theory of an implied contract to pay him the value of his services. If he cannot prove an agreement to pay so much per unit of time worked, the jury fixes a fair value.

If, however, the employee bringing suit has worked under a collective agreement, then according to the custom or usage theory he may look to that agreement for the terms covering his employment, as long as he can prove that he had such terms in mind when he was hired. Apparently it makes little difference under this theory that an employee claiming the benefits of a collective agreement does not belong to the union—at least if the agreement does not specify that its terms cover only members of the union. Such stipulations are rare, if they exist at all. But whether or not he is a member of the union, only the employee claiming rights under the agreement may enforce such rights by court action. The union has no rights under the contract which it may have enforced at law. It is free to help the individual prosecute his law suit. But it may procure enforcement only through the more primitive self-help method of striking.

A second category for the judicial enforcement of collective agreements—the *agency* theory—is no improvement on the custom or usage theory. According to this approach, a union acts as the agent of its members to bargain with the employers over the conditions of their labor. Courts accepting this theory unfortunately attempt to apply the conventional rules of law governing agency relationships in the business world. Hence they assert that the union, as such, is not the real contracting party, since it is only an agent. Here again, only individual employees with grievances may press claims under the agreement, their ultimate recourse being personal litigation in the courts. And since they theoretically bring suit as "principals" of the agent union, only members of the union may secure from the courts compliance with the terms of the agreement. Presumably members employed after the agreement has become effective may not acquire rights until they have ratified its provisions. And for that matter, in the absence of a clear-cut principle of majority rule such as we know it today under NLRA developments—either stated in the union's constitution and effected thereunder by a vote of the membership ratifying the bargained agreement or arbitrarily imposed by the courts—any member may disclaim a term of the agreement or repudiate a subsequent collectively bargained adjustment affecting his rights, unless his personal ratification was secured.

Little hope lies in the trend toward the third category for the judicial enforcement of collective agreements—that called the *beneficiary* theory. Under this development, copied directly from conventional contract law prevailing in some of our states, a union enters into a contract with an employer for the benefit of those workers whom the contracting parties intend to cover. Although the employees benefited are not parties to the contract at all, they may nevertheless secure judicial enforcement of its terms under this theory. Here the union is necessarily a party to the collective agreement, although many unions so recognized under this theory have no separate legal personality except that lent them by the courts in order to make the theory work.

Under this theory an employee may secure judicial enforcement of the collective agreement in his own behalf even if he is not a member of the union, as long as he can show that it was the intention of the contracting parties to allow him the benefits of the contract. But this theory, like the others, is hopelessly involved with legalistic paraphernalia, bad enough in the contexts where it was originally conceived and utterly out of place in the field of labor relations. The third party beneficiary theory in the law of contracts—a far from universally accepted piece of judicial legislation, adapted to the intricacies of mortgages and suretyship—provokes the most ridiculous legalistic speculations when it is grafted onto the field of labor relations.

It is not profitable to discuss further any of these judicial theories. Some consideration of them was necessary to show the futility of adapting common-law principles, developed for another purpose, for use in the labor relations field. It is probably unfair to blame our courts for having done no better, since they are not supposed to cut new paths. Their function may include occasional stretching of legal principles to encompass new situations. But the social change has been too rapid and violent in this field to allow for the slow process of judicial adaptation. Even if judges were inclined to cut through the conventional legalisms and achieve rules to govern the enforceability of collective agreements, they are not expert in labor matters and would probably disagree among themselves as to how they should be handled. Furthermore they would not have the power to set up effective ancillary procedures like arbitration. These common-law theories which they developed are inadequate because they do not allow for suits by unions against employers nor for suits by employers against unions and individual employees under these agreements.

What we need immediately is a thoroughgoing legislative treatment specifically designed to make collective bargaining and the resulting agreements work smoothly and efficiently. And the less such legislation depends for its measures on the conventional law of contracts, the better it will be. Perhaps it would be wise for legislatures to assume in this task that collective agreements closely resemble treaties of peace, requiring sanctions to compel all parties concerned to observe their freely made commitments. They might, indeed, bear in mind Justice Jackson's observation, in his opinion in *J. I. Case Company v. NLRB*, that the term "trade agreement" is more appropriate than "contract," as well as his suggested analogy between these agreements and certain types of fixed schedules of terms controlling individual contracts. In this recent case he likened these collective labor agreements, in their practical effect at least, "to the tariffs established by a carrier, to standard provisions prescribed by supervising authorities for insurance policies, or to utility schedules of rates and rules for service, which do not of themselves establish any relationships but which do govern the terms of the shipper or insurer or customer relationship whenever and with whomever it may be established." He also called attention to the fact that in some European countries a privately negotiated trade agreement of this sort, when approved by an appropriate government agency, becomes a "governmental regulation ruling employment in the unit." Apparently he envisioned individual employment relationships—contracts of employment, if that is preferred—created between employer and employee, automatically including the terms set forth in the controlling trade agreement.

Legislatures should note that Justice Jackson was suggesting only a rough analogy between collective agreements on the one hand and tariffs, standard provisions, and rate schedules on the other. Unlike these situations, collective agreements are bargained out between private persons—unions and employers—who regard themselves as parties to these agreements, with rights and obligations apart from those of the individual employees. The final agreement is intended to reflect the mutual intentions of the parties, indicating that which each was able to secure from the other in a series of horse trading conferences which involved all sorts of concessions and compromises. The extent to which this might be true naturally depends on the relative bargaining strength of the parties—the willingness and ability of the union to strike and the ease with which the employer might resist such pressure. On the other hand, to pursue Justice Jackson's analogy, the terms of a collective agreement are usually applied to all employees in a particular bargaining unit.

However a legislature may go about setting up a procedure for the application and enforcement of collective labor agree-

ments, it is faced with the fact that thousands of these agreements now exist in some sort of practical working order. Collective bargaining practices now in everyday use are far ahead
of anything the courts and the legislatures have ever conceived
or even pondered about. Hence, projected legislation will have
to be planned in accordance with these developments, reflecting many of the techniques already adopted by employers and
unions as well as some of those imposed by the National War
Labor Board.

For instance, in the garment and soft coal industries, the employers and unions concerned have long since worked out for
themselves fairly adequate procedures to dispose of contentious issues arising under their collective agreements. In each
the collective agreements involved are either industry wide or
cover large blocks of an industry in a particular locality, usually
master agreements between associations of employers on the
one hand and national unions of affiliated locals on the other.
While the garment industry has tended to secure the interpretation and application of master contracts through the use of
a privately retained impartial umpire, the soft coal industry
depends on the decisions of regional joint boards composed
of employers and union representatives, with ultimate recourse
to arbitration, if necessary. But these are voluntary arrangements. Their success lies in the civilized determination of the
contracting parties to make them work, as the only practical
alternative to chaos. They amount to a type of self-govern-
ment, without legal sanctions, existing within a political government which should provide adequate sanctions to insure
the operation of such arrangements throughout industry in
general.

The first thing to decide in any projected legislative program
concerning collective bargaining agreements is whether or not
the collective bargaining process should itself be regulated.
This process, which results in collective agreements, must be
considered in sharp contradistinction to the application and
enforcement of such agreements after they are once achieved.

Regulation of the collective bargaining process happens to be one of the most fundamental issues in the contemporary labor relations field. Traditionally in this country the private parties concerned have conducted the negotiation of collective bargaining agreements, government having intervened through mediation and conciliation merely to get the parties together on some mutually satisfactory compromise basis. The backbone of collective bargaining has always been economic coercion, which includes union recourses like strikes, boycotts and picketing, as well as employer recourses like shutdowns, lockouts and farming out work. Naturally a good deal of collective bargaining takes place around a conference table, but those who believe that such parliamentary procedure is all there is to collective bargaining are just kidding themselves. Possibly the word "bargaining" is a misleading term for this whole process, and terms like "hold up" or "starve out" may be more accurate. But such speculation seems beside the point at this late date.

A question of primary political importance is whether or not employers and unions are willing to abandon their traditional techniques of bargaining in exchange for the terms of employment which some appropriate government agency might believe suitable. And if they are not willing to abandon these traditional techniques, should they be made to do so in the general public interest? Although these speculations might not have been taken seriously before the war, they must now be carefully considered in view of the remarkable performance of the War Labor Board. That board's function was to do the collective bargaining for employers and unions who could not manage to do their own. It undertook this task on the assumption that a nation at war could not afford the disruptions which the traditional collective bargaining process might occasion. Its success was due largely to the fact that employers and unions co-operated in accepting and following the policy pronouncements and decisions of the board. Many people have been so favorably impressed by this experience that they would like to see something of the sort set up as a permanent institution. But there are a number of angles they may have overlooked.

In response to the first question above, it seems unlikely that many employers or unions would wish to abandon the traditional techniques of collective bargaining. Most employers would probably like to see the economic bargaining devices of unions completely abolished by law, but they know that this is politically impossible. Indeed, most of them would regard as highly undesirable the only form of government which would make suppression of that kind possible. Quite obviously, the unions do not want to give up their traditional bargaining techniques like the strike. Some employers and a few union leaders might be willing to take a chance on government-imposed collective agreements, but only on the gamble that a particular political administration would lean more toward their side than the others'. This possibility of politically influenced bias, however, is probably what makes most employers and labor leaders nervous about government-conducted bargaining. They would vastly prefer to take their chances on private bargaining, even with all of the trouble that that choice inevitably entails.

As to the second question, in the absence of a paramount national emergency it is almost impossible to justify governmental assumption of the collective bargaining function, even for the purpose of obviating the wasteful and disruptive strikes and boycotts associated with private bargaining. This is so, chiefly because there are no known standards by which government supervised collective bargaining can be conducted. Naturally standards of some sort could be adopted by Congress. That is what everybody is afraid of. If it goes that far, Congress might just as well fix prices and wages and be done with it. We could, of course, have our economists draft standards to govern collective bargaining.

Then the questions would arise: Which economists? And, who would select them? Would they be those reflecting employers' beliefs, those reflecting the sentiments of organized labor, or those reflecting one of the intermediate philosophies? Would the test of competing economic theories be their relative worth, if there be anyone to make the choice, or would it be a show of hands on the floors of Congress? In a country whose only labor policy so far is to have no labor policy, these would be difficult questions to answer. Indeed, any answer would imply a kind of regulation completely at war with the prevailing notions of free enterprise so deeply entrenched in the minds of both employers and organized employees. Each group would like regulation of the other, even if that meant some invasion of free enterprise; but, in the last analysis, they would all agree that complete free enterprise for every economic undertaking is better than none for anybody.

Naturally, a middle course suggests itself. And it is no idle speculation to foresee the possibility of something like the "codes of fair competition" current in the NRA days of 1933. This time, however, the main object would be to fix uniform labor standards throughout the various industries, with allowances for local and regional variations warranting occasional differentials. And organized labor would enjoy parity with the employers in establishing these industry-wide codes. Inevitably an undertaking of this kind would require price fixing of commodities, and the distinction between such a setup and a planned, noncompetitive economy by direct legislation would be hard to discern. One obvious distinction might win the approval of some employers and labor leaders. In a scheme of this sort the bargaining function would still be present, making it possible for employer and employee groups to negotiate compromises. The final result would be called a collective agreement. The only possible catch might be that the government would resolve all failures to reach decisions, a factor which might easily keep one side or the other from committing itself, depending on the known political temper of the administration in power. And since such arrangements would necessarily have to cover entire industries, the expectation of securing a united labor front through unions now competing in the same field seems hopeless.

ISSUES ARISING UNDER COLLECTIVE AGREEMENTS—GRIEVANCES AND THE INTERESTS OF NONMEMBERS

Although it may be incorrect to assume that projected legislation will not include government regulation of the collective bargaining process, this assumption is necessary for a profitable inquiry into the application and enforcement of collective agreements. Any legislation concerning this intensely practical matter must be carefully adapted to practices already established either by custom between employers and unions or in accordance with the law. For instance, it will have to provide that all members of a given bargaining unit are covered by any collective agreement negotiated, since the NLRA already stipulates that the bargaining agency selected by a majority of the employees in a unit is the exclusive bargaining representative for all of them. And new legislation of this type should reflect all implications of the majority rule idea if it is to be completely consistent with the policies of the NLRA. Practically, this means giving unions a separate legal identity for all general purposes—to contract, to sue and be sued—possibly subject to their having registered with some state or federal agency in accordance with certain stipulated formalities. Or it could mean establishment of a series of specified detailed union privileges covering the same ground, not subject to modification through judicial interpretation but less flexible in their application than more generally described powers. Incidental to this, unions must be allowed to bind all employees in the units they represent, whether such employees be members or nonmembers, to any commitments they may negotiate with the employers concerned.

Many may think this last provision an extraordinary power to grant a union over employees' vested interests, such as accumulated seniority rights of great value to them. But unless unions have this power, assuming that they must use it impartially for the benefit of the employees as a whole, they will not be able to operate for the best interests of all concerned. A possibly unusual illustration—a situation which has nevertheless actually occurred in the railroad industry—indicates why this is so. Suppose two companies of equal size, producing the same kind of goods and having adjacent plants, decide to merge into one company, whether for purposes of efficiency and general economy or for other reasons. A part of this merger may be a consolidation of similar departments in order to avoid duplications of machinery, transportation, and supervision. Also assume that each company had been under separate but practically identical collective agreements with the same union. Omitting any consideration of how necessary reductions of the working force might be effected, how would the seniority list in a given department of the new company be drawn, assuming that the personnel in the formerly separate departments were placed together in the new consolidated department?

Presumably the union could cancel the old contracts and negotiate another with the new single employer. If it did this, could it negotiate a new seniority list for the department in question, dovetailing the two old lists so that the service of each employee in the new department is properly reflected in his relative position on this list? Many of the individual employees would no doubt complain, if this were done, that they have lost their positions of relative advantage on the seniority list. Thus, one who had been tenth on the old list in his former job, now may be eighteenth on the new list. Actually he would have gained by the change, assuming that the new department is just twice as large as either of the old ones, although this factor should be immaterial if his relative length of service is accurately stated. At any rate, if the union were not allowed this power to negotiate reasonable adjustments over the objections of the employees concerned, adequate collective bargaining in this instance would become impossible.

It might be thought necessary in a case like this to allow the individual employees an opportunity to secure a judicial declaration of what should have been done and whether their relative seniority positions should have been maintained, but this would seem most unfortunate. Naturally these employees should have the opportunity to prevent an arbitrary disposition of their rights, just as minority stockholders of a corporation may complain of the unwarranted excesses approved by the majority. But that is far different from substituting a court's notions of proper collective bargaining for those authorized by legislation. In such a situation, the court should be confined to reviewing the union's exercise of authority, remaining free to declare the particular negotiation an excess of power only if it found that the union and the companies had exceeded the scope of bargaining authority set forth in the statute. And similar treatment would be appropriate for other kinds of negotiations between a union and an employer, such as agreeing to a wage cut in the face of adverse economic conditions otherwise endangering continuation of operations. For it would seem that a far-reaching application of the majority rule principle is imperative to successful collective bargaining, even if it means vesting *all* bargaining power and representation in the unions, leaving the employment interests of individual workers completely in their hands. If any of the employees dislike the representation that a majority of their fellows have selected, they are always free to campaign for another union or for no union at all, or to find work elsewhere.

Acceptance of these conclusions should not imply a denial of opportunities for individual employees in bargaining units to secure redress for violations of their established rights under collective agreements. Certainly such opportunities should be available to all individual employees, but great care is necessary to determine what these rights are, how they arise, and a practical procedure for their adequate enforcement. Any claims asserted by individual employees working under a collective labor agreement will presumably be made against their employer. Among such claims would naturally be included demands for wages earned but either not paid at all or not paid in proper conformance to the established rate, to the number of hours worked, both straight time and overtime, or to the scheduled job classifications. In as much as claims of this type are more or less routine—frequently arising from bookkeeping errors in the employer's office, in time reports submitted to the office, and in particular employees' own faulty memoranda of time worked or misconception of their rights with respect to accurately kept personal memoranda—little harm and much good accompanies their direct submission to management by the individual employees. They are usually straightened out on the spot, to the mutual satisfaction of everyone concerned. In a way, such claims do not really involve the employees' rights under the collective agreement. They more closely concern his rights created in his personal "contract" of employment, since they do not reflect a misinterpretation of the collective rights so much as they indicate, rather, a misapplication of conceded rights to individual situations through erroneous conceptions of facts.

Now this is a broad statement. But it is intended only to suggest a valid distinction between claims made under clearly understood contract rights with respect to which a misconception of the actual facts exists, on the one hand, and claims made, on the other, under ambiguous or disputed contract rights with respect to which the facts are conceded. It is obvious that the clear categorical distinction between these two situations may easily become lost in particular cases, and occasionally it may seem to be only one of degree. The distinction is suggested only to show that there are certain types of cases easily and adequately cleared up by individual complaints made directly to management. As long as everyone concedes that such adjustments are not in themselves "bargaining," it is hard to see how their occurrence detracts from the function of the union as exclusive bargaining agency. Obviously, if such claims are not promptly and easily settled to the mutual satisfaction of the parties immediately concerned, they become grievances under the collective agreement as a matter of course. And while the union might appropriately have handled them in the first instance, at this stage its intervention becomes imperative.

These conclusions, regarding the power of a union acting as exclusive bargaining representative to dispose of all the details of employment which affect individual employees in a particular unit, have been subjected to serious question in a recent decision of the Supreme Court—*Elgin J. & E. Ry. Company v. Burley*—handed down in June, 1945. This case arose under the Railway Labor Act and thus may not drastically affect the administration of collective agreements and union bargaining power in industry in general, because of the peculiar conditions prevailing in the railway labor scene. Nevertheless, it is a most disturbing invasion of the principle of majority rule and may have repercussions endangering the salutary developments of recent years in this direction.

In this case it appeared that certain individuals employed by the Standard Oil Company had operated railroad equipment in that company's yard in Whiting, Indiana. During 1934 the railroad took over these yards and the operators in question became employees of the railroad, as well as members of the appropriate brotherhood with which the railroad had a collective agreement. Four years elapsed thereafter before the railroad finally conceded that these employees should be governed by a certain provision of this agreement dealing with starting time. In the meantime, these individuals, through the union, had filed claims for penalty back pay with the Railway Adjustment Board, contending that the railroad owed them these accrued sums totaling around $65,000, under the terms of the agreement. In 1938 the railroad offered a settlement of these claims to the union, on the understanding that its acceptance would wipe out the claims for good. The officials of the union agreed to this settlement and the claims were formally withdrawn from the Adjustment Board.

Thereafter the individual employees concerned filed new claims for the penalty back pay incurred because of the railroad's noncompliance with the agreement. Naturally the railroad pleaded the settlement of these claims with the union as a defense to their renewal. The Adjustment Board thought this defense good, so the individuals brought suit in the federal courts. Eventually five members of the Supreme Court held that the settlement by the union was no bar to their suit, while the four dissenting justices thought it should be a bar. Justice Rutledge, speaking for the majority, said that since the individuals had not expressly authorized this settlement, the Court must conclude that the union had no power in itself to settle already established claims for past money due over the heads of individual members of the unit, even conceding that it had the sole and exclusive power to bargain out conditions of employment to operate prospectively.

Justice Frankfurter, speaking for the minority, declared that this was not a simple case of a principal (the individual employees) attacking the unauthorized act of an agent (the union). He insisted that developments in American unionism have been consistently in the direction of exclusive bargaining power in the unions representing employees. Also he pointed out that employees in the past have been dealt with severely for bargaining directly with individual workers who were represented by unions. He deprecated the distinction between bargaining over future terms of employment and the settlement of past due claims in favor of individuals. Thus he intimated that this decision is a severe setback to the principle of majority rule in American unionism and that, as a consequence of it, employers will be forced to abandon direct dealings with unions and to seek recourse to litigation as the only safe method of procedure in handling union affairs. The Court later consented to a reconsideration of this decision. But in March, 1946, a majority of its members reaffirmed its original position in this case, in spite of the fact that the United States government, several of the railroad unions, the AF of L and the CIO all joined with the railroad company in urging a reversal. The uncertainty resulting from the Court's qualified adherence to its original position in this case has apparently disrupted settled practices under the Railway Labor Act sufficiently to require Congress immediately to pass legislation neutralizing the effect of the *Burley* decision.

Any supposed denial of rights under a collective agreement to individual employees or to whole groups of employees— constituting either a part of the bargaining unit or the entire unit itself—gives rise to a grievance or a series of grievances. Such grievances *must* be clearly distinguished from individual or group demands for additional rights, frequently wage increases, not already established in the existing agreement. The latter type of demand is not, strictly speaking, a grievance at all. It is, rather, a new collective bargaining demand and, while there is no harm in its being made during the life of an agreement, such a demand does not arise under the terms of the agreement. Indeed, its pursuit by self-help bargaining techniques such as the strike may be in direct violation of already established contract provisions.

Now the prosecution of a true grievance arising under a collective agreement—either on behalf of an individual employee, of a group of employees, or of the entire unit—may accurately be described as a type of bargaining in itself. That is to say, it is bargaining expressly contemplated in the grievance procedure. Such a process is different from *collective* bargaining—which term is used to denote the negotiations leading up to the collective agreement, itself. Nevertheless, the process of handling a grievance is a kind of bargaining, since it normally looks toward a settlement either by the employer's eventual acknowledgment of its justice, by some compromise, or by some further step such as arbitration when the employer stands pat and the union refuses to admit that it is wrong.

One may well ask by what right a union shall intervene between the employer and the individual employees or groups of employees in order to represent the latter in handling their grievances. Why should an individual employee not be free to settle on any grounds agreeable to him, or to dismiss entirely, any grievance he has raised concerning his personal interests? And why should an employer not be free to deal in this way with the individual employee? Why is not a union's collective and representative function fulfilled when it has bargained out an agreement? There may be many answers to these questions. One of them certainly is that this additional representative function is customarily undertaken by unions, quite often in conformance to express provisions in the grievance procedures outlined in collective agreements. And it is much better that way for practical reasons. Most individual workmen are not able to deal with such matters. They may be skilled craftsmen or they may be common laborers, but whatever they are, they frequently lack the interpretative and forensic abilities to deal with business matters of this sort.

Then again, the whole point of collective representation in the first place was to avoid direct dealings between an employee and his employer because of the inequality in their relative bargaining power. This point might be lost if the employer were permitted to deal with individual employees directly for the purpose of settling grievances which arose under an agreement bargained collectively between him and the union. Furthermore, the union itself, on behalf of all the employees in the unit, has a very real interest in seeing that the terms of the agreement are observed in their practical, day-to-day application. Hence, it can hardly be expected to risk dubious precedents resulting from individual bargaining or to stand by and see what it fought for in the agreement being whittled away by the employer's settlements with relatively helpless individuals.

A very real problem occurs when nonmembers of the union raise grievances under the contract. Although it would be a stupid business practice, some people might suspect that a union would not prosecute such grievances faithfully, concluding that nonmembers should, therefore, be encouraged to settle their complaints with management. And this feeling of suspicion may be heightened where it appears that a favorable settlement of a nonmember's grievance would in some way be disadvantageous to a member of the union. Such a situation might easily arise over conflicting seniority claims between a member and a nonmember. Again, the answers to this problem may be manifold, but a few adequate answers seem apparent.

An established union in an open shop is anxious to convince nonmembers of its value to them in order to secure their membership. One of the best ways it can do this is by faithfully servicing their grievances. Such an undertaking may be difficult, when success means depriving a union member of some benefit he enjoys through the employer's misapplication of the contract. Any union representative is likely to hesitate before going to bat under such circumstances. Fortunately, however, such cases seldom arise, since the average employer may be trusted not to make many mistaken applications of the contract in favor of union, as against nonunion, employees. But even if he does, it seems fairer in the interests of expedience to allow the union the sole right of handling grievances with the employer, in view of the harm to collective representation which may ensue from any other course. After all, a nonunion employee in such a plight belongs to a group in which the majority has selected the union as their exclusive bargaining representative. Under the principle of majority rule, it seems fair enough to make him accept the imperfections of that system along with its benefits, one of which is the very provision which has given him the right to raise a grievance in the first place. Furthermore, he is free to join the union any time he concludes that his nonmembership is disadvantageous to his interests.

Many unions, certified as exclusive bargaining representatives of all employees in open shops, bitterly resent the ability of nonmembers to enjoy all the benefits of collective bargaining without contributing in any way to the support of the unions who secured these advantages. These nonunion members of the bargaining units accept seniority, vacations and wage increases, expecting to have all of these advantages secured to them in strict accordance with the terms of the agreements. Yet they did not contribute to the expense of the original bargaining negotiations and paid nothing toward the upkeep of these contracts. As the union men see it, these free riders make nonunionism pay dividends, for they earn just as much as the union members and are able to keep in their pockets what their organized fellow workers pay out in dues. Of course, the unions realize that if collective bargaining is going to be effective, it must introduce uniform standards throughout a unit, for union and nonunion employees alike.

When a union is unable to secure a closed shop contract in a unit, its members know that the price they must then pay for the advantage of exclusive bargaining rights in that unit is the overhead cost of this privilege. Unions nevertheless prefer it that way to allowing a cleavage between higher union and lower nonunion standards of employment in the same unit. While this divergence of standards might induce nonunion employees to join the organization, past experience indicates that it might eventually insure the undermining of union standards and, possibly, of the union itself. For the introduction of lower nonunion standards might give the employer an incentive to hire only people willing to work under such standards. Unions have bitterly fought this sort of thing for decades. They found in the past that the closed union shop was the only protection against it. For if all employees belonged to the union, they worked under union standards and the employer could not introduce lower standards to compete with them.

Under the NLRA, however, unions know that their standards cannot be undermined in this way, even in an open shop, now that their collective agreements introduce uniform standards. This is something for which they are thankful. But they and their dues-paying constituents now fail to see why the nonunion employees should not share the cost of achieving these benefits. The way to make them share, of course, is to get the closed union shop and establish union membership in good standing as a condition of continued employment. During the next few years, this element of union discontent is bound to intensify the drive for closed union shop contracts. The inevitable clash might conceivably be settled without conceding the closed shop by checking off from nonunion employees' pay amounts equivalent to union dues and assessments and paying this money over to the unions. Perhaps a less shocking compromise would be for each employer to pay this checked off money to some charity.

Either way would deprive the nonunion employees of their advantage over union workers and would serve to keep labor standards uniform. But only the former method would keep the unions from pressing for the closed shop and, under the present state of our law, both methods would possibly render the employers liable to their nonunion employees for the amounts checked off. Hence, we may expect determined union drives for the closed shop or for legislation permitting employers to check off the equivalent of union dues and assessments from the wages of nonunion employees, to be paid to the bargaining representatives acting for them. And if the unions base this legislative demand on the legal theory of an implied contractual right to compensation for services rendered and a corresponding obligation for services accepted, society cannot afford to laugh this off. They will be deadly serious about it.

In the meantime there will remain the practical difficulties apparent when a union is obliged to prosecute grievances filed under a collective agreement by nonunion employees. But the foregoing discussion may indicate reasons why we should not feel too sorry for these employees. If collective bargaining and collective representation are to become the future basis for industrial democratization, in which the majority rule is to prevail, then society should no more pity these nonunion employees than it does a citizen denied social benefits because he refuses to pay his taxes. People who think unionism is bad for our economy will naturally disagree with this because it would tend to force all nonunion employees into the unions representing them. But in light of what has been happening in the development of labor policy affecting unions, they must concede that a trend of this sort is politically foreseeable.

ARBITRATION—ITS SCOPE AND POSSIBLE LEGISLATIVE BACKGROUND

The state courts afford individual employees no practicable recourse in the pursuit of their rights under collective agreements. Rather than go to the extreme of suing in the courts, most of them would prefer to pocket their losses and wait until justice is less expensively and more conveniently achieved. Yet this is all that our law at present provides. Even this recourse is uncertain and enshrouded with conflicting legalistic theories. And if a union were willing to bring suit on grievances arising under collective agreements, either on behalf of individual employees or for a whole bargaining unit, it is doubtful under existing judicial authority if it might do so. There are isolated instances of unions securing judicial aid in compelling employers to comply with collective agreements. But there is little reason to believe either that such precedents will be generally followed or that they point the way to a proper solution of this vexing problem.

The fact remains that the courts do not provide either an adequate or appropriate method of applying and enforcing collective agreements. Employers and unions are aware of this. Just as the merchants in the medieval fairs set up their own informal "courts" to adjust their mutual differences on the spot, so a few employers and unions have established their own procedures for settling disputes arising under collective agreements. The "law merchant" was eventually absorbed into our common law after some centuries had elapsed. In time our common law might adapt itself to the practical needs of labor relations and reflect some of the techniques developed by these employers and unions. But society cannot wait for this to happen, even if it wanted the courts to assume control of applying and enforcing collective agreements. Only the legislatures are able to initiate these settlement procedures for general application throughout industry. And if they are to be uniform, Congress is the only legislature up to the job.

Arbitration affords an expeditious and inexpensive procedure for the settlement of labor grievances. Yet most employers and most union leaders are suspicious about arbitration—at least, until they have tried it. The nature and scope of this process must be carefully defined before their suspicions are allayed. Now, arbitration is an informal procedure for deciding disputed issues. While it *can* be used as a substitute for collective bargaining, in order to break a deadlock in negotiations between employers and unions over the terms of a collective agreement still in the making, its use for this purpose hardly seems to be real arbitration at all. This is the sort of thing the War Labor Board did as a substitute for collective bargaining over the terms of agreements during the war. But nobody thought of the War Labor Board as arbitrating disputes!

Indeed, it is practically impossible to arbitrate deadlocks of this type in the absence of generally conceded standards of decision. Real arbitration would properly seem to imply the disposition of a dispute in accordance with some standard— possibly a law, a trade practice or a provision in a contract— which the parties to the dispute concede to exist, although they cannot agree upon what it means or how it is to be applied in the particular case. Collective bargaining over the terms of a collective agreement, on the other hand, is not a process involving the application of a standard of any sort to a specific situation. Collective bargaining is, rather, an attempt to establish standards—the standards of employment which are in themselves the subject of dispute.

The only conceivable standards that might govern collective bargaining negotiations are general economic standards, and the consensus around the table on these may be easily imagined! To be sure, arbitrators could establish standards if they had to do so. But it seems absurd to let them draw upon their personal notions of economic values in order to break collective bargaining deadlocks. Indeed, this could hardly be termed the application of external standards, no matter how objective the arbitrators might be. Congress, presumably, could legislate standards through the exercise of its political process. But if it went this far, it would probably not leave their application to private arbitrators. More likely, it would set up an administrative commission under which so-called "arbitrators" would decide particular cases in accordance with these standards, their "awards" being subject to the commission's approval. At any rate, employers and labor leaders might well remain suspicious about arbitration in view of the current loose usage of that term in connection with resolving collective bargaining disputes. Rather than entrust their affairs to such an ill-defined procedure, they would understandably prefer to fight for what they can get by recourse to traditional collective bargaining techniques. And dressing up this process in the cloak of "fact finding" provides a poorly disguised substitute, hardly adequate to allay these suspicions.

In a labor relations context, arbitration more accurately implies the interpretation and application of an already achieved collective agreement in the disposition of specific grievances raised under that agreement. There the arbitrator is at liberty to act only within an area that the parties to the agreement had ample opportunity to define in considerable detail. Of course, employers and unions cannot possibly anticipate all possible exigencies and provide for them in their agreements, and what they do cover in advance is frequently couched in ambiguous language. Amazingly different and conflicting interpretations can be read by opposing counsel into apparently clear sentences or phrases used in the agreement to express the mutual intentions of the parties. Sometimes whole sections appear to have been written with such ambiguity that they suggest the studied effort of the parties to remain unclear, each in the possible hope that a decisive meaning will ultimately be supplied in his favor. But the arbitrator has to give meaning to the provisions of the agreement as he finds them, after the parties have had a chance to argue their respective interpretations before him. At least he has something fairly definite to apply to specific fact situations brought before him. And when the terms of the agreement are not as definite as they might be, the parties have only themselves to blame if they do not like the construction which the arbitrator puts on them.

But even this limited scope of arbitration seems too broad for many employers and labor leaders. They still fear the discretion which an arbitrator may exercise over their affairs in accordance with his personal opinions and economic predilections. Nevertheless, a few employers and unions have for some years voluntarily submitted their grievances to arbitration. And during the war many of them did become accustomed to arbitration, after it was included in their agreements by the War Labor Board. As a result, it seems likely that some sort of limited voluntary arbitration will generally prevail in the future as the final step in the prescribed grievance procedures of most collective agreements.

In a system of uniform arbitration lies the only real hope for the smooth operation of an industrial society governed by the terms of collective agreements. The foregoing discussion certainly indicates the impracticability of direct recourse to the courts for the settlement of disputes arising from these agreements. Such a recourse is expensive and time-consuming at best. In any event, our courts are not geared to handle matters of this nature. Only our legislatures can create the necessary procedures and sanctions behind a successful system of arbitration. If this system is to be uniform, then Congress should assume exclusive jurisdiction and promulgate a consistent procedure, including provisions for the enforcement of awards. That uniformity is essential seems obvious, in view of the present-day organization of industry in far-flung corporate units covering vast areas of the nation. A union and an employer operating under a master agreement covering plants in several states could hardly be expected to conform to as many different procedures in the application of that contract— a likely consequence if projected legislation is left to the various state legislatures.

But a vast program of this kind must be approached with great care, for several aspects of it are bound to make unions and employers very nervous, indeed. Most of this feeling of distrust arises from the fear that arbitration will become compulsory. Too many people immediately jump to the conclusion that this process necessarily means the compulsory settlement of *all* labor disputes—even those involved in collective bargaining—and they shudder at the idea of having to live under agreements ultimately written by arbitrators. These fears will hardly be justified if employers and unions are assured that compulsory arbitration will be confined to the interpretation and application of privately negotiated collective agreements, especially if it appears that they will be left free to choose their own arbitrators.

Legislation introducing arbitration should simply require it as the final step in the grievance procedure of every collective agreement, available for the resolution of all differences between employers and unions which arise under their mutually negotiated collective agreements. Employers and unions already know that there *has* to be some convenient and expeditious method for clearing up not only the routine grievances but also the more fundamental issues so frequently arising under collective agreements. They know that these agreements as a rule exist only from year to year, and that it might take twice the life of any such agreement to secure an interpretation and application in a court, if a decision on the merits could be secured at all. As long as they are assured that the scope of compulsory arbitration is defined as suggested, they will accept it with a good grace. For any opposition to such limited arbitration would imply that they do not wish to observe their collective agreements but would prefer recourse to primitive trial by combat—a procedure which society may grudgingly tolerate while an agreement is in the making but which it can no longer afford to condone after an agreement is reached.

If employers and unions are first assured that compulsory arbitration will be thus limited in scope, they can then divert their energies to seeing that the proposed statute contains adequate provisions. For instance, they could suggest that arbitration awards should be enforceable only by court orders after a judicial review of the awards. They might publicly explore the purpose and extent of such judicial review—whether it would be on the merits of the arbitrator's award, on the arbitrability of the issue decided, or on the authority of the arbitrator to act as he did under the proposed statute, regardless of how he decided the issue on its merits. For the employers and unions concerned might wish some protection against an arbitrator's assumption of power to pass on matters properly the subjects for collective bargaining or to exercise authority in a manner not consistent with the stipulated procedures. Conceivably, they might try to exclude from arbitration any issue that depends for its disposition on the application of some state or federal law or administrative decision covering the subject matter in issue. And they might debate sanctions against the failure of either employers or unions faithfully to abide by their undertakings in collective agreements to settle all of their differences under their mutually accepted grievance procedures, including arbitration.

It would be unfortunate if some of these provisions were actually adopted. Of course, the judicial enforcement of arbitrators' awards is essential, for if the losing party can successfully defy an award, the whole procedure would be jeopardized. On the other hand, it is natural to expect that Congress would not make awards automatically enforceable by court decree without some sort of judicial review. But the whole purpose of arbitration would be defeated if the losing party

were permitted to retry his case before a court. If this procedure is to work at all, it must depend on faith in the arbitrator's judgment.

Even if a court should disagree with an arbitrator's award
in a particular case, either on his statement of the facts and
the issue, his interpretation of the evidence offered, or his
construction and application of the contract, that does not
mean that the court is right and the arbitrator is wrong. The
award should still be enforced if the court finds that the arbitrator has not abused his authority as defined in the proposed
statute. And the award should stand even if the court believes
that the arbitrator has made a decision on an issue which it
believes not to have been arbitrable at all under the agreement. After all, an arbitrator should be quite capable of deciding that matter himself. If he is honest and sufficiently
clearheaded, he will recognize the nature of such an issue and
will not hesitate to deny a decision on its merits. Under the
projected statute a court should deny enforcement of an award
only if it finds that the arbitrator has clearly abused his power
in a capricious and prejudicial fashion or has not faithfully
adhered to the procedures stipulated by Congress.

A statutory provision denying an arbitrator the power to
decide issues which depend for their settlement on the interpretation and application of state or federal laws or administrative
rulings would be most distressing. It is true, some people believe that it is bad practice for an arbitrator to accept jurisdiction over such issues. But if, as frequently happens, the
parties voluntarily submit to arbitration an issue requiring the
interpretation of some law, it is hard to see what harm can
accompany this practice. Under compulsory arbitration it might
be reasonable to make such awards unenforceable unless the
reviewing court agrees with the arbitrator's view of the law
in question. But this is not really necessary in most cases, because the arbitrator cannot by his award foreclose official consideration of such situations.

For instance, if he has before him a grievance based on the

alleged discriminatory discharge of an employee and he decides that the discharge was not discriminatory but was for proper cause, nothing he has done can foreclose the NLRB from thereafter concluding otherwise. Similarly, if an arbitrator gave an award to a union on the basis of the Wage and Hour Act, involving rates and back pay of employees who are really under the jurisdiction of the Interstate Commerce Commission and excepted by a ruling of that commission from the terms of the Wage and Hour Act, the employer could secure an official disposition of this case in his favor. The fact remains, however, that many employers and unions prefer to submit these issues to arbitration in order to expedite their settlement. In 99 cases out of 100 they would accept the award, whether or not they agreed with it.

A section in an arbitration statute providing penalties against failures of the parties to abide by those terms of a collective agreement outlining the settlement of disputes which arise under the contract would have to be carefully drawn. Incidentally, this suggests one of the practical problems involved in the enforcement of labor agreements—the fact that it is much easier to compel compliance by an employer than it is to compel compliance by a union. If an employer fails to observe some provision of benefit to an employee or to the union, he can be compelled to make amends by back pay or some other tangible adjustment. But if a union or a group of employees violate some term of the contract designed to secure advantage to the employer, it is almost impossible to impose a remedy or even to enforce future compliance, except by negative actions such as discharges and disciplinary layoffs. This may be due to the nature of a collective agreement, since it is a document in which are scheduled the terms of employment given by the employer to his workers. In short, the employer is conceding something and the employees are receiving something. What they give in return is, primarily, their labor. Hence, about the only kind of undertaking they can enter into collectively concerns their supplying of services.

Off hand, this suggests the no-strike pledge for the duration of the contract. Such a pledge may, of course, have reference to collective bargaining strikes in pursuit of advantages not already granted in the agreement, or it may have reference only to strikes called to secure a favorable settlement of some grievance or issue arising under the terms of the agreement, for the disposition of which a procedure is set forth in the agreement itself. About the only practicable measures possible against bargaining strikes in violation of a collective agreement are injunctions and actions at law for money damages. Abrogation of the entire contract is frequently spoken of as a possible device to discourage bargaining strikes in violation of a no-strike pledge. But this would be a ridiculous penalty, since nothing would be gained by it except a good deal of grief. In any event, these sanctions could not be administered by an arbitrator, even if they were provided for in controlling legislation.

A union's promise not to strike in order to secure the settlement of grievances and other issues arising under an agreement, however, is an entirely different matter. An arbitrator can fairly easily administer and enforce an undertaking of this type. If a union has called a strike or slowdown in violation of such a promise, the arbitrator can uphold the company in whatever appropriate steps it took to discipline the employees involved, such as layoffs or discharges. Moreover, in subsequent proceedings before him, involving the issue which occasioned the work stoppage, the arbitrator may give the award to the company because of the union's breach of contract, regardless of what he may think of the grievance on its merits. Of course, the arbitrator would impose this penalty only when it was requested by the employer in such a case. Where, on the other hand, an employer "struck" by refusing to take a grievance to arbitration, the arbitrator could be authorized by statute to hear the grievance from the union in the absence of management and to render an award in the union's favor if he took its views on the merits of the case. This would certainly be a sufficient sanction against an employer, as long as the union was permitted in this way to raise the grievance and secure a decision.

This discussion may seem to indicate that the *only* suitable function of a labor arbitrator is to interpret and apply the terms of collective agreements. But there are other situations where arbitration has been and will continue to be exceedingly useful and appropriate. Suppose that a bargaining strike is settled by a truce which provides that the employer in question will adopt rates equal to those paid for similar work in another plant organized by the same union. Because of variations in figuring rates in the two plants, due to different base rates and incentive plans, the parties are unable to complete their negotiations and agree to submit the effect of their truce to an arbitrator. An issue of this sort is reasonably suited to arbitration, because it involves the interpretation of an interim agreement, although it is a definite part of the collective bargaining process leading up to a final agreement.

Another type of arbitrable situation is the old-fashioned type of jurisdictional dispute. Yet this has nothing to do with the terms of any agreement. To use the classical example, suppose a dispute arises between the carpenters and metal workers on a construction job, concerning which union shall have the work of hanging metal doors. The carpenters claim they have always hung doors, even if they were formerly made of wood, and the metal workers claim that they have always handled metal, whether it was in fixtures, window sashes or anything else, admitting, however, that they have never before hung doors. Even though there are few standards to guide him in this sort of situation, an arbitrator could adequately dispose of a dispute like this on the basis of testimony and findings concerning the background and history of the two unions concerned, with particular reference to their craft functions. Legislative authority for arbitration of these jurisdictional disputes, with a provision enabling enforcement of awards by injunction, should obviate one of the most wasteful and inexcusable types of strikes.

Aside from situations like these, opportunities for arbitration are rare in the absence of established collective agreements. Of course, if employers and unions *agree* to submit any conceivable issue to "arbitration," using that name to describe the method they choose for breaking a deadlock, they can no doubt get a settlement. After all, an arbitrator can undertake to pass on a requested wage increase with reference to the rise in the cost of living and to alleged reasonable standards of living, if the parties ask him to do it. Perhaps under such circumstances it is not even a misnomer to call this process "arbitration." But it seems wise to keep in mind that this method of settling such an issue is not arbitration as it has become known through practice in recent years. In any event, it would be a mistake to compel by statute the submission of such cases to so-called arbitration. If the government wants to provide an agency to settle issues of this kind without recourse to strikes, that is another matter. But the process would then more accurately be called compulsory "collective bargaining."

It is not appropriate in this book to discuss in detail the techniques and procedures of arbitration. An undertaking of that sort could easily fill a volume in itself. This brief account of arbitration can be justified only to suggest a practical device for interpreting and applying collective agreements. Individuals and groups of employees, or even unions representing them, cannot be expected to take their cases to courts, particularly under the present primitive stage of the common law concerning the enforcement of collective agreements. If a procedure is to be developed by legislation, it should be an adequate one, practically suited to handle specific requirements. Since there is great need for uniformity of procedure— particularly in view of the sectional and nation-wide character of so many corporate employers and affiliated unions—

federal legislation equivalent in jurisdictional scope to the NLRA seems imperative.

Such legislation must carefully define the character of issues to be covered by compulsory arbitration. While it should no doubt state certain standard requirements as the basis of this procedure, it must leave employers and unions somewhat free to develop arbitration procedures of their own by mutual consent. It would be rash to suggest that state legislatures should not enact labor arbitration statutes, just as several have adopted state labor relations acts to perform locally the same function carried out nationally under the NLRA. But, in the interests of uniformity, Congress might well provide for federal judicial review of state court judgments enforcing or refusing to enforce arbitration awards in industries over which it has jurisdiction.

These are speculative issues, and they may seem to raise considerations far off the beaten path of the law. But the labor relations situation in this country is becoming increasingly complicated. Actual employer-union relationships in collective agreements are being created too rapidly for our existing legal machinery to accommodate. While the procedural developments which have occurred during the war may not be to everybody's liking, some of them seem much too valuable to lose through Congressional inaction. Everyone directly interested in these matters must face the fact that collective bargaining and collective agreements are here to stay. Everyone should realize that to avoid industrial chaos, a practical and effective procedure must be devised to make collective agreements stable and operative. In any event, now is the time for everyone interested to speculate on these matters, for the mold of our future law of labor relations is about to be cast.

CHAPTER XIV

WHERE DO WE GO FROM HERE?

The problem to be solved, either as a matter of theory or as a matter of practical necessity, is at bottom always and everywhere the same. How can the right of combined action be curtailed without depriving individual liberty of half its value; how can it be left unrestricted without destroying either the liberty of individual citizens, or the power of the Government? To see that this problem at the present day presents itself everywhere, and has nowhere received a quite satisfactory solution, is of importance.—Dicey, *Law and Public Opinion in England*, 1919.

ASIDE from any of their questionable practices, labor unions must appear to all fair-minded citizens as necessary and valuable social institutions. In an industrial society where the means of production and distribution are under private control, they seem to be the only alternative to direct regulatory legislation as a means of insuring to individual workers completely fair consideration from their employers. Naturally, some employers have always been considerate and responsible toward their employees. But many have taken advantage of their superior economic position to get as much as they can from their employees for the least possible return in the form of either wages or job security.

Working people are by nature inclined to resent paternalistic solicitude in their behalf almost as much as they dislike oppression. They have always entertained notions about their "rights" in an industrial system in which employers have refused to recognize these rights as valid. With their new-found strength in unionism, they believe that they are now

413

in a position to establish some of these rights and to enforce them through the exercise of economic pressures. And in a world run on harsh and impersonal principles governing the distribution of wealth, who can really condemn them for copying the same methods employed by some of our great industrial leaders of the past when they band together in order to wrest from society a larger proportionate share of the national income, what they call a higher standard of living?

Perhaps the most apparent fault in this union philosophy is the failure of associated employees to appreciate that the establishment of a right of any sort inevitably implies the creation of corresponding duties. In any free society this must always be so. The history of industrialism in this country shows that the public has been constantly concerned with imposing on all kinds of private enterprise the duties of consideration toward consumers in exchange for the recognition of such rights as the ownership and control of the means of production and distribution. At times the public seemed to have been fighting a losing battle, for corporate enterprise has frequently waxed so great and our controls over its freedom of activity have occasionally been so ineffective that it has been free to treat the consumer and the investor almost as it wished to treat them.

But the public has asserted itself in statutes like the Sherman Act and its amendments, the Securities and Exchange Act, and the Holding Companies Act in attempts to protect consumers and investors by imposing legal duties in connection with the use of corporate power. Unfortunately, such controls have been necessary, since it is a ubiquitous trait of human nature to use power for all it is worth in the promotion of selfish purposes. Indeed, it may be argued that such uses of power are not even socially wrongful as long as society tolerates them, however harmful to the public interest they may be. This is because society has the burden of establishing its rules of conduct to curtail the abuses of economic power which endanger the interests of the community.

For many decades it has been recognized that while society has benefited from industrialism, it has been inclined to disregard the security of workers and their families. At common law an employer discarded an injured employee as an economic liability, not being required to assume any financial responsibility for the consequences of industrial accidents. To some extent, however, it has at last been decided to have society accept responsibility for such casualties, instead of leaving the injured workers and their families to bear those losses unaided. The various states have inaugurated a system of workmen's compensation acts, designed to place the burden of such losses directly on industry as an overhead operating cost. This falls indirectly on the public in the shape of "hidden taxes" reflected in slightly increased prices of commodities. This insurance idea of socializing risks which individual workers and their families were not in a financial position to administer has been greatly extended under modern social security laws to include unemployment compensation and pensions against improvidence in old age.

On top of all this, society has eventually recognized the right of workers to combine and to use the economic power of combinations for the achievement of more desirable conditions of employment and security against the arbitrary disposition of their job interests. This step has also cost society a great deal in the shape of "hidden taxes." And society is beginning to ask itself if this last concession is not likely to become more costly than it is worth. Realistic people know, however, that society cannot expect a return for any of these concessions—particularly in the shape of self-imposed limitations on the uses of economic power by unions—unless it demands such a return in its laws. A rough analogy is the imperfectly conceived program of obligations and duties which it has already imposed on the powers enjoyed by corporate enterprise. After all, society pays for what it supports in the way of aggressive institutions of all sorts. Even if it has benefited in untold numbers of ways from great corporate enterprise, it is surely entitled to keep such combinations in hand on a social basis.

In so far as working people are more economically independent and secure as a consequence of social legislation and labor unionism, to that extent all society benefits. Such advantage is the return to which society is entitled for creating and maintaining these institutions. Consequently, whether or not society made a bad bargain for having allowed these concessions, the only additional things which it could expect in return are the responsible and socially considerate use of the economic and security devices it has created and tolerated in labor's behalf. If it wants these additional returns, it must demand them in clear and well-articulated terms. For instance, if it believes that working people are abusing unemployment compensation, it should say so and do something about it. If it believes that unions are abusing their economic bargaining power, it should say so and do something about it.

The labor unions know what they want. In view of the state of our present law, they are with some reason going about getting it in a strictly logical fashion. We may all agree that it is foolish of them to take undue advantage of the economic power within their grasp. But the pressure on the unions from beneath is enormous. They cannot afford *not* to do almost exactly what they are doing today, if they are to survive as popular representatives of their constituents. Actually, it is society's function at this time to tell the unions directly—and their constituents through them—what they may and may not do with the new-found power that society has at last given them with so free a hand. It is up to all of us to tell the unions what their corresponding duties are in clear and unambiguous laws.

Before doing this, however, we must pause to reflect what we have irretrievably let ourselves in for, as far as unionism is concerned. We have created and tolerated a social institution directly at odds with what we have always traditionally cherished as the social good under the theoretical principles of classical economics. Of course, we made exactly this same mistake with corporate enterprise in the first place, although we have somewhat half-heartedly attempted to reconcile that development with the old principles of economics. Now we must ask ourselves, are these old principles of economics still sufficiently valid in the sort of world we inhabit to require strict observance?

Is the ideal of a competitive system composed of relatively small units of production any longer worth considering as practicable, especially in view of the fact that combination has gone as far as it has in many of our industries? Is anticompetitive combination a more suitable form of enterprise in an industrial world dedicated to mass production, such as that we now inhabit? Even if we conclude that it is not, although so many believe it is, can we as a practical matter do anything about atomizing our industrial system and re-creating old-fashioned competition at this late date? Are we not compelled to accept the industrial world as it is and subject it to intelligent control and regulation in the interests of the public good? If we accept corporate enterprise as it is, are we not obliged to accept unionism much as it has become, subjecting it also to a series of intelligent controls and regulations in the interests of the public good?

The answers to these questions require a little honest thinking. Our whole trend has been away from the ideal of old-fashioned competition as an instrument for the service of the consuming public. Perhaps this was because unfettered competition has been carried on so ruthlessly that it has frequently occasioned more harm than good. Also, free competition carried to its logical conclusion inevitably has meant combination and the suppression of competition. For the arbiters of our policy in the past were unable to see the value of competition to the competitors if they could not come out on top and stay there. Hence, it might easily be concluded that absolutely free competition is no longer possible and that if there is to be competition at all in the idealistic sense, it must be a controlled and regulated competition. Indeed, because of the administrative difficulties involved in maintaining an absolutely free competition based on a multitude of small units, society may reasonably decide in favor of combination with regulation.

Now labor unionism is a frankly monopolistic and anticompetitive institution, even if its major undertakings have been carried on and justified in the name of competition. This has been competition to suppress or combat competition, exactly as it always used to be in big business. In our study of unions, we have seen that a local in a particular plant would strive for the closed shop because it could not tolerate the competition of nonunion labor standards under the same roof. Then, the established affiliated locals in a given industry could not tolerate the competition of nonunion labor standards in unorganized units of that industry, any more than their unionized employers could. So they were compelled to campaign for the universal closed shop in the particular industry if they were to survive at all. We must therefore concede that unionism, as an institution designed to achieve and maintain higher than open market standards of employment, cannot exist as long as competing nonunion labor remains available. And this is true on a nation-wide basis, since our present-day scale of industrial, commercial, and transportational organization virtually makes the entire country one vast market.

It is now a commonplace to think of unionism affiliated on a nation-wide basis as a device primarily for eliminating the competition between union-made and nonunion-made goods in the same markets. Can we any longer honestly conceive of unionism as something dissociated from this objective? Those who answer this question in the affirmative will have a tremendous burden of proof to discharge. They might more profitably ask why our government ever permitted this anticompetitive development to take place under the policies of the Sherman Act? The answer to this question is that during the 1920's the Supreme Court did undertake to stop it by virtue of the Sherman Act.

But in 1940 a later personnel of the Court realized that it could be stopped under the antitrust laws only by denying the very existence of unions as they had developed (and probably had to remain if they were to exist at all) in a highly nationalized system of industry. By that time, perhaps understandably, the Court was reluctant to assume the responsibility of carrying out the task which Chief Justice Taft had so willingly undertaken almost 20 years previously in the *Coronado* cases. After all, even he had impliedly admitted that the difference between strikes for higher wages and for extending union organization was one of degree. The later personnel of the Court were of the opinion that this degree had by then become imperceptible, particularly in view of the policies expressed in intervening legislation like the Norris-LaGuardia Act and the NLRA.

If the Court had stopped its tolerance at that point, leaving the unions free to pursue organization upon a national basis for the purpose of eliminating nonunion competition through the unionization of industry, in spite of the Sherman Act, society would still have had enough legal protection under that act against many undesirable union practices. But in the *Hutcheson* case the Court felt impelled to divorce labor unions completely from any sense of responsibility toward the conduct of national commerce. This decision alone left society and the free flow of interstate commerce more at the mercy of organized economic power than they had ever been since the days preceding the passage of the Sherman Act.

Indeed, it is hard not to agree that by now so much water has gone over the dam that society must accept it as gone by default and take nationally affiliated unions for what they are. What this means as a practical matter is that we have obligated ourselves to tolerate in our midst a monopolistic and anticompetitive institution wielding enormous economic power. This does not mean, however, that we are helpless in dealing with this power or in subjecting it to whatever convenient restrictions we consider necessary for the public good. Nevertheless, if we are to regulate this power, we have to promulgate these regulations in new legislation, and this law should be in the nature of policing regulations designed to prevent particular harmful interferences with the conduct of national commerce. The real difficulty is to decide how far to go in order to protect commerce and at the same time to allow large unions a legitimate use for their lawful power.

In 1935, Congress concluded that organizational strikes were so harmful to commerce that their causes must be outlawed. Hence, it passed the NLRA to prevent employers from interfering with the organization of their employees into unions. To a large extent this measure was successful in obviating organizational strikes and in freeing commerce from the burdens it would otherwise have sustained. Now commerce has again been threatened by strikes which are just as harmful as those obviated in 1935. This time, however, it is unlikely that our representatives in Congress will regard employers as the guilty ones. Conceivably there may be some people who believe that Congress should allay this newly threatened harm to commerce by setting up a commission empowered to prevent a new type of unfair labor practice,—the refusal by an employer to accept "reasonable" union demands. But many people today are inclined to believe that the unions themselves are the guilty ones in threatening to strike for the purpose of procuring concessions which they have no right to ask. And they are of the opinion that Congress should this time devise some sanction against unions when they threaten to burden commerce with their recourse to self-help.

Everyone must realize that society has irretrievably committed itself to the right of union people to strike. It is not only politically impossible, but also dangerous socially, to abolish completely the right to strike. Indeed, any legislation of that far-reaching character would probably be held unconstitutional by the Supreme Court. Certainly the complete suppression of the right to strike would in our times create a condition closely akin to involuntary servitude and it would undoubtedly lead some members of our Supreme Court to call it the deprivation of a fundamental constitutional liberty. The most Congress could do in this direction would be to require the deferment of strikes pending some designated procedure for the settlement of particular disputes. If such procedure should not bring about the desired settlement, there is no feasible method that would permit us to outlaw strikes and, at the same time, remain a completely free people.

A procedure of this type has until recently obviated serious strikes in the railroads, since the passage of the Railway Labor Act in 1926. However, its cost has been an almost routine concession to the unions of the bulk of their demands. Something of the sort might be tolerated for settling the labor disputes in any public utility whose prices are fixed by public action, but its toleration in an industry operating on a free enterprise basis is highly questionable. Yet this is one of the things which society must ponder.

Even if Congress undertakes a program to defer industrial bargaining strikes which might adversely affect commerce, leaving the right to strike as the last resort, it will have a large order on its hands. For it will be obliged to afford some bargaining substitute reasonably guaranteed to result in agreements. Anything comparable to the procedure under the Railway Labor Act would not seem adequate for industry in general. And fact-finding commissions reporting the results of their investigations either to the president or to the public in general will do little more than show up the weak points of one or the other party's position. Both of these methods logically would presuppose power in the government to make the final decision on the basis of somewhat arbitrary standards— either those articulated in legislation or those entertained personally by the officials entrusted with the task.

A more likely method than these is recourse to codes of fair employment resembling those of the NRA days of 1933, which the parties would bargain out with the assistance of government. But here again, the final decision would lie in the hands of government, and this process would inevitably imply toleration of price fixing as well as the standardization of employment conditions. Still, this device would make more practical sense than either of the other two, because it would require adaptation on an industry-wide basis—a feature which would tend to reflect realistically what is already occurring to some extent in the private bargaining conducted in the coal, clothing, automobile and steel industries. Furthermore, it would enable adjustments to be made among different units of a given industry on the basis of local conditions and other justifiable competitive differentials. And it would make possible a separate consideration of the needs of small business units in contradistinction to those of large units—perhaps even in separate codes to apply to their situations.

Recourse to such codes would mean the end to the concept of old-fashioned competition which so many people still nostalgically cherish. But it might also mean the end to the bitter bargaining disputes so disruptive of commerce. For there would be little point in Congress going this far if it did not at the same time, in the interests of public convenience, require unions to abide by the outcome of such government sponsored industry-wide treaties. Presumably such codes would at first deal only with money items like wages and vacations, leaving to particular employees and their unions the determination of other items like seniority and discipline. Eventually, however, all matters normally covered by collective agreements would tend to become standardized. And it would be only a matter of time before commodity prices would also be fixed, with the unions naturally playing a role in that process, as well.

This seems not an unlikely outcome of big corporate enterprise dealing with big unionism. In view of the tendency of any such scheme toward wage and price fixing, with the con-

sequent disappearance of competition, before going this far
Congress should ask itself whether or not these disadvantages
are outweighed by the corresponding advantage of obviating
periodic disruptive industry-wide strikes. In the meantime,
while the answer to this question is being pondered, there
might with assurance be undertaken the imposition of some
sort of compulsory settlement of bargaining disputes in the
utility field, much as has been done with the railroads. This
procedure might well be extended to include any vital industry
or service without the daily functioning of which the health
or safety of the community might be jeopardized. The monetary cost of such procedures would be great, indeed. Yet this
cost might be far less to society in the long run than the
total harm otherwise likely to ensue from wasteful strikes.

But these considerations are all speculative. Whatever may
be done in the future to solve the problems arising from disruptive bargaining strikes, it is now possible to state with fair
assurance what should be done about certain specific union
practices which are harmful to the community, aside from
bargaining strikes. Roughly, these practices may be divided
into two categories—the first including interferences with a
sound and orderly economy—what we mean when we speak
of the free flow of commerce and free markets—and the second
including interferences with the administration of an established statutory policy governing the organization and representation of employees. Measures to control or forbid these
practices should be devised with specific reference to each
of them, precisely as the amendments to the Sherman Act have
dealt specifically with the undesirable commercial practices of
corporate enterprise. In dealing with such matters Congress
should in no way be deterred by anything the Supreme Court
has recently said or decided. After all, the development of a
uniform labor policy is the peculiar business of Congress alone.
It cannot afford to have its prerogative to establish a work-

able policy of this sort in any way pre-empted by a judicial body whose function it is to follow the lawmakers and not to lead them.

A program of the sort referred to under the first category would not, of course, strike at the basic problem of monopoly and the suppression of competition. Rather, it would be in the nature of a set of policing rules intended to see that the monopolistic institution of unionism did no more harm than was necessarily inevitable from the pursuit of its normal objectives. When Thurman Arnold was assistant attorney general in charge of the antitrust division, he suggested the use of the Sherman Act to prevent five typical union practices that he believed too harmful for continued toleration. Under the present Supreme Court views, all of these practices are now lawful, with the possible exception of one of them. Implicit in Arnold's program, however, was toleration of what he regarded as legitimate organizational pressures of certain kinds —practices admittedly monopolistic and anticompetitive but nevertheless too intimately inherent in established unionism to be dissociated from it. In conceding this scope for legitimate union pressures, it appears that he adopted the general views entertained by Justice Brandeis in his dissenting opinions in the *Duplex* and *Bedford Cut Stone* cases.

The first union practice Arnold thought should be held unlawful was economic pressure to prevent the use of cheaper materials, improved equipment, and more efficient methods. Thus the carpenters' union, which has a virtual monopoly on carpenters' jobs in the building industry, won't let its members work on certain cheap and greatly improved building materials. In this way it compels unionized general contractors to use the more traditional materials in the interest of holding at a high level the amount of work to be done and of keeping its members employed. Since the services of this union are required for almost all construction work, this attitude has jeopardized modern housing developments to the detriment of potential home builders both in enjoyment and in money saving.

In this way the union is serving only its vested interest in the number of construction jobs available for its members. Also protected from the competition afforded by cheaper methods and materials are its own interests and those of unionized woodwork mills in their established production systems.

Adherence to this policy, of course, invites the creation of a new industrial union to make and install new materials and to undertake new methods—a competitive pressure which might go far to alleviate the existing distress in the building trades. Another instance of this sort is the prohibition by a building trades union to permit the use of automatic cement-mixer trucks on construction jobs, a labor-saving device which substantially decreases the cost of building. In outlawing any union pressures tending to discourage labor-saving devices, Congress might have to consider a program of technological displacement compensation. At the same time, it may be that if such devices really save substantial amounts of money, the corresponding impetus to building would quickly absorb such technologically displaced employees. In any event, these uses of union power for purely selfish ends greatly harm the public interest in cheaper and more adequate living facilities, and their compulsory discontinuance is imperative.

The second practice Arnold thought unlawful was the compulsion imposed by unions to hire unnecessary labor. Thus a truckers' union has fostered a practice whereby its unemployed members met trucks entering New York City and compelled each truck driver to hire an unnecessary extra driver while in the city limits. This was the practice deemed by a majority of the Supreme Court in *United States v. Local 807,* under the federal antiracketeering act, to be an example of a bona fide labor organization "lawfully carrying out the legitimate objects thereof." Justice Stone, on the other hand, thought that the compulsion to hire such an extra driver in order to avoid a possible assault would, if sanctioned as lawful, "render common law robbery an innocent pastime." Obviously, the undertaking by the musicians' union to compel the hiring of unnecessary orchestras and to forbid broadcasting by amateurs is not in this class. But both are examples of uneconomic conduct, serving only the interests of the unions and their members and either harming or contributing in no way to the public convenience.

The third practice Arnold thought subject to restriction is the systematic use of union power for extortion and to compel payments of graft. Actually, he had in mind the activities of those illegitimate organizations, traveling in the guise of legitimate unions, which offer "protection" for sale to employers and utter dire threats of what will happen if they do not pay the suggested "premiums." But it is not always easy to detect the distinction between legitimate and illegitimate unions. And payments of graft or extortion are almost as easily enforced through the imposition of economic pressures as by a "pineapple" thrown into the front door of a store. A statute aimed at this practice would have to be carefully worded if it is to be effective in restraining only the people and practices at which it is aimed!

A fourth practice deemed undesirable by Arnold is the use of economic and other coercion by unions to compel the observance of illegally established commodities prices. Here a union may easily conceal its pressures under the cloak of organizational campaigns against competing nonunion enterprises.

For instance, suppose the milk dealers of a large city illegally agree upon a certain price per unit of milk, while certain independent dealers from outside bring in their milk for direct sale in stores at a much cheaper price. Obviously, this competition may seriously undermine the maintenance of the illegally fixed price, a factor as distressing to the union of milk drivers as to their employers, since adherence to this price may be the only way in which their wages can be kept at a high level. In view of the permissible ambit of union economic activity, it might seem necessary to rest statutory liability for this union practice on proof of connivance with the local dealers in maintaining prices. But this would not follow if it appeared that the cheaper milk is purveyed directly from stores to consumers and is not delivered to homes—a situation excluding any union interest in controlling house-to-house delivery employment standards, as such. Under these circumstances it would appear that the union is engaged in eliminating a competitive enterprise merely in the interests of maintaining an illegal monopoly price. Hence this activity would fall outside of any policy warranting the use of economic self-help in the protection of union employment standards. Since it could serve only the vested interests of the local dealers and the union and would be harmful to the public interest in cheaper milk, a practice of this sort should most certainly be prevented.

The fifth union practice deprecated by Arnold involves undertakings to disrupt already established collective bargaining relations—the sort of thing which occurs in connection with interunion disputes. As this practice is closely connected with the organizational techniques to be discussed presently, its further consideration will be deferred at this time. In the meantime, it must appear that a legislative program on the basis only of Arnold's suggestions would be incomplete. Experience indicates other specific union practices that Congress might reasonably undertake to prevent in the future.

For instance, the deliberate interference by unions with commodities already in or intended for the channels of commerce has always been most troublesome. Of course, the recognition of big unionism inevitably implies the acceptance of their economic embargoes deliberately used in bargaining and organizational strikes to impose financial embarrassment on the particular nonunion employers under fire. In a country where unionism and its normal activities are not only taken for granted but also seem actually to be approved, perhaps we cannot afford to deprecate the imposition of such economic pressures on employers who systematically resist the organization of their employees or oppose normal bargaining with unions established in their plant. But if a union deliberately prevents an employer from shipping certain goods (to quote Chief Justice Hughes in the *Apex* case) "either by their illegal seizure for that purpose, or by the direct and intentional obstruction of their transportation or by blocking the highways of interstate intercourse," such conduct might well be considered a violation of some federal law.

Physical interferences of this sort are probably contrary to local law in most states, but local enforcement authorities cannot always be counted on to maintain the same respect for the channels of commerce that Congress might require. But a federal law prohibiting these interferences would have to be carefully drafted in order not to forbid the use of legitimate union economic embargoes. If confined to the prevention of physical interferences, such a statute could not possibly embarrass unions in the discharge of their normal programs. Nor could the physical interferences at which it would be aimed afford any ground for invocation of a broader statute, such as the Sherman Act, against the offending union.

A recent Supreme Court decision suggests another way in which Congress should prevent unions from adversely affecting participation by others in commerce. Thus, in *Hunt v. Crumboch,* already referred to in another connection, a truckers' union forced an owner of a fleet of trucks out of business by forbidding any of its members to work for him, well knowing that the only interstate haulage available was for concerns already committed to dealing only with unionized truckers. Although the truck owner in question wished to sign a closed shop contract with this union, it would not deal with him at all because of a long-standing grudge—the union's belief that one of his officials had murdered one of its members. This arbitrary use of union power is inexcusable. It is roughly on a par with the enforcement of a closed shop contract by a union arbitrarily denying membership to employees it does not like.

Although the Supreme Court has made it plain that it will not tolerate a closed union under such circumstances, it refused to declare this conduct of the truckers' union illegal under the Sherman Act. Conceivably such a decision involves an unconstitutional construction of the Norris-LaGuardia Act and Section 20 of the Clayton Act—the statutes construed and applied to remove the truckers' union from the effect of the Sherman Act. At least, such a construction seems no more constitutional than a decision interpreting a federal or state law to let a union deprive the Negro members in a bargaining unit of fair and equal representation or the right to work at all. In any event, this situation invites legislative restriction against the arbitrary abuse of union power to exclude anyone from a field of endeavor in which he is entitled to participate.

An instance of a union economic embargo which Congress should certainly outlaw appears in the electrical workers' case, *Allen Bradley Company v. Local Union No. 3*. This decision has also been discussed elsewhere. There a local union, which controlled all employment in the manufacture and installation of electrical equipment in the New York City area, would allow no outside manufactured equipment to be sold in the New York market. This embargo was placed on union-made and nonunion-made equipment alike. It was effected by the refusal of the installation electricians to handle any equipment not locally produced by their fellow members. The tight market control which ensued was very harmful to local consumers and beneficial only to local union members and their employers. It is true that the Supreme Court disapproved of this practice in so far—but only in so far—as it depended on the co-operation of employers. But nonetheless, it left the union free to use its own economic strength, quite adequate to the occasion, in continuing this anticompetitive embargo.

Here is a use of union power indistinguishable from the illegal abuses of corporate power to control markets. Under present law the union may establish and maintain a protected market for its own interests, deliberately excluding the equipment of even unionized competing outsiders so that the employment standards of its members will not suffer harm. Furthermore, this particular union rigorously excludes from membership any electrician who does not enjoy some close connection with a person who is already a member. This ability to exclude workers from gainful employment occasionally enables unions to control whole fields of enterprise, as in the building industry. Indeed, by decreasing the number of trained craftsmen available, it may have sufficiently harmful repercussions on commerce to justify Congress in treating its continuance as it should the controls of commodities markets, mentioned above.

One more specific union practice concerns a union's endeavor to maintain perfectly lawful commodity or service prices at a high level. An instance of this occurred in England where coal miners were paid on a sliding scale in correspondence to the market price of coal. Believing that the market price per ton had fallen too low because of the abundant supply of coal on the market, the union deliberately undertook to drive the price up again by periodically stopping production. This venture into an economy of scarcity for the purpose of securing higher piece rate pay the House of Lords thought unlawful in *South Wales Miners' Federation v. Glamorgan Coal Company.* Under our own law this practice would be perfectly proper.

Another instance of this sort of thing occurred in Minnesota where a unionized employer undertook to charge less per unit for laundry service than a local association of laundry men had agreed upon under a state statute permitting them to fix prices. His union employees were paid in part on a percentage commission basis. Conceiving that this decrease in price operated as a cut in their net earnings, they struck to compel compliance with the uniform price schedule. This practice the Minnesota court thought proper under their local broad definition of a labor dispute and under the state unfair trade practices act, observing that this latter statute "recognizes that there is such a thing as too much competition" and that "the economic reaction upon its labor of ruinous or excessive competition in a given trade or industry is obvious."

Practices of this type are more or less implicit in some of the market restraints which unions have occasionally imposed in order to provide a stable basis for their own wages. If they do this sort of thing in interstate commerce with the connivance of their employers, presumably both are subject to the penalties of the Sherman Act. Hence, if the practice is concededly wrongful under such circumstances, the fact that unions may at present pursue it alone with impunity seems little reason why Congress should continue to allow them to indulge in such conduct so obviously contrary to the public interest.

While the foregoing list of anticompetitive union practices may suggest a formidable legislative program for Congress to undertake, the prohibition of none of these items should in any way interfere with the pursuit of legitimate union objectives. They are all forms of indulgence which no one would hesitate to condemn when undertaken by anyone but labor unions. It may well be that the public can ill afford any longer to support an inconsistent policy that allows one group to engage in specific conduct admittedly unlawful when carried on by others.

But this legislative program is hardly complete without consideration of another series of questionable union practices which have grown up during the past few years. These include the exercise of normal union pressures under circumstances that render them exceedingly harmful to others and of no great value to the offending union itself. Under our present state of the law, these practices are generally regarded as permissible. While they are more or less intimately connected with the extension of organization, they should not be entitled to the protection which our prevailing policies imply since they are not essential to what may be called legitimate union expansion.

The new type of so-called jurisdictional dispute—more accurately termed the interunion dispute—is a course of conduct that eventually is certain to prove more harmful than beneficial to unions and is occasionally disastrous to employers. There are several aspects of this sort of thing not essential to legitimate union pursuits. Indeed, they tend to destroy already established relationships between employees and bona fide unions. This situation occurs when the members of one union refuse to handle or to install materials produced by a manufacturer who is committed to bargain and has actually entered into an agreement with another union. For instance, a manufacturer of wood trim is organized under the procedures of the NLRA by a CIO woodworkers' union. His market consists of general contractors who employ only AF of L carpenters. These AF of L carpenters refuse to handle or install the manufacturer's products simply because they are made by workers belonging to a rival union. No doubt, the AF of L union wants the manufacturer to hire only its members and wants his employees to shift their allegiance from the CIO to the AF of L union.

Obviously, the manufacturer is helpless in the face of this pressure. And under prevailing policy it is questionable if even his employees may change their affiliation during the life of an existing agreement. In any event, an embargo of this sort virtually puts the manufacturer out of business and sets completely at naught the parliamentary organizational procedures of Congress in the NLRA. Up to the present it has been condoned under liberal theory as legitimate competition —an attempt by the AF of L union to improve its interests by imposing its organization on a plant through the exercise of purely economic coercion. But previous application of that theory has always presupposed an employer able to respond to the pressure by conceding to the demands of the aggressive union.

Since the NLRA became law, however, the employer under fire can no longer make that choice. And under the same act he has a duty to refrain from bringing any pressure on his employees concerning what union they should join. Assuming that they had not already chosen their union, they might presumably be in a position to respond to the pressure by suing for peace with the boycotting union.

But even if this were so, there are still two objections to such use of economic pressure. First, the employer would be in an ambiguous position if the continuance of his enterprise were thus left to the choice of his employees. Second, this practice plays havoc with the fundamental basis of the NLRA that the employees in a plant have the right to organize autonomously and freely to choose a bargaining representative with whom their employer must deal for at least a year.

In view of this discussion, no room is left for the type of competitive pressure described above. Its justification under the liberal common-law theory seems clearly rebutted by the supervening statutory policy underlying the NLRA. The sweeping provisions of the Norris-LaGuardia Act, however, have disabled the federal courts from enjoining practices of this sort, although the terms of that act were obviously not passed with the subsequent organizational policies of the NLRA in mind. But however apparent it may be that Congress virtually made the Norris-LaGuardia Act of 1932 an anachronism when it passed the NLRA in 1935, the Supreme Court has nevertheless used the anti-injunction statute to hamstring itself in dealing with this situation under the Sherman Act. Here it is clearly incumbent on Congress to perfect its partially inarticulate policy underlying the NLRA by passing legislation declaring unlawful any organized pressure of this sort and by amending the anti-injunction act to allow adequate judicial enforcement of this proposed new legislation.

Another similar objectionable practice occurs when a union, after it has lost an election conducted by the NLRB, exerts pressures through picketing and other means against an employer and his employees. Suppose, in such a situation, that an AF of L and a CIO union had contended for the right to represent the employees in a particular bargaining unit and that the AF of L had won the election, thereupon being certified to the employer and making an agreement with him. If the CIO union subsequently pickets the plant, causing considerable harm to the employer and the employees through loss of business, it may not be enjoined from doing so under the Norris-LaGuardia type of anti-injunction act since it is engaged in a "labor dispute." Nevertheless, such picketing is a plain defiance of Congressional policy and is the sort of ridiculous state of affairs tending to make so many people impatient with the haphazard course of labor legislation in this country.

Here again, the trouble is due to the effect of an anachronistic statute antedating the creation of the current policy of Congress in the NLRA. The employer can do nothing about this situation. His interest in continued stable production ought not to be left to the willingness or unwillingness of his employees to give in to the outside pressures. Furthermore, even if his employees do give in and shift their affiliation to the out union, assuming that they may lawfully do so at all, the forsaken AF of L union would promptly retaliate by establishing a picket line in its turn. Then the employer and his employees would be right back where they started.

Obviously, Congress should declare such defiance of a board certification unlawful and should amend the Norris-LaGuardia Act to make it enjoinable. One difficulty about this, however, is that under the Supreme Court's present views such picketing, if it is peacefully conducted, is "freedom of speech," guaranteed as such in the Constitution. Moreover, the Court might hold Congress unable under the 5th amendment either to make this picketing enjoinable or even to re-define the scope of a labor dispute in order to do so. It is hard to believe that the Supreme Court would use the Constitution to maintain such a contradictory situation in the teeth of specific legislation by Congress to the contrary. But if it means what it has said in its extraordinary achievements to date, no other outcome seems logically possible. Yet Congress plainly has no other course available if we are to achieve anything like a sensible control over the irresponsible use of union power in cases of this type. Should the Supreme Court nevertheless persist in its indefensible position, experience has shown that the matter will eventually be adjusted politically.

Congress might fare better in outlawing the use of other

pressures such as the boycott to defy a board certification. For instance, take the newspaper case of *Star Publishing Company v. NLRB,* where a CIO union won the bargaining rights for the entire plant, including the circulation department which the AF of L teamsters' union wanted to represent. When the NLRB would not allow the employer to give the AF of L union bargaining rights over this department, the teamsters' union refused to handle his papers. And since the CIO union was unable to get the papers delivered, the employer was compelled to shut down. It seems absurd that Congress should refrain from making unlawful such a defiance of the NLRB's certification. Yet here again it may run into difficulties if the Supreme Court decides to extend the constitutional umbrella already raised over picketing to include such a "liberty" as the teamsters' concerted refusal to handle the employer's newspapers.

All of these same observations are germane when, after one union has won a board election and is certified to the employer, the losing union successfully stalemates bargaining by threats to boycott the employer and to strike his other stores or plants elsewhere in which it happens to represent the employees, if he bargains with the certified union. After all, the Supreme Court has recently declared in *Franks Brothers Company v. NLRB* that an employer must bargain with the certified union, even if the conduct of the losing union has caused a drastic depletion in the membership of the certified union. Here again Congress must make the conflicting policies of its two outstanding labor relations statutes consistent if it expects the everyday relations of employers and unions ever to assume an intelligible balance.

When amendments of this sort have been considered, it has been apparent that our labor unions and their liberal supporters have ignored many of the difficulties inevitably imposed on a community by unrestricted union power. No doubt they will exercise tremendous political pressure against any attempt by Congress to inaugurate a program of reform dealing with some of the specific practices outlined above. Yet if they are smart, they will see the good sense of having to live within the boundaries of law and order. In the long run they will benefit quite as much from such restrictions on their power as will the balance of the community. Perhaps it is expecting too much of them, however, to hope that they can see matters in their proper perspective when they review the events of the past decade as seen through the reports of the Supreme Court. When things are going their way, they might argue, why should they make any concessions, particularly when it is more than likely that the highest court in the land may well declare invalid any legislative attempts to curb their unrestrained use of economic power.

In spite of Congress' best intentions from now on, it appears that the fate of our future labor relations policy lies in the hands of the Supreme Court. What that Court may do next is hard to tell. In view of the power it has already asserted over the legislative prerogative to shape a workable labor policy, it must be conceded that Congress is in a dubious position. For the Court seems determined to foster a uniform labor policy of its own conception for the nation as a whole, regardless of the wishes of Congress, and the state legislatures and courts. And in doing so it seems to care little that it is building on the liberal policies first enunciated by a Congress which might wish to reconsider and revise some of those policies. This may seem an extreme assertion to make, but it must be recalled that the Court has already taken some extraordinarily forced and inconsistent positions to place our labor relations law where it now stands.

Consistent with these developments, the Court has taken a position upholding federal legislation which denied an employer the right to speak to his employees about the merits or demerits of unionism in his own plant, while at the same time it has overthrown legislation which denied outside union

officials the right to speak to these same employees about the
merits or demerits of their employer. People don't understand
these things when they see them put that way. They appreciate
the reasons behind the NLRA and the necessity of allowing
employees to organize without any interference from their
employers. They also realize why some courts and legislatures
might similarly want to curtail the exertion of organizational
pressures, including the unrestrained discussion of the employers in question, by outside unions or employees. What
they can't see is why the Supreme Court should fail to recognize either that both of these legislative measures are entitled
to judicial respect as expressions of politically articulated desires of the community or that they are both invalid as unconstitutional restrictions on freedom of speech. But how the
Court—and under its decisions, organized labor—can have it
both ways is becoming increasingly hard to comprehend as
time goes on.

In the meantime the general public is disturbed about two
other matters which they believe are simple enough to solve
but which their representatives in Washington apparently
find too complicated for solution. These are, first, the seeming inability to make unions abide by the terms of their collective agreements and, second, the creation of union responsibility not only to employers and others for harm caused either
by the organization or its individual members, but also to
their own constituents through periodic accounting and a more
democratic internal control. For some unexplainable reason
the popular mind seems obsessed with the idea that the incorporation of unions will solve these matters. Incorporation or
some type of registration would certainly put unions on a
more businesslike footing, but the former alone would give
them a separate legal identity in which they may contract,
sue, and be sued. Hence mere registration would be insufficient
without an additional statutory identity for these purposes.

In two recent decisions the Supreme Court has cast much
uncertainty on the power of a state legislature either to require

the incorporation or registration of labor unions or to insist
that paid organizers and business agents of unions be licensed.
In *Hill v. State of Florida* it declared invalid a Florida statute
making it a misdemeanor for a union to operate without having registered with the secretary of that state, disclosing certain
specified information. Another provision of this same statute
was declared invalid because it required any business agent of
a union to have been an American citizen for more than ten
years, not to have been convicted of a felony, to be a person
of good moral character and, in any event, to be approved by
a designated state board, before he could perform his duties
within the state. These exactions a majority of the Court held
improper because they interfered with an existing exercise of
the constitutional commerce power of Congress embodied in
the National Labor Relations Act. That federal statute established the full freedom of workers in choosing their own collective bargaining representatives. Congress had placed no restrictions on this freedom of choice. Since it had the exclusive
jurisdiction under the commerce clause to regulate the organization and bargaining of employees engaged in units operating
in interstate commerce, the Court declared, no state legislature
could pass any valid law interfering with the guaranties set up
by existing Congressional regulations.

In *Thomas v. Collins* a majority of the Court had previously
declared that the state of Texas could not validly require a
union agent to secure a license (which would have been
issued as a matter of course, on request) before he solicited
members for his union. R. J. Thomas, president of the UAW
and a vice-president of the CIO, deliberately went to Texas to
break this law in more ways than one. He solicited a member
for the oil workers' union and was promptly arrested. The
Court majority invalidated this licensing statute as an invasion
of freedom of speech contrary to the 14th amendment. But a
vigorous dissenting minority insisted that Texas had as much
right to license a union organizer as it had to license salesmen,

doctors, lawyers and other business and professional workers.

While this protection of union organizers from licensing requirements might be strictly confined under the 14th amendment to the specific verbal act of solicitation, the prohibition in the Florida case against state registration and licensing acts is much broader. Nevertheless, while it is clear that the constitutional protection afforded in the Texas case also operates as a restriction on Congress, that in the Florida case does not. Since this latter protection was afforded under the commerce clause, it remains apparent that Congress is completely free to place any registrational limitation it pleases on the privileges it has already established in the NLRA. Justice Frankfurter, dissenting in the Florida case, thought that the state of Florida was still free to speak on this subject of registration in the absence of any Congressional provision covering it. Indeed, he even went so far as to assert that any state was free at any time to enact registration and licensing statutes of this sort deemed essential for local protection against abuses in fields over which Congress had the exclusive power to act under the commerce clause.

The fact remains that under these two decisions, the power of the states and of Congress as well to license union organizers is questionable under the 14th and 1st amendments of the federal Constitution. At the same time, it remains clear that, while the Supreme Court has forbidden states to require either the registration or incorporation of unions engaged in representing the employees of companies operating in interstate commerce, Congress has full and complete power to enact such provisions of a uniform nature as long as it does not encroach on the privilege of union officials to speak freely to workers.

In the matter of compelling a union to abide by the terms of its agreement, there is little that Congress or state legislatures can do besides giving every union, both national and local, such a separate legal identity and then making it subject to civil suits, either for damages or injunctions. Possibly legisla-

J. L. LEONARD
DEPARTMENT OF ECONOMICS
UNIVERSITY OF SOUTHERN CALIFORNIA

tion in this direction could impose liability on the national or international union organization for stated instances of harmful activity irresponsibly undertaken by its affiliated locals. But if this is done, it must be clearly understood that there are corresponding remedies which the unions themselves may pursue against employers for *their* breaches of agreements, either in suits for damages or for injunctions. Perhaps a more practical incentive to union and employer responsibility under collective agreements would be the creation of a uniform procedure—some sort of terminal arbitration—for the prompt and expeditious handling of issues arising under collective agreements, with judicial enforcement of the awards rendered.

An established procedure of this sort should go far to prevent serious breaches of collective agreements since it would have obviated the need for their occurrence. If such a procedure is established, naturally unions may be expected to take their contractual commitments as seriously as other people do. So far, they do not seem to be convinced that society has taken this matter very seriously, since no body of law surrounding the application and enforcement of collective agreements has as yet been built up. Certainly, the conventional law of contracts is in no way appropriate for the administration of these agreements. Furthermore, the unions themselves are somewhat unenthusiastic about most of the suggestions dealing with their responsibilities under their agreements, because they believe that once a program of regulation and control is undertaken, their power to effect advantageous changes will largely be lost. From the perspective of time, and in view of past restrictions on unionism in this country, one can hardly blame the unions for approaching this matter with a great deal of caution.

The responsibility of unions to their memberships for their internal operation has become an issue of primary importance because of the great power over the affairs of others with which society has entrusted these organizations. In view of the developments of the last few years, it seems inevitable that the unions will soon be representing the interests of all workers in most fields of industry. To the extent that they will assume such a gigantic fiduciary undertaking, they must be subjected to fairly stringent laws of stewardship concerning not only financial affairs but also the administration of individual employment rights under collective agreements. Already our courts are awakening to the need for fair and impartial representation by unions of all workers in the bargaining units which they represent. They are beginning to insist on free and open membership whenever such unions secure complete control over available employment through closed shop contracts. Just as private corporate enterprises must render periodic accountings to their stockholders, and as large insurance companies and banks are under public scrutiny to prevent the misuse of other peoples' money, so labor unions must eventually submit to similar controls.

The discussion in this chapter may seem to imply that there are few things that Congress can do aside from outlawing specific abuses of union power to hurt commerce and to interfere with established organizational and bargaining systems. With the exception of attempts to canalize collective bargaining into some sort of parliamentary procedure and to see that collective agreements become conveniently and expeditiously enforceable, there probably is little else that Congress can do right now. What direction these latter developments will take is now largely a matter of speculation. The Ball-Burton-Hatch bill, now pending in Congress, seeks to create settlement procedures for collective bargaining disputes with fact-finding commissions and the temporary suspension of recourse by unions to self-help. This is essentially a mediation device and does not specifically contemplate the resolution of bargaining issues by the government as a last resort. It does, however, provide for the voluntary arbitration of bargaining disputes, with fairly broad powers to the arbitrators, judicial review of their awards, and ultimate enforcement. And in the case of enterprises affected with a pronounced public interest, such as utilities and even the distribution of milk, it recommends a technique of disposition approaching the much talked of compulsory arbitration for bargaining disputes.

With respect to the application and enforcement of existing collective agreements, it suggests a procedure roughly equivalent to compulsory arbitration, although it allows great latitude for individual employees to settle their grievances by dealing directly with their employers. At the same time, this bill proposes several qualifications of the NLRA, greatly modifying the remedial powers at present exercised by the board under that act, introducing unfair labor practices for employees and unions, prohibiting interferences with representation proceedings, and dividing the administrative functions of the NLRB, as modified, between two different and separate boards. The purposes of some of its sections are not clear, although the net effect is to compel unions to abandon recourse to self-help for organizational and bargaining purposes in favor of the more civilized parliamentary procedures suggested in the bill and already existent, to some extent, under our present laws. And on one of the new proposed boards it places the task of curtailing union recourse to self-help, under ambiguously stated circumstances, through civil suits for injunctions. In this connection, there is proposed an amendment of the Norris-LaGuardia Act to relieve federal courts from its restrictive terms when they are asked by the board to grant injunctions against unions.

Nowhere in the bill does there appear a hint that Congress has heeded any of the demands now being urged by unions that they be given some share in the management of industry or that security should be afforded to employees in the shape of guaranteed annual wages. Naturally, the backers of this bill have not undertaken to suggest an industrial relations blueprint of the future. Their chief interest has been to introduce procedures to stabilize present union achievements of power, and to fit into an established free enterprise capitalistic system the lawful and proper exercise of such power.

But eventually the unions may be pressing legislative programs of their own. And they will not be very much like the Ball-Burton-Hatch bill. They will no doubt assert demands for legislative recognition of employees' and unions' stakes in the industrial system. While they will hardly go as far as to claim a share in the physical properties of plants and equipment, they will most certainly condense the vaporous claims to property rights, aired at the time of the 1937 sit-down strikes, into demands for a share in the operation of industry as a process in which they are participants and in which they claim to have as much at stake as the stockholders have. However revolutionary such claims might appear to most members of the public, they cannot afford to dismiss them as the mere effusions of crackpots when, as, and if they are made. It is true that such demands would threaten the very foundations of a capitalistic industrial society, geared at present to operate only in response to the profit motive. For it would be difficult to see how the inducement of profits could continue to support such a system when investors of capital might not be allowed the exclusive prerogative of operating their properties through their own managerial representatives.

At present these demands seem fantastic. Yet we must keep our minds sufficiently open to consider seriously their possible submission. This seems especially so in light of what has been transpiring in England. We live in an industrial age, the like of which has never before existed. In a manner of speaking, we are sailing on uncharted seas—socially, economically, and politically. The livelihoods of more and more millions of people remain dependent on the operations of relatively fewer owners of property. From developments we have seen in our own lives, we have some basis for reflecting on the possibilities of political power in the hands of those millions. After all, while man cannot live on bread alone, economic security takes him a long, long way, and it has probably become his chief aim in life. If the great bulk of our community insists upon a direct share in shaping the course of their economic destinies, it may shortly become the task of our leaders of industry, as well as of our representatives in government, to devise ways in which this participation may take place on a practicable basis. For if they do not, the unions and their members may eventually show that these matters can be settled at the polls.

We live on the frontier of an economy of plenty. Our industrial capacity promises an abundance for all. Fulfillment of this promise would certainly be the attainment of justice in anybody's language. And whether or not we achieve it in our law depends upon what we decide as a people for the solution of our greatest internal problem—the creation and the distribution of wealth and our national income. To a large extent our economy of the future will be determined by the struggle going on between the elemental forces presently comprising the organized factions in our industrial society—management and labor.

We must constantly remember at the outset that there is no logical or ultimate solution. Indeed, we are hardly able to define the inarticulate social premises on which a logical answer could be based. Our public leaders are still floundering in a sea of inconsistencies, uncertain of their next turn, while the participants of the struggle are still engaged in almost primitive forms of trial by combat. At times we comfort ourselves with the belief that the most obstreperous management and labor groups are experiencing a normal adolescence—that each is secretly measuring the other to see how far the opponent will go or how long he can last. And we are encouraged by the relative maturity already achieved in the relationships between employer and labor groups in a few of our industries to believe that the shyness between these new acquaintances will disappear as they all grow up together and begin to appreciate their community of interests.

Any laws by which they shall live and share the results of their common efforts must conform to their joint views. But this does not mean that society can turn over the show to organized management and labor so that they can run it in accordance with their combined notions of what is fitting and proper. It is manifest that the future economy of the country is to be molded through the manipulations of great special interest groups. And of course, as in the past, the farmer will certainly insist upon his seat at the council table. And the consumer may even try to tag along through the development of a co-operative movement, cutting across the ranks of the other factions, as well.

But such a development cannot be allowed to eclipse the greatest organization of all—the government—through which the resultant of these factional pressures can alone be articulated into an orderly and mature process of law. In the last analysis, this means that the American people must have the final word in passing on the proposals offered for the future by these groups. Here is where the American people must realize their responsibilities and have something ready to say.

In making up their minds, they must recognize in realistic terms the factors involved in the struggle. They must approach all nostrums and the special pleadings on both sides of the fence with a spirit of healthy skepticism. They must entertain a certain amount of faith in the fundamental integrity of each of the factions and must retain a great deal of faith in their own ability to realize a sane and adequate balance of interests. And they must remain ever ready to accept experimentation all along the line, pliant enough to discard the useless but firm enough to hang onto what is good in terms of the general interest. The policies reflected in our labor law of the years to come can be made workable and just. Whether or not they will be depends largely on the patience, the wisdom, and the understanding that each of us may contribute as a citizen in a real industrial democracy.

EXCERPTS FROM THE CLAYTON ACT, OCTOBER 15, 1914, C. 323, SECS. 6 AND 20, 38 STAT. 731 AND 738

SECTION 6 That the labor of a human being is not a commodity or article of commerce. Nothing contained in the antitrust laws shall be construed to forbid the existence and operation of labor, agricultural, or horticultural organizations, instituted for the purposes of mutual help, and not having capital stock or conducted for profit, or to forbid or restrain individual members of such organizations from lawfully carrying out the legitimate objects thereof; nor shall such organizations, or the members thereof, be held or construed to be illegal combinations or conspiracies in restraint of trade, under the antitrust laws

SECTION 20 That no restraining order or injunction shall be granted by any court of the United States, or a judge or the judges thereof, in any case between an employer and employees, or between employers and employees, or between employees, or between persons employed and persons seeking employment, involving, or growing out of, a dispute concerning terms or conditions of employment, unless necessary to prevent irreparable injury to property, or to a property right, of the party making the application, for which injury there is no adequate remedy at law, and such property or property right must be described with particularity in the application, which must be in writing and sworn to by the applicant or by his agent or attorney.

And no such restraining order or injunction shall prohibit any person or persons, whether singly or in concert, from terminating any relation of employment, or from ceasing to perform any work or labor, or from recommending, advising, or persuading others by peaceful means so to do; or from at-, tending at any place where any such person or persons may lawfully be, for the purpose of peacefully obtaining or communicating information, or from peacefully persuading any person to work or to abstain from working; or from ceasing to patronize or to employ any party to such dispute, or from recommending, advising, or persuading others by peaceful and lawful means so to do; or from paying or giving to, or withholding from, any person engaged in such dispute, any strike benefits or other moneys or things of value; or from peaceably assembling in a lawful manner, and for lawful purposes; or from doing any act or thing which might lawfully be done in the absence of such dispute by any party thereto; nor shall any of the acts specified in this paragraph be considered or held to be violations of any law of the United States.

APPENDIX B

EXCERPTS FROM NORRIS–LAGUARDIA ACT, MARCH 23, 1932, C. 90, SECS. 4 AND 13, 47 STAT. 70 AND 73

SECTION 4 No court of the United States shall have jurisdiction to issue any restraining order or temporary or permanent injunction in any case involving or growing out of any labor dispute to prohibit any person or persons participating or interested in such dispute (as these terms are herein defined) from doing, whether singly or in concert, any of the following acts:

(a) Ceasing or refusing to perform any work or to remain in any relation of employment;

(b) Becoming or remaining a member of any labor organization or of any employer organization, regardless of any such undertaking or promise as is described in section 3 of this Act;

(c) Paying or giving to, or withholding from, any person participating or interested in such labor dispute, any strike or unemployment benefits or insurance, or other moneys or things of value;

(d) By all lawful means aiding any person participating or interested in any labor dispute who is being proceeded against in, or is prosecuting, any action or suit in any court of the United States or of any State;

(e) Giving publicity to the existence of, or the facts involved in, any labor dispute, whether by advertising, speaking, patrolling, or by any other method not involving fraud or violence;

(*f*) Assembling peaceably to act or to organize to act in promotion of their interests in a labor dispute;

(*g*) Advising or notifying any person of an intention to do any of the acts heretofore specified;

(*h*) Agreeing with other persons to do or not to do any of the acts heretofore specified; and

(*i*) Advising, urging, or otherwise causing or inducing without fraud or violence the acts heretofore specified, regardless of any such undertaking or promise as is described in section 3 of this Act.

SECTION 13 When used in this Act, and for the purposes of this Act—

(*a*) A case shall be held to involve or to grow out of a labor dispute when the case involves persons who are engaged in the same industry, trade, craft, or occupation; or have direct or indirect interests therein; or who are employees of the same employer; or who are members of the same or an affiliated organization of employers or employees; whether such dispute is (1) between one or more employers or associations of employers and one or more employees or associations of employees; (2) between one or more employers or associations of employers and one or more employers or associations of employers; or (3) between one or more employees or associations of employees and one or more employees or associations of employees; or when the case involves any conflicting or competing interests in a "labor dispute" (as hereinafter defined) of "persons participating or interested" therein (as hereinafter defined).

(*b*) A person or association shall be held to be a person participating or interested in a labor dispute if relief is sought against him or it, and if he or it is engaged in the same industry, trade, craft, or oc-

cupation in which such dispute occurs, or has a
direct or indirect interest therein, or is a member,
officer, or agent of any association composed in
whole or in part of employers or employees engaged
in such industry, trade, craft, or occupation.

(c) The term "labor dispute" includes any controversy
concerning terms or conditions of employment, or
concerning the association or representation of persons in negotiating, fixing, maintaining, changing,
or seeking to arrange terms or conditions of employment, regardless of whether or not the disputants
stand in the proximate relation of employer and employee.

TABLE OF AUTHORITIES CITED

CHAPTER I

page 22, line 23, et seq. The *Philadelphia Cordwainers'* case, *Commonwealth v. Pullis* (1806), as reported in Commons and Gilmore, *Documentary History of American Industrial Society*, volume 3, pages 59–236.

page 26, line 2. Quoted from *People v. Melvin*, 2 Wheeler Crim. Cas. 262 (Ct. Gen'l Sessions, N. Y. C., 1810).

page 26, line 5. *Commonwealth ex rel. Chew v. Carlisle*, Brightly, 36 Pa. N. P. (1821).

page 26, line 34. *People v. Fisher*, 14 Wend. 10 (Sup. Ct. N. Y., 1835).

page 28, line 3, et seq. *Commonwealth v. Hunt*, 4 Metcalf, 111 (Mass. 1842).

page 30, line 1. Landis and Manoff, *Cases on Labor Law* (1942), Historical Introduction, 35.

CHAPTER II

page 31, line 13. *Mogul Steamship Co. v. McGregor, Gow & Co.*, C. A. [1889] L. R. 23 Q. B. D. 598; H. L. [1892] A. C. 25.

page 35, line 9. *Allen v. Flood*, H. L. [1898] A. C. 1.

page 40, line 17. *Quinn v. Leathem*, H. L. [1901] A. C. 495.

page 45, line 36. *Leathem v. Craig*, Irish Reports, Queen's Bench Division [1899] 667, 701 et seq.

CHAPTER III

page 53, line 17. *Bowen v. Matheson*, 96 Mass. 499 (1867).

page 55, line 26. *Carew v. Rutherford*, 106 Mass. 1 (1870).

page 58, line 26. *Thorne v. Motor Trade Association*, H. L. [1937] A. C. 797.

page 58, line 33. *Rex v. Denyer* [1926], 2 K. B. 258.

page 60, line 5. *Vegelahn v. Guntner*, 167 Mass. 92 (1896).

page 62, line 21. *Plant v. Woods*, 176 Mass. 492 (1900).

page 68, line 15. *Berry v. Donovan*, 188 Mass. 353 (1905).

page 69, line 18. *Pickett v. Walsh*, 192 Mass. 572 (1906).

page 76, line 23. *Curran v. Galen*, 152 N. Y. 33 (1897).

page 77, line 5. *National Protective Assn. v. Cumming*, 170 N. Y. 315 (1902).

page 80, line 25. *Jacobs v. Cohen*, 183 N. Y. 207 (1905).

CHAPTER IV

page 89, line 6. For instances, see *Letts v. Kessler*, 54 Ohio St. 73 (1896) and *Burke v. Smith*, 69 Mich. 380 (1888).

page 89, line 30. *Huber v. Merkel*, 117 Wis. 355 (1903).

page 90, line 11. Cf., *Tuttle v. Buck*, 107 Minn. 145 (1909).

page 90, line 20. *Dunshee v. Standard Oil Co.*, 152 Iowa, 618 (1911).

page 93, line 27. *Lumley v. Gye*, 2 E. & B. 216 (1853).

page 96, line 34. This somewhat fictionally graphic account is based on a reference in Frankfurter and Greene, *The Labor Injunction* (1930), 23, and authorities cited.

page 98, line 29. In *Truax v. Corrigan*, 257 U. S. 312 (1921).

page 99, line 23. Frankfurter and Greene, *The Labor Injunction* (1930).

page 101, line 8. *Taliaferro v. United States*, 290 Fed. 906 (C. C. A. 4th, 1923).

page 104, line 10. Section 20 of the Clayton Act, cited and quoted in Appendix A, page 447.

page 104, line 16. The Norris-LaGuardia Act is cited and, in part, quoted in Appendix B, pages 449–51.

CHAPTER V

page 108, line 9. In *Dorchy v. Kansas*, 272 U. S. 306 (1926).

page 110, line 20. See *DeMinico v. Craig*, 207 Mass. 593 (1911).

page 119, line 20. See *Plant v. Woods*, 176 Mass. 353 (1900), and *Berry v. Donovan*, 188 Mass. 572 (1906), both discussed in Chapter III.

page 121, line 11. See *Bossert v. Dhuy*, 221 N. Y. 342 (1917).

page 125, line 18. *Iron Molders' Union v. Allis-Chalmers Co.*, 166 Fed. 45 (C. C. A. 7th, 1908).

CHAPTER VI

page 132, line 15. *Macauley Bros. v. Tierney*, 19 R. I. 255 (1895).

page 133, line 14. *Bohn Mfg. Co. v. Hollis*, 54 Minn. 223 (1893).

page 133, line 17. *Thorne v. Motor Trade Association*, H. L. [1937] A. C. 797.

page 134, line 26. *Auburn Draying Co. v. Wardell*, 227 N. Y. 1 (1919).

page 136, line 18. *Seattle Malting & Brewing Co. v. Hansen*, 144 Fed. 1011 (U. S. C. C., Calif., 1905).

page 138, line 3. *Gompers v. Bucks Stove & Range Co.*, 221 U. S. 418 (1911).

page 141, line 30. E.g., *A. T. & S. F. Ry. v. Gee,* 139 Fed. 582 (U. S. C. C., Iowa, 1905).

page 141, line 32. See *Gevas v. Greek Restaurant Workers' Club,* 99 N. J. Eq. 770 (1926).

page 145, line 22. *Exchange Bakery & Restaurant v. Rifkin,* 245 N. Y. 260 (1927).

page 147, line 30. *Goldfinger v. Feintuch,* 276 N. Y. 281 (1937).

page 153, line 26. *McKay v. Retail Automobile Salesmen's Union,* 16 Calif. (2d) 311 (1940).

CHAPTER VII

page 158, line 2. *Stillwell Theatre, Inc. v. Kaplan,* 259 N. Y. 405 (1932).

page 159, line 25. Section 20 of the Clayton Act is cited and quoted in Appendix A, pages 447–8.

page 161, line 24. *Duplex Printing Press Co. v. Deering,* 252 Fed. 722 (C. C. A. 2d, 1918).

page 162, line 36. *Duplex Printing Press Co. v. Deering,* 254 U. S. 443 (1921).

page 172, line 14. *American Steel Foundries v. Tri-City Central Trades Council,* 257 U. S. 184 (1921).

page 172, line 25. *Truax v. Corrigan,* 257 U. S. 312 (1921).

page 174, line 25. *Lumley v. Gye,* 2 E. & B. 216 (1853).

page 175, line 16. In *Adair v. United States,* 208 U. S. 161 (1908) and in *Coppage v. Kansas,* 236 U. S. 1 (1915).

page 175, line 28. In *Coppage v. Kansas,* 236 U. S. 1 (1915).

page 179, line 18. *Hitchman Coal Co. v. Mitchell,* 245 U. S. 229 (1917).

page 180, line 2. *Interborough Rapid Transit Co. v. Lavin,* 247 N. Y. 65 (1928), as to which see *Interborough Rapid Transit Co. v. Green,* 227 N. Y. Supp. 258, 264 (N. Y. Sup. Ct., 1928).

page 180, line 35. For a reference to sources on this incident, see Frankfurter and Greene, "Congressional Power over the Labor Injunction," 31 *Columbia Law Review,* 385, 387 (1931).

page 181, line 15. *R An W Hat Shop, Inc. v. Sculley,* 98 Conn. 1 (1922).

page 198, line 24. *Senn v. Tile Layers' Protective Union,* 301 U. S. 468 (1937).

page 199, line 6. *New Negro Alliance v. Sanitary Grocery Co.,* 303 U. S. 552, 304 U. S. 542 (1938).

CHAPTER VIII

page 201, line 1. 26 United States Statutes at Large, 209 (1890).

page 206, line 29. *Loewe v. Lawlor,* 208 U. S. 274 (1908), commonly known as the *Danbury Hatters'* case.

page 210, line 12. *Duplex Printing Press Co. v. Deering,* 254 U. S. 443 (1921).

page 211, line 6. *United Mine Workers of America v. Coronado Coal Co.,* 259 U. S. 344 (1922).

page 216, line 27. *Coronado Coal Co. v. United Mine Workers of America,* 268 U. S. 295 (1925).

page 219, line 23. *Bedford Cut Stone Co. v. Journeymen Stone Cutters' Association,* 274 U. S. 37 (1927).

page 221, line 13. *United States v. Brims,* 272 U. S. 549 (1926).

CHAPTER IX

page 238, line 9. *Republic Steel Corp. v. NLRB,* 311 U. S. 7 (1940).

page 238, line 18. *NLRB v. Fansteel Metallurgical Corp.,* 306 U. S. 270 (1939).

page 239, line 16. *Phelps Dodge Corp. v. NLRB,* 313 U. S. 177 (1941).

page 239, line 22. *H. J. Heinz Co. v. NLRB,* 311 U. S. 514 (1941).

page 245, line 26. See *AF of L v. NLRB,* 308 U. S. 401 (1940).

CHAPTER X

page 254, line 26. *Morehead v. New York, ex rel. Tipaldo,* 298 U. S. 587 (1936).

page 255, line 3. *West Coast Hotel Co. v. Parrish,* 300 U. S. 379 (1937).

page 255, line 4. *Adkins v. Childrens' Hospital,* 261 U. S. 525 (1923).

page 255, line 5. *NLRB v. Jones & Laughlin Steel Corp.,* 301 U. S. 1 (1937).

page 255, line 30. *Apex Hosiery Co. v. Leader,* 90 Fed. (2d) 155 (C. C. A. 3d, 1937).

page 256, line 2. *Leader v. Apex Hosiery Co.,* 108 Fed. (2d) 71 (C. C. A. 3d, 1939).

page 256, line 8. *Apex Hosiery Co. v. Leader,* 310 U. S. 469 (1940).

page 262, line 2. *Eastern States Retail Lumber Dealers' Association v. United States,* 234 U. S. 600 (1914).

page 269, line 39. *United States v. Hutcheson,* 32 F. Supp. 600 (D. C. Mo., 1940).

page 269, line 33. *United States v. Hutcheson,* 312 U. S. 219 (1941).

page 274, line 28. Wisconsin Laws of 1931, Chapter 376.

page 279, line 14. *Allen Bradley Co. v. Local Union No. 3, IBEW,* 325 U. S. 797 (1945).

page 280, line 18. *Allen Bradley Co. v. Local Union No. 3, IBEW,* 145 F. (2d) 215 (C. C. A. 2d, 1944).

page 284, line 29. *United States v. American Federation of Musicians,* 318 U. S. 741 (1943), affirming 47 F. Supp. 304 (D. C. Ill., 1942).

page 285, line 7. *United States v. International Hod Carriers' etc., Council,* 313 U. S. 539 (1941), affirming *United States v. Carrozzo,* 37 F. Supp. 191 (D. C. Ill., 1941).

page 285, lines 27 and 28. *United States v. Building & Construction Trades Council,* 313 U. S. 539 (1941) and *United States v. United Brotherhood of Carpenters & Joiners,* 313 U. S. 539 (1941), both affirming lower court decisions.

page 285, line 36. *Hunt v. Crumboch,* 325 U. S. 821 (1945).

page 287, line 8. *Milk Wagon Drivers' Union v. Lake Valley Farm Products, Inc.,* 311 U. S. 91 (1940).

CHAPTER XI

page 290, line 3. Quoted from *Consolidated Edison Co. of N. Y. v. NLRB,* 305 U. S. 197 (1938).

page 291, line 5. *Consolidated Edison Co. of N. Y. v. NLRB,* 305 U. S. 197 (1938).

page 292, line 19. *Int'l Ass'n of Machinists v. NLRB,* 311 U. S. 72 (1940).

page 293, line 26. *NLRB v. Fansteel Metallurgical Corp.,* 306 U. S. 240 (1939).

page 296, line 3, *NLRB v. Mackay Radio & Telegraph Co.,* 304 U. S. 333 (1938).

page 296, line 34. *Phelps Dodge Corp. v. NLRB,* 313 U. S. 177 (1941).

page 301, line 4. *NLRB v. Newark Morning Ledger Co.,* 120 F. (2d) 262 (C. C. A. 3d, 1941), cert, denied, 314 U. S. 693 (1941).

page 303, line 20. *NLRB v. Jones & Laughlin Steel Corp.,* 301 U. S. 1 (1937).

page 303, line 31. *National Licorice Co. v. NLRB,* 309 U. S. 350 (1940).

page 304, line 35. *J. I. Case Co. v. NLRB,* 321 U. S. 332 (1944).

page 307, line 15. *Medo Photo Supply Corp. v. NLRB,* 321 U. S. 678 (1944).

page 308, line 31. *Order of Railroad Telegraphers v. Railway Express Agency, Inc.,* 321 U. S. 342 (1944).

page 312, line 17. *NLRB v. Appalachian Electric Power Co.,* 140 F. (2d) 217 (C. C. A. 4th, 1944); *NLRB v. Century Oxford Mfg. Corp.,* 140 F. (2d) 541 (C. C. A. 2d, 1944).

page 314, line 6. *Franks Bros. Co. v. NLRB,* 321 U. S. 702 (1944).

page 314, line 17. *Great Southern Trucking Co. v. NLRB,* 139 F. (2d) 984 (C. C. A. 4th, 1944).

page 314, line 33. *NLRB v. Star Publishing Co.,* 97 F. (2d) 465 (C. C. A. 9th, 1938).

page 316, line 10. *Fur Workers Union No. 21238 v. Fur Workers Union, Local No. 72,* 308 U. S. 522 (1939), a memorandum affirmance of case with same title in 105 F. (2d) 1 (C. A. D. C., 1939).

page 319, line 29. In re The Maryland Drydock Company and Local No. 31, 49 NLRB, 733 (1943). But see In re Union Collieries Coal Company & Mine Officials' Union, 41 NLRB, 961 (1942). And also see *Jones & Laughlin Steel Corp. v. NLRB*, 146 F. (2d) 833 (C. C. A. 5th, 1945).

page 323, line 27. In re Jones & Laughlin Steel Corp., 66 NLRB, No. 51 (1946).

page 324, line 14. In re Packard Motor Car Company & Foremen's Association of America, 16 LRR, 168 (1945), and ibid., previous citation.

page 325, line 11. See *NLRB v. Virginia Electric & Power Co.*, 314 U. S. 469 (1941).

page 326, line 4. *Wallace Corp. v. NLRB*, 323 U. S. 248 (1944).

page 332, line 13. *Hunt v. Crumboch*, 325 U. S. 821 (1945).

CHAPTER XII

page 337, line 27. *Pierce v. Stablemen's Union*, 156 Calif. 70 (1909).

page 338, line 27. *American Steel Foundries v. Tri-City Central Trades Council*, 257 U. S. 184 (1921).

page 338, line 36. *Senn v. Tile Layers' Protective Union*, 301 U. S. 468 (1937).

page 341, line 30. *Thornhill v. Alabama*, 310 U. S. 88 (1940).

page 345, line 17. *Gompers v. Bucks Stove & Range Co.*, 221 U. S. 418 (1911).

page 345, line 20. *American Steel Foundries v. Tri-City Central Trades Council*, 257 U. S. 184 (1921).

page 345, line 23. *Senn v. Tile Layers' Protective Union*, 301 U. S. 468 (1937).

page 350, line 21. *American Federation of Labor v. Swing*, 312 U. S. 321 (1941).

page 351, line 6. *Milk Wagon Drivers' Union v. Meadowmoor Dairies, Inc.*, 312 U. S. 287 (1941).

page 352, line 9. *Hotel & Restaurant Employees' Union v. Wisconsin Employment Relations Board*, 315 U. S. 437 (1942).

page 352, line 12. Wisconsin Statutes, 1939, chap. 103.62 (3).

page 353, line 9. *Allen-Bradley Local No. 1111 v. Wisconsin Employment Relations Board*, 315 U. S. 740 (1942).

page 354, line 9. *Bakery & Pastry Drivers Union v. Wohl*, 315 U. S. 769 (1942).

page 357, line 9. *Goldfinger v. Feintuch*, 276 N. Y. 281 (1937).

page 357 (line 29. *Carpenters & Joiners Union v. Ritter's Cafe*, 315 U. S. 722 (1942).

page 362, line 28. *Cafeteria Employees' Union v. Angelos*, 320 U. S. 293 (1943).

page 366, line 10. Mozart G. Ratner and Norton J. Come. "The Norris-LaGuardia Act in the Constitution," 11 *George Washington Law Review*, 428 (1943).

page 368, line 10. *McKay v. Retail Automobile Salesmen's Local Union*, 16 Calif. (2d) 311 (1940).

page 371, line 15. *Steele v. Louisville & N. R. Co.*, 323 U. S. 192 (1944), and *Tunstall v. Brotherhood of Locomotive Firemen & Enginemen*, 323 U. S. 210 (1944).

page 372, line 10. *Wallace Corp. v. NLRB*, 323 U. S. 248 (1944).

page 372, line 35. *James v. Marinship Corp.*, 155 P. (2d) 329 (Calif. Sup. Ct., 1944).

page 373, line 31. *Bautista v. Jones*, 155 P. (2d) 343 (Calif. Sup. Ct., 1944).

CHAPTER XIII

page 381, line 11. *Young v. Canadian Northern Ry. Co.*, 1931 A. C. 83.

page 381, line 23. Judicial developments in the United States are described in detail, with authorities cited, in Rice, "Collective Labor Agreements in American Law," 44 *Harvard Law Review*, 572 (1931).

page 384, line 33. In *J. I. Case Co. v. NLRB*, 321 U. S. 332 (1944).

page 394, line 10. *Elgin, J. & E. Ry. Co. v. Burley*, 325 U. S. 711 (1945).

page 395, line 34. *Elgin, J. & E. Ry. Co. v. Burley*, 66 Sup. Ct. 721 (1946).

CHAPTER XIV

page 419, line 2. *United Mine Workers of America v. Coronado Coal Co.*, 259 U. S. 344 (1922); *Coronado Coal Co. v. United Mine Workers of America*, 268 U. S. 295 (1925).

page 419, line 4. *Apex Hosiery Co. v. Leader*, 310 U. S. 469 (1940).

page 424, line 11. Arnold, *The Bottlenecks of Business* (1940), pages 251-2.

page 425, line 29. *United States v. Local 807*, 315 U. S. 521 (1942).

page 428, line 2. *Apex Hosiery Co. v. Leader*, 310 U. S. 469 (1940).

page 428, line 21. *Hunt v. Crumboch*, 325 U. S. 821 (1945).

page 428, line 34. *Wallace Corp. v. NLRB*, 323 U. S. 248 (1944).

page 429, line 14. *Allen Bradley Co. v. Local Union No. 3, IBEW*, 325 U. S. 797 (1945).

page 430, line 20. *South Wales Miners' Federation v. Glamorgan Coal Co.*, [1905] A. C. 239.

page 430, line 30. *Lichterman v. Laundry & Dry Cleaning Drivers Union*, 204 Minn. 75 (1938).

page 435, line 2. *NLRB v. Star Publishing Co.*, 97 F. (2d) 465 (C. C. A. 9th, 1938).

page 435, line 23. *Franks Bros. Co. v. NLRB*, 321 U. S. 702 (1944).

page 438, line 3. *Hill v. State of Florida*, 325 U. S. 538 (1945).

page 438, line 24. *Thomas v. Collins*, 323 U. S. 516 (1945).

INDEX

Allen v. Flood, 35
Allen Bradley Co. v. Local No. 3, 279, 429
Allis-Chalmers Co., 125
Amalg. M. C. & B. W. N. A., 43
American Federation of Labor (AF of L), 138
NLRA: secured passage of, 226
Am. Steel Foundries v. Tri-City T. C., 172
Angelos, Cafeteria E. U., 362
Annual wage, 442
Anti-injunction acts
see Injunctions
Antiracketeering act, 425
Antitrust act
see Sherman Act
Antiunion promise
Definition, 174–5
Legislation against, 174–7
Norris-LaGuardia Act, 184 ff.
Apex Hosiery v. Leader, 255 ff.
Arbitration
see also Collective agreements
Collective bargaining in, 402 ff.
Compulsory, 442
Federal system of, 404
Function of labor arbitrator, 410–11
Judicial review of awards, 406–7
Jurisdictional disputes, 410
Scope of, 411
Arnold, Thurman, 424 ff.
Auburn Draying Co. v. Wardell, 134

Ball-Burton-Hatch bill, 441–3
Bargaining unit
see National Labor Relations Act
Bautista v. Jones, 373
Bedford Cut Stone case, 219
Bentham, Jeremy, 52
Berry v. Donovan, 68
Black, Justice, 281, 327, 355, 359
Blacklist, 58
Bowen, Lord, 48
Bowen v. Matheson, 53
Boycott
Definition of, 34, 120
Labor, 106 ff.
Secondary, 34, 58, 121, 134 ff.
Brampton, Lord, 41 ff.
Brandeis, Justice, 108, 168, 179, 194, 220, 223, 334, 338, 369, 424
Bridges, Harry, 245
Brims, U. S. V., 278
Burley, Elgin J. & E. Ry. Co. v., 394

Carew v. Rutherford, 55
Carlyle, Thomas, 20
Case bill, 324
Chapman, Judge, 54 ff.
Civil rights doctrine
Clayton Act, 171 ff.
Explained, 81–2
Clark, Judge Charles E., 280 ff.
Clark, Judge W., 302
Clayton Act
see also Injunction
Effect of, on Sherman Act, 270 ff.

461

Clayton Act (*Continued*)
Labor sections, 447–8, 159 ff.
Section 6, 209–10
Closed shop, 116–18
Contract for, unlawful, 68
Free riders, 399
Legality of strike for, 63, 77, 115
Open unions under, 326 ff.
Universal, 144, 192
Collective agreements
see also National Labor Relations Act
Administration of, 386
Agency theory in suits on, 382
Analogy to schedules, etc., 384–5
Arbitration, use of in, 396 ff., 402 ff.
Beneficiary theory, 383
Congressional power to regulate, 379 ff.
Custom or usage theory, 381
Free riders, rights of nonmembers under, 399
Majority rule in, 390 ff.
Mergers in, 391
Nature of, 305
No-strike pledge in, 408–9
Collective bargaining
Arbitration to achieve, 402 ff.
Elements of, in labor disputes, 387
Government intervention in, 388
NRA of 1933; codes of fair employment analogized to, 389
Combination
Legality of, 33
Necessity of, for labor, 62
Commerce
see also National Labor Relations Act
Protection of, 427 ff.
Common law
Defined in contrast to statutes, 17

Commonwealth v. Carlisle, 26
Commonwealth v. Hunt, 28
Competition, 61, 84
Codes of fair employment and, 421–2
Massachusetts conception of, 68–9, 72
Sherman Act and, 202–4, 216 ff., 260–64
Union theory of, 74–5
Congress of Industrial Organizations (CIO), 223–8
see also Political action committee
Consolidated Edison Co. v. NLRB, 291
Conspiracy
see also Criminal conspiracy
Civil conspiracy, 33
Constitutional law, 336, 366
see also National Labor Relations Act
Contracts
See also Collective agreements, Freedom of contract
Inducing breach of, tort of, 93, 179
Coronado cases, 419
see also Sherman Act
Coronado case (first), 211
Coronado case (second), 216
Council
Affiliated labor unions, 130
Building trades unions, 127
Criminal conspiracy
Decline of, in America, 30
Early American cases, 22 ff.
Genesis and theory of, 18–19
Curran v. Galen, 76

Danbury Hatters' case, 206
Democratic National Convention, 83
Dicey, A. V., 413
Douglas, Justice, 355, 357

Due process
see Constitutional law
Duplex P. P. Co. v. Deering, 162 ff.,
210

*Eastern States Retail Lumber Deal-
ers'* case, 262
Economic interest, 156
Elections
see National Labor Relations
Act
Equity, 95–6

Fact-finding
see Strikes
Fansteel Met. Co. v. NLRB, 293
Frankfurter, Felix, 99, 104, 185,
269 ff., 286, 289, 298–9, 351, 353,
358–9, 363, 395, 439
Franks Bros. Co. v. NLRB, 314, 435
Freedom of contract, 18
Freedom of speech
see also National Labor Relations
Act, Picketing Employer's right
of, 436–7
Free enterprise, 87

Gallup poll, 348
Gibson, Chief Justice, 26
*Glamorgan Coal Co., South Wales
M. F. v.*, 430
Goldfinger v. Feintuch, 147, 357
Gompers v. Bucks S. & R. Co., 138
Gompers, Sam, 138, 159 ff.
Gray, Judge, 80

Halsbury, Lord Chancellor, 36 ff.
Hand, Judge A., 284
Herschell, Lord, 37 ff.
Hill v. Florida, 438
Hitchman Coal Co. v. Mitchell, 178
Hobbes, Thomas, 378

Holmes, O. W., Jr., 31, 60 ff., 98,
200, 253, 369
Hoover, President, 180
Hough, Judge, 105
Hughes, Chief Justice, 265–6, 303,
428
Hunt v. Crumboch, 285, 287, 428
Hutcheson, U. S. v., 269 ff., 366, 419

Illegal purpose doctrine, 50, 90
Test for legality of strikes, 30, 60,
81
Inducing breach of contract
see Contracts
Industrial revolution
Background of modern law, 14
Factory system, 21
Injunction
Abuse of, 95 ff., 104
Amendment of Norris-LaG. Act
to prevent interunion disputes,
433
Anti-injunction acts, 159 ff.,
173–4, 185–7, 198
Comparison between Norris-LaG.
and Clayton acts, 194–5
Norris-LaG. Act, 184 ff., 191, 254
Preventive remedy, legitimate use
of, as, 99
Sherman Act, 272–3
Interunion disputes, 247 ff., 413 ff.

Jackson, Justice, 287, 304, 329, 355,
384
Jacobs v. Cohen, 80
James v. Marinship Corp., 372
J. I. Case Co. v. NLRB, 304, 384
Jones & Laughlin Steel Co., 324
Jones & Laughlin S. Co. v. NLRB,
303
Jurisdictional disputes, 410
see also Interunion disputes

Jurisdictional strikes
  see also Strikes
  Jurisdictional strike defined, 71–2

Labor dispute
  Businessman-worker, 377 ff.
  Defined in Norris-LaG. Act, 189 ff.
Labor unions
  see Unions
Landis, Dean James M., 29
Legislation, economic policy, 84
Levy, Recorder, 24
Liberty of contract
  see Freedom of contract
Local 807, U. S. v., 425
Loewe v. Lawlor (sub nom. Danbury Hatters' case), 206
Lumley v. Gye, 93, 179

Malice
  In labor litigation, 35–6
  In tort liability, 89
  Effect of, on otherwise lawful conduct, 89 ff.
Malthus, 20
McKay v. Local Union No. 1067, 153, 368
Meadowmoor Dairies, M. W. D. Union v., 351
Medo Photo S. Co. v. NLRB, 307
Milk Wagon D. Union v. Lake Valley F. P., Inc., 287
Mogul S.S. Co. v. McGregor, 31
Monopolies
  Unions as, 418, 429–30
Motive
  see Malice
Murphy, Justice, 284, 342, 355, 357, 372

National Labor Relations Act (NLRA), 225, 228, 230, 234, 236, 239, 251, 254, 333

Administrative functions of board, 233 ff.
And bargaining unit, 240 ff.
Certification and, 315, 434–5
Closed shops and open unions, 326 ff.
Collective agreements, 290 ff.
Courts and, 250–2
Description of, and terms in, 229 ff.
Discretion of board in allowing remedies, 238–9, 293 ff.
Elections, how conducted, 243 ff.
Employer acceptance of union to represent employees, 228 ff., 291
Employers and, 248, 313, 324–5, 436–7
Instatement of applicants denied employment, 296 ff.
Interunion disputes, 317 ff., 433 ff.
Majority rule and, 303 ff.
Political background, 226 ff.
Power of board after collective agreement made, 300 ff.
Practical working of, 235 ff.
Reinstatement of discharged employees, 296 ff.
Representation cases, 239 ff.
Section 8, 231–2
Section 10 (c), 237
Shift of union allegiance, 309 ff.
Sit down strike and, 293
Supervisory workers under, 319 ff.
National Labor Relations Board (NLRB)
  see National Labor Relations Act
Nat'l Licorice Co. v. NLRB, 303
Nat'l Protective Assn. v. Cumming, 77
National Recovery Act (NRA)
  see also Collective Bargaining
  Codes of fair employment, 421–2

National Recovery Act (*Continued*)
Influence on NLRA, 223
Negroes
see Racism, Railway Labor Act
New Negro Alliance v. S. G. Co.,
199
Newark Morning Ledger v. NLRB,
301
Norris-LaGuardia Act, 366
see also Injunction, Labor dispute
Sections 4 and 13, 449–51

Order Ry. Telegraphers v. Ry.
Express Agency, 308

Packard Co., 324
Palles, Chief Justice, 45
Parker, Chief Justice, 77
Parker, Judge John J., 180
People v. Fisher, 26
Petrillo, J., 284
Phelps Dodge Corp. v. NLRB, 296
Philadelphia Cordwainers' case, 22
Picketing, 359, 434
Definition of and law concerning,
141 ff.
Peaceful, 60, 142–3, 339, 342 ff.,
347–8 ff.
Pink tea, 172
Reactions to, 346–7
Stranger, 142
Supreme Court and, 361–2, 369
Sympathetic pressures induced by,
359
Sympathetic response: legality of,
369
Tort and, 337 ff.
Pickett v. Walsh, 69, 114
Pierce v. Stablemen's Union, 337
Pitney, Justice, 170 ff.
Plant v. Woods, 62 ff.

Policy
see Legislation
Political action committee, 117
Pound, Judge, 132, 158
Property
Importance of, in labor law, 18
Ownership of, as bargaining control, 175–6

Quinn v. Leathem, 40, 121

R An W Hat Shop v. Sculley, 181
Racism, 369 ff.
Railway Labor Act
In general, 394, 421
Negroes and, 370 ff.
Reed, Justice, 357, 363, 366
Registration of Unions
see Unions
Restraint of Trade
see Sherman Act
Ritter's Cafe, Carpenters and J.
Union v., 357
Roberts, Justice, 275
Roosevelt, President F. D., 254
Rutledge, Justice, 395

Scrutton, Lord Justice, 158
Seattle M. & B. Co. v. Hansen, 136
Secondary boycott
see Boycott
Senn v. Tile Layers' Protective
Union, 198, 338–9
Shaw, Chief Justice, 28
Sherman Act, 267
see also Injunction
Amendments to, 424 ff.
Boycott cases under, 258–65
Clayton Act: effect of, on, 269 ff.
Competition and, 216 ff.
Coronado cases and, 259–61
Hutcheson v. U. S., 269 ff.

Sherman Act (*Continued*)
    Labor and, 205 ff., 279
    Policing measure, 256–7
    Restraint of trade and, 202 ff., 208
    Text of first two sections, 201
Sibley, Judge, 378
Sit down strike, 255, 443
    see also NLRA
Southern Trucking Co. v. NLRB, 314
Star Pub. Co. v. NLRB, 314, 435
Steele v. L. & N. R. Co., 371
Stone, Justice and Chief Justice, 239, 256 ff., 299, 307, 371, 425
Strikes
    Abolition of right to strike: political impossibility of, 420–1
    Codes of fair employment to obviate, 421–2
    Fact-finding commissions and, 421
    For unlawful objectives, 107–8
    Immediate conditions of labor for, 106 ff.
    Jurisdictional, 113 ff.
    Legality of, 30, 57, 104 ff., 107
    Nature of, 107
    Postponement of, 421
    Sympathetic, 108, 129–30
    Technological change, 111
Supervisory workers
    see also National Labor Relations Act
Supreme Court, 436
    see also Picketing
Swan, Judge, 281
Swing, AF of L v., 350
Sympathetic pressures
    Conscription by neutrals: appeals by strikers, 137 ff.
    Picketing and, 150 ff., 154
Sympathetic strike
    see Strikes

Taft, Chief Justice, 212, 419
Technological change
    see Strikes
Thomas v. Collins, 438
Thomas, R. J., 438
Thornhill v. Alabama, 341
Torts
    Defined, 32
    Law of, in relation to labor, 88 ff.
Trade Associations
    Blacklist, legality of, 58
Trade Disputes Act, 14
Trilogy, House of Lords law of, 46 ff.
Truax v. Corrigan, 172

Unions
    Aims of, 415, 442, 443
    Anticompetitive aspects of, 418
    Benefit of, to society, 416
    Compliance by, with agreements, 439–40
    Incorporation of, 380, 437
    Legislation to curtail abuses by, 424 ff.
    Licensing of organizers, 439
    Policy for future of, 443
    Price-fixing and, 426–7, 429–30
    Registration of, 438
    Responsibilities of, 414, 440–1
    Status of, 380
United Automobile Workers, 318
United Farm Equipment Workers, 318
United Mine Workers, 178, 211, 323
U. S. v. Am. Federation of Musicians, 284
U. S. v. Int'l Hod Carriers Union, 285
Unity of interest, picketing cases, 149

Vegelahn v. Guntner, 60

Voltaire, 349

Wage fund theory, 20, 66
Wagner Act
  see National Labor Relations Act
Wallace Corp. v. NLRB, 326, 372
War Labor Board, 387, 402

*Wisconsin E. R. B., Hotel & Rest.
  Employees Union v.,* 352
Wohl, Bakery & Pastry Drivers'
  Union, 354

"Yellow dog contract," 298
  see also Antiunion promise